THE LAST CANYON VOYAGE

# THE LAST CANYON VOYAGE

## A FILMMAKER'S JOURNEY DOWN THE GREEN AND COLORADO RIVERS

Charles Eggert

THE UNIVERSITY OF UTAH PRESS
*Salt Lake City*

The Defiance House Man colophon is a registered trademark of The University of Utah Press. It is based on a four-foot-tall Ancient Puebloan pictograph (late PIII) near Glen Canyon, Utah.

Library of Congress Cataloging-in-Publication Data

Names: Eggert, Charles, 1918-2005, author.
Title: The last canyon voyage : a filmmaker's journey down the Green and Colorado Rivers/Charles Eggert.
Description: Salt Lake City : The University of Utah Press, [2020] | Includes bibliographical references. | Summary: "Recounts the last of the few river trips to follow Powell's path down the Green and Colorado before those rivers were dammed" —Provided by publisher.
Identifiers: LCCN 2019053502 (print) | LCCN 2019053503 (ebook) | ISBN 9781607817345 (paperback) | ISBN 9781607817352 (ebook)
Subjects: LCSH: Eggert, Charles, 1918-2005—Travel—Colorado River (Colo.-Mexico) | Eggert, Charles, 1918-2005—Travel—Green River (Wyo.-Utah) | Motion pictures—Colorado River (Colo.-Mexico) | Motion pictures—Green River (Wyo.-Utah) | Colorado River (Colo.-Mexico)—Description and travel. | Green River (Wyo.-Utah)—Description and travel.
Classification: LCC F788 .E29 2020 (print) | LCC F788 (ebook) | DDC 917.91/304—dc23
LC record available at https://lccn.loc.gov/2019053502
LC ebook record available at https://lccn.loc.gov/2019053503

Errata and further information on this and other titles available online at UofUpress.com

Printed and bound in the United States of America.

*Being left behind to wait was the hardest part, and so this book is dedicated to*

BETTY, KIP, AND SEB, AND TO MY MOTHER.

# CONTENTS

*Editor's Note* ix
*Acknowledgments* xi
*Foreword by Roy Webb* xvii

Introduction by Alfred E. Holland Jr. 1
1. The Idea 32
2. Don Hatch 38
3. Cid Sumner 44
4. Last Preparations in Vernal 57
5. Meeting in Green River 63
6. Getting Ready to Launch 71
7. On the River at Last 89
8. Shakedown 97
9. Red Canyon and the First Rapids 109
10. Brown's Park and the Gates of Lodore 118
11. Hell's Half Mile 127
12. Rippling Brook 140
13. Echo Park and Harper's Corner 142
14. Photographing the Yampa River and Jones Hole 152
15. Whirlpool and Split Mountain Canyons 163
16. Vernal Interlude 174
17. Uinta Basin 187
18. Desolation Canyon 194
19. McPherson Ranch 204
20. Gray Canyon and Green River, Utah 214
21. Labyrinth and Stillwater Canyons—Cid Leaves the Expedition 234
22. Cataract Canyon 247
23. The Big Drops, Dark Canyon Rapid, and Hite 267
24. Hite to Ticaboo Creek 273

25. Glen Canyon 282
26. Hidden Passage 293
27. Rainbow Bridge to Lee's Ferry 303
28. *L'Envoi*—Grand Canyon 320

Endnotes by Roy Webb 327
After the River by Sarah McDaniel Holcombe 343
Color Insert following page 108

# EDITOR'S NOTE

Charles Eggert quoted extensively from the journal of Major John Wesley Powell, which was titled *Canyons of the Colorado* and published in 1895 by Flood and Vincent Publishing in Meadville, Pennsylvania. It was again published in 1961 by Dover Publications, Inc., New York, under the title *The Exploration of the Colorado River and its Canyons* by John Wesley Powell. Dover Publications has since released newer editions. The book is currently in print.

# ACKNOWLEDGMENTS

This book would not have been published without the help of many friends and admirers of my father.

Cid Ricketts Sumner was the first person to review this manuscript. Her participation in the expedition brought a focus to what otherwise would have been just another bunch of boys playing in boats. Her maturity, good humor, and placid disposition were essential, and her friendship with my father grew and lasted as long as she lived. Her influence in my father's life is indelible.

The youngest member of the trip dedicated the rest of his life to the restoration and preservation of riparian ecology. Bruce Lium's interest in this book and his continuing friendship with me has been an inspiration and an impetus to bring this book to completion. He is an example of how the river changes those who experience its magic, and how that can lead to a life of service to our wild rivers and the communities that depend on them.

Don Hatch and his crew carried my father and his passengers safely through some of the world's worst rapids and they all had a hell of a good time doing it. The friendships formed with the entire Hatch clan continued for many years afterward. Since then Hatch River Expeditions has divided into two companies; trips in the Upper Basin are now run by the O.A.R.S. organization and Hatch River Expeditions covers the Grand Canyon. Both organizations have continued to extend to me and my family their appreciation for what my father did for the river running community. There is no better way to begin a lifetime of river adventures than to start with an experienced guide service.

Most of the images in this volume were by my father or his assistant, Tony Tuttle, but Philip Hyde took several images on the 1956 trip through the Grand Canyon that are included here. Many thanks to David Leland Hyde for his permission to use them; the image of the three travelers at the end of the book is the period that completes the sentence.

My father signed the first contract for this book in 2004. Since then his friend and editor John Alley has shepherded this manuscript through two publishers. The first was Michael Spooner of the Utah State University Press, who graciously and generously allowed John to take the book with him to the University of Utah Press.

Before his retirement, John confidently handed the book to another editor at the University of Utah Press, Rebecca Rauch, a former river guide who understood as well as anyone the importance of bringing my father's story to the river community. The result of her patient persistence is in your hands. Thank you, Reba.

Ms. Rauch handed the manuscript to Tracy Wilson for copyediting. My dad was a photographer and a conservationist, and although he wrote well, there were a lot of little things that needed correction. Working with her has been an absolute delight. Her very detailed and careful improvements to the manuscript have made it much better without changing my father's voice.

The Department of Special Collections, a part of the Marriott Library at the University of Utah, is under the skilled direction of Greg Thompson. He and all the members of his staff have carefully and competently cared for my father's films, photographs, and writings, preserving them for future generations of researchers and anyone curious about the history of the Great Basin. It is reassuring for me to know that my father's work will not end up in the dustbin of history.

The cover image of my father in Dinosaur National Monument with his Cine Special camera was resurrected by Jessica A. Booth of the University of Utah Press. The color slide was so badly degraded that the image was almost entirely red. Her skill at using editing tools brought the lost image back to life. Ana Wolpin, another accomplished graphics artist refined the coloration just a bit to my complete satisfaction. Ms. Booth's layout of the cover makes a memorable first impression.

The contributions of three more of my father's friends have brought to this manuscript background, context, and history. The importance of their contributions cannot be overstated.

Sarah McDaniel Holcombe came upon this manuscript while researching her hometown author, Cid Ricketts Sumner. We still laugh about her tentative, formal, and respectful initial contact with me. Her enthusiasm and superb powers of writing and observation have helped guide me through the task of assembling this book. The poignant afterword is the result of her dogged research and is an essential part of a complete understanding of the expedition. My father heard Cid's voice again in Sarah's southern accent, and delighted in her unselfconscious laughter. Sarah's devotion to this project is as selfless an act of generosity and love as I could ask for.

Alfred Holland forged a deep friendship with my father. Their correspondence and many conversations over the years revealed a background I knew little about. It is from his biographical introduction that I have gained a much deeper understanding of who my father was and what made him so. Al's experience as a former river guide and historian gave him a unique perspective on why this book should be a part of the history of the Intermountain West. During the 1998 rafting trip with friends and family through Lodore, he was thoughtful enough to bring along and read aloud passages from my dad's writings. Hearing those words in that place gave all of us a deeper connection with history and my father. Al's acknowledgment of my father's importance to the river community gave him the reassurance that his life's work still had meaning. The last gift that Al and his wife, Candy, gave to my father was a box of their homegrown oranges, a delicacy that my father relished in his last days.

I inherited the task of preparing my father's book for publication. I thought my part of that work would be to write a forward that would explain why, after so much time since its creation, the book still had relevance. It came as a lightning bolt that the best person to answer that question had been hiding in plain sight for almost a decade. Reba Rauch suggested to me that we ask Roy Webb to write it instead. There could not have been a more qualified person for the task, and with delight (and my great relief) we asked him if he would consider writing it. Roy had started the process of pulling my father out of the obscurity of retirement and back into the community of river runners and historians that celebrated him like a long-lost hero. Roy had written many books about the history of the river runners and made it part of his life's work to document and preserve the records of people whose experiences had been shaped by this extraordinary landscape. His foreword tells us why this book is fitting addition to the history of the Green and Colorado Rivers. He also worked closely with Reba to select and caption the images in this volume. His attention to detail and accuracy are the mark of a true and competent professional. My father would be very proud of what all these fine people have built around his manuscript.

My dad would be quick to thank the community of professional river guides for their enthusiastic reception for him and his work at the 2000 Upper Basin River Guides training seminar in Green River, Utah. They had the unique pleasure of seeing the old Charlie at his finest, performing to his best audience ever, showing his film and lecturing about his adventures to the delight of a much younger crowd. I believe that it was the happiest moment of his professional life.

River guides know better than anyone else what it is like to experience the beauty and the timeless wisdom of the river. Their job is not just to ferry their guests safely down the river but bring to them a much greater appreciation for the history, geology, and ecology of the canyons. They are the living repositories of the stories of the river runners before them, and they enhance their guests' understanding and appreciation of the river experience. It was my father's hope that this book would become a well-worn addition to their ammo boxes. The lives these guides live after the river, and the lives of the people they carry on their journeys are all influenced by the sweet song of the canyon wren, the roaring of rapids, and the stillness of an evening watching the moonlight creep across the canyon walls as the river gently glides by in the darkness with the distant business of the rest of the world finally silent. Who knows where these changed souls will end up? Perhaps as a river restoration contractor, a historian, a teacher, a writer, a poet, an activist, and maybe a politician, all having gained the strength of resolve to bring others along in the effort to preserve the experiences of renewal and inspiration found in these canyons.

In a greater sense this book tells all of us of a time before our destruction of the planet was so obvious, when our innocence was still in place and we thought things would always remain the same. We know now this is not so. Since this book was first conceived and written, we have seen vast areas of these lovely canyons changed forever by our exploitation of the river. Understanding what this place was like before the dams were built can be a force for changing our attitudes about our responsibility to the places we love, wherever they may be. Future generations will not likely experience the beauty of Glen Canyon as the Garden of Eden it once was, rather as a guidepost for our careful consideration of our place in the natural world. It may serve as a warning and challenge to all of us to do our part to preserve and resurrect these places of tranquility and replenishment.

Sebastian Eggert
Mount Rainier National Park
July 22, 2019

# FOREWORD

*by Roy Webb*

I first met Charles Eggert over the telephone. I got a call in my office at the University of Utah's Marriott Library; when I answered, a querulous voice on the other end asked, "Why are you leaving me out of that book you're writing!?" At the time I was working on my second book, *Call of the Colorado*, a thematically arranged photo history of river running on the Green and Colorado. The book was arranged into chapters addressing different motivations for river running: Explorers, Scientists, Adventurers, Outfitters, and Photographers. As a photographer and filmmaker, Eggert felt he should have been included. His friend Don Hatch, whom I worked with on my first book, *If We Had a Boat*, told Eggert I was working on a book that included photographers. Eggert and I talked at some length, and I learned that all of his personal papers were in the attic of his home in Rhinecliff, New York, up the Hudson River from New York City. That, I told him, was the reason that historians had forgotten his many contributions to Colorado River history: writing history requires sources that are available for research. Thanks to his phone call and our subsequent conversations, I was able to make sure his contributions were included in the book.

Eggert and I kept in touch over the next few years, and in 1997, our daughter Rachel's tenth birthday wish was to go to New York City. So my family and I visited New York City over Thanksgiving, where we saw the Rockettes, the Christmas decorations, the toy stores, the delis, the Macy's Day Parade, and the Plaza Hotel, (Rachel had memorized the book *Eloise*). One day I left them in the museums and stores and took a train up the Hudson River Valley to Charles's hometown of Rhinecliff. He picked me up at the train station in Rhinecliff in his red Corvette. We had lunch with George Washington and spent the rest of the day at his home, the carriage house of a long-vanished mansion, talking about the river and looking through boxes and boxes of, to use a professional archival term, stuff. Many phone calls and many emails and many questions later, Charlie agreed to donate his extensive personal archive, consisting of boxes of correspondence, business records from his lecture tours, journals, promotional materials, copies of his films, a large collection of still photographs, and ephemera such as the Eggert-Hatch Expedition flag and Froggy, a toy frog that was the trip mascot, to the Special Collections Department of the University of Utah's Marriott Library. The Charles Eggert collection is a cornerstone of the Utah River Running Archives.

Also included in this vast collection were copies of a book manuscript Eggert had written with the title *Forbidden Passage* (now retitled *The Last Canyon Voyage*). Charlie had written *Forbidden Passage* after he ended his long run of lecture and film tours, but for various reasons, detailed in his archival papers, the book was never published. As I read the manuscript, I realized that this was a hidden gem that deserved a wider audience than the occasional researcher who might stumble across it while conducting research in the library.

Eggert and I worked together on his collection by means of letters and telephone calls for the next several years. He was, rightfully, concerned that it be well treated and made available for future scholars. In 1998 Eggert came to visit Salt Lake City, his first trip west in many years. He came to the Marriott Library to check on his collection and was pleased to find it being well taken care of. Two years later, in 2000, I helped re-create part of his 1955 expedition on a Don Hatch River Expeditions trip through the Canyon of Lodore, with Don Hatch, Eggert's son Seb, Al Holland, and others. There were many stories and much hilarity around the campfires, and Eggert was finally able to run the rapids he had filmed from shore almost half a century before. The shots of whiskey below Hell's Half Mile were purely medicinal.

That same year, Eggert was invited to participate in river runners' gatherings in Green River and Moab, Utah, where he showed and narrated his films *A Canyon Voyage* and *Danger River*. Eggert beamed with pride as he was recognized as a pioneer of river running and accepted as an elder of the close-knit tribe of river guides. Charlie moved west to be with his son Seb toward the end of his life, and we kept in touch. At that time, all of us at the library were working on arranging and describing his archival collection, and Charlie was always full of much-valued advice. We were all sad to hear of his passing in the winter of 2005, but he died secure in the knowledge that his archival treasure trove was in a good place. And indeed, his films and photos continue to be seen to this day. *Wilderness River Trail*, *This is Dinosaur*, *A Canyon Voyage*, and *Danger River* have been shown at many gatherings of river guides and historians; and at the celebration of the fiftieth anniversary of the establishment of Canyonlands National Park, I showed a later film, *The Sculptured Earth*, that he made in the early 1960s during the push to establish Canyonlands.

*The Last Canyon Voyage* provides a perspective on an event unique in both time and place. The canyons of the Green and Colorado were facing a virtual death sentence; when Eggert, Hatch, and their crew went down the rivers in 1955, the legislation authorizing the building of both Flaming Gorge Dam on the Green River and Glen Canyon Dam on the Colorado had been signed, and plans were underway to begin construction. After 1956, the long series of canyons along the two rivers would be forever changed, the canyons flooded and the rivers tamed. It is also an exceptional point of view by a very observant participant. Charles Eggert's experienced filmmaker's and photographer's eye shows through in his descriptions of the people and places that are the basis for the book. Along with Cid Sumner's *Traveler in the Wilderness*, it is one of only two books that document the 1955–56 Eggert-Hatch Expedition, which itself was very important to the history of the Green and Colorado Rivers. Within less than a year after the boats were pulled out of the water, and everyone involved on the two trips moved on with their lives, the first blasts had echoed through both Flaming Gorge and Glen Canyons, and the construction of the great dams that would forever change the face of the rivers had begun. Remote and unknown places that had only recently emerged from obscurity were about to once again become blank spaces on the maps of the West, giant reservoirs that covered the canyons like nothing had ever been there before. By making the last films before construction on Flaming Gorge and Glen Canyon Dams began, Charles Eggert saw an opportunity to not only record history, but to make history, and he seized it.

The Eggert-Hatch Expedition had two avowed purposes: to make the last film documenting the river's course before the dams were begun, and to retrace John Wesley Powell's pioneering journey of 1869. In 1955, the canyons of the Green and Colorado, Powell's route, were virtually unchanged from when he passed through them eighty-seven years before. Even today, some of the landscapes in remote and seldom-visited areas of Wyoming, Colorado, and Utah don't look much different from when Powell passed through. So for those unfamiliar with the region, what follows is a brief description of the canyons and valleys that Powell and then the Eggert-Hatch Expedition traversed. Before I launch on that short verbal expedition, honesty to the reader compels me to point out the excellent, hand-drawn maps that Eggert created to accompany *Forbidden Passage,* which are found elsewhere in this book.

When the Eggert-Hatch Expedition launched from Expedition Island in Green River, Wyoming, in June of 1955, the town was a little bit bigger, and quite a bit busier, but it was still a railroad town, not that far removed from the hell-on-wheels boomtown it had started out as in 1868. For the first seventy miles below town, the Green River flowed through open country, lined with low rolling hills of gravel, sage, and cactus. Jackrabbits, prairie dogs, and antelope watched travelers on the river from the banks. The only real changes along the river by 1955 were small ranches with cattle, sheep, and horses; ferries and fences; and even a little town, Linwood, at the mouth of Black's Fork. The mosquitoes were the same, as were the characters who lived in those remote ranches, and whose memories sometimes reached back to the Shoshone and the mountain men, well before Powell.

Below Linwood the Green River entombed itself in the first of a long series of canyons; it would pass through ten different canyons before meeting the Colorado River in southeast Utah. The first three were short, spectacular, and very different from each other. Flaming Gorge was the entrance to the whole series, where the river ran up against a flaring red cliff. At the time the Eggert-Hatch Expedition passed through Flaming Gorge, the Green was still untamed by dams. When the snow in the mountains of western Wyoming melted, levels in the river could rise to as much as 25,000 cubic feet per second, or cfs; by contrast, today the standard release from Flaming Gorge Dam is 1500 cfs. The river was muddy, the currents were strong, and the turbulence as all that water tried to force its way into the narrow opening of Flaming Gorge, creating whirlpools, boils, and eddies, gave rise to the legend of the dreaded "Green River Suck." Supposedly an impassable cataract that had claimed the lives of many men and animals, the "Suck" was a figment of a mountain man's imagination, but the stories about it were passed along to anyone daring to float the Green River through the upper canyon. No doubt Eggert, Don

Hatch, and their crew heard some variation as they readied their boats in Green River.

Horseshoe and Kingfisher Canyons were just long curves of calm water through differing geologic layers; between the two was Hideout Flat, where hidden trails crossed the river. The Uinta Mountains were long the haunts of outlaws like the Wild Bunch and the Tip Gault gang, valued by them for their remote location on the borders of Utah, Colorado, and Wyoming. The river struck the spine of the Uinta Mountains and turned due east into Red Canyon, cutting through Uinta Mountain quartzite, hard red rock that produces difficult rapids. Skull Creek Rapid had been the scene of at least one recorded fatality, and the next, Ashley Falls, was the biggest rapid on the entire Green River. Passing it safely was considered a significant benchmark by early river runners, who often stopped to add their names to William Ashley's at the "river register" on the rocks by the rapid. Red Canyon had its charms too, lovely little side canyons with clear, cold, trout-filled streams like Carter, Currant, and Allen Creeks, but after passing Red Creek Rapid—where there were many accidents over the years—river runners were not unhappy to see the end of Red Canyon. Today Flaming Gorge Dam, built in the 1950s in the middle of Red Canyon, floods all of these canyons to within a few miles of the town of Green River.

The river flows calmly in Brown's Park, then and now a remote open area of scattered ranches. Once the home of the Wild Bunch and other outlaws, now it contains a number of wildlife refuges. The Canyon of Lodore, named by one of Powell's men in 1869 after a cataract in the Lakes District of England, has always been a test of boats and boating skills. It is less than twenty miles long but choked by numerous difficult rapids with intimidating names like Disaster Falls and Hell's Half Mile. It is cut through the same Uinta Mountain quartzite that forms Red Canyon, but runs north to south, so it is often gloomy and atmospheric. After a calm interlude in the magnificent, hidden gem, Echo Park, where the Yampa River joins the Green at the end of Lodore, the river runs through Whirlpool Canyon, the open Island and Rainbow Parks, and Split Mountain Canyon, all within the boundaries of Dinosaur National Monument. The Green debouches into the open Uinta Basin, and for the next hundred miles the river rests from all that frenetic activity, in big looping curves through cottonwood bottoms and sloughs. Although not right on the river, the town of Vernal, Utah, was the home of Don Hatch and Hatch River Expeditions, so the travelers were able to take a short break and regroup before continuing their journey.

As the Tavaputs Plateau of central Utah begins to rise, the Green begins to cut down through it. Desolate at first, Desolation Canyon soon turns into a magnificent wilderness of deep canyons, wildlife, abandoned Fremont Indian ruins and pioneer ranches, and continual whitewater rapids. Desolation, and a smaller canyon downstream, Gray Canyon, are so remote that they were the hideaways of outlaws for many years, and the Outlaw Trail ran along the Green's shores in this area. After the Green exits Gray Canyon under the towering Gunnison Butte, it passes the old Ute crossing, also used by the pack trains of the Old Spanish Trail, and the little town of Green River, Utah. Another railroad town, the hamlet of Green River, looks little different from when the Eggert-Hatch Expedition passed through in 1955. Established as a crossing of the Green by the Denver and Rio Grande Railroad in 1883, Green River went through various booms and busts in its history. Oil, uranium, military bases, even peaches came and went, making and losing many fortunes. Today, bypassed by I-70, Green River is trying to emulate the tourism boom that is enriching Moab, Utah, a few miles to the south along the Colorado River, but so far, "the world's best melons," produced by abundant Green River water, a long growing season, and good soil, are the only consistent success story in town.

The last two canyons of the Green River, before it meets the Colorado in Canyonlands National Park, are the exquisite Labyrinth and Stillwater Canyons. The Green runs beneath towering sandstone cliffs, calm as a lake, through the heart of Canyonlands National Park. One of the most remote areas in the lower forty-eight states, the tranquil waters of both canyons tempted local entrepreneurs in Green River and Moab to try to establish a steamboat line between the two towns around the turn of the twentieth century. The paddlewheel boats would haul freight, mining supplies, and tourists from the railroad in Green River down to the confluence, then back up the Colorado to Moab. Originally, the plan was to haul fruit and produce from Moab back up to the railroad for shipment. Alas, despite much effort and money expended on numerous craft, none was ever able to make it back and forth on a regular basis; the rivers were just too shallow. Today the scenery and easy water make Labyrinth and Stillwater Canyons a favorite destination for canoeists and kayakers seeking a family-friendly wilderness river trip.

It was in the middle of Stillwater Canyon that Don Hatch and Charles Eggert decided that Cid Sumner, the only woman on the 1955 trip, should not continue through Cataract Canyon, which lay just below the confluence of the two rivers. Cataract has long had a reputation as "the graveyard of the Colorado," and the men felt it was just too dangerous for a woman. Such attitudes were not uncommon then; it wasn't until well into the 1980s that women were accepted as equals to men on river trips, and the misconception that women are not able to handle wilderness travel persists to this day. In accepting and then embracing Cid Sumner's participation in the expedition, Eggert was ahead of his time, but he was still concerned about her safety in the rough rapids of Cataract Canyon. So despite Cid's protests, she was flown out in a light airplane from a small airstrip at Anderson Bottom, planning to rejoin the party at Hite, at the beginning of Glen Canyon. Before the lower end of Cataract Canyon was covered by Lake Powell in the 1960s, there were forty-five miles of continuous, increasingly difficult rapids. An unknown number of prospectors, trying to reach the gold mining areas of the lower San Juan River and Glen Canyon, were lured by the placid waters to their doom in Cataract; hence the reputation. Later accidents, capsizes, and even a few deaths among recreational river runners in the canyon have done nothing to lighten that gloomy notoriety, and even with the lower thirty miles flooded, Cataract is still approached only with caution by the hundreds of recreational and commercial river runners who float it every year.

Cid Sumner rejoined the party at Hite, a tiny hamlet populated by a few uranium prospectors at the time, where there was a ferry across the river, and Glen Canyon begins. It was a long, calm stretch of the Colorado River, featuring sinuous, sweeping curves beneath golden sandstone walls. Its name came from the many side canyons, with pockets of trees; clear streams; and mysterious, charming glens and grottoes. Glen Canyon has always had an almost mystical effect on travelers; it seemed a world outside normal, everyday existence, a desert Eden. The impression made on the members of the Eggert-Hatch Expedition was no different. Charles Eggert and Cid Sumner's accounts of their time in Glen Canyon are lyrical, impressionistic, and the other members were similarly affected. The name for Eggert's manuscript, *Forbidden Passage*, was derived from a small, narrow passage along the river, where visitors had to swim through waist-deep water to reach a hidden, vaulted chamber. Eggert, an artist at heart, was almost overwhelmed by his experiences in Glen Canyon. Glen Canyon is today the subject of a great deal of controversy regarding its flooding by Lake Powell after the construction of Glen Canyon Dam. Those who knew it, and many who are too young to have visited, still mourn the loss, while thousands flock to Lake Powell for the water-based recreation and stunning beauty.

At Lee's Ferry, the foot of Glen Canyon and the start of river trips through the Grand Canyon, Don Hatch looked at the water levels—9,000 cfs—and felt that it was not safe to continue because the water was too low. Accordingly, boats and equipment were stored in the government buildings at Lee's Ferry, goodbyes were said, and the party broke up, vowing to meet again the next year and finish retracing Major Powell's route.

When they met at Lee's Ferry in the summer of 1956, however, only a few members of the original party were there: Charles Eggert, Don Hatch, boatman Bruce Lium, and Fred Wood. There were others who joined them for the ten-day voyage through the Grand Canyon, but the participants in the trip did not mesh as well as the 1955 crew had. The sense of purpose, even of mission, that they had felt the year before just wasn't there. In the conclusion of *The Last Canyon Voyage*, this sense of loss shows in Eggert's final chapter, about the 1956 Grand Canyon voyage. The Grand Canyon, one of the natural wonders of the world, and one of the premier whitewater rivers to be found on earth, is given short shrift in a chapter of only a few pages.

There is no way, at this remove, and with Charles Eggert long gone, to explain this. One of the original goals of the trip, to retrace Powell's route, had become less important, and Eggert knew that unlike the canyons they had traversed the year before, the Grand Canyon was not then threatened with flooding by dams and reservoirs (although it would be in the 1960s, and Eggert threw himself into the fight to defeat those projects). He might have felt that he could come back anytime and relive his experiences in the Grand Canyon and perhaps write about them. Their passage through the Grand Canyon was hot, with high water making the rapids especially difficult, and everyone was worn out by the time they reached Lake Mead. Long river trips are exceptionally arduous, even today, and people simply get on each other's nerves after so many days spent together. Surely that fatigue affected Eggert as well and could be reflected in his writing. He had a wife and young children at home, he was already planning the lecture series using the two films that resulted from the expedition, and likely felt he needed to get back to making a living and get on with his life.

Whatever the reasons might have been, when they assembled at Lee's Ferry in 1956 for the continuation of the trip, it just wasn't the same. The final blow came when Don Hatch, the coleader and Eggert's good friend, took him aside after they had entered the Grand Canyon and told Charles that he would not be with them for the entire Grand Canyon traverse. Don's father, Bus Hatch, had been hired by Lowell Thomas to go to Pakistan and run the Indus River for a Cinerama film, and Bus needed Don's help to run the boats. Don had to hike out of the Grand Canyon at Phantom Ranch, with Smuss Allen, a longtime Hatch guide, hiking in to replace him. With the departure of Eggert's good friend Don, the heart seemed to go out of the expedition and out of Charles Eggert.

These speculations may not justify why Eggert did not devote the same energy into writing about the Grand Canyon portion of the trip in *The Last Canyon Voyage*, but they might explain it. And it should be noted that *Danger River*, Eggert's film documenting the Grand Canyon river trip, was well done and well received. He showed it and the companion film, *A Canyon Voyage*, in venues all over the country for many years. He obviously put a lot of his creative energy and effort into the films, so perhaps he can be forgiven for neglecting the Grand Canyon in his written version. In the end, it must be up to the reader to draw their own conclusions as to why Eggert glossed over the last part of the expedition. After the sense of pioneering and the camaraderie of the 1955 trip, the Grand Canyon—especially without his friend Don, and other members of the crew from the previous year—must have seemed like an anticlimax.

As a companion to Eggert's films, or on its own, *The Last Canyon Voyage* is vital to our understanding of what the land and the people along the rivers were like in those days before the upper canyons of the Green, and Glen Canyon, became blank spaces on the map, as they had been for millennia before the 1950s. Eggert, a trained and talented photographer, was able to describe the canyons, the towns, the people who lived along the river with a precise eye, leaving us a priceless record of rural Wyoming, Colorado, and Utah in the middle of the twentieth century. With the publication of *The Last Canyon Voyage*, the final piece of Charles Eggert's long history of environmental activism, filmmaking, and his impact on the Green and Colorado Rivers has fallen into place, and his legacy is secure. The University of Utah Press is to be commended for rescuing a hidden gem from the proverbially dusty archives and bringing it to light.

Photograph of Charles Eggert taken by Philip Hyde. Copyright © 1956 Philip Leland Hyde Photography, used with permission.

# INTRODUCTION

*by Alfred E. Holland Jr.*

## Passions and Their Pursuit

Charles Eggert embraced passions and their pursuit with a fervor seldom equaled. He found beauty everywhere he looked—his wife, Betty, and their two sons—Charles Christopher "Kip" and Robert Sebastian "Seb"—elegant music by classical and Romantic composers, dance, photography, handsome men and women, historic structures in the Hudson River Valley, the wild landscapes of the West, conservation, performance, and speed. He was easily distracted, yet he remained committed for as long as the distraction endured. Nonetheless, each of his diversions allowed him to inflame two or often more of his fervors simultaneously. Charles Eggert faced a quandary throughout his life, an identity crisis arising from his adoption as an infant. He devoted tremendous energy to an unsuccessful effort to discover his parents, finally dismissing the quest by reciting the explanation he had learned from a Coney Island fortune teller who told him he was the result of a tryst between a British soldier and a Dutch princess, "and that's all you should know."

Charles Eggert knew he was human, especially when he could savor the joys of his emotions and enthusiasms at their greatest intensity. In his conservationist cinematography he managed to pursue more of his compulsions simultaneously than in any other of his endeavors. His films show the consequences of not merely indulging, but harnessing passions and their pursuits. Charles Eggert lived eighty-seven years riding his ardors and chasing his dreams, sixty of those years proudly identifying himself as a conservation cinematographer. *The Last Canyon Voyage* is his journal from the peak adventure of that career, his voyage down the Green and Colorado Rivers in the summer of 1955. This brief introduction seeks to explain his life before and after his historic voyage.

## Youth

Charles Eggert's parents Charles J. and Louisa Tekla Estrel Eggert had been married for a dozen years when they adopted the newborn boy in 1918. Louisa, sixteen years Charles J's junior, opined the hard life she led prior to marriage had ruined her chances to bear children. Born into a Catholic, Bavarian immigrant family, she learned English in school and began a life as a domestic immediately upon completion of the eighth grade. Her marriage, however, changed her life substantially. She never worked outside her own home after 1906. Her son recalled a meticulously ordered home—every window shade drawn down to the same level, both sides of every pane clean and bright, but not a book in the place. Charles J. Eggert, of Lutheran, Prussian parentage, left school after the fifth grade to find work in the paper mills on the western shores of Lake Erie. His practical papermaking expertise led to his position as one of the five founders of the then largest manufacturer of corrugated box board in the United States. By the time young Charles joined the family his father earned a comfortable living superintending the paper mills subsequently acquired by Consolidated Paper Company in and around Monroe, Michigan. He worked fifty weeks per year, heading off to work each morning in a three-piece suit, white shirt, and tie, but changing when necessary into overalls. He commuted to work in a Model T and purchased a new Cadillac every two years. Each summer he loaded his family into that Cadillac, drove three days north to Sault Ste. Marie, and sat down in his chair to watch the ore ships pass through the locks at the outlet to Lake Superior. Charles J. Eggert worked himself to death at this regime, dying January 11, 1929. He left his heirs, Louisa and young Charles, substantial holdings in Consolidated Paper stock, a paid-for brick home on the outskirts of Monroe, and a "summer place" on the Lake Erie shores at Avalon Beach.

Young Charles's raising was unusual beyond his comfort. Although neither of his adopted parents attended church services, he attended

Charles Eggert riding his bicycle at about three years old. Photograph courtesy of Sebastian Eggert.

Episcopal services each Sunday with his stepaunt Elisabeth Agnes Estrel. Elisabeth was the daughter of his mother Louisa's father and his second wife. Louisa's father had remarried shortly after her mother died of complications from Louisa's birth. Louisa and her stepsister developed a close relationship, so close that Elisabeth actively participated in raising young Charles, who called her Aunt Nena. She called him Lamie. Her intimate involvement in raising him led to her participation in one of the most traumatic experiences of his youth—a tonsillectomy. Charles had been sick with a persistent sore throat for months. In his feverish delirium he asked for watermelon to soothe his throat in the middle of winter. Somehow the family acquired a melon, he resumed eating, and the adults planned the surgery. Enticing him with the ruse of an expedition to buy watermelon seeds for his own garden, his mother and aunt, the two most trusted women in his life, led him to a surgeon's office where he was gassed with ether and awoke vomiting blood.[1] For the remainder of his life Charles Eggert loathed the smell of ether, loved the taste of watermelon, and warily distrusted women, but he never suffered tonsillitis again.

In first grade Charles's teacher, Miss Goodman, introduced him to Camille Saint-Saëns's *Danse Macabre* and Nikolay Rimsky-Korsakov's *Scheherazade*. His aunt Nena cultivated young Charles's curiosity and fed his growing appetite, introducing him to broadcast performances and recordings of orchestral music, especially works by Johannes Brahms, Ludwig van Beethoven, and Pytor Ilyich Tchaikovsky. Aunt Nena was provocative in her day. Eggert subsequently described her as an aggressive flapper who smoked cigarettes and drove her own automobile, to the consternation of her Monroe neighbors, and who sought to inject culture into her artless stepsister's family. Under his aunt Nena's guidance, he became a rabid listener, commandeering the family radio to hear the scheduled broadcasts, until his fifth-grade teacher played Franz Liszt's "Mephisto Waltz" and asked her students to express the music's meaning through motion. Eggert dates his delight in the dance to that fifth-grade introduction. In April 2000 he wrote, "The dance interested me—and still does—because of the welding of music and bodily movement. Most of us tap our foot or jiggle our fingers to rhythm. The dance is an expansion of that. The body expressing the music is the ultimate to me. Music is my very soul and my super-sensitive body has always called out to express what the ears were taking in."[2]

The Eggerts lived in a sturdy, "foursquare," brick-veneered home at 511 North Monroe Street, "three lots from the city line." The city line marked an abrupt division between residential development and a mixture of active and abandoned burial grounds, field, pasture, and forest. Young Charles and his super-sensitive body reveled in the outdoor activities beyond the paved streets. He and a neighbor played in the cemetery when no burials were underway, then surreptitiously redistributed the flowers mourners had placed at graves to those otherwise neglected. He gathered chestnuts in the late fall with his uncle Al, hunted squirrels year-round, and traipsed along behind his neighbor Carlie Lown, who tended a small farm across North Monroe Street. The woods beyond the cemetery teemed with life: massive maples and oaks and elms, soaring hawks and eagles, jabbering jays and crows, singing wood thrush and orioles, spectacularly plumed pheasants, and skittering quail. In those woods he found one of his characteristic multiple pleasure phenomena—the delightful music from birdsong, the panic from flushing a pheasant, the "ominous and forbidding" darkness beneath the canopy, the stark realities of birds of prey, and the sweet meats of roasted chestnuts. Those emotions could be savored in at least quick succession, if not simultaneously, and young Charles developed a taste for the pleasures offered by the outdoors, even in winter.

In summer he hung his woolen knickers in the closet, folded up his ever-present V-neck sweater, cast off shoes and boots, and donned his overalls. Once school let out, he followed his family to their summer place at Avalon Beach. Charles Eggert grew up around boats and water. When the Raisin River flooded, so did the Eggerts' basement in Monroe. Young Charles climbed into one of his mother's washtubs and made the most of the inconvenience, splashing about in the couple feet of water singing "Row, row, your boat." At the Avalon Beach house he spent his summer days paddling an orange Old Town canoe, rowing his mother out to the fishing grounds in a flat-bottomed boat, and in his teens piloting an outboard-powered speedboat. He became so strong a swimmer that once, when a stout wind came up out of the west, he returned to shore by tying his canoe's line around his waist and swimming back rather than paddling. He long loved Kenneth Grahame's *Wind in the Willows* and took to heart the advice Water Rat gave to Mole, "Believe me, my young friend, there is *nothing*—absolutely nothing—half so much worth doing as simply messing about in boats."[3]

## Adolescence

Not long after his father's death in early 1929, Charles and his mother sold their home in Monroe and moved to Toledo, Ohio. Charles attended Scott High School, competed on the swimming team, and met Betty Rose Blair in study hall in 1934. Charles was smitten by sixteen-year-old love. Betty remained to be convinced.

Her parents likewise had a summer place at Avalon Beach, so Charles and Betty could pal around together year-round. They dated off and on through high school, and became "steadies" after graduation. Charles acted in plays, trained in ballet, and continued to listen voraciously to symphonic music.

Seeking further training in theater and dance, Charles found an opportunity through an advertisement in *Theater Arts* magazine. He enrolled during three summers at the Phidelah Rice School of the Spoken Word in Oak Bluffs on Martha's Vineyard. Rice ran the summer stock theater on the island off Massachusetts and her School of the Spoken Word augmented that enterprise.[4] One of his memorable assignments entailed declaiming Alfred Lord Tennyson's "Crossing the Bar" in all its Victorian, feigned detachment from the angst accompanying death foreseen. Eggert learned the projection, modulation, and diction skills upon which he based his professional speaking voice as he sought to incorporate the emotional content of Tennyson's approaching death into his presentation.

> Sunset and evening star,
>     And one clear call for me!
> And may there be no moaning of the bar,
>     When I put out to sea,
> But such a tide as moving seems asleep,
>     Too full for sound and foam,
> When that which drew from out the boundless deep
>     Turns again home.
>
> Twilight and evening bell,
>     And after that the dark!
> And may there be no sadness of farewell,
>     When I embark;

For though from out our bourne of Time and Place
  The flood may bear me far,
I hope to see my Pilot face to face
  When I have crost the bar.[5]

During the summer of 1935 Charles Eggert toured the capitals of Europe, visiting museums, attending operas and concerts, and living footloose and fancy-free; then he returned to the States, intent on making his mark in theater and the dance. He studied briefly at the Pasadena Playhouse, then moved to New York City. He joined the Museum of Modern Art for the print of Picasso's *Woman in White* the museum offered new members, and caught the eye of Acting Secretary Allen Porter, who was manning the front desk at the moment. Eggert had long appreciated handsome men as well as beautiful women, and Porter's invitation to meet for cocktails served as the entrée into a social scene Eggert later described as a "posh Midtown East Side social set" comprised of fellow well-heeled aesthetes. The group of friends he acquired in New York City included both married couples and a smattering of gay men, both discreet and flamboyant. They attended ballet, symphonic, and opera performances, then retired to the best restaurants and saloons to discuss what they had seen and heard. Eggert's aesthetic sensibilities matured in the context of his new-found friends. Living and loving as fast as the dividends from the cardboard manufacturer allowed, young Charles Eggert managed to ignore the Great Depression and other world affairs. His pursuit of performance, whether in theater or in dance, helped satisfy his craving for attention, his lust for music and zeal for movement, and his hedonistic inclinations.

Cosmopolitan New York City was a far cry from Monroe, Michigan, or Toledo, Ohio. Eggert's interests in the arts had marked him as unusual in his youth. In early adulthood he found his way to a community that shared his pursuit of the arts with similar zeal. He gradually began to believe he, too, could become an artist. His patrimony offered financial security sufficient to buffer him from fiscal collapse. As he matured, he recognized he might put his extraordinary privilege to some higher use than the gratification of fleeting urges. But he had neither found his muse nor his medium by the end of the thirties.

Then the war broke out in Europe in 1939. When he was required to register for the draft on October 16, 1940, he recalled, "Suddenly I found myself obligated to someone else—my government—who was telling ME what to do and no ifs, ands, or buts under penalty of the law!"[6] The Selective Training and Service Act organized the drafting of two million men for active duty and reserves from the sixteen million men who registered in 1940. Facing odds of one in eight, Charles Eggert felt vulnerable, exposed, and alone. His memories of his high school sweetheart, Betty Blair, then attending Columbia University in New York, resurfaced and he resumed his courtship. He had substantially matured during his time in New York City and when he proposed, she accepted. They wed on Friday the thirteenth of March 1941 in St. Thomas Church on West 53rd Street at Fifth Avenue.

## World War II

The prospect of being drafted to fight in trench warfare terrified young Charles. Availing himself of contacts with pioneering aviation engineer Grover Loening, Charles wrangled enrollment in Roosevelt Aviation School's airplane mechanics training program out on Long Island "in hopes," he recalled later, "the draft would consider me more useful repairing airplane motors than killing Germans in messy trenches in France.... But I couldn't tell the difference between a piston and a cylinder and dropped out." His high blood pressure disqualified him from volunteering for his next choice, the US Coast Guard, which he "thought would be the safest place to be in the armed forces, for who would have the audacity to attempt invading our shores." He then chanced to meet the captain commanding the US Naval Recruiting Station. Plying that connection, Charles D. Eggert enlisted in the naval reserves on November 4, 1941, as a Photographer's Mate 3rd Class. By early December he worked the midnight-8:00 a.m. watch at the recruiting station at 50 Church Street, photographing new recruits as they enlisted. On December 7, 1941, a neighbor awoke him in the early afternoon, telling him to turn on his radio. Eggert since recalled, "I tuned in the CBS New York Philharmonic broadcast in time to hear the announcement of the bombing [of Pearl Harbor] from the stage at Carnegie Hall."[7]

In the spring of 1942 Photographer's Mate Eggert shipped out from Norfolk aboard the USS *Nitro* (AE-2), a refrigerated munitions transport vessel relict from the First World War, in a convoy of five ships,

Charles Eggert as a youth rowing a boat near his family's summer shack at Avalon Beach on Lake Erie. Photograph courtesy of Sebastian Eggert.

including two destroyers, for San Juan, Puerto Rico. He spent most of his time photographing vessels and the diligent labors of sailors stationed in the Caribbean, then was assigned to the Public Relations Office of the 10th Naval District, where his principal duty was to document visits by dignitaries, politicians, and USO entertainers. His most memorable assignment was to photograph First Lady Eleanor Roosevelt during her visit to Puerto Rico beginning March 8, 1944.[8] In as much as Eggert's uniform had no pants pockets, he kept his extra flash bulbs in his socks for handy access. Mrs. Roosevelt noticed him grabbing them as she was posing for the obligatory photographs with Governor Rex Tugwell and asked, "Young man, did I just see you take a flashbulb from out of your stocking? What an odd place to carry them." Eggert replied, "With no pockets, Mrs. Roosevelt, where else could I store them?" A week later in her "My Day" column for March 15 she mentioned the meeting:

> The Army and Navy photographers, as well as the press photographers, have been very busy on this trip, and I was enormously amused at seeing young Charles Eggert of the Navy suddenly dive down for his extra flash bulbs, which he kept in his sock. The Navy uniform does not have any convenient pockets for

Charles Eggert met Eleanor Roosevelt during his time as a photographer for the navy during World War II. Photograph courtesy of Sebastian Eggert.

> photographers. I have watched him ever since with the greatest amusement. He has now entered into the joke, and reminds me that one of the things which will make me remember Puerto Rico is the peculiar way in which the Navy photographers carry their flash bulbs![9]

Following VE Day, the navy transferred Eggert to New Orleans, where he rejoined his wife, Betty, celebrated Christmas with a tree decorated with paper doilies, and was mustered out of the naval reserve. They set up housekeeping in a home Betty had purchased in 1943 in Barrytown, New York, and Charles opened a photography studio in nearby Red Hook. His studio survived on graduation and yearbook photographs, an occasional fashion assignment, and debutante portraits, but did not thrive through its first couple of years. For the first time in Charles Eggert's life things did not work out well of their own accord. He began to have serious second thoughts about his life and its purposes. World War II's four-year interruption had put an effective end to his aspirations as a dancer; but he might yet find a career in music.

**Postwar Malaise**

Betty, Charles, and their two-year-old son, Kip, moved in 1947 to Westport, Connecticut, where Charles took a job as a recording engineer with Mirko Panyko, a custom manufacturer of closet-sized, big-ticket, high-fidelity equipment in nearby Fairfield. Each weekend Charles recorded the Saturday evening broadcasts of the NBC Symphony and the Sunday afternoon broadcasts of the New York Philharmonic onto sixteen-inch vinyl disks Panyko distributed to his customers. Panyko pioneered 33N rpm recording two years before Columbia issued its first long-playing records but his "instruments" were so expensive he abandoned their manufacture and shifted his engineering genius to the television field in the middle 1950s, about the time, Eggert groused, "NBC threw out the Toscanini-made NBC Symphony for Lawrence Welk and his accordion-based band."[10] Eggert worked for Panyko for three years, from 1947 through 1950, and rekindled his passion for symphonic music. In the fall of 1948 he enrolled at Bard College in Annandale-on-Hudson, New York, to study music composition and conducting, commuting by train between his studies in the Hudson River Valley and his work and family in Connecticut.

As he rode those trains his introspective bent turned sour and he gradually became engulfed in a creeping malaise. The responsibilities attending marriage and fatherhood constrained his spontaneous pursuits of pleasures. His financial struggles as a photographer, then as photo editor for a Westchester County society magazine, nagged at his confidence. As war had broken out and he had faced induction, Charles Eggert had felt alone. Now that the war had ended he realized that he had considerable company in his disquietude. Watching his fellow commuters riding back and forth to New York City, he had deep second thoughts about the American dream as he had understood it. World affairs struck him as especially grim and foreboding.

The war fought for President Franklin Roosevelt's "Four Freedoms" seemed increasingly to have been fought for naught. The United Nations

Security Council permanent members' veto power, he opined, "spelled doom as far as the effectiveness of the organization was concerned. Concerted as the Allies were throughout the war, here we were once again falling back on nationalism by establishing a way out if one of us didn't like what was happening. Had we not learned a lesson from the League of Nations?" He shuddered at the consequences of "zapping Palestine off the map" and asked, "hadn't we learned from the Treaty of Versailles that cutting up countries solved no problem but rather, caused more violent ones?" Charles Eggert was at this stage in his life "questioning the purpose of life, having come out of a war which formulated ideals of high hope and 'a bright new world' which, once back into it, I found enormous disillusionment."[11]

Eggert saw his typical neighbor, both from Fairfield, Connecticut, and Barrytown, New York, commuting daily from his "beyond-his-budget estate . . . to work at his big city job which he hated, . . . hating to face his overspending wife and the prospect of keeping up with the Joneses next door. I was damned if I would join that rat race." His fellow travelers' refusal to make eye contact, their blank faces and habitual refuge in their fortress of privacy in public struck him as particularly dehumanized.

Although he arrived at it a little earlier than typical, by 1949 Charles Eggert was in the throes of a midlife crisis. Then he met a real cowboy and saw in his eyes something missing from those flaccid-faced commuters. City-boy Charles Eggert found his first real cowboy as only he could—at the rodeo in Madison Square Garden, where he had taken his four-year-old, cowboy-besotted son, Kip. Eggert recalled squiring his son around that early October 1947,

> We covered the territory—front row seats, back stage, and even after, a look-in at the real cowboys as they hung out in the bar at the hotel across the street from the Garden. This was a whole new world to me, and in the eyes of its inhabitants, there was a "look" totally absent in the eyes of those commuters. These Westerners saw something in life which I needed to see.[12]

Through social contacts with the Panykos, Charles Eggert learned of an invitation-only dude ranch operated by Bill and Rowena Paton near Shell, Wyoming. After successfully finagling an invitation through the good offices of several friends, Charles, Betty, and Kip Eggert headed off to Wyoming in the summer of 1949 and, he said, "fell in love with the area." The Paton ranch was nestled into the mouth of Shell Canyon at the western foot of the Bighorn Mountains and surrounded by spectacular scenery. The Eggerts stayed a week, then took off for Yellowstone National Park. Rather than returning directly to Connecticut from Yellowstone, they headed back to stay a few more days with the Patons and promised to return the next summer.[13] In the spring of 1950 they returned, this time leaping at the opportunity to lease a twenty-acre spread known as Cottonwood Ranch on Trapper Creek, south of Shell.

## Epiphany

Launching from their Cottonwood Ranch base, the Eggerts returned to Yellowstone and rented a cabin at Canyon Village on the rim of the Grand Canyon of the Yellowstone. There he found his calling, decided on his medium, and found the focus he had discerned in the bull- and bronc-riders' eyes. One morning Charles Eggert, who had little interest in hiking and loathed the early morning, awoke at dawn "with a not-to-be-denied necessity to hike to the bottom of the canyon." When he later recalled his hike he wrote,

> The deeper I hiked into the canyon, the more overcome I was of the stillness beyond the roar of the falls as I came closer—the vastness of the landscape as the colors became alive with the sun's rising—the purity of the air—the fresh smell of dawn as it lay heavily on the morning dew. I felt my presence as never before as I measured its insignificance against where I was. I felt ME for the first time and perhaps this was why this place was . . . preserved [so] souls like me could find ourselves and ponder our purpose in the world.
>
> This was a feeling of such intensity, yet totally indescribable. But, as I climbed up toward the rim, I knew I had to somehow spread this message of self-recognition and re-creation I felt and where it might be found; that the National Parks were places of re-birth, were far more valuable than merely "scenic freaks" and must be preserved for others to find what I had found.

> How was I to do this? That camera hanging from my neck. From my eye to its, I would make my purpose in life an attempt to show and feel through my photographs what I had seen and because of it, what I had felt so that others might follow and find it, too.[14]

Charles Eggert made good on his promises made to himself after this epiphany. He returned to Connecticut, quit his job as Mirko Panyko's recording engineer, moved his family back to their Barrytown home, opened a new photography studio in Barrytown, and continued his studies at Bard. His schooling posed formidable challenges. Music composition proved both difficult and unrewarding; consequently, his ardor for his studies began to flag. Conducting, on the other hand, delighted Eggert's entire being. For one thing, it placed him in the very center of an orchestra with all eyes and ears attending to him and his musicians' performance. In addition, directing an orchestra offered him the opportunity to combine physical movement and musical interpretation in performance, offering an alternative to the dance. Eggert continued to practice conducting into his eighties, working himself into a full sweat directing masterful performances to the music from his stereo.

Flush with newfound purpose, Eggert read Freeman Tilden's *The National Parks* as soon as it was published.[15] He absorbed Tilden's lesson on preservation of not only the freakish features, such phenomena as the geysers, mud pots, and fumaroles of Yellowstone, but also the crystalline blue of Crater Lake, the massive granite walls of Yosemite Valley, and the spectacular vistas of Grand Canyon. Naturalists might explain the bison, bears, elk, and eagles; geologists, volcanologists, and hydrologists, the mysteries of rock, fire, and water as sculpted and sculptor; Eggert sought a way to convey spiritual rebirth, the rescue from the abyss of morose depression he had enjoyed that early morning beneath Yellowstone Falls. On his thirty-fourth birthday he wrote to master photographer Ansel Adams explaining that he sought to become an effective guide for the uninitiated visitors to national parks. He closed his rambling letter with the following question: "What would you do to become acquainted with a Park?"[16]

Adams advised Eggert to put his zeal to good use and learn of the major conservation issues of the day by contacting the "leaders of the

Conservation Movement": the Sierra Club, the Wilderness Society, and the National Parks Association, adding, "I suggest you join these worthy organizations and get into the conservation swim. Ask them what they really need."[17] Eggert promptly wrote off, volunteering his photographic services and membership support to the organizations Adams had suggested. Fred Packard, executive secretary of the National Parks Association, enthusiastically replied before the end of January and alerted Eggert to the brewing controversy over the Bureau of Reclamation's plan to build between one and three dams within Dinosaur National Monument as part of the Colorado River Storage Project.[18] Within a week Packard enticed Eggert to travel to Washington, D.C., and accompany him to a news conference by director of the National Park Service Conrad L. Wirth in order to be introduced.

## Moviemaker

During conversations after the conference, Connie Wirth asked Eggert whether he took movies in addition to stills and if he was interested in shooting some film for the National Park Service in Dinosaur National Monument. Eggert enthusiastically accepted the invitation, lied about his moviemaking experience, and took the color film Wirth offered. He promptly ran out to buy an Eastman Cine Special movie camera. When the academic year at Bard ended in May of 1952, Charles Eggert left without graduating and headed to Dinosaur National Monument. Jess Lombard, one of two Park Service officers in the monument, showed him around and accommodated the travel trailer Eggert and his family lived in while making the film. He shot the five hundred feet of 16mm Kodachrome film the Park Service had loaned him and fifteen hundred feet more he purchased. He hired a plane and flew over the monument, drove almost every road within its boundaries, and ran a short river trip on the Yampa and Green Rivers through Echo Park to their confluence, where the Bureau of Reclamation proposed to build the keystone dam and reservoir.

Jess Lombard came along on this run with riverman Bus Hatch through the heart of the monument and strongly encouraged Eggert to visit the stunning Gates of Lodore. The Gates had been named by John Wesley Powell in 1869 during his first descent of the Green and Colorado

Rivers. They are the consequence of the Green River incising a spectacular gorge, Lodore Canyon, through the eastern flank of the Uinta Mountains. Eggert met Bus Hatch's son Don at the Gates and they boated two miles down into the canyon, as far as Little Stinker, a good-sized boulder in the middle of the river at the mouth of the Winnie's Grotto side canyon.[19] While motoring down and back they discussed their shared dream of rerunning the Powell trip before the dams proposed for the Green and Colorado's canyons were built. Don Hatch promised Eggert, "Charlie, when the right time comes we'll do it."[20]

Eggert returned to Barrytown and spliced together his film *This Is Dinosaur*. In keeping with the National Park Service's objectives, it features polite introductions to the scenic wonders of the monument, clear and brief explanations of the geological history, several scenes of pretty flowers and flowing waters, and a brief shot of a doe swimming across the river, then bounding up the rock-strewn hillside. For its musical soundtrack he commissioned Clair Leonard, one of his former professors at Bard, to improvise on the college chapel's organ. Leonard and Eggert screened the film in the chapel, timing with a stopwatch. Then Eggert started up the tape recorder and preserved Leonard's decidedly avant-garde and spare melodies.

Because of the interagency rivalry between the Bureau of Reclamation and the National Park Service, both arms of the Department of the Interior, the Park Service insisted the controversial proposal to build a dam or more within the monument not appear at all in *This Is Dinosaur* but that the film nonetheless extol the wilderness values threatened by inundation. Eggert succeeded at that difficult assignment. Executive Secretary Fred Packard of the National Parks Association answered, on December 30, 1952, a query from Richard Pough of the American Museum of Natural History in New York about Eggert's request to show *This Is Dinosaur* at the museum. Waxing a bit eloquent on Charles Eggert's recent history as a conservation cinematographer, Packard remarked,

> When I introduced him to the National Park Service people here, they provided him with some color film to take for them out there [Dinosaur National Monument], expecting him just to make the pictures for someone else to work up into a usable film.

> To their surprise, he came back a month or so ago with a complete film on Dinosaur, narrative, sound track, music, etc.—and it was superb! As a matter of fact, he has shown such originality in it that he has taught the Park Service something about nature presentation. Without mentioning the problem itself, he answered all of the points our opponents have raised—beauty, park values, accessibility, the boat trip, etc. I have no hesitation whatever in recommending it be shown, as well as the excellent slides he took at the same time."[21]

In *This Is Dinosaur* Charles Eggert had taken a major risk; satisfied his several cravings for scenic wonder, musical delight, photographic craftsmanship; and forged himself a new identity as a cinematographer. Although he had battled disappointment, this film restored his enthusiasm for life and work. *This Is Dinosaur* is not only a very well made film, but also marks a significant advance in park and monument publicity cinema for its grace in teaching moral values in addition to the scientific lessons. In the process he had also been swept up by the preservationist zeal motivating the activists campaigning to keep dams out of national parks and monuments. He organized in New York the first chapter of the Sierra Club outside California, sought venues to show *This Is Dinosaur*, and began work on a film on Acadia National Park in Maine. Charles Eggert had become a conservation and preservation evangelist, one who, at Ansel Adams's suggestion, had brought his photographic skills "into the conservation swim." The conservation and preservation movement enjoyed explosive growth in the early fifties. Eggert was both one of the first to enlist and among its most enthusiastic and effective recruiters.

During the summer of 1952, shortly after Eggert had finished his filming in Dinosaur National Monument, a second party came to visit and descend the river through the monument, an extended-family vacation led by Dr. Harold "Pops" Bradley, recently retired physiological chemistry professor at the University of Wisconsin Medical School and member of the Sierra Club Board of Directors. His sons numbered among themselves a remarkable array of interests and professions. Steve Bradley managed the Winter Park ski area on the continental divide above Denver, Colorado. When the snow melted, he floated the runoff in foldboats, then fiberglass kayaks (his own innovation). His brother David was a member of the California Academy of Sciences. William was a geology graduate student. Richard Bradley taught physics at University of Montana. In the fall Pops showed his film to anyone who would provide an audience and a few minutes, both in Madison and in the San Francisco Bay Area. Newly appointed executive director of the Sierra Club David Brower saw the Bradley film and took note of how effectively it cultivated enthusiasm against the proposed dams in Dinosaur National Monument. In the middle of the winter he attended the Wildlife Conference, where he saw Eggert's presentation of *This Is Dinosaur* and hatched one of his best ideas—hire Charles Eggert to make an advocacy film for the Sierra Club, one that would "call a dam a dam" rather than maintaining the decorum the National Park Service prudently required.

David Brower and Charles Eggert wrote back and forth throughout the winter and spring of 1952–53, laying plans for the new film. Eggert, his cameras, and four thousand feet of 16mm Commercial Kodachrome joined, on June 13, 1953, the first of five trips the Sierra Club ran through Dinosaur National Monument that summer. The club floated the river during the heat of the day, explored side canyons early and late, and indoctrinated the visitors at nightly campfires, an organization scheme and purpose familiar to Sierra Club members since it had been practiced by Dave Brower's mentor, William Colby, and John Muir before him on similar-sized "high trips" into the Sierra Nevada. The only major difference was that this time the expeditions used Bus Hatch's boatmen and surplus bridge pontoons rather than the wranglers and packhorses familiar in the Sierra Nevada. At the end of their trips the Sierra Clubbers went home and wrote impassioned letters to their senators and congressmen. Eggert went home and began to edit the film he had exposed. After arduous debates with Brower over the soundtrack, content of the narration, and even the sequence of scenes, Eggert delivered *Wilderness River Trail*, complete with new Clair Leonard accompaniment and Dave Brower narration.

His film did a better job of explaining a river trip than any other. Its scenes chronicle the automobile and truck travel from town to the river, the organized confusion of rigging the boats, loading the gear, piling the passengers aboard, and the subsequent serenity of drifting with the current downstream, leaving no tracks through the wilderness other than the boats' wakes. *Wilderness River Trail* is an impassioned piece of remarkably effective propaganda built upon the cinematic techniques Eggert developed in *This Is Dinosaur*. It confronts head-on the dam boosters' assertion that filling the canyons would facilitate recreational uses of the dangerous and isolated canyons in the heart of Dinosaur National Monument with images of men, women, and children frolicking, cooking, dining, contemplating, and otherwise enjoying the canyons from the rivers at their bottoms. As early as 1959 scholars studying the political wrangling over the Colorado River Storage Project identified *Wilderness River Trail* as one of the key tools the "Dinosaur Cooperators," the rag-tag alliance of conservation and preservation organizations opposed to the Echo Park dam and any others in the monument, marshalled in their battle against the Bureau of Reclamation.[22] In appreciation, the Sierra Club bestowed its first-ever honorary life membership on Eggert.

## "The Powell Stunt"

In November 1954 Charles Eggert began to plan his epic journey down the Green and Colorado Rivers from Green River, Wyoming, to Lake Mead, Arizona, broaching the idea to Bus and Don Hatch in Vernal, Utah. Bus ignored Eggert's letter, and Don replied with some serious second thoughts that focused on the expense of such an expedition and on the logistical challenges it posed.[23] During the time since Powell's first run in 1869 only a few similar transits of the canyons between Green River and the mouth of the Virgin River had been made: Powell's second geological and geographic exploration of 1871–72; two or maybe more descents by Nathaniel Galloway in the late 1890s, a trapper and prospector from Vernal, Utah; the George Flavell voyage of 1896; the Julius Stone voyage of 1909, guided by Nathaniel Galloway; Ellsworth and Emery Kolb in 1911, photographers with a shop on the South Rim of the Grand Canyon; Haldane "Buzz" Holmstrom's solitary descent from Green River to Boulder Dam in 1937; and Norman Nevills's publicity stunt trip in 1940.[24] Eggert proposed an innovation. He intended to film the canyons of the Green and Colorado in a special 16mm wide-screen format and then take the record of the last free-running days of the great river of the West on tour as a travelogue. The "rerun of the Powell stunt" as Bus Hatch disparaged it, offered nearly everything Eggert yearned for—a chance to introduce audiences to the glories of the wilderness, to return to the stage he so desperately missed, to return to the West, and the opportunity to ensconce his name in the record of major Colorado River explorers, the last of them to boot. The fight over dams in Dinosaur National Monument had been settled in a compromise of sorts. The Colorado River Storage Project's dams planned within the monument's canyons had been removed from the project, but their storage capacity had been replaced by planning a taller, thus deeper, dam at the foot of Glen Canyon on the Colorado River and a dam in Flaming Gorge, upstream from Dinosaur National Monument on the Green River. Eggert rejoiced in having helped preserve Dinosaur's canyons and mourned the looming losses to the other dams. His travelogue could show people across the country what was soon to be lost in hopes that they would resist and oppose additional destruction of free-running rivers in the West. His expedition offered him the last chance to see those canyons unspoiled and to run the rivers that had carved them in their natural, free-running state.

Don Hatch, on the other hand, faced the daunting problem of leaving his father alone to manage their river running partnership for most of the season and of convincing Bus that was a good idea. In preparation for those discussions Don prepared a generously profitable estimate of expenses for a forty-day trip totaling nearly $4,000 and tasked Eggert with raising at least ten paying guests.[25] Eggert responded with a suggestion to lengthen the trip to sixty days, reduce the number of paying guests to eight, and set the fare at $700 each, but confessed he had not yet elicited a single commitment.[26] After dithering back and forth without securing any customers for nearly three months, Eggert, because he recognized it as "a place to get odd-ball people to do odd-ball things," arranged for a classified advertisement to run three weeks in succession in the *Saturday Review*. It read:

> EXPLORE WITH TOP BOATMEN and renowned wilderness photographer down the Green and Colorado Rivers. Expedition leaves Green River, Wyoming June 10th on sixty-day journey to Lake Mead through sixteen fabulous canyons including Grand Canyon. Relive voyage Major Powell made in 1869. Requirement: ruggedness! Inquire: Charles Eggert, Barrytown, New York.[27]

Several would-be adventurers replied to Eggert's solicitation and received in the return mail his four-page, thrill- and trepidation-packed description of the expedition's plans and requirements. Some applicants set even cosmopolitan Charles Eggert back for their outrageous gay flirtation or macho braggadocio. Two enquiries, however, caused him great pause. Patricia Fretwell, wife of the leader of Explorer Post 20 of Los Alamos, New Mexico, asked about the trip on behalf of her husband and herself. Eggert politely but firmly replied, "you'll note that we have said we are limiting our party to 14 men. We do not mean we have closed the door to the female of the species. However, we'd like you to very seriously consider the various situations we will encounter on the journey."[28] Eggert had no way of knowing he was turning down one of the most experienced female whitewater boaters in the United States, but he managed to run her off, along with her husband James H. "Stretch" Fretwell. Explorer Post 20 under Stretch Fretwell's leadership trained a remarkable cadre of young men as boatmen. Their influence on river running, beginning in the late 1960s, persists to the present. Mrs. Fretwell's enquiry helped soften Eggert up for a second query, however, this one from one Mrs. C. R. Sumner who was extraordinarily well-spoken on the page, writing, "I am old enough not to be disturbed in the company of men, no matter what their physiological necessities might be."[29] In addition to Mrs. Sumner, Eggert rounded up a few more paying customers: Fred Wood, a book peddler from Bridgeport, Connecticut; Bob Parsons, Fred Wood's brother-in-law and pathologist from Oakland, California; and Leslie Emsden, an English physician. He borrowed $18,000 from the First National Bank of Red Hook, New York, to finance his travels, cameras and film, and postproduction and presentation expenses, and launched from Green River, Wyoming, at 9:45 a.m. on June 11, 1955.

On the other side of the continent the *New Yorker* of the same date printed a generous description of the Eggert-Hatch Expedition's plans, and Lowell Thomas announced the party's embarkation on his news broadcast that evening on CBS.[30] In 1998 Eggert identified three major stimuli behind his trip in 1955, inspiration from Wallace Stegner's book on Powell, *Beyond the Hundredth Meridian*,[31] a compulsion to see all the canyons of the Green and Colorado River system, and "to travel the last untouched trail in America" that "would soon be destroyed in part by reservoirs. I wanted to record it for posterity before it was gone."[32] Eggert's head boatman, Don Hatch, who shared Eggert's desire to experience the threatened canyons one last time, recorded his initial impression of the trip in his journal: "Used 4½ gals. Gas. Sissy crowd—all except boatmen. Big boat towed bad. Charlie 'wishy washy' still . . . hope passengers leave at Jensen. Hate commercial trips anyway. Beautiful sunset. 3 picts. Heavily loaded." The Hatch boatmen on the trip included Bruce Lium, a seventeen-year-old college student from Salt Lake City, and Leslie Jones, an engineer for the Utah Highway Department. Hatch's spirits quickly rallied as he, Lium, and Jones settled to the familiar routine of hosting guests on the rivers. By June 14, as the party camped in the rain at the Gates of Lodore, he reported the "Crew lively & in good spirits."[33] Don's observations kept close records of the water stage and documented his worries that he and the expedition might lose their race with the river, that the high water might outrun them and leave them with too little river to ride at the downstream end of their journey. As *The Last Canyon Voyage* relates, they lost the race but succeeded in floating and photographing the canyons of the Green and Colorado rivers and in cementing treasured and enduring friendships. As the party disembarked at Lee's Ferry they vowed to return the next season to finish the trip. Eggert, Hatch, Lium, and Wood made good on their promises in 1956.

No trip on the Green and Colorado Rivers has produced as much literary and cinematic output as the Eggert-Hatch Expedition of 1955. Charles Eggert quickly edited and assembled *A Canyon Voyage*, again featuring a score by Clair Leonard, and took it on tour. He unofficially premiered it at Bard College on November 12 and 13, 1955. Realizing it opened with entirely too much dry discussion of geological process, he reworked its beginning sequences, then officially premiered the film at the Cosmos Club, Washington, D.C., on November 21, 1955. John Wesley Powell, on an inspiration from Clarence Dutton, had founded the Cosmos Club in the fall of 1878.[34] Howard Zahniser, one of Eggert's associates from the Echo Park Dam fight and executive secretary of the Wilderness Society, plied his influence as a member of the Cosmos Club to wrangle an invitation for Eggert to present his new work in those august environs and to join the organization. Three weeks later Eggert presented *A Canyon Voyage* to the Explorers Club in New York and was similarly initiated into that group. Between December 15, 1955, and February 29, 1960, Charles Eggert presented *A Canyon Voyage* to sixty-eight audiences, whose members paid him between $100 and $500 per performance for a total revenue of $17,519, hardly a resounding business success. The film he made from his 1956 voyage through Marble Gorge and Grand Canyon, *Danger River*, netted a far smaller gross, fifteen showings for $3,320.[35] Eggert's financial independence allowed him to pursue his dream of filming and showing the canyons of the Green and Colorado to audiences all over the country. *A Canyon Voyage* is Eggert's masterpiece. Almost all the shots are handheld and rock steady. His adept use of the 2x1 aspect ratio of his lenses to convey the grandeur of the canyons, a technique he acquired and mastered as he floated down the river, is particularly successful. Eggert's voice was an instrument, and he had mastered it. Eggert's early career as a moviemaker had been one of dizzyingly rapid maturation and success. That growth rate proved, to widespread disappointment, impossible to sustain.

Such miniscule returns on so large an investment of time and borrowed money increased the tensions in Charles and Betty Eggert's marriage, but nothing like Charlie and Betty's purchase August 10, 1961, of Wyndclyffe, the outlandish mansion and estate on the Hudson built for and at the whim of Elizabeth Schmermerhorn Jones and her brother Edward in 1853. Even Eggert's ample assets could not finance restoring the woe-befallen relic of so ostentatious an age. The Eggerts turned a fair gain on Wyndclyffe; from an initial purchase price of $12,500 they subdivided the estate on three separate occasions and then sold the derelict mansion for $85,000 on October 6, 1971.[36] They were distracted from the Wyndclyffe project by another restoration project, the Federal period home Maizefield in Red Hook, New York. The entire family worked on its restoration, a far more feasible project. The boys were assigned to strip off the wallpaper. The product of their labors won listing in the National Register of Historic Places on November 26, 1973. Shortly thereafter the Eggerts received a printed but anonymous card reading, "The Park Service is pleased to announce your property has been selected as a game preserve and the first shipment of 5,000 buffalo will arrive Tuesday at 3:25 a.m." Hours of mirthful speculation have ensued conjuring friends in the Park Service who might have been the culprit. On a more serious note, living in and around an architectural restoration project had a major influence on both of Charles and Betty's sons. Charles Christopher "Kip" worked as a sculptural wood craftsman in the Hudson River Valley and Robert Sebastian "Seb" operates an architectural millwork shop in Port Townsend, Washington. Neither of them ever cared for wallpaper thereafter.

While engrossed in his restoration endeavors, Eggert again tried his hand at authorship. He penned three manuscripts for three publishers, all tentatively titled *Forbidden Passage*. Eggert won, before he launched, a contract from Alfred Knopf to write a children's book recounting the Eggert-Hatch Expedition of 1955. His memoir of the journey missed the children's literature mark by a wide margin, and Knopf turned it down. That work is the heart of this volume. His second piece admiringly tells the story of Powell's 1869 trip with good-natured judgment and balanced personal interjections from the 1955 expedition. He hustled it to *American Heritage*, but the magazine could not figure out how to serialize or shorten the sixty-three page manuscript, which was too long for an article and too short for a book. Through Dave Brower's literary agent, Perry Knowlton, Eggert submitted the piece to Walker Publishing. Jake Page, editor at Walker, suggested Eggert follow the model of a recent American publication of the Gospels of Matthew, Mark, Luke, and John, and publish side by side the germane sections from the Powell Expedition's journals and his own.[37] Eggert eagerly began the writing in 1971, got as far down the river as Ouray, Utah, and his life and marriage disintegrated. Notwithstanding his editor's plea to "KEEP GOING, PLEASE !!!" on the last page of the unfinished draft, Eggert never finished the piece. In 1998 he rued, "I have such a guilt over this unfinished work, I can't describe it! But nothing seems to get my enthusiasm up to continue on and at this point I feel it is too late."[38] When Sarah Holcombe chanced to read what Charlie Eggert always called the "Knopf manuscript" during her research for a biography of Cid Sumner, she and Roy Webb initiated publication of the volume in your hands.

Cid Sumner's contemplative memoir of her adventure with her rugged men friends, *Traveler in the Wilderness*, bookends Charles Eggert's films with its Easterner's introduction to and zealous infatuation with the wilds of the arid West. Published both in the United States and in England, it sold well. River runners and wilderness enthusiasts continue to savor her eloquence.[39] She was a successful author, writing and publishing eleven novels and three works of nonfiction in a thirty-two-year professional career.

Tony Tuttle, Eggert's assistant on the 1955 voyage, returned to finish at Bard, headed off to California to continue his career in the theater and to the fast times Eggert had known two decades earlier. Abruptly shifting from actor to author, Tony published his first novel in 1966. *This Time in Twilight* is a fictional account of dark and complex social dynamics played out in a canyon doomed to inundation. It sold better in England than in the United States, but never sold a thousand copies in the two markets combined.[40]

## Second Coming at Canyonlands

By 1962 Charles Eggert had redirected his energies to historic preservation and real estate speculation in the Hudson River Valley until Secretary of the Interior Stewart Udall, acting on the urging by Superintendent Bates Wilson of Arches National Monument, began actively campaigning for the creation of a Canyonlands National Park from the expansive public domain surrounding the confluence of the Green and Colorado Rivers southwest of Moab in southeastern Utah. Recalling Eggert's aesthetically delightful yet successful propagandizing during the Echo Park Dam fight and the eloquent lessons on preserving spectacular landscapes from development taught by *A Canyon Voyage*, Udall hired Charles Eggert to shoot, edit, and produce a film to promote the new park's creation. Unlike the Dinosaur contest, the proposal to create Canyonlands National Park did not antagonize another branch of the Department of Interior, so Udall encouraged Eggert to create an advocacy piece. Charlie spent forty-two days traipsing behind their guide, Bates Wilson, aboard jeeps, on horseback, and afoot. Through forty-eight minutes *The Sculptured Earth* extols the values of the region as an archaeological and aesthetic treasure, as a geological and geomorphological laboratory and classroom, and as a preserve of glorious desert biota, as Eggert resurrected the exhortations and much of the outline of *Wilderness River Trail*. Over a score, again by Clair Leonard, Eggert closes *The Sculptured Earth* with an evangelical message familiar since his epiphany in Yellowstone, now augmented by the wilderness and historic preservation endeavors of the decade since: "Let us protect this land from the spreading maw and sharp talons of civilization as one of our great national parks, where values are measured not in dollars but in solitude, in exaltation, and in spiritual re-creation."[41] Charlie Eggert stuck with a successful design and succeeded yet again. His success can be measured, at least in part, by the political controversy in subsequent Utah elections.

Utah's electorate was deeply fissured by the proposal to establish a national park, removing 257,640 acres of unknown resources from potential exploitation. As a general rule, in the Congressional elections of both 1962 and 1964, Republican candidates for Congress opposed the park's creation and Democratic candidates supported it. In that tense political context, when Democratic secretary Udall asked to premier *The Sculptured Earth* at the University of Utah's largest auditorium, Republican governor George D. Clyde, in a fit of partisan pique, forbade such political use of state property. Eggert, Udall, and several National Park Service staffers quickly arranged to screen the film at the Hotel Utah to repeat sold-out crowds.[42] As influential Utahns—ranging from David O. McKay, president of the Church of Jesus Christ of Latter-day Saints, on down to mere voters—expressed their favorable impression of the park from Eggert's film, the Utah congressional delegation adopted a more compromising stance and ultimately allowed the legislation through Congress in early September 1964. Within two weeks President Lyndon B. Johnson signed the park into existence.

**Dams in Grand Canyon**

When the proposal to build two dams in the Grand Canyon surfaced in 1965, David Brower cast about looking for film footage showing the threatened reaches, recalled Eggert's *A Canyon Voyage* and *Danger River* films from 1955 and 1956, and began a whirlwind cut, splice, and edit ordeal to produce from the lecture-circuit movies what Eggert since called "a Sierra Club cinemascope propaganda piece against the Marble and Bridge Canyon dams." The dam opponents showed the new *A Canyon Voyage* continuously in a hearing room in the Capitol and at the National Press Club. The two veterans of the Echo Park Dam fight collaborated on the script Brower read for the narration. It opens with an homage to John Wesley Powell's farsighted understanding of the West and the problems posed by aridity, then segues into reminding the senators and representatives that the Bureau of Reclamation had been "stopped by a Congress that stood firm for the National Park System" in Dinosaur National Monument. The narration returns to the iconic image of Powell over scenes from "Glen Canyon, where all the glens are gone now. All lie buried under the rise and fall of Lake Powell, which drowns what Powell liked best there." The script gave Theodore Roosevelt the last word in the film as Brower intones Roosevelt's familiar and most apt, "Leave it as it is. You cannot improve it. The ages have been at work on it and man can only mar it." Charlie Eggert, with a glistening twinkle in his eye, delighted in terming his friend Dave Brower's rhetorical flourishes "calling a spade a steam shovel," but here Brower declaimed the doctrines of their passionately shared creed, which held that "90 percent of the American Earth is more than enough to sustain a lasting civilization and 10 percent invested in wilderness is needed to sustain meaning in that civilization."[43]

## Life After His Second Coming

The uproar Brower instigated over the proposed dams in Grand Canyon proved too much for the Sierra Club's Board of Directors to countenance and cost Brower his job as executive director. Undismayed, he became president of Friends of the Earth and joined the boards of directors of and allied closely with the John Muir Institute for Environmental Studies and the League of Conservation Voters. Charles Eggert briefly worked for the Friends of the Earth during 1970 and 1971, then was dismissed by that organization and divorced by his wife, Betty, in the worst years of his life. He trained as a National Park Service ranger, including law enforcement training, to make himself into what he called a "pine tree pig." Assigned to guard his old acquaintance Eleanor Roosevelt's home, by then the Franklin Delano Roosevelt Library and Roosevelt-Vanderbilt National Historic Site, Eggert took refuge in the Park Service and later credited it with helping him preserve his sanity.

The twentieth anniversary of the founding of Canyonlands National Park in 1984 brought him out of his near seclusion in the Hudson River Valley and back to eastern Utah. He traveled to Canyonlands to show his *The Sculptured Earth* and basked in the first accolades and applause he had enjoyed in nearly twenty years. On the way Charlie, Kip, and Seb dropped in unannounced on Don Hatch in Vernal, Utah. Hatch, ever resilient to surprises, took the Eggert men through Split Mountain Gorge the next day to show Charlie's boys what was behind their father's obsession with rivers and canyons. Flush with delight reliving old adventures and successes, Charlie called on Dinosaur National Monument. He was heartbroken to note they had no idea who he was and how he

Charles Eggert (L) and Don Hatch at Split Mountain boat ramp on the Green River during a reunion in 1984. Photograph courtesy of Sebastian Eggert.

was associated with the preservation of the monument's canyons. That heartbreak drove him back into near seclusion in the Wyndclyffe carriage house he and Seb had remodeled and retained when the rest of the property had been sold in 1971.

When Roy Webb wrote his biography of Bus Hatch in 1989, Bus's son Don sent a copy to Charles Eggert. As was his compulsion, Charlie immediately repaired to the index to find his name. *Riverman: The Story of Bus Hatch* has no index so Charlie had to read it cover to cover.[44] In the entire discussion of the Echo Park Dam fight, a key episode in Bus Hatch's personal and commercial life, Eggert found nary a word about *This Is Dinosaur* nor about *Wilderness River Trail*, let alone his name. Eggert was furious, and in a maniacal rage he fired off a letter to Webb, a prolific river historian and first-rate media archivist at the University of Utah's Marriott Library. Roy coolly replied, "How can historical researchers study you to write your story into the books when you keep all your records squirreled away in New York?" Webb's courtship, featuring his plan to deliver a talk on the Eggert films to the Colorado Plateau River

Guides training seminar in Moab, eventually convinced Charles Eggert to donate his films and papers to the Marriott. While researching in the Hatch River Expeditions Papers at the Marriott Library in 1997, I stumbled upon some of the Don Hatch–Charles Eggert correspondence planning the 1955 expedition and let out a most unprofessional whoop and holler. Roy's casual mention that Eggert had just that year donated papers to the library led to establishing the lengthy email correspondence upon which this brief biography has so thoroughly depended.

Although it had taken decades, river people finally discovered Charles Eggert and came to appreciate his important contributions. Eggert basked in the new rays of attention. In 1998 Don Hatch River Expeditions hosted him and many members of his family on an Eggert-Hatch reunion and memorial celebration trip through Lodore Canyon. Charlie, eighty years young, noted that this time he finally got to ride through the rapids. He had walked around them all in order to photograph them in the past. He resuscitated *A Canyon Voyage* and dusted off his long-forgotten narration for a performance May 6, 2000, in the theater of the John Wesley Powell Museum in Green River, Utah, as the main event at the Colorado Plateau River Guides spring seminar. He stole the show, reduced work-hardened boat folk to tears with his images of drowned Glen Canyon, and received his first standing ovation. The following Sunday he repeated the performance at a rally in Moab for the decommissioning of Glen Canyon Dam and reunited with his old friend Dave Brower for the first time since 1971.

Charlie once mentioned the four things he had done in his life about which he was most proud: his roles in preserving Dinosaur National Monument and in establishing Canyonlands National Park; his honorary life membership in the Sierra Club, the first ever bestowed, awarded for his *Wilderness River Trail;* and his and Betty's restoration of Maizefield.

Eggert underestimated his significance. The conservation and preservation movement in the United States underwent a marked change in the decades immediately following the Second World War. Charles Eggert's influence on the direction of those changes, particularly his development of a new style of film in order to influence policy even at the national level, has been too often overlooked. Following Eggert's successful *Wilderness River Trail*, the Sierra Club became a remarkably active producer of propaganda films but never asked him to do another. The Sierra Club's embrace of new media constituted an important dimension of its rapid transition from a remarkably insular California mountaineering club into one of the most effective national-scale activist organizations in the environmentalist camp in the 1950s and 1960s.

Charles Eggert had the good fortune to be adopted into a family that provided him with nearly a lifetime of financial security. His personal experiences growing up in the 1920s and 1930s presaged the great increase in leisure available to Americans in the booming years following the Second World War. He experimented with a broad array of leisure and recreational activities, taking some so seriously they became professions: theater, dance, music, photography, wining and dining, and fast cars and boats. Yet, he sought the deeper understanding, the longer view, that focus on the infinite horizon he saw in the rodeo hand's eyes. Returning from his epiphany at Yellowstone Falls, he sought out a way to do good work doing good works. Finding his subject, however, entailed something of a protracted courtship between man and water. Young Charles learned the basics as a child "messing around in boats" on the shores of Lake Erie. As he started his own family in the Hudson River Valley, that stately stream, although it spawned an entire school of landscape painting, had little to say to him. The young streams outside his cabins at the Paton Ranch and Cottonwood Ranch grabbed his attention, chattering incessantly about their clear and sweet waters, their savory trout, the austere landscapes they had sculpted, and bragging about the comfortable environment in the valley bottom in contrast to the arid hillsides. Swept off his feet, Charles Eggert was thoroughly seduced, so much so that when he learned from Conrad Wirth of the threats to the Yampa and Green Rivers in Dinosaur National Monument, like Lohengrin defending fair Elsa's honor in Richard Wagner's opera of the same name, he immediately joined the battle. Eggert made much of his opportunity and dedicated his remarkable creativity and some of the best years of his life to advancing the conservationist and preservationist causes of preserving and revering free-flowing rivers in their spectacular landscapes. In this sense he exemplifies the changing environmental movement of midcentury America. He was a man very much of his time and place at the outset of the modern environmental movement. At the same time, he marked the end of an era, the era of grand expeditions.

His 1955–56 descent of the Green and Colorado Rivers was the last expedition mounted to transit the entire reach between Green River, Wyoming, and the mouth of the Virgin River in Nevada. Expeditions' purposes had changed during the eighty-six years between John Wesley Powell's geographic exploration and geological investigation in 1869 and Charles Eggert's sentimental and cinematic journeys in 1955–56. In addition to Powell's and Eggert's respective objectives, Robert Brewster Stanton had surveyed the canyons for a railroad route; Nathaniel Galloway had prospected and trapped his way down the river, then led Julius Stone and friends down the river for the sheer joy of the experience; Clyde Eddy and his band of college boys seemed to have been on a joyless quest to prove their manhood. In each instance the leaders invested substantial personal resources in their voyages of discovery. Charles Eggert's expedition succeeded in seeing the canyons of the Green and Colorado before they were defiled with additional dams, and was the last to be able to do so. He wrote of his memories of Glen Canyon and Rainbow Bridge in 1958, after construction had begun on the dam, "If there is weeping to be done, cry over the destruction of this place! . . . We were among the last to know . . . it. Our sons would not know it, and we tried to forget how rich an experience was being taken from them."[45]

One additional item belongs on Charles Eggert's list of notable accomplishments. The Eaton-Eggert family plot in Monroe, Michigan, contains a headstone engraved Charles D. Eggert, 1918-19. Charlie celebrated the passing millennium with especial glee, outliving by half a decade the stonecutter's expectations. He died December 21, 2005, satisfied that during his fourscore and seven years on Earth he had helped make our home a better place.

*One*

# THE IDEA

It was in the spring of 1952 when I first mentioned the idea to anyone. Don Hatch and I were perched on a rock ledge high above the Green River, silently looking into the awesome purple chasm of Lodore Canyon. As we listened to the roar of a rapid far below us, I asked, "How would you like to go down it all the way?"

"To Mead?"

"Yeah, from Green River, Wyoming, to Lake Mead—the Grand Wash Cliffs—the way Powell did."

"That's always been a dream of mine," Don said, "but I've never found a good reason to do it—except just wanting to."

"Isn't that reason enough?"

"Not in Dad's book. That'd be a doggone expensive deal—take a long time too." Don turned to me. "Charlie, you realize that'd be more than a thousand miles? It would take from forty to sixty days—and there's another problem: the river would never be right."

"What do you mean, 'the river would never be right'?"

"The water volume in the river, I mean. If you started up here in high water, by the time you got to Grand Canyon, the river would be too low. If you started really early up here—so the spring runoff would hit the Grand when you got there—the going would be too rough for too long on low water at this end."

"Well," I said, a bit exasperated, "Powell did it! Did it twice!"

"Yeah," Don answered with a chuckle. "Powell did it all right. And he's about the only one who ever has! Matter of fact, I guess only about

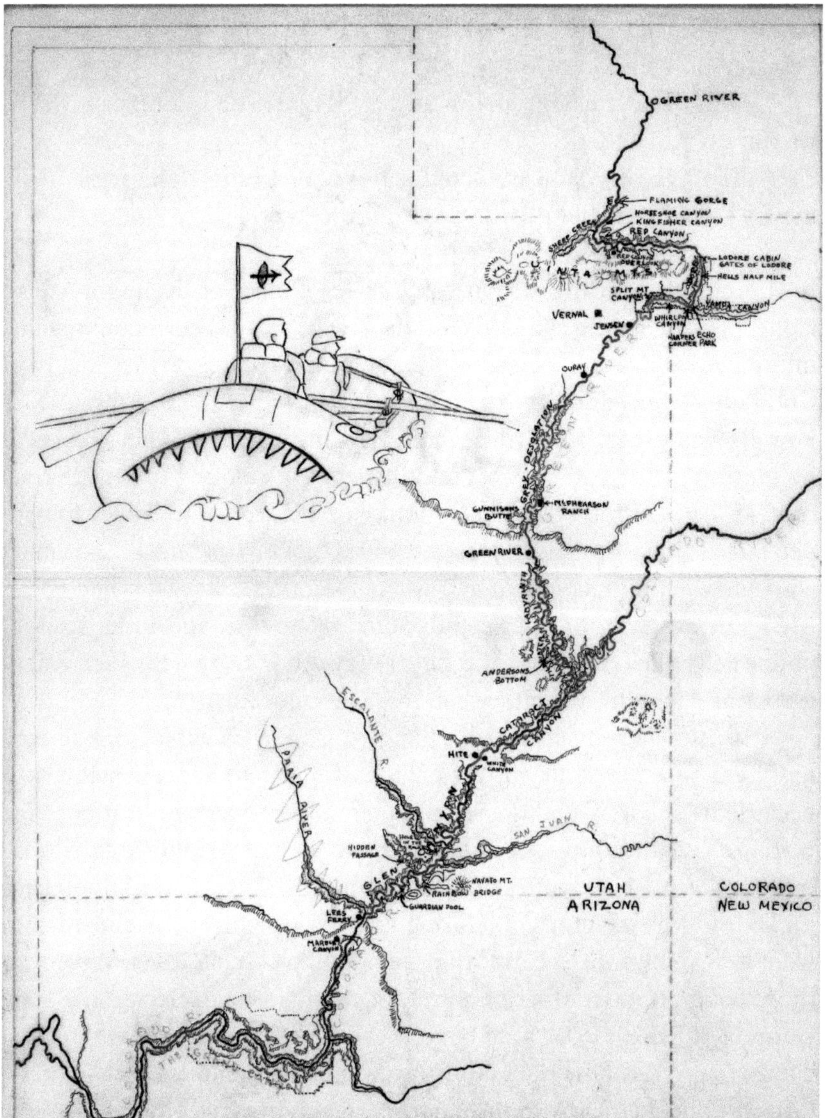


A hand-drawn map by Charles Eggert showing the route of the entire river trip during 1955–1956, starting at Green River, Wyoming, and ending at Lake Mead, on the Arizona-Nevada border.

six expeditions have made it all the way down since then. Not that others haven't tried," he added after a pause. "Some of them never even got *this* far." He pointed to the canyon. "In fact, a boat is piled up on the rocks at Disaster Falls right now."

"Well," I said, pushing all this aside, "I'd like to do it someday. Maybe we can do it together."

"Yeah, Charlie," Don answered as he got up to stretch his legs. "Yeah, maybe someday we'll find a reason—and we'll do it."

In the fall of 1954, the reason came. The chances of the Eighty-third Congress passing the Upper Colorado River Storage Project bill seemed imminent.[1] That would mean building at least two dams on the Green and Colorado Rivers, and the chances of ever traveling Major John Wesley Powell's wilderness river trail would be gone forever. So far as I knew, no motion picture existed that told the story of running the entire river route of 1,030 miles. Were such a film to be made, it would have to happen soon.

One evening I sat down and wrote Don that the reason had come. My letter began a long series of letters, telegrams, and long-distance phone calls to Don in Salt Lake City. Every intricate plan for such a dangerous and lengthy adventure had to be discussed.

If an adventurer sets off on a dangerous journey with a look of contentment that hides all outward signs of fear and apprehension, it is because he is happy that the seemingly endless toil, complications, and worry of organization have at last come to an end. When we shoved off on the Green River on the morning of June 11, 1955, I could look back on six months of intense planning and organizing and feel glad they were over. When we left our campsite behind at Green River, Wyoming, there were no more worries about whether we had selected the right equipment, whether the food boxes were watertight, whether there were enough supplies of the right kind, or whether the members of the expedition would get along with one another.[2] There was nothing now to face but the challenge of the adventure itself, and we would have to face that with what we had in the boats.

Just what were the adventure and the challenge? Our maps gave us an indication. In Salt Lake City is a master set of maps, consisting of thirty-six sheets, which mark the course from Green River, Wyoming, to Temple Bar on Lake Mead in Arizona. These maps record the experiences and knowledge gained by various expeditions that have traveled all or part of the Green and Colorado Rivers, from Major Powell's first expedition in 1869 (put down on the maps by later historians) to the most recent attempts. We had had five sets of photostatic copies of the master set made, and I had spent long hours studying the notations written on them. At mile point 743½ was noted, "Bert & Wayne capsized (7-8-49)"; at mile point 744½, "Bert last seen entering rapid by Wayne," and at mile point 760, "Bert's wrecked boat left here—erected stone monument around an oar—Placed 'In Memoriam' in jar at base of monument."[3] There were other grim indications of the challenge. "Stanton's Point—Peter Hansbrough [*sic*] drown ten miles above—buried by 700' column" was printed beside mile point 763.[4]

Possible campsites—and impossible ones—were also marked: "Good campsite on nice rock ledges—good drinking water" was a notation at mile point 582 in Glen Canyon. At mile point 702 was a warning: "Dangerous campsite—watch canyon in case of flash flood, falling rocks." "Don't drink water from these creeks!" advised one entry with arrows pointing to two spots near mile point 664.

At mile point 86 on sheet three, our map stated, "Theodore Hook's disaster site—1869—Drowned following Powell."[5] On sheet twenty-eight, at mile point 782, we added these words to the map from a report we received just before shoving off: "Boyd Moore drowned May 26, 1955."[6] From sheet three to twenty-eight, from mile point 86 to 782, from 1869 to 1955, the story was the same—one of challenge and tragedy. During the many years and over the many miles, men had set off to confront the world's most dangerous river. Few had won; many had lost.

The journals of the men who had made the run—or part of it—made it seem no less dangerous or easier than our maps indicated. These journals are tales of struggle and suffering, of fear and anxiety. The account of Clyde Eddy's run from Green River, Utah, to Black Canyon in 1927 is no less frightening than Powell's journey in 1869.[7] Yet the anxiety I first developed from reading these accounts was subjugated by the task of organizing our own expedition. The fear of the river was overcome by the fear of wrong decisions, bad planning, or poor judgment. These, above all, were the things that had defeated the others. The fear that gripped me when we started was the fear of fear itself. As coleaders of the expedition, Don and I would not be allowed the luxury of fear, for were it to be revealed at any time, it would most certainly travel down the ranks of our crew like a fuse on a stick of dynamite, and the entire expedition would explode in chaos.

When I had had time to take my thoughts from planning the expedition to the experience before me, I had felt many moments of fear and hesitation. As I spent hours studying the maps, I wondered what notations our expedition would add to them. How far would we get?

As I traveled across the great plains of Nebraska in my Jeep station wagon on my way to Vernal, Utah, where I would join Don Hatch, the other two boatmen, and one of our passengers, I felt a compelling desire to turn around and go back—back to the security of my home and family. It was late afternoon, which always to me is the loneliest part of the day, and big, dark storm clouds covered the horizon ahead. For a moment, I felt I was heading straight for doomsday. But then I remembered why I was doing it. This might be the last chance I would ever get to travel the wilderness river trail of Major John Wesley Powell and find it almost as untouched as it had been in his day.[8] Civilization is rapidly spreading its sharp talons in the name of progress and development across the land, and there are few opportunities to follow historic trails and experience them as the original explorers did. Today it would be very hard to imagine what it was like when John Colter took his fabulous lone journey up the Bighorn and Wind Rivers and became the first white man to see what is now Yellowstone National Park.[9] It would be impossible to follow the course of Lewis and Clark up the Missouri and across the continent and see it as they did.

The wilderness river trail of Powell was, in 1955, the last untouched—or relatively untouched—historic trail in the United States. I wanted to follow it and see it as Powell had before it was too late. George Mallory, when asked why he wanted to risk his life climbing to the top of a mountain, said, "Because it is there!"[10] My reason was the opposite: because it would not be there.

I'm glad that the momentum of the complications and details of organizing the expedition—plus the inspiration of the reason for undertaking it—kept me going west that afternoon on the plains of Nebraska, for on October 15, 1956, President Eisenhower, from his desk in the White House, pushed a button. It set off twin blasts of high explosives that rocked the stillness in two of the West's remote canyons, Flaming Gorge and Glen Canyon, and sent tons of rock into the Green and Colorado Rivers. The blasts signaled the construction of two huge dams that would forever block the passage of travelers on the wilderness river trail of Major John Wesley Powell. Our expedition was the last to make it.

*Two*

# DON HATCH

Vernal, Utah, is an oasis, particularly if you have traveled six days to get to it from the Atlantic Coast in a Jeep station wagon.[1] I passed the city limits sign at 10:30 a.m., having left Rawlins, Wyoming, before sunrise. Coming to the first street running north, I rounded the corner as fast as my little Jeep could go. I was a day late! There was the Hatch house at last—the only one in the block with a big picture window that looked out on nothing but a weed-filled vacant lot. It seemed to me that window was meant more for people to look into than out of. But Bus Hatch, besides being the head of the Hatch River Expeditions—a summertime enterprise—was also a contractor, and I suppose his window was partly advertising.[2] It also helped people to locate him, for during the river running season, the Hatch house was always teeming with activity, inside and out, with people inquiring about, just returning from, or waiting to go on a river trip through the canyons of Dinosaur National Monument.[3] Although the Hatches occasionally ran trips down the Snake River, or the Salmon, or sometimes through Grand Canyon, the canyons of the Upper Green and Yampa Rivers were their specialty.

As I pulled up in front of the house, I expected everyone to notice me. After all, here was one of the men who were going to make that fantastic and dangerous journey all the way down the rivers. Certainly they had heard about our expedition! I supposed it was the talk of the town. But no one looked up as I crossed the lawn, no one noticed my manner of great importance. I went into the house unannounced. Frank Hatch greeted me with a matter-of-fact "Well, so you got here."[4] I expected to find Don but learned he was at the warehouse getting our equipment ready. Naturally, he'd be there working; there were all these last-minute preparations!

Without the fanfare I had expected, I left just as unnoticed as I had arrived. Did the Hatches resent that I was a day late? I did feel guilty leaving Don alone to work on the boats, buy the supplies, and entertain one of our passengers, a Mrs. Sumner. Perhaps they thought I had slowly ambled along, enjoying the scenery. Little did they know how fast I had driven west to get here as quickly as I could. What with all the car trouble I had had, being just a day late was nigh to miraculous!

When I got to the warehouse, which looked more like a deserted lumberyard than anything else, I spotted Don in the backyard working over something. Turning into the driveway and going as fast as the situation would allow, I drove up right behind him and gave a loud blast on the horn. Without so much as a flinch, Don turned around and said, "Well, how-de-do! Where have you been?"

He knew perfectly well where I had been. Hadn't I called him from Rawlins the night before, and here it was just noon? I had made darned good time! His nonchalance made me feel as though I had just come across the street to borrow a screwdriver! But this was his way; he never got excited over anything, and this helped make him one of the best boatmen on the river. It put his passengers at ease in the tight spots where worry or hysteria might mean disaster.

"I hope this is the right size," he said, pointing to a large marine plywood box that was lined on the outside with foam rubber and covered with canvas. In it we would carry the twenty thousand feet of 16mm color motion-picture film and other assorted film we would be using during the voyage. The box had been built with more than extra precaution; it had to be waterproof, even if dumped into the river, and buoyant. Eight clamps held the lid down solidly. Because color film deteriorates rapidly in heat, we hoped to keep the interior of the box cool by soaking the outside foam rubber lining with water. The outer canvas lining held not only the foam rubber in place; it also soaked up more water and slowed down evaporation. There was extra room inside the box to store microphones, maps, and other important items that we could least risk ruining. Leaning over the box and driving tacks into the canvas was a young and, I thought, rather fat fellow, wearing a white cowboy hat.

"My! It's a big thing—looks heavy," I replied, half meaning the box and half the person leaning over it.

"Bruce," Don said as an introduction to one of our boatmen. Bruce![5] I was disappointed.

"But he'll work that weight off on the river," Don added, apparently reading my thoughts. Did I reveal them so obviously?

Bruce chuckled at Don's remark, then wiped his hand on his pant leg and extended it to me. "Hi-ya, Charlie," he said, taking a very firm grip. He looked at me as if he was really glad to meet me.

"The boats are over here," Don said as he took me to a heap of what looked like a rubber junk pile. Nothing appears more desperately helpless than a deflated rubber boat, and what was to be the *Brontosaur*, our twenty-seven-foot boat, looked more desperate and dilapidated and dirty than any I had seen before.[6] I don't know what I had expected: a bright, shining galleon in full sail perhaps?

"And these are the angle irons that will support the food boxes off the bottom of the boat," Don said. He explained that these 8 × 5½-foot angle-iron frames would be suspended with nylon straps a foot and a half above the rubber bottom of the big boat. On the frames, we would load all our food boxes and equipment, leaving the bottom free and flexible in the event that we hit rocks. Also because all the weight would be suspended, the boat would remain free to twist and bend and ride the surface of the big rapids' waves instead of plowing into or under them. "Gotta make a couple more before we start—Dad broke them on his last trip through Lodore," Don explained. "Doggone it, I can't keep Dad's hands off our equipment. That's why the *Bronto* looks so scuffed up. She was freshly painted when I brought her over from Salt Lake. But it was a good thing he went ahead and tried her out," he continued. "It saves us some failures."

Well, that was true, but I resented anyone using our equipment. I wanted to start out with everything looking new.

"He broke an oarlock too, so we're improving that design," Don said, breaking into my thoughts. "Better to find these things out now than out on the river. I'm making some new frames too—shorter and stronger." After a pause, he went on, "Bruce went with him. He's just learning to run the river, and, Charlie, he's going to work out fine—real fine!"

Don knew I was disappointed that we couldn't get Bruce's older brother, Clark, to come with us. Clark was twenty-seven, with experience as a boatman and maturity that would mix better with us older folks. Bruce was only seventeen. Among the many things I would learn on this voyage was that maturity cannot be judged by age alone—if it can be determined by age at all!

My thoughts now turned to Mrs. Sumner, who was our only woman passenger.[7] I had planned to meet her the night before at the Vernal airport. When I knew I couldn't make it and had to stop for the night in Rawlins, I telephoned Don to meet her in my place. "She's already here," Don said over the phone. "Yeah, she came in early by bus this afternoon. She's sitting right here across from me."

Walking back to the Jeep, I asked, "What about Mrs. Sumner?"

"I put her up in the Dinosaur Motel—it's as good as any in town," Don said.

"I know *that*," I said. "You told me over the phone. How *is* she?"

"How is she? She's okay," Don replied matter-of-factly. "She'll make out."

"Think she'll make it down the river?"

"We'll see" was his answer. He changed the subject. "As long as you're headed to town, I'll go along. I've got to get some big bolts."

There was no further conversation about the voyage, and it seemed we were both avoiding the subject because it was so big. As for this woman who was going with us, Don would leave me to my own impressions. Together we would compare them when we both knew the important thing: whether she was capable of making it down the river or not.

I headed for the motel after leaving Don in front of the hardware store. He would walk back to the warehouse. I arrived at the motel office, announced myself, and said that Don Hatch had made a reservation.

"Oh, yes," the lady at the desk said, "that was for last night."

"Didn't he cancel it?" I asked. "I told him over the phone to do that."

"No, he didn't, but that's all right—I didn't fill up last night anyway."

"I'll be glad to pay you for it," I insisted, but she refused.

"You're one of the party that's going all the way down the river, aren't you?" she asked. "Gosh, I envy you. I wish I could do it—it has always been a dream of mine to go into those canyons."

"Haven't you been in the canyons at Dinosaur?" I asked.

"Oh my, no! I'll see those when they put the reservoir in there."

*Then it will be too late,* I thought, but I kept quiet because I didn't want to get into an argument over Echo Park Dam at this moment.[8] "Is Mrs. Sumner here?" I asked, changing the subject. If the Echo Park project hadn't come into the conversation, I would have been more hesitant to inquire about Mrs. Sumner. I wanted to delay the meeting. So often when you anticipate an event strongly, the event itself turns out to be a big disappointment. Now that the time of meeting Mrs. Sumner was upon me, I wanted to slow it down.

"Yes, she's in number twenty-eight," the clerk told me. "Wait, I'll give her a ring." She plugged in the wires at the switchboard and rang the room. There was no answer. "Must be out someplace," she said in a disappointed tone.

I wasn't disappointed. I was relieved! I wanted to put off seeing this woman, for I feared she would turn out exactly as I had pictured her. Mrs. Sumner's sprightly letters certainly indicated she was charming and intelligent, but then letters can be carefully measured documents. I was sure that Mrs. Sumner would turn out to be one of those very masculine women whom men loathe. She'd be one of those types who wear their hair in a tight bun at the nape of the neck, or worse, in small buns covering the ears that used to be called, in the twenties, "cootie garages." No doubt she'd be wearing a heavy tweed suit, even on this hot day, and she'd have on cotton-ribbed stockings and low-heeled brown shoes that lace up the front. She'd probably have a hard face, with a thin, unlipsticked mouth and a few bristly hairs growing on her chin, and she'd greet me for the first time with a gruff "Pleased to meet you—when do we get started?" "We," of course, meaning "I." Wasn't this the type, after all, the kind of woman who would tackle the kind of adventure we proposed?

These images of Mrs. Sumner having gone through my head in a quick flash, I now ventured to ask, "What is she like?"

"She's very attractive," the woman replied. "Is she really going with you? My! What courage!"

*Obviously she'd have courage and ought to look like it,* I thought, remembering the mental picture I had just conjured up. I fished for more details. "She's probably looking over the town," I said. "How will I recognize her?" (Obviously I'd recognize such a formidable woman!)

"Well," the motel clerk began, "she wears her hair in a little bun on top of her head." (I was right! A bun!) "She has gray hair." (Oh? Gray hair? I expected brown.) "And she's wearing a dark suit." (Of course—a dark suit on a hot day like this—and probably tweed too, though I didn't ask.) "She's very good-looking," the woman continued, "quite tall and stately." (Stately? Same as formidable—and good-looking, well, that depends on your definition of what good looks are!)

The clerk seemed finished with her description, so I took my key and checked into my room. I unloaded my bags, changed my shirt, which by now was soggy with perspiration, and shaved in preparation for meeting Mrs. Sumner. I deliberately moved about slowly to pass the time and give her a chance to return and perhaps call on me first. When an hour passed with no word from this woman, I walked around the wing of the motel and found room twenty-eight. The door was closed, and all was quiet inside. Was she there? I knocked, and a voice said, "Come in," with an inflection that left me with the impression that entering was an option for the caller to decide upon: enter or not as you wish. I wasn't quite sure I wanted to open that door, and I wished she had given me a command instead of leaving the choice up to me.

*Three*

# CID SUMNER

I opened the door. Just getting out of her chair and collecting a notebook and loose papers from her lap was Mrs. Cid Ricketts Sumner. "I'm Charles Eggert," I announced.

"Why, Charles, here you are at last!" she exclaimed. I detected a slight trace of a southern accent in her voice. Yes, here I was at last, and I was so taken by surprise at her appearance that I hardly knew what to say. She was tall with a surprising figure for a woman of sixty-four! She was also much younger looking than I had expected. Her gray hair was casually tossed. The knot was there, but it wasn't large, and it wasn't tight against the nape of her neck. Her gray hair set off a soft, rosy complexion, and her eyes had a pixie twinkle in them. They were decidedly smiling eyes. She was wearing a frilly white blouse that was quite sheer and a black skirt of some lightweight material, certainly not tweed! She had on medium-height walking shoes and nylon stockings—flesh colored. She was beautiful, and I was at once reminded of my mother.

I fumbled for something to say. "You sure pulled a fast one on us, coming in by noon on the bus," I finally managed to get out.

"Yes," she answered, "I wanted to see the country—you can't do that very well from a plane—so I took a bus from Denver over the mountains. I've never been in the West before, and I want to see it all!"

"Well, let's see it!" I said. "But first come and have some lunch with me. After that we'll ride out to Dinosaur National Monument."

"Now just don't worry about me," Mrs. Sumner said. "I know you have thousands of things to do, so you go right ahead. I'm very comfortable here."

"No," I insisted, "you come along with me. I have some business out at Dinosaur, and I planned to take you with me. I want to give you a preview of the canyons." Also I needed time with this woman before we left; as soon as possible, I wanted to get some idea about whether she could "take it" on the trip.

After lunch in a little restaurant next to the bus station, we started our twenty-five-mile drive out to Dinosaur National Monument. On the way I told Mrs. Sumner how I had come to think of it as my favorite place. I'd made two films there, and I had come to know it pretty well. "As a matter of fact," I told her, "the whole idea of this trip was born there."

As we went on, I spoke of those times in the wilderness where I had found myself spending days and nights alone, miles and miles from the nearest human being. Hardly anyone came to Dinosaur then. The experience of sitting alone by my campfire on the banks of the river, surrounded on all sides by canyon walls, gave me a wonderful sense of existence. I seemed to be a part of eternity, and I felt the presence of the eons of time it had taken to carve the landscape. It was so still and quiet there—a kind of quiet I had never experienced before.

Across the river from my campsite in Echo Park was a great rock fault, probably a hundred million years old. I told Mrs. Sumner how I had sat looking at it until I could hardly see it in the darkness. I felt the great power of forces deep in the earth that had shoved it up from beneath the overlying rocks and exposed it to the sun. I wondered then, as I sat in the twilight that had turned the rocks to flame red, what it must have been like when it happened. Now it seemed so still. Soon the moon came out, and the walls of the canyon reflected its cold, blue light. A splash in the water reminded me of the river. Everything was not at peace, nor still and unchanging. The splash came from a falling rock. Nature's forces were always at work, changing the scene. The river—the river was cutting always deeper and deeper into the channel it had begun more than ninety million years ago. And the wind, armed with sharp particles of sand, was still carving the fantastic and grotesque shapes on the canyon walls. Time was ticking away as certainly as the shadows were changing the outlines of rocks around me. But here in the wilderness, I felt I had all the time in the world; indeed, time was spread out all around me—a hundred million years and more of it—and I felt a bit of eternity.

"You know, Mrs. Sumner," I said, "being alone in a place like that makes you aware of the important values in life."

"Yes, it does." Then she added, "Please call me Cid."

Just then we hit a hard bump that signaled the end of the macadam and the beginning of the dirt road into the monument. The bump also brought me back from my "eternity" into the present. It also knocked us both out of our comfortable-as-possible position in the front seat of the bouncy Jeep.

The road, cutting through a small hill, emerged on the Green River. "There she is!" I said.

"Our river?" Cid asked—as though we already possessed it. "It looks very placid here." She was right: it was placid. The Green gave no indication of the turmoil it could conjure up in the canyons a few miles above. It was a big river here, wide and graceful, as it flowed around a great bend. Logs, the flotsam from spring floods above, were floating lazily downstream, but even spread out as the river was with such a large volume of water, the fast current carried the logs past us rapidly. The river was high from the melting snows in the mountains, and it looked as I imagined it had ninety million years ago—before the Uinta Mountain uplift occurred.[1] Eons ago the Green was a quiet stream meandering through a great swamp covering the entire Great Basin from Wyoming to Arizona. Dinosaurs roamed about, feeding on the succulent plants that grew there. The swampy waters gave buoyancy to the huge brontosaurs that sometimes weighed as much as ninety tons!

Then came a slow uplifting of Earth's crust. Great mountain escarpments were shoved toward the sky, vast plateaus were lifted, and the swamp was drained and dried up. The dinosaurs either perished or were driven away to other feeding grounds. All this happened gradually—so gradually that the Green River retained much of its original course. As the land rose, the currents became stronger. The draining swamplands poured silt and debris into the river and gave it tools to cut deeper and deeper into the land as it rose higher and higher. Thus, the river carved out a path through a mountain range and into the plateaus of the Great Basin, forming the eighteen canyons we intended to travel through.

"In a few miles, we'll see where the river pours out from the mountains as Split Mountain Gorge," I said. I was driving more slowly now so Cid could see between the openings of the ridges to our left that formed the many layers of upward-tilting strata.

"I've never seen such colors!" Cid said. "Reds, oranges, purples—why, Charles, some of those rocks are even blue!"

"That's the Morrison Formation, the blue-colored rock. There's where they find the dinosaur fossils," I explained. Out of the corner of my eye, I spotted a small animal moving on a tiny hill. "Look," I whispered as I stopped the car, "there's a prairie dog." We waited quietly for a few minutes. Presently several curious little animals popped their heads out of their holes, climbed out, and stood on their hind legs looking at us. "Looks like they're having a party—let's get out and join them."

As soon as I opened the car door, the animals scampered down their holes. Cid went over to one and peered into it, hoping to get some response. Either the little dog was too shy or not at home.

"Want to hold ninety million years in your hand?" I asked. She gave me a puzzled look. "Here—hold a bit of eternity," I urged. She took the rock I handed her. "It's a bit of dinosaur fossil I found lying on the ground."

"How can you tell?"

"Look at the detail—see all the bone fibers there?" I pointed to the tiny fibrous pattern. "Nature preserved them so completely that doctors can tell that dinosaurs had rheumatism!"

Cid gave me an incredulous look. After examining the rock more carefully, she gave it back to me, and I threw it on the ground. "So others who come later can find it and hold it too," I said in answer to her puzzled look. "We're in part of the National Park System. That's what it means—to protect these things so we all can come to look and feel. Besides, it'd be against the law to take it."

We walked up a long, sloping hill spotted with scraggly sagebrush. The small cacti we carefully avoided were exploding their delicate red and yellow blooms. Soon we reached the crest. I had been waiting for this moment. Cid was intently looking for fossils, petrified wood, and interesting stones lying on the ground. Quietly I said, "Cid, look ahead." She raised her eyes, and for a moment she couldn't speak because she was so flabbergasted by the panorama. She put her hand to her mouth as though to hold her heart in.

Below and beyond us spread the spectacular beauty and magnificence of the Uinta Mountains and the narrow slit of Split Mountain Canyon. The walls of the canyon rose straight up a thousand feet from the river's edge. The jagged head of Split Mountain was combed by soft white clouds and beyond were the summits of other mountains, snowcapped from the winter. Hugging the base of Split Mountain were the rainbow-colored ridges of uplifted strata that ran east to the base of Blue Mountain, ten miles beyond. To our left, we could see into the sharp curve of the canyon, from which poured the Green River. The rapids within the canyon, hidden from our view by high walls, echoed in our ears. The whole scene was a shock to the eyes, an explosion of color and geological upheaval.

"I don't believe it. I just *don't* believe it!" Cid exclaimed. "Charles! We're not on Earth; this must be some distant planet!"

"This is Dinosaur," I said proudly.

The road into the valley below is a steep, twisting one with many hairpin turns and drop-offs of a hundred feet. It is narrow and does not have the security of a guardrail. As we started down, I thought to myself that this would be a good test of Cid's courage—for she was sitting on the side of the Jeep with most of the drop-offs. I would be able to tell easily how frightened she was by observing how far toward my side of the Jeep she leaned. I warned her as we started down that the road might be a little rugged.

"I've been on some pretty rough roads in Mississippi where I was born and raised. But," she added as she looked cautiously over the side of the Jeep, "they were in flat country—certainly nothing with drop-offs like this!"

As we drove down, down, down, winding and twisting, with the Jeep in low second gear to hold us back, only occasionally did I notice that she was leaning in toward me. Soon we were at the bottom, where the road flattens out into the valley. We drove into a little side road on the bottomlands, between the river and the canyon wall. In and out among the sagebrush we weaved, surprising white-faced cows peacefully grazing on the succulent grass that the shadows of the high sage protect from the hot sun. Several cows stood frozen in the middle of the narrow dirt road, spellbound by the sudden sight of us. I banged my hand on the outside of the door. "The only way you can scare them," I explained as the cows took off into the sagebrush. "The horn doesn't affect them in the least."

"What are you looking for?" Cid asked, observing that I was straining my eyes to examine the canyon wall to our right. "Surely not for cows!"

"Petroglyphs.[2] They're around here someplace." Petroglyphs, I explained, are carvings that prehistoric Indians made hundreds of years ago. There were many in the monument, but the ones I was looking for were exceptional—groups of horses in full gallop; their design had all the beauty and delicacy of ancient Chinese Tang horses. Tragically, they have been nearly destroyed: destroyed by thoughtless people who use them as targets for rifle practice! Great holes have been gouged into the horse figures by well-aimed bullets.

"The Park Service just doesn't have the funds to staff enough rangers to patrol the place, and unfortunately, a few people don't feel enough responsibility to themselves—or others—to protect these wonderful things."

Presently I found the wall where the carvings were. When we got out of the Jeep, Cid started ahead while I was getting my camera. "You'd better let me go first," I cautioned, implying that I could make out the easier trail for her. I really meant that I could frighten away any rattlesnakes that might be lying in our path—or if not frighten them away, at least have the protection of my high boots. I avoided the subject of snakes at this point. I had plans to broach that subject in the future. Cid followed me through the sagebrush to the talus slope at the bottom of the cliff.

"I'll climb up and point them out to you. This is rough stuff to climb," I said as I began to make my way up the rocky slope to the petroglyphs. When I reached the top, I turned around and saw Cid following my tracks up. *Well,* I thought, *let's see how she makes it!*

Cid Ricketts Sumner was already on trial; the tests had begun here and now—at her own choosing. As I watched this elderly woman climb cautiously up the tumbled rocks of the talus, my thoughts went back to weeks ago—to the ad I had placed in the *Saturday Review* for passengers to make the voyage with us. My ad stated, "Requirement: ruggedness!"

I received replies from all over the country. The majority were requests for jobs with the expedition—paying jobs—in spite of the fact that I had advertised for passengers, not employees. I was surprised at the lengths to which most of the answers went to prove the writer's ruggedness.

"As to ruggedness," wrote one fellow, "during one of my summer vacations, I was employed as a fire tower relief man."

Another wrote, "Am sure that I can fulfill the requirements of ruggedness, having spent a cruise in the marine corps and worked in heavy construction for some time."

From one fellow, I received a complete biography of his rugged qualifications (as though he doubted them himself, the way he labored the point). These were among the things that he thought qualified him: Being one of the youngest colonels in the marine corps, serving a stretch in the Foreign Legion, possessing the Navy Cross, Order of the British Empire, Legion of Honor, Croix de Guerre with Palms and Stars, etc. On several occasions, his personal history went on, he had been wounded in combat and escaped from a Nazi death camp after fifteen months of starvation diet, beatings, and torture. He wrote, "I spend much of my free time hiking and camping in wilderness areas often under conditions so rugged that I go it alone because I can't find anyone willing or able to travel as fast, as far, and as light as I sometimes do."

His qualifications certainly indicated he was a man we were looking for! They were greater than those of our boatmen and me put together! But when I received no answer to my reply where I outlined our objectives and the hazards we expected to face while traveling down the world's most dangerous rivers, I began to wonder whether we were attempting too much.

One shy fellow wrote me, "Will you plan to use good, strong boats like Powell's?" with no mention of ruggedness at all.

Another reply, not so shy, described the writer as everything wrapped into one. He claimed he was a rugged, outdoors type; unpredictable guy; TV, radio, screen actor; vocalist, dancer, cowboy, sailor, frogman, artist, color photographer, novel illustrator, writer, fisherman, hunter, model, set designer, and color technician. His hobbies consisted of handicrafts, horses, sailing, swimming, ballet, bullfighting, cockfighting; the intense study of American Indians, Aztecs, Mayans, Incas, Polynesians and Orientals; zoography, ornithology, ichthyology, psychology, theology, and philosophy.

As I read these "qualifications" that he thought made him eligible to travel with us, I wondered why he hadn't put them in alphabetical order! This writer would have undoubtedly been a very interesting character to have along except for certain other stated qualifications, tastes, and character implications that deserve no mention in this narrative. His reply to my ad went unanswered. It was the only one that did. I was astonished to receive such a blatant exposure of character.

But I was amazed, to a lesser degree, by many writers' frank revelations of their personal life and problems. From people I didn't know, I received details I would mention only to my most intimate friends. In many of these letters, I read longings to escape from the utter boredom of existence, high-pressure living, or the "civilization" where they found themselves trapped. As I read their letters, I often thought of my peaceful times in the quiet wilderness. This was the thing these writers were seeking. There was an almost pathetic longing to get back to nature from which all men have sprung, to places where they might find quiet, solitude, and peace; places where they could stand up against the forces of the earth and understand themselves better.

"I'm rugged," wrote one man from Oregon, "but there must be more. Please fill me in on the details," his short letter requested.

Indeed, there were details to be filled in! Because I expected a number of replies to my ad, I had prepared a form letter containing the additional details. Necessary equipment and personal supplies, required inoculations and physical examinations were listed. "We must have men willing and able to get along under all kinds of circumstances and conditions, men held together by a common interest: the success of the expedition. The first requirement is to have a tough hide, psychologically as well as physically," my form letter stipulated.

My letter made no mention of women, nor did I expect to get inquiries from them. But I did. Don and I had decided we wouldn't consider women for the expedition. Not only did we feel they would cramp our style, but the trip would be just too hard for them. It was, judging from the lack of answers to my form letter. However, I did receive replies from four women. One wrote, "I believe I could make it. I am twenty-six years of age and full of adventure. My folks are Scottish, and I am very rugged!" A second woman wrote back, "I am rugged as they come! I've been on quite a few trail trips, and I can stand up against any man." The third woman wrote me that she could lift more weight than most men and would therefore be a real asset when it came to rugged work. "I have been a professional wrestler," she informed me to my horror!

One morning a card arrived from woman number four: "Please send me further information about your excursion—cost, equipment, lodging en route, etc. How rugged must one be? I am but moderately so. I am old but intrepid."

I had to read the card twice before I believed it. "Excursion," did she call it? "Lodging en route," did she mention? Obviously, this woman had no idea what we were about to attempt! I debated whether I should even bother sending further details, but one of those unaccountably mysterious things moved me to spend three cents to send her a brochure. I thought, as I sealed the envelope, *this will fix her. Excursion indeed!*

A few days passed, and I had forgotten all about this ridiculous card. Then the follow-up came:

> Dear Sirs:
> Thank you for your folder recently received. I see that I am nothing that you asked for, being a woman, aged sixty-four. I can offer nothing more than ballast, a good spirit, and some skill as a cook. I am a writer—see *Who's Who*—and would expect to write up the expedition from my point of view, one woman to many rugged men.
>
> If at the last moment you need my money and are willing to take a chance, let me know, will you? I'd fly out to Green River.
>
> My life is of little importance and I would try not to be a nuisance. I have been a medical student, I am old enough not to be disturbed in the company of men (no matter what may be their physiological necessities). My children are of age and independent, no one needs me, I am at that place in life when I can feel altogether reckless, adventurous, ripe for whatever fun can be wrung from existence. Do not imagine that I am trying to commit suicide via your expedition. I love life and people and shall to my last gasp. When I go abroad I carry a note saying, "Just bury me where I fall." This would apply to your expedition.
>
> If you are up this way, drop me a line. I'll give you bed and board. I like your spirit.
> Yours sincerely,
> Cid Ricketts Sumner
> Duxbury, Mass.

Now here was a letter to contend with! She liked our spirit! I liked hers! No sooner had I gotten a copy of *Who's Who* and found that Cid Ricketts Sumner was indeed a writer of considerable note than I put in a long-distance call to Don in Salt Lake City. His reaction to her letter was the same as mine. We were intrigued, and our determination not to have women along wilted fast.

After pondering two days about the risk of having this woman with us, I wrote that we might consider taking her on a temporary basis for the first nine days of the trip; at the end of that time, we would arrive at a civilization point where we could drop her off if we found she couldn't take it. By then we would know whether she could make it all the way or not, for in those nine days we would experience almost all the situations we'd find on the river.

I heard again from Mrs. Sumner the same day I mailed my letter. She wrote, "I've just had a complete physical examination—all normal. My doctor says go ahead, and I really don't think it will be much more rugged than my last year's expedition—riding an Irish hunter across Counties Galway and Connemara. (And I hadn't done any real riding in thirty years!)"

This woman was really turning out to be fascinating! It was her last paragraph that clinched my decision to take her. She wrote, "I have spent a good deal of my life being oil on troubled waters. In short, I think this would all be great fun and you could count on me for aid and encouragement. I can float if dumped in the river, unless made into instant hamburger, and my name Cid is short for Placid."

If there was one thing we needed on this expedition, it was placidity! And we'd need psychological ballast, too, on this long, hard voyage where men's nerves would be tried to the utmost, and an arbiter might well be needed.

Now I was closely watching Mrs. Placid Ricketts Sumner of Duxbury, Mass., as she slowly progressed up the rocky talus slope toward the petroglyphs. In my mind's eye, I pictured her moving over the talus beside a roaring rapid deep within a dark, forbidding canyon.

She climbed deliberately without faltering. She didn't seem like a woman of sixty-four. *She'll make out*, I thought, and I had a moment of pride that I had had the insight to choose this woman as one of our crew.

I liked Cid Sumner. I liked her spirit—and spirit was the most valuable thing we could have aboard our rubber boats.

"Whew! That was steeper than I thought," Cid said breathlessly. (But hadn't I gotten out of breath, too, climbing up?) "They are lovely," she continued. "Petroglyphs, did you call them? Tell me more about them, Charles."

I explained to her that these had been carved here a few hundred years ago. Archaeologists know very little about them—or any of the other drawings in the monument. Doubtless they depict some event in the lives of the people—a hunting incident, for instance, as one of the petroglyphs near us indicated. Carved on the red sandstone wall were several mountain sheep. "Perhaps the artist who carved these horses was making a record of the number of wild ones he had seen here," I guessed.

"What a pity they are so scarred. It is a real crime! Imagine using these beautiful things for target practice!" Cid looked up and noticed another kind of carving, a more recent one. "And who is Mrs. Tietjen?" she asked.

"Mrs. Tietjen" was someone's name carved among the petroglyphs, where it remains to disgrace her until erosion eventually destroys it along with the rest. *Why*, I wondered, *do people carve disgraceful effigies of their otherwise good names in places like this?* I would be ashamed to see mine there! Or if Mrs. Tietjen wasn't responsible for it, who did she know who disrespected her so?

"Watch your step coming down," I warned Cid as we started back. "It's much harder than going up. I didn't expect you to behave like a mountain goat quite yet, or I would have warned you to put your boots on. You have boots, don't you?"

"Yes, I have them," Cid answered, "and I am most certainly going to wear them. I had to go all the way to New York City to find the kind you recommended! I paid enough for them, and I'm determined to get my money's worth!"

Cid and I drove to the entrance of Split Mountain Gorge, where the river was pouring forcefully out from the canyon. We stood at the end of a sandy beach where a cliff protruding into the river blocked further passage into the canyon.[3] To get around this barrier and into the canyon, you would have to go back half a mile and climb nearly eight hundred feet. Beyond us and hidden from our view was a rapid. We could see the tumultuous water pouring before us down the river, still disturbed by the shock of whatever obstruction blocked its course above. We could hear the roar of the rapid echoing from the wall of the cliff opposite us. Near us in the river was a back eddy—a great, slow-moving whirlpool, the result of the rapid above. These back eddies are almost always found at the end of a rapid. They are caused by the widening of the river below the rapid, where the water, after being squeezed into a narrow channel, spreads out again. While the main force of the river continues downstream, much of the remaining volume swirls around in the opposite direction of the flow to fill in the widening riverbed.

These eddies are, at the same time, both dangerous and advantageous to boatmen. By pulling into one as quickly as possible after running the main part of a rapid, the boatman has a chance to slow down before going on—especially if another rapid lies in his immediate future. Often these eddies afford the only chance to land a boat and look over the next rapid. This is their advantage. On the other hand, if a boatman does not judge the power of an eddy correctly, he can be caught in the current of the back-swirling water and carried right back into the rapid he just ran! Or worse, if he loses complete control or cannot fight the swirling current, he may be taken for a wild merry-go-round into the rapid again, back into the eddy, and back again into the rapid—a situation from which he may not escape before his luck runs out. I have often sat beside one of these back eddies watching a log trapped there. The log swirls round and round, seeming never able to escape into the main current to continue its journey.

I raised my eyes from the river and looked across to the other side—not more than two hundred yards away. There the steep wall of the canyon rose straight up. Even when I was looking at it, it was hard to believe such a solid mass of rock could exist. Looking at this buttress of yellow-brown Weber sandstone, Cid said, "I expected the West to be spectacular—but never, never did I believe it would be this big!" She leaned back, craning her neck to see the top. We were engulfed in rock. The sky appeared as a small blue slit between two great walls. "We're in an inferno—a beautiful inferno!" she cried.

"Over here," I said, "there is a cave." In the cliff wall behind us was a long, narrow scoop that the river had hollowed out long ago. Its opening was just high enough for a person to enter. The cave led us deep into the surrounding rock. It was dark and dank inside, and the floor was covered with fine sand. As we stood there, we talked of the ancient Indians who had probably taken refuge in this very spot, just as I had done with my family the year before. Here we—my wife, our young son, Kip, and I—had found shelter from the rain. Protected by the overhanging cliff at the entrance to the cave, we put our sleeping bags on the soft sand. When the sky cleared, we lay looking out on the gorge and at the stars above. We listened to the restless river echoing from the cliffs beyond: the river upon which Kip and I, the day before, had journeyed in a small boat through a few miles of quiet water beyond the rapids; the river beside which, the year before that, I had stood silently all of one Sunday with park rangers watching for floating duffle and bodies of men who had been unlucky in the rapids of Split Mountain Canyon; the river upon which we were now about to set forth.

*Four*

# LAST PREPARATIONS IN VERNAL

After the six days of strain driving from New York to Utah, the bed in the motel felt wonderful, and I fell asleep before I could begin to think of the future. I had a hard time forcing myself to leave its soft comfort on the morning of June 8, but there was much to be done. This was the day we planned to leave for Green River, Wyoming, our starting point on the river. I wanted to get an early start across the Uinta Mountains. But I had been delayed a whole day, so the morning had to be filled with arrangements that should have been made the day before. There was the granting of official permission to run an expedition through Dinosaur National Monument and Grand Canyon National Park. And there were arrangements about a Park Service radio. We would feel more secure with radio communication. We weren't expecting reception down in the canyons, but in case of an emergency, someone could climb up to the rim to radio for help.

"I can't get you a radio to use in Grand," Dinosaur's superintendent, Jess Lombard, said. "They don't have anything that will work down there and, of course, you can't very well climb up to the rim. But," he added, seeing my disappointment, "I'm arranging to have one of our FM walkie-talkies at Lodore cabin for you to use through Dinosaur. We've just installed FM, and I'm anxious to discover whether we can get reception through the canyons. You can help us find out by following a call schedule I've made out."

"How will I get into Lodore cabin, Jess?" I asked. "You remember that Don and I had to break in in 1952?"

"I remember," Jess said jokingly. "I never did get you for destroying government property, did I!"

"The mosquitoes were so bad when Don and I got up there that time that I would have broken into Fort Knox to escape them."

"Well," Jess said, reaching into a drawer, "here is a key—put it in your pocket so you won't forget it this time." He handed the key to me with a slip of paper to sign for it.

"I don't know whether I'd better sign this or not," I told him. "I might lose the key getting dumped in Ashley Falls."

"In that case, we'll send a warrant to you for careless handling of government property." He continued more seriously, "Quite a trip you're making. I knew you'd do it someday. Always had it under your skin since your first trip through Dinosaur, didn't you?"

"Yes, I guess so, Jess, and now that I'm about to do it, I'm a little frightened. I guess you tend to forget how big it all is until you get a glimpse of a place like Split Mountain Gorge again."

"How do you think your lady is going to make out?" Jess asked.

"We don't quite know for sure yet. She seems like quite a gal—she sure doesn't act sixty-four!"

"Don's worried about her."

"I know—I don't blame him. He's a very cautious guy. I think she'll hold her own, though. I don't think she'll cramp our style, either."

"No going off the side of the boat, I'll bet," Jess chided.

"Oh, I don't know. Good night, Jess, that's a perfectly normal function. I doubt we'll have to worry about modesty—she's an adult. We'll make plenty of rest stops anyway. We're not in any great hurry."

Jess and I got down to more serious business. He gave the call letters of the walkie-talkie to me. "Your call letters are KB 7235. Our station letters are still KOD 793. Instructions for operation are marked on the set. I'm sending a ranger up to Lodore in a day or two to check on things, and I'll have him leave the radio under the table in the cabin." Jess continued, "Now, about the members of the expedition. I'll need to have their names and addresses." He got out a pad and pencil.

When he finished writing them down, I said, "We still need a cook. Don had one, but he got scared away. Do you know where we can get a good cook?"

"No, but I'll keep my ears open," Jess answered. "I heard Don's ad for one on the local radio station last night. He told me some sixteen-year-old girl had applied."

"Too young." I laughed. "But if you do hear of one, we could pick him up on the way through Jensen. We expect to get there on the nineteenth."

I also made other arrangements with Jess. A park ranger would drive my Jeep into Echo Park so I could use it during our two days there. After this and other official items had been completed, Jess said, "Well, good luck, fellah!" and gave me a fond pat on the back as I was leaving.

"Thanks, Jess, we can use it."

Next I went to the Utah State Employment Office, where I wanted to get information concerning the insurance for our boatmen. Like other government forms, this one contained questions that just didn't fit our situation. I had to create the proper wording so my men would be covered by insurance in case of accident.

I described the situation to the man behind the counter. "Does this have to do with making another propaganda film against Echo Park?" he asked petulantly.

His remark raised my back fur! I was not in the mood to get into an argument about the Echo Park Dam in Dinosaur National Monument.

"What has that got to do with employment compensation?" I snapped back at him. "Does filling out this form have anything to do with whether I am for or against Echo Park?"

He retreated quickly and stammered, "Well, no—but I just wondered whether you were going to make another of those movies."

"I didn't come here to discuss my motives in hiring these men. I came here to find out how to answer these questions. Does getting state insurance depend on that?"

"No," he answered contritely, "no, it doesn't."

"Well, then," I said with forced calm, "let's get onto these questions—they don't quite fit our situation."

I was still burning up as I headed down the street to the Vernal clinic for my tick shot booster. Inoculations against Rocky Mountain spotted fever are a wise precaution if you travel the wilds of this country in the spring. Utah and Wyoming are sheep country, and the tick, a small, very tough insect, uses the sheep as a host during the breeding season. The tick carries the germs of this dreaded fever. Since we planned to be sleeping on the ground, we were taking a chance of one biting us. Unless attended to immediately, the fever can be fatal. We'd be in no position down in the canyons to care for someone with the fever, so we insisted that everyone in our party be inoculated.

The shot was taken care of in a few minutes, and I was off to Don's house to help with the final loading of the truck. By the time I got there, the shot was beginning to take effect: my arm was getting sore, and my muscles were stiff. The best cure is to give the arm strenuous exercise. I knew I'd have plenty of that when I saw all the activity. Our boats and gear were being loaded on the truck that would haul it north to our starting point on the river.

I have never seen so much stuff! Food boxes, gasoline cans, duffle, wooden planks, pieces of iron, oars, outboard motors: all were piled around the truck. Everyone was helping to load. I spotted Les, our third boatman, immediately.[1] I was shocked, to put it mildly! Some time ago, in Salt Lake City, Les had had an "argument" with a Cadillac while riding his motorcycle. I understood that Les had recovered completely from the broken leg he had received in the accident. Now he was limping badly; indeed, it was more than just a limp—he could hardly stand on his leg! His six feet and 190 pounds were every ounce muscle, but to see this strong body hobbling around made him appear even more helpless and incapacitated. My heart sank to the soles of my boots! How could he make it in that condition? What would the others think when they saw him this way! Already we had one strike against us by not having as many men along as we wanted. With Les in this shape, we also seemed to have someone who was impaired, and perhaps a burden to us right from the start! At that moment, I felt that we must give up the expedition completely. Then Les looked over and saw me.

"Hi, Charlie," he shouted and hobbled over to meet me, a big, broad grin on his face.

"Hi, Les," I answered dejectedly. I couldn't help but comment about his limp right away.

"Oh, the leg's all better," Les explained. "It's this wretched toe—an ingrown toenail. But it will be okay in a day or two."

"I hope so," I said, and I meant every word.

"Well, we're just about ready to shove off." Les turned back to his work. He bent over and picked up the heavy Coleman three-burner stove in one arm and the immense iron grill in the other and hobbled toward the truck. In spite of his leg, Les certainly hadn't lost any of his strength—that was certain!

Don came out of the house looking worried and irritated. "We've got too much stuff, Charlie," he said.

"Well, what can we weed out?" I was thinking of all the additional gear I had in my Jeep.

"That's the trouble: we need it all, I guess. But you'll have to leave your cots behind; that's for sure."

By unpacking my own duffle and getting rid of nonessentials, and sorting through the gear in the Jeep, I managed to lighten the load by at least a hundred pounds. During the weeding out, I got Don aside and said, "Now! What about Les—he's in a hell of a shape!"

"I know it," Don said. "He was okay a week ago when I saw him last."

"I don't know how he can make it limping like that—he'll never get around on those rocks if we have to line the boats!"

"Yeah," Don answered. "If I had known he was in this condition, I'd have gotten another boatman, but he didn't say anything to me about it. I'm mad as the devil at him, but there isn't anything we can do now. But I think he'll work out—look at him!"

I turned to look across the yard, and there was Les doing twice as much work as I could possibly manage with two good legs. I was sure Les wouldn't complain, and I knew he wouldn't allow himself to be a burden. He was certainly no shirker—the work he was doing now proved that. But I thought about the others who didn't know his capabilities. They'd be shocked at seeing him and uneasy—Fred especially, for I figured he was a little apprehensive about the river.[2] Fred was willing to give the river every respect due it, and he felt keenly the necessity for having every point in our favor at the start. Well—there wasn't anything we could do about it now, so what would happen would! The others would get to know Les if they'd just give him a chance. As I was thinking this, Bruce came over.

"Just about all set, Charlie. We've got lots of stuff!" He looked toward the truck.

"You're telling me!" I answered. I had noticed Bruce loading the truck with interest. He was able to heave as much weight as Les. I was a little surprised because he didn't look as if he had Les's strength. "Think you'll make it over the mountains in that?" I pointed to the old, dilapidated truck, which was a converted school bus. The thing was packed to the gills, inside and out. With the two deflated rubber boats, platforms, iron frames, and boxes on the roof, and oars sticking out of the windows, I was certain it couldn't make it out of the driveway, let alone travel the rugged road across the Uintas to Green River.

"We'll make it!" Bruce said with conviction.

They'd make it if Bruce's determination had anything to do with it, but the bus looked as if it was working at cross-purposes. The axles were already straining under the load, and the thing wasn't even moving! What would happen on that rough and rutty road? As I turned to leave, I was convinced I'd never see our equipment again.

*Five*

# MEETING IN GREEN RIVER

This is called the "Vernal–Manila Highway," I told Cid as we bounced, bumped and leapt from one rut to another.[1] "If we get across these mountains and still have our insides, we'll be lucky!"

"A friend told me to sit back and relax on rough roads—like a sack of flour," Cid said. "Ride with the bumps—that makes it easier," she added as she adjusted herself after nearly bouncing out of her seat.

"We should have safety belts to hold us in. I've got to go as fast as I can, where I can," I apologized. "We're so darn late!" I sped up the Jeep on a smooth stretch of the road. Then I slammed on the brakes as we suddenly came upon the dry bed of a creek that had washed out the road in a recent flood. The gear packed in the back bounced and scattered as we hit the gully too fast.

"This is probably the most rocky ride in the country," I said. "We're going directly across the Uintas, and we're passing through more than two hundred million years of Earth's history via the rocks. You'll see signs along the road telling which geological era we're in as we go."

We wound around and cut through the many layers of rock that have been exposed by the uplift of the Uinta range as we climbed higher and higher toward the top of the mountains. Across the Dakota sandstone, the Morrison, Entrada, Wingate, Chinle, Shinarump, Moenkopi, and Weber layers, we climbed. On through the strata, we drove—through older rocks: Mississippian, Devonian, and deep into the Cambrian, each stratum a different color: red, purple, chocolate brown, yellow, gray, orange, white, and even green rocks, each with a different texture.

Soon tall pine trees began to border our narrow road, and we knew we were nearing the top. We had climbed several thousand feet through the cuts and canyons to get above the Uinta Valley we had left behind at Vernal. Through a cool, magical forest, we drove. What a beautiful forest this was: with its tall, deep green pines and aspens in their yellow green spring foliage. Occasionally a deer darted in front of the car, or, rounding a sharp bend, we surprised one warming itself in the sun on the road between the trees. Large meadows, or "parks," where thick, tall grass and wildflowers grew, opened up before us. Presently, at a road junction, we came to a sign that read To Red Canyon Overlook.

"Ah!" I sighed. "Thank heavens! I was beginning to think we were lost."

"What more beautiful place could you pick to be lost?" Cid remarked.

"Now, Cid, we're going to have a *real* look at a canyon." I turned off on the Red Canyon road.

"Come follow me," I instructed when we reached the end of the road. I had been here before, and the way was familiar. The terrain was rocky, with little topsoil, but here and there, where the pines grew thick, dead needles padded the ground with soft, heavy cover. "Watch your step," I said, noticing how gingerly she was walking over the sloping rocks. "Rattlesnakes like to lie under tilted rocks like these, so it is best to use caution when stepping down from the large slabs that slant up from the ground."

Cid stopped in her tracks to consider what I had said. She looked as though she had come face-to-face for the first time with the dangers—at least one of them—of the experience she was about to undertake. Had she not thought of the risks before? Perhaps not so tangibly as now.

"I doubt very much that we'd find a rattler up this high," I said to reassure her, "but it's best to be cautious anyway. Make a habit of it."

After a short hike across the rocks among the tall pines, we came to a gaping crack in the rock floor. The crack was about four feet across and ran several hundred yards on either side of us to the canyon rim. A sign was posted here and read in large letters: DANGEROUS TO GO BEYOND THIS POINT—BEWARE OF HIGH WINDS.

"Come on," I said as I jumped across the great fissure. Cid looked hesitant, but I reached across and offered my hand. She took it and jumped. I kept my hand on her arm, for a strong wind was blowing. A few more steps, and we were at the brink of Red Canyon.[2] Cid approached the drop-off cautiously and looked down—down two thousand feet where the river ran deep in the gorge. The sun's reflection made the river look like a silver thread as it wound its way between the canyon's gloomy walls. She stepped back quickly. She looked shocked. She was speechless. Then, gathering courage, she approached again and looked into the deep abyss.

"Are we going to be down there?" she asked finally.

"That's our river," I answered. "Just think, in a couple of days, we'll be down there! See those tiny riffles? They're big rapids."

Even with the wind blowing through the pines, we could hear their roar up here. The sound vibrated from the canyon walls below us and mingled with the wind as it sang through the trees. We heard a great chorale of Earth as we looked down.

"I must remember this place and look for it as we pass down there on the river," Cid said.

I suddenly thought of the rock we were on. It was almost an island suspended in the sky. One day it would break free and go plunging into the river below with a mighty roar. These tons and tons of rock falling into the river would form another great rapid, or possibly that much rock might create a huge dam, blocking the river completely. Indeed, the crack was so big and wide that the rock might go tumbling any minute. I felt uneasy standing on it. What held it in place now? Perhaps it was in delicate balance, waiting for the next rain or frost, or the next ounce of weight, to remove the last vestige of its hold to the solid rock behind. It might let loose now—or tomorrow, blocking our own passage down the river. Or it could let go just as we were passing beneath it! *Yes*, I thought, *I must mark the spot—or better still, on second thought, forget where it is entirely and be free of the anxiety of looking up as we pass slowly by.*

We crossed the wide fissure again and made our way to another point where we could look down into Red Canyon. The wind blew full force into our faces, bringing with it the poignant smell of pine. This fresh, sweet smell, whenever I experience it, brings back memories of my childhood and the days I spent in northern Michigan. I used to go there every summer, and every summer I bought a pillow stuffed with pine needles. For months after that, through the fragrance of my souvenir pillow, I could enjoy the memory of those wonderful days in the dense northern forests. No matter where I am, when that fragrance is in the air, I recall those early childhood days. So it was now, on this lonely point of rock in the wilderness, two thousand miles and twenty years away, that I remembered that time. Every child should have wilderness memories. Then, as a grownup, he or she will never feel lost and alone in the wild. The scenes of early childhood will come back with the sound of a splashing brook, the warmth of a sun-bathed rock, the call of a blue jay, or a smell in the air. That person will always have the company of known things.

I breathed deeply the pine-scented air as though it was a healing balm to my lungs, lungs filled with the fumes of gasoline exhaust and road dust from the past week, filled with the smog and filth of the air in big cities. Here was real air, bright and sparkling, air filled with just God-given ingredients. City air is poisoned with fumes from cars and factories and thousands of burning incinerators. Soon our city fathers will have to chlorinate their air just as they do their water. Here in the mountain wilderness, the only additives are the sweet odors of nature: pine and sage, wildflowers and mosses.

The shadows of the canyon walls were beginning to throw the river into darkness. The sight reminded me of the late hour and that we must rush on if we were going to get to the Rock Spring airport by 9:10 p.m. to meet two more of our crew, Fred and Tony.

Leaving the canyon, we began the long descent down the north escarpment of the mountains. Presently our "highway" came to a sharp drop-off where a side canyon, cut by a little creek, descended quickly to the valley nearly a thousand feet below. Again, as before, I wondered how in the world the road could get down there. It seemed impossible, but it does it—by a series of very sharp cutbacks and steep dugways down the side of the canyon wall. Following along the road, Sheep Creek makes just as steep a descent.[3]

Sheep Creek should, by all laws, be one great rushing cascade, but it is one of the best-controlled streams I have ever seen. Beavers take care of maintaining it. These clever builders have erected a system of dams that would be the envy of the Bureau of Reclamation (if they haven't seen them, I suggest they do so immediately!). Here the beavers have given us a perfect example of upstream reclamation and flood control. I doubt that there has ever been a serious flash flood in this creek since the beavers took over. Not only have they regulated the stream flow by a progression of dams and reservoirs, but they have controlled the silt and erosion buildup in a stream that otherwise would be notorious for it. The water runs crystal clear. The beavers have provided scores of gentle ponds for their homes where trout abound, the swimming is fine, and recreation is unlimited. What wonderful animals these beavers are! The government ought to employ more of them!

While making our descent, I noticed that Cid was holding on tighter than before. Seeing her made me conscious that I was grasping the steering wheel a bit more firmly than usual too. This was a steep road, and even with the Jeep in low second gear, I found myself having to use the brakes. We were glad to get to the bottom.

"That's the first time I've ever used a car for an elevator!" Cid said with relief.

Now for the most astonishing sight of all along the way! "Watch ahead," I said as we went around a bend. Coming into view was a synclinal fault through which Sheep Creek has cut its path to the Green River. I don't know of a better example of the mighty earth forces than here. The rock strata from hundreds of feet above is suddenly contorted and twisted and bent into a great upside-down rainbow that curves down on one side of the creek and then up again on the other. We stopped the car and got out to get a better look, for in the car we couldn't see the full sweep of this incredible scene. We stood in silence for a while, lost in imagining the prehistoric holocaust that had occurred here millions of years ago. The overpowering sight seemed to forbid speaking.

On the way back to the Jeep, I broke the silence. "I have a theory," I said, "that might make a good short story for you."

"What is it?" Cid asked.

"Well, perhaps the world goes in great cycles," I began, "and every so often civilization and human knowledge get to a certain point, just a little beyond the place where our civilization is now. Man discovers he can split the atom, but he still doesn't have the final knowledge about things. He keeps playing around with these atomic toys until one day, just when he thinks he has the right answer, he hits the correct combination—the right one, that is, to blow everything to hell and gone. He destroys everything on the face of the earth, and so eventually everything starts over again. Life is created anew, the land is again separated from the waters, and finally humankind comes into being, and civilization starts all over. Perhaps if archaeologists started digging into the syncline," I continued, "they'd find a whole city buried, with Empire State Buildings and all."

"Quite an idea," Cid said.

"Well," I said finally, "I wonder whether God looks down on us, and when we have about reached the point where we discover his secrets, he says, 'That'll be all, boys.' I don't think God wants us to know the final answer."

I looked back at those twisted rocks and all at once felt relieved. After all, we hadn't yet invented a bomb that has anywhere near the power to move the earth like this. I shifted the gears and started off feeling secure.

As we crossed the Wyoming state line, we found ourselves back in the present again, having passed through Earth's entire geological history—from the oldest rock back to our present topsoil. At the Utah-Wyoming line, the road widened into a first-class highway, and so I sped up. We had to meet that plane in Rock Springs. And the equipment truck we had left behind in Vernal—by now it must be ahead of us, especially since we had taken so much time at the Red Canyon overlook. But when we came upon no truck, nor even met another car, all the way from Manila to Green River, I began to wonder whether it had made it out of the Hatch driveway.

It was eight o'clock when the first sight of the lights of Green River came into view—lights which looked magically out of place in this vast land of rolling hills, sage, and buttes. The sun had taken a long time to set behind the Great South Pass, but now the stars were out, and the lights of the town looked like their reflections on the desert. Green River was a lonesome-looking place in this vast nothingness.

With great excitement, Cid and I crossed the bridge over the Green, but we were too much in a hurry to stop and see "our" river and our starting point on it. We sped to the motel to verify our reservations and then moved quickly on to Rock Springs at sixty-five miles an hour—which was *very* fast in a Jeep station wagon!

"I'm sorry to whiz you along like this," I shouted to Cid over the deafening whine of the transmission, "but those boys will think we have abandoned them if we don't meet that plane."

We had fifteen miles to go from Green River to Rock Springs, and we made it in fifteen minutes. I kept a lookout for the airport, hoping it would be at the west end of town so we could avoid having to drive through. This would give us an added few minutes to catch our breath before the plane arrived. But no airport, so we stopped in a gas station for directions.

"It's about five miles beyond the other side of town," the attendant told us. "Follow US 30, and you'll see the sign—you can't miss it."

I've always been suspicious of that phrase, "you can't miss it." It usually means "you'll be lucky to come upon it by accident." At any rate, the directions were simple enough, and allowing time to get across town and five miles beyond, we should just make it. How could anyone miss an airport anyway with all the lights around it?

Well, it can be done, and we proved it; we missed it by fifteen miles, or thirty, if you count the backtracking. All of the lights were turned off in the administration building except for one in a back room and one in the front corner of the building where Fred and Tony were standing when we pulled up beside them, a half hour late.[4] They looked forlorn indeed, as though they had lost their last friend and been cast destitute upon the desert. They had expected to be taken in hand by their guide and mentor and led safely across the Great American Desert and through the dismal abysses of eighteen mighty canyons. But this friend of Odysseus wasn't there to meet them! A thousand thoughts must have gone through their heads while they were waiting under that lone light, whose rays quickly faded into the dark mysterious hills and buttes beyond. From here they couldn't even see the friendlier lights of the town just beyond the hills.

What a relief when they recognized the Jeep! They ran to us quickly as I jumped out of the car. I welcomed them to the wide-open spaces and explained in one breath why we were so late. We gathered up their gear and piled it into the Jeep, leaving just enough room for them to squeeze into the back seat. Introductions were made, and the process of finding out about each other began.

"What brings you to these canyons?" Cid asked Fred, whose glasses reflected the dashboard lights and made him look like a great owl sitting in the dark of the back seat.

"Well," said Fred, "I read Chuck's ad in the *Saturday Review*, and here I am." He gave a nervous chuckle. "The West has always been a hobby of mine," he went on to explain.

"Hobby?" Cid sounded slightly shocked.

"Yes, I've never seen very much of the West, but over the years I've collected every book I could get my hands on. Major Powell has always been a sort of hero to me—matter of fact, I had just finished reading Wallace Stegner's biography of him—*Beyond the Hundredth Meridian*, it's called—when I saw Chuck's ad."

"Have you read it, Cid?" I broke in. "I brought it along."

"So did I." Fred laughed.

"No—no, I haven't," Cid said, "but I've seen some of our canyons!"

Tony spoke eagerly: "What are they like?"

"They are great monstrous, marvelous jokes the gods of the Indians left as a warning to the rest of humankind," Cid answered.

"Have you fellows eaten?" I interrupted.

"Oh, yes," Tony answered, "on the plane—but that was hours ago!"

"Cid and I haven't had a thing—so let's have a drink in celebration and then get some food," I suggested.

"A drink is a very good idea!" Cid said. "I could use one after that ride!"

Over our drinks, conversation went on about the past—and the future; about the boats, the boatmen, and the expedition. It went on at the café where we ate and during our ride back to Green River. Fred and Tony asked many questions, and I detected just a bit of apprehension in their voices. Cid, on the other hand, asked none. She had resigned herself to whatever was to come long before.

It was late, very late, when I finally rolled into bed. It had been a full day, and I was dog-tired. The next day, our day of departure on the river, would be even fuller, and before I could begin to think of all the problems, I fell into a deep sleep.

*Six*

# GETTING READY TO LAUNCH

The next thing I knew, I was grabbing the alarm clock. I fumbled for the knob to quiet its hysterical clanging. The thing frightened me half out of my wits. I thought that some screaming monster had pounced on me. With my heart pounding in my throat, I fell back on my pillow. As I lay waiting for the thumping to stop, I tried to remember where I was. The room was strange. What was all that junk that I saw in the half light of dawn? Two guns stood in the corner. A big brown bag lay across the baggage rack. My duffel bag—my guns—a motel room in Green River: I gradually remembered. This was the day; we'd be meeting another passenger from California; we'd be packing our equipment aboard the boats; we'd be camping beside the river! I closed my eyes and thought of what wonders and terrors lay ahead.

I roused with a start and took my watch from the side table. It was 8:30 a.m.! How could that be? I'd set the alarm for 6:00. Had I dozed off? Of course I had—while I was thinking about today and tomorrow. I jumped up and called to Tony in the next room. I rushed into the shower. As the clean, warm water poured over me, I thought to myself, *Enjoy this—it'll be the last warm shower in a long, long time.*

Tony had to be called three times before he came to. I dressed hurriedly, ran out to awaken Fred, and found him just getting up. I walked over to Cid's room and knocked on the door.

"Come in," she said, again with that curious questioning intonation. She was sitting at a desk, dressed in her river clothes—dungarees, sneakers, a man's white shirt. Even so she looked chic.

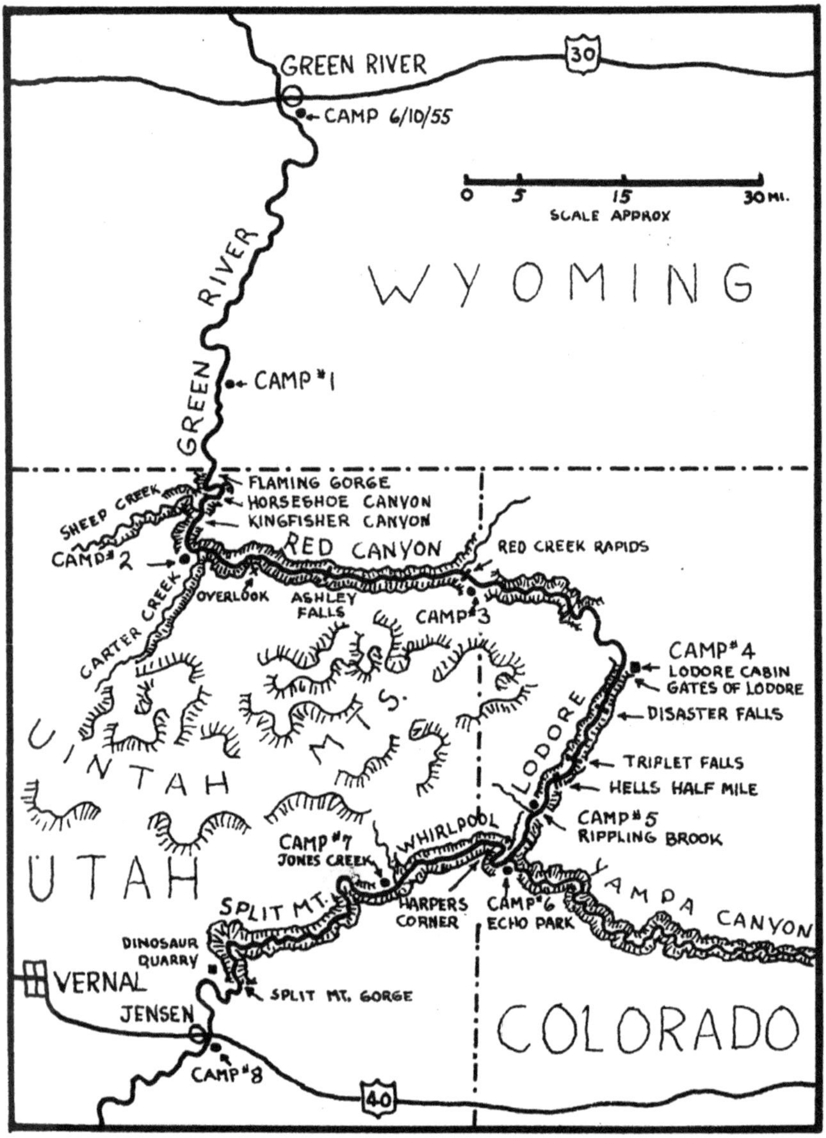


A hand-drawn map by Charles Eggert showing the top-most section of the 1955 river trip, including camp locations.

"Dressed already?" I asked in surprise.

"Why Charles, I've had my breakfast already."

"Breakfast!"

"Yes," Cid said, matter-of-factly. "I hiked down the road to a little diner I had noticed last night and had my cup of coffee. It's down about a mile. I was nearly blown across the desert by the wind, though! It was quite a place," she continued, "full of truck drivers and cowboys. They all looked at me curiously, coming in there off the highway at 6:30 a.m. I'm sure they thought I was hitchhiking to Salt Lake City. One driver even offered me a ride back into town, but I wanted to get the fresh air. With that wind, I certainly got it—mixed with blowing sand!"

I was amazed by these early morning exploits of Cid's, and I could only say sheepishly that we hadn't had our breakfast yet. "We're just about to go—come have a second one with us," I said.

"Shall I leave these things here?" she asked, pointing to her gear, neatly organized and stacked against the door.

"We'll pick it up after breakfast. I'll get Tony and Fred and meet you at your door."

I thought it would be better to go into town to eat. There was a greater chance of meeting Don or the other boatmen. We had not gone three blocks before we ran into Don's wife, Jerry. I pulled to a quick stop. "Hi! Where's everybody?" I shouted across the street to her. Jerry told us that Don was over at the grocery store. Where the boatmen were, she did not know because Don had been unable to find the boats.

"Unable to find the boats!" I exclaimed. "Didn't you follow them over?"

"No," Jerry answered, "we left long after they did." Just then Don came up the sidewalk. He looked annoyed. I got out of the Jeep and quickly crossed the street to him.

"Where are the boats?"

"Golly, Charlie, I don't know." He looked worried. "I've been up and down the banks of that river three times this morning. Not a trace of that truck—and I ought to be able to spot a truck!"

"Well, maybe they stopped along the road for the night," I said with more assurance than I felt.

Don answered that this might be so, but both of us thought it unlikely. Surely they must be around someplace—or they'd show up soon; no need to worry about that yet. "Where's a good place to eat?" I asked.

"Right around the corner, across from the railroad station—Teton Café," Don answered. "I'm buying supplies at the store on the corner. I'll be down in a little while."

I remembered Cid, Fred, and Tony, who were leaning out of the Jeep to catch what we were saying. "Come over and meet Fred and Tony," I told Don. By the time he had crossed the street, the concerned expression was gone from his face. As he greeted Cid again and met Fred and Tony, he seemed to have that reassuring air that convinced me that he was the right head boatman for this journey. In a pinch, he always took the lead at being calm and collected, inspiring in others the faith that was so necessary on a dangerous journey. Only to me did he confide his worries.

We all ordered vast quantities of food for breakfast, as though it was the last meal of our lives. Don came in while we were on our third cup of coffee. "Still can't find them," he said. "I told Bruce to leave a message at Western Union when they got in."

Now that the others knew, we all began to talk of what might have happened. There could have been an accident, but Don wiped that idea out; surely he would have seen an accident on the way over the mountains. It could have been sabotage; there were several dam proponents in the Echo Park controversy who might carry things that far. I remembered my conversation in the employment office. Then, too, hadn't someone thrown a brick through the window at Don one night while he was working on the boats at the warehouse? It could be sabotage, all right, and we gave that serious thought.

All we could do was continue to search. I took the left side of the river, Don the right. We drove everywhere we could with the Jeep. Where we couldn't see the bank, we hiked, but still no boats. They should have been at the Powell Memorial on a small island near the center of town—where we had told the boatmen to go—but there wasn't a trace of them. We ran into Don several times, again discussed the situation, invented new theories, and continued the search. The Western Union office was checked so many times in hopes that Bruce had left word that the operator must have thought we were all insane. It finally got so that when he saw us drive up, he simply looked out the window and shook his head.

It would soon be time to meet the eighth member of our expedition, Fred's brother-in-law, a doctor from California.[1] He would be arriving on the Union Pacific train, the City of San Francisco. I left Fred and Cid at the station to meet him while Tony and I went to the railroad bridge over the Green River to photograph another streamliner, the City of Los Angeles, which was due in just ahead of Doc's train. This shot was to tie Major Powell in with our story, for as he set off on the river on May 24, 1869, the first transcontinental passenger train crossed the railroad bridge at Green River. In the film of our voyage, we, too, would greet a transcontinental train as we shoved off. This was important enough to delay our search for the boats; Don continued alone with that.

Tony and I set up the cameras and waited for a shiny streamliner to round the bend in the west and approach the bridge. We couldn't have had worse luck! The first train that came along was not a bright, shiny one. Rather, it had old-fashioned cars; apparently it was a local. A bright yellow streamliner did arrive next—but from the wrong direction, so the proper approach shot couldn't be made. The next train to round the bend was a freight. That wouldn't do. It passed over the bridge, and, at the same time, a freight came onto the bridge from the opposite direction and stopped. As it stood there, the City of Los Angeles arrived. Not only would that be unphotogenic, but the freight was between us and the passenger train! Our only chance now was to get pictures of Doc's train—if that freight would get out of the way! According to the schedule, Doc's train was scheduled to come in right after this; it would be the last transcontinental train from the west we could photograph; there wouldn't be another chance, so we waited with fingers crossed. Just in time, the freight cleared the bridge, and the sleek passenger train where Doc was gathering up his gear rounded the bend and crossed the open bridge—with both cameras buzzing!

We packed the cameras and started for the station. As I came out on the main street, Don's car was speeding toward me. Bruce was sitting in the front seat! I hadn't for one moment forgotten the lost boats while waiting for the trains. My anxiety turned to anger, and the more I thought about it, the madder I got. The train mix-up had only aggravated me more. How could anyone get our carefully laid plans confused? I jumped out of the Jeep and approached Bruce. "You'd better have a clever answer about where you've been!" I said.

"Well, Charlie, it was this way," Bruce began calmly, seemingly unaware that I was angry. He explained that the truck driver had gotten his instructions confused. The driver, who knew no more about Green River than did Bruce or Les, had taken them to the place where he thought we meant to meet—a spot where Bus Hatch had launched his boats a few years back. Then the driver insisted that he had instructions from his boss to return to Vernal that same night, which he did in spite of the protests from the two boatmen. The driver had taken them up a deserted road behind the railroad yards over the hills to a point three miles south of town. Only now had Bruce been able to walk into town and find the Western Union office. We hadn't searched that road; it seemingly didn't go anywhere near the river.

I was so relieved that I forgot all my anger. We sped to the station to meet Doc. When we got there, we found him waiting with Cid and Fred. I liked Doc the first moment I saw him. He was tall and sturdy. He wore glasses over eyes spaced wide apart. On either side of his face, I saw crow's-feet wrinkles, formed there not by age but laughter. The broad grin on his slightly oversized mouth wrinkled his entire face. I had expected to see him dressed in city clothes since he had come from San Francisco, but instead he had on khaki pants, a khaki jacket, a cap, and boots. He carried a duffel bag and a fishing rod. I knew that here was a man out for fun. I felt confident that he knew more about wilderness living than Fred did, and he would be a big help in breaking Fred into the life we were about to experience. Fred had never slept in a sleeping bag before. I was concerned about Fred; at times he seemed a little doubtful, a little worried about what lay ahead. Although Doc could be only a temporary member of the expedition, I felt that his presence would do much to help Fred gain the confidence he might need.

Besides, Doc was jolly, and he fit in right from the start. His laugh was too loud—it burst from him like an explosion—but it was hearty and contagious. Fred had that laugh too. Between the two of them, the railroad station reverberated as I told them about the trouble we had had with the trains and the most important news of all: that we had found the boats! Doc, of course, had heard about this problem immediately from Fred and Cid. There was no doubt that Fred and Cid had been concerned; their faith in Don and me as leaders had been slightly shattered by such a preposterous situation. If Doc's faith in us was tested over losing our boats even before we got started, he didn't show it. He was eager and happy about the voyage, and he had a vitality that gave us the feeling that we were about to embark upon something wonderful. With his arrival, the day picked up decidedly, and with the assurance that now we had a doctor aboard the expedition, we all felt better.

At the café, we had discovered another bit of information that disrupted what I had thought to be well-laid plans. No one was coming with the truck to drive my Jeep back to Dinosaur National Monument. I had very definitely planned to use it while we stopped on the river there. Don thought of a solution: get his father to fly up to Green River to pick it up. Don called and found that because of plane schedules, Bus couldn't get up before the next morning, the morning we planned to be on the river headed toward the canyons. There was nothing to do but wait. We'd have to pick up Bus at Rock Springs, just as we had Tony and Fred. Don announced that he also wanted to delay for a few last-minute improvements on the equipment—we needed another angle-iron support. Much food still had to be bought, along with personal items either not known about before or forgotten. It seemed best to take it easy, wander about town, shop for odds and ends, and get away on the river whenever we were finally ready.

I thought that time would never come! We decided to move from the motel to the river to get the "feel" of camping and discover what else we might need during those many nights out we had before us. Good thing we did. We found we lacked many things. It was amusing to see our passengers grasp the seriousness of our voyage now that they were becoming acquainted with the boats and equipment. But mostly the sight of the river—which all of them were close to for the first time—made them think twice and realize that this was indeed an expedition and not an armchair tour. This would be no excursion, and there would be no lodging en route except whatever each of us could carry from the boats to the shore.

Our first camp beside the mighty Green was completely isolated from civilization even though it was only three miles from town. It was just as wild and desolate as any place along the river, and the sound of the water rushing and boiling gave us all a sense of what we were about to attempt. This was the same river we had seen from the bridge, from above at Red Canyon, but now we were living beside it, where we could dip our hands into it or even fall in if we weren't careful climbing around on the boats. Here we could look downstream with our sight uninterrupted by roads or buildings and almost see ahead the 1,030 miles we intended to travel. Cid Sumner must have thought about those miles as she stood beside the bank during our first evening. She had seen a glimpse of the canyons—two of them at any rate. Only she knew a little of what was ahead.

One of my anxious moments came and passed without the reaction I had expected—the meeting between Les and our passengers. I had worried even more about this since our lost boat affair. If our passengers' confidence hadn't been shaken by that or the other indications of disorganization that had surfaced during the day, I was certain it might be when they saw Les with his bum leg. This might be the last straw.

Too often we judge people at first sight without waiting until we see who they really are and what they are made of. I am sometimes guilty of this myself, and so I wondered what the others' reactions to Les's almost useless leg would be. At first appearance, before they saw his strong arms pull so ably on the oars as I knew they could, he seemed hardly capable of running a violent river.

When we got out of the Jeep, Les was working on the floor inside our big boat. He was out of sight until we reached the shore. When he heard us coming, he bobbed up, slid over the side of the boat, and warmly greeted us with a big smile. He immediately took Cid by the arm and said, "Come aboard, Mrs. Sumner, and see how she floats!"

After a moment of looking over the *Brontosaur*, Cid asked, "But where am I to sit?" noting that there were no seats in the boat other than the cross boards where the boatmen sat to row.

Les said with a laugh, "Why, you sit where you always do!" This broke the ice. So far as I know, no one ever noticed Les's other injuries: his broken nose or his badly scarred left eye—at least not until he had overcome them with his warm and kind personality; at first his leg was a subject of clinical curiosity to Doc. Later, it became a matter of great concern in the success or possible failure of the expedition.

Everything that had been unloaded from the truck seemed to be lying about helter-skelter. The two Evinrude motors were still in their boxes, unopened. Food boxes lay strewn about. No one knew quite where the cooking utensils were. It seemed hopeless to attempt to cook a meal; most of our food supplies were still at the store waiting until the last possible moment before being exposed to the elements. There was no time for organization, so I suggested we get our sleeping bags ready so we could hop into them without having to scramble around later in the dark. Eating in town seemed the simplest way for tonight.

Each of us picked a spot he or she thought the most comfortable and began to build a nest. I put my tent up and was driving the last stake into the ground when I looked over at Cid. She was having trouble. She seemed utterly confused about making her camp. The only thing she had done was put up her cot, where she was sitting with a hopeless look on her face.

"What's the matter, Cid?" I asked when I got over to her campsite. "Can't you figure this out?"

"Well, it does seem a little complicated," she answered apologetically.

"I'll show you how to do it this time," I said. I rigged up a curious arrangement that suspended the pup tent above her cot. At one end, a T-bar held the tent over the cot. I attached a rope to the top of the other end of the tent. Then I tied the rope to the nearest handy object. This time it turned out to be a sturdy tree that was conveniently close by. Later, during the voyage, this rope was attached to a variety of things: tamarisk bushes, driftwood, hanging rocks, and, on more than one occasion, an oar stuck into the ground. The bottom of the tent hung a few inches below the edge of the cot. It made a conveniently private wilderness boudoir, and I was very pleased with my quickly concocted arrangement. (I didn't confess to Cid that I knew no more about this curious setup than she did!)

My only worry was that it didn't seem very windproof. Looking at it, I had a vision of Mrs. Sumner being carried off up the canyon under the full sail of the tent like Mary Poppins. I tried to hide my amusement over this image and, with my ingenuity, said, "Looks kind of floppy—you can make improvements as we go along." But my mental picture of her in flight must have shown, for Cid suggested that it might be wise to tie a rock to her leg to hold her down. "That's one of the improvements I was thinking of," I said, and we both laughed heartily.

The next day was full of waiting, frustrations, last-minute problems, and solutions. Bus Hatch arrived by plane as scheduled to return my Jeep to Vernal. That was the only schedule that we managed to keep. The Teton Café again became our headquarters. From breakfast on, one or more members of the expedition occupied our "office," sitting at a big round table by the corner window. From here we could keep track of the activities of the others.

We tried to help Don finish buying food. This resulted in utter confusion. We either duplicated items on his list or, as we looked over the shelves, spotted some goodies we thought we ought to have, and this swelled the food boxes and the budget. We had enough candy to supply several expeditions and picked up enough cans of soup to float our boats. Don would have nothing to do with dehydrated food in spite of the fact that taking it would have solved enormous weight and space problems. Nor did we think it wise to have it because we would have to un-dehydrate it with silty river water, which was going to be our major supply. We knew we'd come upon clear creek water and springs only occasionally and could not carry a large supply on the boats. We had no refrigeration, so it was necessary to have all our foodstuffs in cans or dried.

In the grocery department of the store where Major Powell, too, had supplied his expedition, we bought literally hundreds of cans of food. For our main meals, we took beef stews, canned beef and hamburger, spaghetti and meatballs; whole chickens, tuna with noodles, Spanish rice, soups, vegetables, white and sweet potatoes, and puddings for dessert. For our lunches, we took a variety of canned fish—tuna, sardines, and shrimp; beef tongue, Spam, ham, peanut butter, sandwich spreads, cheeses, and various condiments. Bisquick, canned sausage and bacon, and dry and cooked cereals were purchased for breakfasts. Among the odds and ends were canned fruits: peaches, pears, and pineapples; a variety of powdered soft drinks, peanuts, dried apricots and apples, coffee, tea, cocoa, canned and powdered milk, and cream. The only fresh foods we took were onions, carrots, lettuce, oranges, and eggs. I was willing to agree to powdered milk, but I was stubborn about powdered eggs. I had had enough of them in the navy! So we took a chance on fresh eggs.

"Well," Don said, to conclude the argument, "the eggs won't be a waste; when they hatch, we can broil the chickens!"

Doc had a good suggestion: take along live ducks. They could be tethered by string to the boats and float along with us until needed. That way they'd take up no room whatever, and they would help us along down the river. "Provided they go the same direction we do," Don added. My real shock over the quantity of food we were taking came when I saw Don walk down the aisle with twenty loaves of bread! They were piled so high in his arms that we couldn't see his head.

"Good night!" I exclaimed, "I thought it was only going to take us nine days to get to our next supply point!"

"Well, he answered, "the bread will just about last us until then."

The store in Green River was more than just a grocery; it was a modern version of the old-fashioned general store. The place carried, as well as groceries and meats, saddles, hardware, furniture, and clothing. Several old characters still sat around the cracker barrel and took great interest in us. Their fathers would have remembered Powell in 1869 and been among those who had waved him down the river into the great country beyond: the south desert, the canyon country.

When we found we were being more of a hazard than a help to Don's shopping, we dispersed to talk with the old men and buy things in other departments. Cid purchased another air mattress. Her leaky plastic one couldn't be patched. Other forgotten items were purchased—hats, cups, extra socks. Cid found a remnant of white nylon that she had no particular use for. "It's just pretty," she explained, "and I can't resist a bargain." As it turned out later, she couldn't have purchased a more useful item!

After checking our lists, I discovered we needed more salt tablets, so I went across the street to the drugstore. While I was waiting for the tablets to be wrapped, I felt strangely aware of something staring at me from over my shoulder. I looked up, and there was our mascot! I knew it the moment I saw him. He was a toy rubber frog standing on a shelf, and with his big, bulging eyes, he had a definite personality.[2] His body was half the size of his head, and with his mouth wide open and red tongue sticking partly out, his broad smile covered his whole lower face from ear to ear. Two red dots marked his nose. He stood erect upon two broad feet, and his arms, which terminated with big hands, reached out defiantly from his sides. He wore a pair of red shorts. Altogether he had an expression of joyful expectation. From the tip of his toes to the top of his eyes (they stood above his forehead), he was not quite a foot tall. He was indeed a jolly amphibian, and the expression of character that some designer had built into his hollow, rubber form, would make him the perfect mascot. Indeed, he later seemed almost to come alive as we coursed our way down the rivers, and our affection for this simple rubber toy grew and grew until Frog seemed to be one of us.

I didn't realize how much personality he had acquired or how much of our affection he possessed until long after our voyage was finished.

When I came to gather up my equipment after a lecture in Chicago, Frog, who was always introduced during the show, was missing. Someone had walked off with him! I felt a deep pang in my heart for the silly thing and kept telling myself all the way back to New York what a silly fool I was for being so upset over a toy! Hadn't I replaced him that very day with another just like him that I had found in a Loop drugstore? He was worth only $2.04, tax included. Or was he? He had become a symbol of an experience, with scars just as we had from the voyage. Could this bright, shiny new frog, which was still wrapped in tissue paper in a box on the backseat, replace him? Yes, I could tell a little white lie to my audiences and introduce this new one as Frog, our mascot, but inside I could not lie. This was not the Frog who had commanded the helm of the *Brontosaur* or had had his paint rubbed off from tight cords bound to his neck and legs so he wouldn't be washed overboard, or whose bright colors had dulled from the blasting sand and baking sun.

I never discovered what his Chicago adventure had been, but one morning not long after, he showed up in a box mailed to me from there. He had returned! Been returned by someone who appreciated sentimental value, and we all greeted his reappearance as though a good friend had come back.

I bought the toy immediately and could hardly wait to show him to our group at the Teton Café. "We have another member in our party," I said slyly as I sat down at the table to order a three o'clock lunch. Everyone's ears pricked up to hear this astounding news. "Folks," I said solemnly as I bent over to pick the toy out of the bag, "I want you to meet—Frog, our mascot!" With that I squeezed his stomach, and he let out a loud squack. His reception was a roar of laughter and delight. I passed him around to everyone. Each person tried out his squack, and we made such a racket that everyone in the café came over to join in the fun. When the hilarity of meeting this creature quieted down, we went on to more serious business.

"Guess we'd better get to the legal matters," I announced. There were documents to be signed releasing me from any responsibility in case of accident or illness during the voyage. Everyone had understood beforehand that this was a cooperative expedition where they assumed their own responsibilities; it wasn't a guided tour. I read the long document aloud and made sure all understood it before they signed. "In consideration of ONE DOLLAR ($1.00) hand paid to me . . . the receipt whereof is hereby acknowledged with other goods and valuable consideration, I do hereby remise, release, and forever discharge until the end of the world," the document read. The wording had the air of doomsday about it! As each person signed, another witnessed it while I paid out a silver dollar.

The next document to be signed was a photographic release, giving me permission to take pictures of each person for commercial purposes. I had to pass out another silver dollar to make this one legally binding. It was also making me insolvent!

"Now," I said, "I have another document. This one is going to cost you a dollar. You'll need this to hunt in certain areas we'll be passing through." The document read,

> This License entitles the holder to hunt, pursue, shoot, and remove from that area known as Dinosaur Control Area of Uintah County, Utah, which is in the vicinity of Dinosaur National Monument, the following types of reptilian wild game:
> A. TYRANNOSAURUS REX—1 only (Adult Male).
> B. DIPLODOCUS GIGANTIGUS—1 only (Either Sex) and not less than 5,000 lbs. Live weight.
> C. STEGOSAURS—2 only (Males) any size.
> D. PTERODACTYLI—4 only (without young).
> The holder of this license agrees to remove all such game, legally bagged by him under the proper restrictions, properly preserved and in sanitary condition within 5 days of time of reptile's death, and further agrees to have said game inspected by the Utah Game Warden before removal.
>
> Signed———.
> ISSUED BY AL E. OUP
> Deputy Lizard Warden

I signed each permit and recovered seven of my fourteen silver dollars. There was so much passing around of documents, borrowing of pens, and collecting of silver dollars that Cid was utterly confused and told me later she'd like to know, just out of curiosity, who had come out ahead, she or me!

Time passed quickly, and the hour to depart from the town of Green River, Wyoming, came. Last telegraphs were sent, and final goodbyes were said over the long-distance telephones. The food and supplies were packed in Don's car and my Jeep, and we headed for the river. No one took a backward look as we passed over the hill and into the desert country. There was no ceremony, no brass band, as we took our leave of town for the final journey to the boats on the river.

Don's wife bid us goodbye as soon as her car was unloaded. We then unloaded the Jeep, which Bus Hatch was waiting to drive away. A solemn atmosphere spread over the camp as he prepared to leave. Each of us seemed to find some reason or other to delay his departure a bit longer. Even Bus found excuses to hang around. We made several unnecessary trips down to inspect the boats with him, although we knew they were already in seaworthy shape for the voyage. We all sensed that Bus's departure would break our last contact, and we would be wholly on our own with no other choice but to go down the rivers. The thought of the rivers and the hazards must have been in everyone's mind as we stood around delaying Bus Hatch. He, I think, sensed it too, and his stalling was meant to give any of us a last chance to change his or her mind and back out. I, too, found reasons to hold up his departure, and at the last minute—when Bus had already started the engine—I stopped him to take a last look inside the Jeep to see whether anything had been forgotten. Something had been forgotten: I discovered the wicks for the Coleman lantern hidden under the backseat. Finding them was such a surprise that I forgot my real motive in holding him up that final time.

The tailgate of the Jeep was closed for the last time, and Bus started off in a rush. I sensed he went fast to get away before anyone called out, "Wait!" We all cheered and waved him away, and when he was out of sight, we each went to our own campsite as though each of us wanted, at that moment, the security of our small possessions here in the wild desert of Wyoming.

There was nearly an hour of absolute quiet in camp. Tony bunked at a distance behind my tent. He spent his time writing a letter to his girl, and I wondered when he thought he'd get it mailed. Fred and Doc had pitched the tent they were sharing close to mine. Fred spent the hour sorting his clothing. His actions were so slow that I wondered whether he was trying to make each minute into 120 seconds. Doc had his sleeping bag outside the tent in the shade of a cottonwood. He was napping; probably dreaming of fresh trout. Les and Bruce were down at the boats.

Neither spoke a word to the other. Cid was hidden away in her boudoir, perhaps reading or writing her notes—or perhaps thinking of the river as it poured out of Split Mountain Gorge 185 miles downstream. Don, like a purser on an ocean liner bound across the sea, was working on papers. As I watched him make checkmarks with his pencil, I imagined him checking off some great passenger list to see whether everyone was on board. Once in a while he looked over at one of us as if to verify that this passenger or that one was in the right stateroom.

Doc's voice finally broke the silence. "Fred's got a bottle!" he shouted. "Who wants a cocktail?"

We all jumped up and gathered around the table. Bruce pronounced himself too young to drink hard liquor. Beer was enough for him. He ran down to the river and brought up a can that had been cooling in the water. Les came hobbling along with a gallon glass jug of a strange mixture of fruit juices for his own—singular—taste. Les was what one might call a high Mormon: he kept strict habits according to the LDS Church.

When the drinks had been poured, Fred said, raising his tin cup high into the air with care not to spill any of the contents, "Here's to the river!" We all gave a cheer.

"Here's to the Eggert-Hatch River Expedition!" shouted Cid as a second toast. Don added, "Long may it float!" We all laughed, and his remark seemed to break the last bit of tension. For the first time, I felt we were a tightly knit group bound by one purpose—the success of the voyage.

We got down to the business of food. The three-burner Coleman stove was set on the two boxes the motors had been in. The griddle was in place, and the thick steaks (fresh meat from town) were put on to sizzle. The aroma floated in the air and mingled with the strong smell of boiling coffee. These were mixed with the odor of sage, which seemed to become stronger as evening arrived. My nostrils began to dilate just as they had from the pine smell in the forest two days earlier. The smell of cooking camp food is another of those wilderness experiences to which nothing can compare and which makes living outdoors unforgettable.

We had only one small disaster. Tony had built a wood fire and sat the coffeepot atop it to boil. As the wood beneath burned away, the pot tipped over, and we had to start a new brew.

We talked around the open campfire until long after the last star had lighted up. There was a conscious avoidance of the subject of the river.

The camp at Green River, Wyoming, getting ready for launch of the river trip. Leslie Jones, a Hatch boatman who made part of the trip, is cooking on the stove.

Instead, we talked of smaller matters. Les and Bruce had already gone down to the boats, where they chose to sleep. "It's cooler down there," Les had explained. But that couldn't be the reason, for it was already near freezing, and we had gotten our warm coats to wrap around ourselves. His real reason, I knew, was to act as guardian over the boats. He wasn't ready to trust them on the river yet, even though they were firmly tied.

It was Don who gave the final signal to hit the sack for the night. "Tomorrow'll be a busy one," he said, getting up and stretching the kinks out of his legs. We followed his lead and headed toward our private little "homes" as though Don had given an order. We needed an order, for we seemed lost about what to do; we were hesitant to spend our first isolated night with the river.

I had just settled down and was thinking how comfortable my campsite was when suddenly a roar of laughter came from Fred's tent. It was as though a balloon of boisterous humor had suddenly burst in the dead quiet of the night. There was no first snicker or giggle to warn of its coming; it simply exploded and filled the whole desert with sound. They laughed so hard, Doc and Fred together in that little tent, that I was sure it would fall over on them—indeed, I thought it had! But when I looked out, their tent was still up, and I could see them bouncing about in the shadows of their flashlights on the tent wall. I couldn't figure out who was laughing at whom, but I could visualize the tears running down both their faces from laughing so hard and feel the aching they must have felt in their sides. The rest of us had no idea what they were laughing at, but it was so obviously funny that we all became infected and began to laugh too. Even Bruce, down at the boat, began to chuckle.

"What's so funny?" I yelled.

"Yes," shouted Cid from far off. "Tell us the joke!" But they were laughing so hard that they were beyond conversation. All we could get out of Fred was, "Doc—those—" and then he would break out in a side-splitting roar, and we could learn no more.

Gradually the outbursts came after longer and longer intervals, and the quiet began to take over. Soon the sharp little cracks of twigs breaking under the tired bodies of people as they made a last adjustment in their sleeping bags had stopped. All was silent—silent at last. I heard Fred's heavy breathing in his tent. I began to hear other sounds too, as my ears became adjusted to the subtle noises of the wilderness after the hubbub of civilization, just as the eyes become adjusted to the darkness after the brightness of light. I heard the last short chirps of a bird as it, too, settled in its nest for sleep. In the distance, a loon was calling into the darkness. Her call was suspended upon the light breeze, held there so the loon could hear the melancholy notes she sang.

I lay with my head in the open door of my tent, gazing at the stars that lit the night sky in place of the moon. It was cold and crisp, and in the light of the stars, I could see my breath. I felt relieved of the day's trials. The feeling was like the soothing calm you feel when a sharp pain stops. The boats were floating safely by the bank of the river, tied securely to a tree and watched over by alert boatmen. Our last tie with civilization had been broken, and we had waved our last goodbye. There was no turning back now, no debating in our minds whether we should go on or not. From now on there was just one course to follow—the river—and there were no doubts. We were all heading down through the rapids and the forbidding canyons. The official beginning of the expedition would not happen until tomorrow morning, but it had started with our last look at the Jeep as it passed over the hill. All of us must have felt the same that night as we sighed our last deep breath before giving ourselves up to sleep. We had made our choice.

*Seven*

# ON THE RIVER AT LAST

Major John Wesley Powell wrote in his journal on May 24, 1869: "The good people of Green River City turn out to see us start. We raise our little flag, push the boats from shore, and the swift current carries us down."

So began one of the most daring and heroic journeys of exploration in American history. Of the thousand-odd miles that Major Powell and his nine men were to travel, white men had seen not more than a hundred before. Yet enough was known to create rumors and weird stories of fearful whirlpools that flowed with tremendous velocity and sucked men and boats to the bottom of the river, never to be seen again. There were places where the river disappeared completely underground, pulling boats down along with the water. There were stories of great waterfalls too, and men who had come to the brink of the canyon, vainly endeavoring to reach the water below, only to perish with thirst in sight of the river that roared its mockery into dying ears.

Today we know that none but the first and last tales are true, but the major and his men must have thought hard about these things that May 24. They must have pondered the legend an old Indian had told Powell as a warning not to enter the canyons. Long ago, the legend went, there was a great and wise chief who mourned the death of his wife and would not be comforted until Ta-vwoats, one of the Indian gods, came and told him she was in a happier land and offered to take him there so he might see for himself and, upon his return, cease to mourn. The great chief promised, and so Ta-vwoats made a trail through the mountains that intervened between that beautiful land where his wife was and the desert home of the poor chief, Nu'-ma. Ta-vwoats led Nu'-ma through the great gash he had made through the land, and when they returned, the deity exacted a promise from Nu'-ma that he would tell no one of the joys of the land that he had seen lest others, through discontent with the circumstances of this world, should follow the trail to the happy land where the chief's wife now lived. Then the god sent a raging river through the gorge, a river to engulf anyone who tried to pass through. The wrath of the gods would be upon any who entered there.

The old Indian who recounted the legend warned Powell more than once not to enter the canyons. The Indians, he said, considered doing so disobedience to their gods and contempt for their authority, and he believed that surely they would punish Powell and his men.

We, too, remembered the rumors and ancient Indian legend as we erected our little expedition flags on the boats and prepared to enter the swift current on June 11, 1955. Indeed, the wrath of the Indian gods had been focused upon many who had entered the canyons. In 1955 the Indian god Ta-vwoats was still forbidding people to travel that beautiful passage he had cut for Nu'-ma. His favor had been granted to only a few. Were we to be among them?

We knew there were no great waterfalls. We knew, too, that the river did not disappear underground. Major Powell had discovered that in 1869. Now the entire river route was mapped, and as I settled myself into position in the sixteen-foot rubber boat, I clutched the maps in my lap, feeling security from them. But was that feeling warranted? My memory went back to the great fissure Cid Sumner and I had seen at the rim of Red Canyon. Perhaps by today it had fallen (for there had been rain and frost in the mountains since we had left that spot). Would we face an impassable waterfall? There were hundreds of places where this very thing could happen. The river changes every year, every day, and in flood times, every hour. It is forever at work cutting the rocks, widening its bed here, narrowing it there. Our maps could at best give us a general idea of what was ahead. We could never be certain. The most dangerous thing we could do was assume certainty about the river. Even at night, bedded down on its banks, we could not feel secure, as we learned nine hundred miles later. It is then—when you feel safest—that the river lashes out and strikes. Or is it the wrath of the Indian gods? Is Ta-vwoats still there watching his canyon trail to the beautiful land? Perhaps.

The large *Brontosaurus* rubber raft tied up at Green River, Wyoming, put-in for the river trip.

Breaking up our first camp was a bedlam of confusion. Everything was piled on the banks beside the boats. Where would it all go? The nine food boxes were fitted into the angle-iron frames. Then the one-and-a-half-foot pipes were unscrewed from our table, and it was placed across the aft end of the *Brontosaur*, where it became a camera platform. Gasoline cans were stowed under the oarsmen's seats. What was left over, we loaded into the small boat. We must have had a ton and a half of supplies and baggage, and as more was packed into the *Brontosaur*, she sank deeper into the water. We were glad that the river was high—even though the big boat drew only four or five inches of water! There were no rapids for the first two days, so it was unnecessary to tie things down as securely as we needed to later on. Gear was also piled atop the food boxes between the two boatmen, Les and Bruce, on the *Brontosaur*. Cid chose this as her place aboard the big boat. Fred and Doc made comfortable seats on the platform, using the gear there as backrests. Tony and I remained on shore to photograph the departure of the *Brontosaur*. We would ride with Don in the small boat. The two 7.5-horsepower Evinrude motors were

The trip underway, riding on the *Brontosaurus* on the Green River. Shown in the front of the photograph is Cid Ricketts Sumner, while Charles Eggert is the photographer at the back of the boat. Photograph courtesy of the Leslie Emsden Digital Collection, Special Collections, J. Willard Marriott Library, University of Utah.

mounted on it, and we could easily catch up to them. At 9:45 a.m., with much shouting and waving of flags, Cid, Fred, Doc, Les, and Bruce set off. None of us knew then that this would be the last voyage to follow the entire river route of Major John Wesley Powell.

The sky was a vivid blue, so bright it almost hurt our eyes to look at it. Small fluffy clouds floated in it and made it seem even larger and deeper. The scenery away from the banks was very colorful: buttes of buff and red with yellow, spotted with the olive green of sage, topped by strange rock castles, where I imagined the Indian sentries stood watch for trespassers on Ta-vwoats's forbidden passage and warned him of their coming. Vistas were Cinerama-like, and as we passed downstream, they stayed with us, ever changing as the river angled and twisted through them.

Bruce spent most of the morning with a paintbrush while Les leisurely rowed, keeping the big boat straight in the river. The decor on the *Brontosaur* had been scuffed up on the trial runs, so Bruce repainted the big sign on the side of the boat announcing who we were. He brightened and sharpened the big yellow teeth that were outlined in red by a huge mouth that extended around the front of the boat. Above the mouth were painted two large eyes. A similar design was at the back end, so we looked the same, coming or going, and the only way we could tell which was the front was by Frog, who was tied securely there. The *Brontosaur* looked like a great monster in the water, and she rode so low that the mouth in front seemed to be swallowing mammoth gulps of water.

Fred and Doc were overenthusiastic with their picture taking, and I shouted a warning to them not to photograph every butte we passed or they'd be out of film before we got to the first canyon, Flaming Gorge, fifty miles downstream. Even I found it hard to resist turning my camera on many of these colorful geologic monuments.

We had far less trouble our first day than Major Powell's men had had. They first ran onto a sandbar and had to push off. Then they broke an oar trying to avoid a rock, thus crippling the boat, which struck another rock and tossed two men overboard. Our troubles were small ones. We had to readjust the weight of the small boat and the pitch of the propellers of the motors so they would have the proper bite in the water. The towline to the *Brontosaur* was made of nylon cord, divided in the center to form two lines whose ends were attached to either end of the motor mount. This arrangement, we thought, would create an even pull. Don rigged up a fancy arrangement to detach the lines in case of an accident. If someone pulled a single nylon string, both lines were supposed to come loose from the small boat immediately.

Neither the divided line nor the emergency pull cord worked, however. The big boat whipped around behind us in spite of the double line, and when we attempted a sharp turn, one of the lines got tangled in the left propeller. Don pulled the emergency cord, but the lines didn't come loose, and so we sheared a pin. During lunch Don changed to a single

Cid Ricketts Sumner in camp on the Green River in 1955. Note the simple headdress she adopted for the trip to cope with the sun, heat, and bugs.

towline attached between the two motors. This simplified the emergency detaching too. One motor, we discovered, would steer the boat, so the other was locked into a straight course. The two motors, when they were synchronized at the same speed, droned on hypnotically as we sped through the water.

In the afternoon, the wind died down, and we felt the desert heat for the first time. Cid dug into her gear and pulled out the nylon remnant she had purchased in Green River. She fringed the edges and made it into a veil. To protect herself from the sun, she wrapped it fully around her face and head, leaving only her dark glasses peering out. She looked exactly like the Invisible Man.

We traveled thirty-six and a half miles our first day.[1] It was late afternoon when we stopped on a large island for our river camp number one. We arrived ashore hot and exhausted, and all we could do was throw our gear on the bank, pick a spot to put it, and sit listlessly staring across the river. Perhaps it was the excitement and tension of the first day that caused us to feel that way, but even more likely, it was heat exhaustion that got us. At any rate, I got the salt pills out of the medical kit, and a daily minimum of two per person was prescribed from then on. The boatmen were the only ones with energy. They forcefully busied themselves setting up the commissary and began to cook supper. We had failed to mark the food boxes, so nearly all of them had to be unloaded and opened to find the evening menu that Don had planned. While the boatmen cooked, the rest of us decided to go for a swim. We hoped the cold water would bring us back to life after the heat of the afternoon. It did the opposite: it made us more enervated than ever. Our supper was ready long before we were, and by the time we got seated around the platform, it was cold.

We ate in the light of a lingering sunset—one of the few we saw on our long voyage deep within the canyons—and it was a spectacular one. The clouds hung low, and they looked like flames in the western sky. To the east, purple clouds lay forbiddingly on the horizon, and in the south, the sky was black. I began to fear we were in for a storm, but the blackness must have been the shadows of the Uinta Mountains on the clouds. The sky cleared almost as soon as the sunlight disappeared from the clouds. It was night, and with it came the stars.

As soon as the dishes were washed, we all retired exhausted. I lay with my head sticking out of the door of my tent. For a long time, I watched the stars. I could not sleep in spite of my weariness. I could only think—not of all the problems, nor whether we should have made the choice of tackling them or not. These problems had left with the Jeep the night before. I thought now of why—why were we doing it; why were we all here together on the world's most dangerous river? These were not the kinds of disturbing thoughts that had kept me awake night after night during the weeks before but a peaceful, logical probing. Why were we here together tonight, here beside the river where we were perhaps destined to suffer untold hardships?

I got up and walked to the river's edge. I wanted to get closer to this thing whose magic drew us together, whose hidden powers had made us choose to remain instead of turning back when we had had that last moment of choice. Perhaps being close to it would give me the answer. In the distance as I stood there, I could hear over the hill behind me the faint yelp and then the cry of a coyote, which was soon answered by another, farther off. At my feet, I felt the current moving; the ground seemed to shudder with the river's surging, inexplicable force. Out on the stream, I could hear a soft splash, then a deep, sighing swoosh as the water turned over from the rising of strong currents deep below. Downstream I could hear the river play over small rocks. The water seemed to chuckle as it played around the bulky sides of the *Brontosaur*.

I sat on my haunches and put the tips of my fingers into the water. It was cold from the fresh melting of snow from the mountains above. It felt soothing and seemed to draw me closer to the silent land beyond. The reflections of the stars were caught on the ripples and tossed back to where they had come from.

I watched the reflections downstream in the current. I looked up to see the high bluffs and buttes to the south. Their shapes were even weirder and more eerie than in the daytime. They looked like an ancient, tumbled city brought down by a prehistoric Sampson. Some of the formations still had many pillars left standing. In the darkness beyond them, I could imagine the canyons that the horizon hid from my view. I thought of the ones I knew—the bright red of the canyon Cid and I had looked down into, the gloomy purple chasm of Lodore, and the sunny, yellow brightness of Yampa. And I thought of the ones I didn't know, canyons with forbidding names: Desolation, Gray, Cataract. I listened again to the sound of the boiling turmoil of the angry river I had heard long ago as Disaster Falls echoed up and down the canyon. I remembered hearing it with Don that evening when he had said, "That's always been a dream of mine—but I've never found a good reason to do it—except just wanting to."

*Eight*

# SHAKEDOWN

As soon as we settled ourselves into the boats for our second day on the river, I moved next to Don with my notebook and pencil in hand. "We've got to do something about camp organization," I said, opening my notebook. "What do you say we assign specific jobs to each person? Maybe that will make things more efficient."

"Good idea," Don answered. "We've got to get earlier starts if we're going to get all the way down this river."

"Let's make a breakfast duty list first. Bruce is always the first one up, so let's make him breakfast cook. Besides, he makes good pancakes," I said, remembering them from this morning. "Tony can start the fire and see that water is put on to boil." I wrote all this down. Setting the table and getting the food out were assigned to Fred and Cid, and Doc would wash the dishes. Don, Les, and Bruce were left to check the boats and the run of the day. I had cameras to check and prepare with Tony, but we all would clean the campsite and see to it that nothing was left behind. Don was designated to make a final check to see that everything was aboard.

Our evening camp duties were detailed next, and they ran much the same as for breakfast. Poor Doc, he got the dishwashing job both times. Perhaps it was his profession that made us think of him for the job; we knew that with Doc washing, our dishes would come nearer to sterilization!

The river was lazy, and the scenery lulled us on. We were pleased with the way the two 7.5-horsepower motors towed all the weight, and

Don Hatch cooking on a grill over an open fire in camp on the river.

we were glad to be making such speed, for we were anxious to get into the canyons.

Not many miles beyond our lunch site, we went around a wide curve, and at the end of it, the high riverbanks opened out. Suddenly, before us, in full majesty, the Uinta Mountains spread out. The snow-covered crests glistened in the sun. They seemed exceptionally bright because behind them, and moving toward us, were heavy, deep purple clouds.

"Hurrah!" I shouted back to the *Brontosaur.* "There they are! We'll be smack in them soon."

"Smack in them soon is right!" Don grumbled. "In those storm clouds. Looks as though we're in for something. Look how fast they are traveling toward us!"

Even though we were still fifteen miles from the mountains, the stiff blast of the wind hit us a few minutes later. The water became choppy, and soon high waves began splashing over the boats. The sun went behind the heavy clouds, and the rain came with violence. The downpour was so heavy that we lost sight of the riverbanks, and the upstream blast of the wind brought our boats to a standstill even though Don had the motors running at full power. We could make no headway, and the boats bounced around in the choppy water. Don huddled under his poncho, while behind us in the *Brontosaur*, Les and Bruce took refuge in the

Don Hatch (L), Bruce Lium (center), and Leslie Jones, on the *Brontosaurus*. All three men were boatmen for Hatch River Expeditions and went on the 1955 trip.

bottom of the boat. Doc, Cid, and Fred huddled among the gear on the platform. They were having a hard time trying to keep the edges of the tarpaulin covering them down.

Suddenly, the left motor started to sputter. Don jumped up to see if the gas line had gotten cinched in the scramble for his poncho. "No! Gas—we're out of gas!" he shouted above the roar of the wind and the pounding of the rain. I grabbed the oars.

"Pull into shore! Pull into shore!" we called to the *Brontosaur*. Bruce and Les grabbed their oars, and together we pulled for shore. We hit with a thud and remained there without making a move until the wind and rain stopped. Poor Tony was huddled on the floor of the small boat, sitting in six inches of water, with a tarp half wrapped around him.

The bad weather left as quickly as it had come. The wind stopped, the clouds went, and the sun came out like a blast furnace to warm and dry us. We climbed from our soaked holes looking as disheveled and uncomfortable as wet cats. "Boy! Things sure happen fast around here!" Tony said with amazement.

The boats were bailed out, the tanks filled with gas, and we were off again. With the wind gone, the surface of the river smoothed out. We quickly approached the mountains. They came upon us like a great monster, their heights rising so quickly that we were engulfed in them before we were quite prepared to meet our adversary—the canyons within them. The river took a sharp turn, and there was our first canyon—Flaming Gorge.[1] We looked amazed upon a whole side of a mountain carved out by the river. In ninety million years of work, the river had cut it asunder, leaving the bare rock a brilliant orange. High above, the orange blended into yellow, which was brilliantly edged by the low-hanging purple clouds that again were filling the sky. Major Powell, who had given the canyon its name, must have seen it in the same light as we did, for it truly looked like a gigantic flame.

For a mile and a quarter, nature gave us this dramatic introduction to the canyon country where we would spend almost all of the rest of our voyage, and Flaming Gorge would stand out in our memories as one of the most beautiful. We were looking back at it as we entered Horseshoe Canyon, and when we looked ahead, we were amazed to find ourselves held between sheer walls not more than a hundred yards apart and rising two to three hundred feet above us.[2] "Want to climb up to look down on the horseshoe curve the river makes?" I asked Don.

"Not unless you want to—there's a good campsite below, Carter Creek—good fishin'," he answered with a glint in his eyes. So we went on, never quite appreciating the river's impressive curve through Horseshoe Canyon.

I pondered whether I should insist on stopping to photograph from above—but it was getting late, and the prospect of a good campsite and a trout dinner enticed me. Don broke into my thoughts with a shout: "White water ahead!" he yelled.

Bruce heard him—or the sound of tumbling water—for he immediately shouted, "Rap-eed! Rap-eed ahead!" Tony jumped up.

"Sit down—you're apt to get bounced out!" Don ordered sharply. The river suddenly flowed faster. Don jerked the towline and set the *Brontosaur* free. We bounced through the rapid like a cork in the small boat. Water splashed everywhere. It was over all too quickly.

"Wow! Quite a rapid," Tony said.

"Nothin'," Don answered with a grin on his face. "There's another coming up around the bend—little too."

We got far ahead of the *Brontosaur*, for Don sped up the motors to get a better ride through the small rapids. We turned a bend and bounced through the second rapid as gaily as the first. When we were through it,

Don chuckled, "The boys back there'll be surprised—bet they don't know that's there." He slowed our small boat down and turned into the back eddy below the rapid, where we remained at a standstill to watch the big boat come lumbering broadside around a curve. "Ha, ha!" Don shouted gleefully. "They're going to get splashed."

Bruce and Les bit the water with their oars in an attempt to straighten out the big boat before hitting the white water, but they were too late. The *Brontosaur* hit it broadside with a hard splash. I could hear the two boatmen shouting instructions to each other while Fred and Doc roared with laughter and Cid yelled, "Hurrah, hurrah! We're getting wet!" Their voices resounded down the narrow canyon, bouncing from wall to wall.

"Why didn't you warn them?" Tony asked with surprise.

"That will teach them to keep on their toes. That splash may save them from getting dumped later on," Don answered seriously.

Don was exhilarated for the first time during the voyage. In Vernal, where we had met, and during the days of final preparation for the expedition, he had seemed depressed and short-tempered. But now I felt his lightheartedness. Perhaps it was because he was in the country he loved and fighting the adversary he felt he was a match for—the rapids. "Eggert," he commanded, "keep on your toes! Don't just gape at the scenery. Where are we anyway?" He shoved the map case to me. I took it, and pretending to raise a spyglass to my eye, I peered ahead. I saw that the river was about to make a broad turn to the left, to head south again. Around the bend was a broad flat on the left bank. I looked down at the map; it was all very simple.

"Mile point 73, sir—Nielsen Flat dead ahead, sir," I answered. "Kingfisher Canyon coming up, Captain."[3]

"Right!" Don replied. "To the head of the navigation class." Then he added, "Bet Les thinks we're approaching Ashley Falls. He's always miles ahead of the rest of us."

"You've been through here before, haven't you, Don?" Tony asked.

"Yeah—helped survey it a few years ago. I spent the whole summer running up and down this end of the river while the 'wreck-lamation' guys tried to find a dam site."

"You helped the dam builders, you traitor!" I said.

"I know it! Didn't have any sense then."

"Did they find one?" Tony asked.

The raft and crew bathed in sunlight in Kingfisher Canyon, Green River, 1955.

"You bet they did—down below here—and they're going to build one. Flaming Gorge, they're calling it, and it's going to flood all of this," Don answered with a sweep of his hand. "Guess I should have dumped them in Ashley Falls."

"Do we come to Ashley Falls today?" Tony asked Don.

"Tomorrow," he answered.

We had rounded the big curve by now, past Nielsen Flat. The walls again rose, and we were in Kingfisher Canyon.[4] The kingfishers have gone since Powell's time, but there were other birds. Several golden eagles soared over the rim of the canyon, looking down upon us in the narrow slot of rock the river had cut. They glided gracefully on the updrafts. Ducks and Canada geese floated along with us as we went, sometimes almost surrounding us like a miniature flotilla. They were so numerous that they hardly seemed worth photographing. There were vultures, too, perched on overhanging ledges, staring down upon us ominously with their eager, hungry eyes!

When we went around Nielsen Flat, we picked up a huge gray heron that we chased many miles down the river. As we neared him, he flew ahead, lit on the riverbank or in a tree, and awaited our approach. Then,

The trip's ten-man raft with crew floating through Red Canyon on the Green River, 1955.

when we got close to him again, he took off, landed farther below, and waited. Eventually he lost us when we went on one side of an island, and he went on the other. I wondered how long he waited for us to pass by.

"Beehive Point and Red Canyon dead ahead!" Don shouted over the roar of the motors. Downstream rose a high peninsula of Weber sandstone, which Powell had named Beehive Point because of the impressive number of swallows nests he had seen there. Swallows still packed their spherical mud nests against the rock wall and made it look like a honeycomb. With their small slots for entrances and so many looking alike, we wondered how a swallow could tell which was his home.

Beyond Beehive Point, we could see the yellow-brown Weber sandstone end and the wine-colored walls of Red Canyon rise majestically and abruptly.[5] In a massive surge upward, the walls mounted to twelve hundred feet and more, with terraces climbing in giant steps. Douglas firs grew on each terrace, and in the late afternoon light, the canyon looked forbidding and gloomy.

"We've got to watch it ahead—couple of nasty little churns coming up," Don said, turning to the boatmen in the *Brontosaur*. "Heads up for the rapids ahead!" he yelled to them. "Stay far right on the third one. We land right below it!"

"Steady as we go," I heard Les advise Bruce as the approaching roar became louder.

Away we bounced through the first rapid. I grabbed my poncho to protect myself from the spray. The water felt cold now that the sun had gone behind the canyon wall.

"Second one coming up!" Don shouted. The river ahead dropped out of sight, and all we could see was the splash of the waves as they ripped between the narrowing canyon walls. In a moment, with hardly time to catch our breaths after the first rapid, we ran swiftly through the second. Almost immediately after it was the third.

"Get ready to grab that line!" Don shouted to Tony in the front of the small boat. He jumped up. "Not now—not now! I'll tell you when. Then jump with it."

"Into the water?" Tony asked in bewilderment.

"No! Ashore—we're landing."

Don hardly had time to get these last words out before we were in the rapid. It was short, but rough, and right in the middle of it, Don suddenly veered our boat broadside as he headed for the bank. We tipped dangerously, and a wave hit us, covering us with water.

"Get ready to jump!" Don ordered. The shore was approaching. "Now—jump!" But between Don's "now" and "jump, Tony leapt from the boat and landed waist deep in the water. The boat ran into him and nudged him ashore.

"Why didn't you wait for us?" Don laughed after Tony had gotten to his feet.

"I thought you said 'jump,'" Tony complained.

"I did say 'jump'—but you'd already gone by then," Don answered.

"Here comes the *Brontosaur!*" I shouted. Les and Bruce were pulling on the oars with all their strength to bring the heavy craft around and across the rapid.

"Get ready to grab their line," Don yelled. We ran down the beach, for we could see they would hit below us. The *Brontosaur* was in the full force of the current and traveling at a fast rate. I ran down the beach with Tony close behind, both of us watching for the opportune moment for Doc to throw us the line. Suddenly, I came to a creek and ran into it. Just at that moment, Doc threw the line. I managed to grab it. Tony grabbed me so I wouldn't be dragged farther into the creek. For a moment, I thought we couldn't hold her, but by this time Don was on the rope too. We checked the big boat's speed and swung her around to shore. The three of us were waist deep in Carter Creek.[6] I suddenly realized how cold the water was.

"Let's get out of here!" I shouted.

"What's the matter, Charlie, not cold, are you?" Les yelled from the boat. With the *Brontosaur* out of the main current, we were able to drag her along the bank to the place where we had beached the small boat. There we tied her to a huge log washed up on shore by higher water.

"Tony, you'd better get to work on that fire—Eggert is about to turn blue," Don said.

"You're wet, Tony; I'll make the fire," Bruce volunteered. He built a fire worthy of Wagnerian gods, and Don, Tony, and I huddled around it while changing to dry clothes. In the shadow of the canyon wall, it was cold, and the sharp wind that always blew upcanyon in the early evening chilled us. Our teeth chattered.

As soon as we were in dry clothes and warm, we scrambled for our fishing tackle. "We'll have trout tonight!" Don said eagerly. He, Doc, and I abandoned camp for the creek.

"I hope dry flies work here," I said hopefully when we got to the first prosperous-looking hole.

"Nope! Worms," Don answered.

"Worms! How are we going to dig for worms around here?"

"Here are some." Don, with a pleased look, reached into his creel and brought out a pint box packed full of them. "Picked them up in Green River before we left." *Well!* I thought, *Next to the river, fish must be closest to Don's heart!* With all the confusion we had had to cope with there, how could Don have taken the time even to think of worms? I took a few, and so did Doc, and we were off on our separate ways to find a likely spot. I could taste the trout already!

*If I could only catch one—just one!* I wished as I watched my line float gradually into a deep hole. Nothing. Not a nibble. I tried again. Still no luck. I walked upstream to another spot and dropped my line into the water. A fish struck! I gave a hard jerk; I wasn't going to let him have a chance! The line and trout went flying from the water into the air—and into a tree behind me. There the line tangled in a high limb with the trout dangling and fighting madly on the hook. I didn't think I had ever seen a fish more out of water, nor one so thoroughly caught! I had to climb the tree to get him, and I had to laugh out loud at myself as I hung over the limb. I thought of my son Kip, who is quite a fisherman (far surpassing his father). What a kick he would have gotten out of this scene!

I managed to catch three fish in two hours, the other two by more conventional methods. I started back for camp wondering how the others were making out. When I arrived, Cid and Fred were bending over the fire, cooking.

"We gave you up," Cid said, "and we've taken matters into our own hands—we're hungry!"

"Caught three," I answered Fred's eager question. He was more anxious about the results of my fishing than what was happening in the pot he was leaning over; that was obvious. I could see that he was disappointed not to go fishing, but I sensed he felt it was more important to remain in camp to help Cid set up, according to those duties we had assigned earlier in the day. I suddenly felt guilty for having run off, but then I had been tense all day, concentrating on photography, and I felt a little justified in playing.

Bruce and Les were down at the boats readjusting lines that had stretched from the twisting of the big boat in its first rapids. Tony was sitting on his bedroll writing. I noticed that the cameras were still lying around on shore beside the boats. "Tony," I said as I walked over to him," I wish you'd take care of those cameras. They should be put in their cases and wrapped in the waterproof bags. It might rain tonight."

"Soon as I finish this letter to my girl," he answered.

"Better now, Tony, while there's still light enough to see what's lying around. Those cameras are your most important concern; they're our reason for being here." I was annoyed that he had neglected his job. I turned back to Cid and Fred. They were busy working on a pot of canned chicken.

"Don will be furious that we used the rice," Cid remarked. "It wasn't included on the menu—but rice is so good with chicken," She continued apologetically, "We should have cooked the rice separately, but we couldn't find another big pot."

I looked into the stewing pot and saw that it held a rather thick mess. I looked over at Fred. He gave me a loud laugh. "He who complains must do the cooking!" he said.

Doc and Don still had not returned when everything was ready to eat. It was almost dark, and I began to wonder what had become of them. *Lost in the reverie of fishing*, I thought. It must either be very good or terrible. There's one way to get them back—the rifle. I went down to the boat and dug out the 30-30 Winchester. This would be as good a use for it as any. I loaded it and went to the mouth of the creek after warning everyone that I was about to make a big noise. I pulled the trigger. What a racket I made! The shot was so loud and sharp that the very canyon walls seemed to quake as it reverberated a thousand times over, traveling down Red Canyon and into Carter Creek Canyon. I suddenly thought in horror that I might have started a landslide. I stood petrified for a moment waiting for the sound of rock thundering down into the canyon. But all was quiet once the sound of the gun had stopped echoing.

"The boys should hear that," I remarked. "They should be able to hear it all the way to Jensen!"

The shot worked, for in a few minutes the fishermen came down the trail into camp.

"Catch any?" Cid shouted to them.

"Not a one!" Doc's tone was dejected.

"Six," Don announced, holding a string of small fish up for all of us to see.

"Well! It's a good thing we didn't rely on you fishermen," Cid said. "We'd have starved! As it is, you can see we have a fine dinner waiting."

"Come and get it!" Les shouted, appearing suddenly from nowhere. As we sat down, I noticed a small bouquet of wildflowers sticking jauntily out of a tin can in the middle of the table, which was covered by a plastic cloth that I didn't even know we had. Our places were set neatly with the forks on the proper side of the plate.

"Well! What style we're eating in tonight!" *Organization does do something*, I thought. Cid dished out heaping plates of food.

"Hmmm—rice!" Don observed.

What with getting soaked in landing and my excitement over fishing, I had not really noticed our campsite until now. It had a majestic setting. We were buried at the bottom of deep red walls with just a slit of night blue where the stars were. I imagined them hung on wires stretched across the rim of the canyon. Deep grass carpeted our campsite, and tall Douglas firs surrounded us. The fresh smell of pine and the peculiarly

Carter Creek camp in Red Canyon of the Green River, 1955. Fred Wood is on the right, and Dr. Robert Parsons is seated.

pungent odor of the many wildflowers made it so fresh I couldn't believe anyone had set foot in this place before us. There were no used tissues to mark someone's bathroom break, no beer cans to tell of others' boisterous presence. Carter Creek camp was as primeval a spot as we'd ever find. I could feel the presence of deer staring down upon our campfire, which reflected its light on the wall behind us and lit the mahogany-colored shaggy bark of the big tree trunks.

At Carter Creek, we must have all felt the same sense of peace I did that night. I felt I was in the right place at the right moment. So often do we think we should be somewhere else, doing some other thing; feel anxious about whether our moments are counting for something; wonder whether they are counting for the right thing. At Carter Creek, there was no watching the clock to see if we were where we were supposed to be.

The creek babbled over the rocks, the breeze sang softly through the pine needles, and the big river murmured gently nearby. Here at Carter Creek, we could say we were at peace with one another, at peace with the world where we live, and we could feel the presence of God.

Boulder Narrows, Mile 18. During the flood of June 1956, this house-sized boulder was almost submerged.

Redwall Cavern, Mile 33. John Wesley Powell estimated this huge natural cavern could hold fifty thousand people, although later scholars have lowered that figure to five thousand.

Landing to scout a Grand Canyon rapid. Boatmen often stop to look at rapids from shore before running them.

Don Hatch overlooking the Little Colorado River, the largest tributary to enter the Grand Canyon. The entire flow of the Little Colorado comes from large mineral springs a few miles up the canyon, which accounts for the blue color.

Landing at Espejo Creek, Mile 67. Below this point, the party encountered more and more difficult rapids, like Unkar and Hance Rapids, followed by the Inner Granite Gorge.

*Brontosaur* running Unkar Rapid, Mile 73. Unkar Rapid is formed by the Unkar Delta, site of the largest concentration of prehistoric Native American occupation in the Grand Canyon.

Charles Eggert with camera, Al Galloway in foreground. Al Galloway's great-uncle, Nathaniel Galloway, was one of the most significant pioneers of white water boating on the Green and Colorado Rivers.

Don Hatch running a Grand Canyon rapid. Don is in a ten-man military surplus boat—the smaller of the boats used by the Eggert-Hatch Expedition—so named because it could hold ten fully-equipped soldiers.

Jack Brennan in his powerboat *JAX*, left, and the *Brontosaur*, right, in Granite Gorge. Jack Brennan, along with his friend Don Harris, operated Harris-Brennan River Expeditions up until the 1960s.

Running Granite Rapid, Mile 94. The pontoons used by the Eggert-Hatch Expedition were military surplus bridge pontoons, adapted for river running by adding a rowing frame and oars.

Tapeats Creek, Mile 133, is a popular stop because a clear, cold side stream enters the Grand Canyon at that point. Boaters stop to get fresh water, fish for trout, and cool off in the creek.

Bruce Lium was the only boatman to complete both the 1955 and 1956 legs of the Eggert-Hatch expedition.

Jack Brennan's power-boat towing the *Brontosaur* below Separation Canyon, Mile 140. Lake Mead backs up into the Grand Canyon as far as Separation Canyon.

*Nine*

# RED CANYON AND THE FIRST RAPIDS

Les had no trouble getting the gang up with his shouts of "Crawl out!" With the prospect of trout for breakfast, we were all up immediately.

"No, no!" I said to Bruce. "Not the Coleman stove this morning. Trout tastes better cooked over a wood fire!" At night we always had a big campfire, and in the morning, a small one sufficient to boil a pot of water, but we never cooked on it. But with the heavy scent of pine, the warmth of the morning sun, and the merry rush of Carter Creek, nothing else would do but a romantic fire to cook the trout! The fire was made, and our big griddle was atop it when I turned and saw Don rolling the trout in cornmeal. "Oh, Don! No! Let's fry them in thick butter just as they are."

"You never fry raw trout!" Don proclaimed.

"We will—I'll cook them myself!" I announced, and due to the half authority of the expedition coleader, four trout were fried in butter, four rolled in cornmeal. The ninth trout had the distinction of having cornmeal on one side, butter only on the other. Our finely drawn line of demarcation made no difference in the outcome. I ruined the trout. My romantic idea of cooking over a wood fire turned out disastrously. There was no way of controlling the heat, and the griddle got too hot. The fish were burned on the outside and raw on the inside. I was the only one who complained, which was my prerogative, since I happened to be the cook!

It wasn't long after we left our camp when we heard a booming roar in the canyon ahead.

"Ashley Falls," Don said as he turned off the motors.[1] He listened intently. Perhaps he was trying to figure out the seriousness of the falls before seeing them. The roar grew louder and louder, and the canyon walls seemed to shake as we came closer. Ahead in the center of the river, we could see a huge rock that blocked the current, sending it to either side in a great heap of churning foam. The white water bounced against the cliffs and poured over the steep drop. The river vanished completely from sight.

We stopped well above the falls on the left side; the other side was sheer rock wall. The boatmen were the first to reach Ashley Falls to look it over. Tony and I scrambled over the huge boulders with the cameras. We planned to photograph the boats going through and be picked up below. Fred and Doc followed, also intending to walk around the falls. Only Cid remained in the boat; climbing over the big rocks would be hard for her, and we weren't going to make her do it unless it was necessary. Don would decide that.

"Let's run the small boat through and find out what's on the other side of that," Don said to Bruce and Les, pointing to the house-sized rock in the center of the channel. We couldn't see what hazard lay behind it. "We'll have to take a chance on the far side of the river," Don explained. "We sure can't run this side." Directly below us were many sharp rocks, the water pouring violently around and over them. I could see why we couldn't run there: the boats would be torn to pieces.

The men had serious faces as they approached the rapid in the small boat. Don entered the falls stern first. That way he could look downstream while he rowed upstream to slow the approach. Pulling the oars against the current also gave him more maneuverability. We held our breaths as they dropped down the falls. Into a big wave they tossed. Water poured into the boat's back end. Then they disappeared behind the rock. It seemed like minutes before we saw them again. They had made it through! We gave a cheer.

After landing below, Bruce and Les started back over the boulders to take the *Brontosaur* through. "We'll take Cid with us, Charlie—too hard for her to climb over this stuff," Bruce said as he passed me.

"Hurray for Cid!" Fred shouted. Cid waved from the boat.

"Watch that current against the big rock," Don shouted last-minute instructions from the small boat, where he remained. "I'll be below to pick you up in case." *In case of what*? I wondered.

Fred Wood and Dr. Robert Parsons scouting Ashley Falls on the Green River. This rapid is now under Flaming Gorge Reservoir.

"We're going to line upstream a ways," Les said as he made his way back, hobbling the best he could over the jumbled rocks. "We need more room to get to the other side to run it."

We could see from where we were perched above the falls that the two men were lining the big boat upstream along the bank as far as they could pull her before setting off. Soon they were as far as they could go—where the canyon wall came down to the water. Les jumped in and took his place at the oars. Bruce gave a hard shove, jumped in, and they were off. They rowed with all their strength to get to the other side before hitting the first drop. As the big pontoon came to the brink, it seemed to hesitate before deciding to drop into the boiling current below. Then it poured over, gathering momentum as it went. As it hit the waves below, it gave a great lunge, dug into the first big wave, rode over the top of the second, and headed for the rock midstream! Les jumped up in an attempt to break the force of the impending crash. Cid, lying flat on her stomach in the center, had her feet in the air. She, too, saw that they were going to hit and planned to do what shoving she could to help soften the collision. They went out of sight behind the big rock. While the *Brontosaur* was hidden behind it, the roar of the falls seemed to become louder as if someone had suddenly turned up the volume. I kept my eyes glued to the camera finder. I was afraid I would run out of film before the boat appeared again. But down she came! We all cheered and laughed with relief as the boat, looking very much like a big caterpillar, rode up and down the heavy waves below.

"All okay!" we heard Cid shout as they continued downstream.

"Darn it!" Fred said as we got into the small boat with Don. "I wish we could have gone through."

"Well," Don answered, "I can get you through part of it." With that he wheeled the boat around and went up to the rapid as close as he could. Then he veered sharply into the full turmoil beside the big rock in the middle. As we hit the current, we could see at last what was behind it. Between the big rock and the right side of the river was another huge boulder, very sharp on top, with water just about covering it. Maneuvering between them had been a hard job for the big boat to do; to get through the narrow channel had taken great skill. We were proud of Bruce and Les.

After we had run some of Ashley and felt its spray, we felt satisfied that we at least had gotten a taste of this famous rapid that Powell had named Ashley Falls because he had found the name Ashley and the date 1825 painted on the cliff. Powell thought that Ashley had been a prospector or trapper, but he was, in fact, another explorer of the West and had traveled by bull boat through these canyons as far as Desolation Canyon, where he left the river. His painted name disappeared long ago, worn away by the elements. On the high rocks above the falls, we had seen the names of other famous river men who had passed through: Stone—1909 was one, on the same trip with Galloway—1909. We decided not to carve our date. We figured that anyone interested in us would know we had gone through.

Don started the motors, and soon we caught up with the *Brontosaur*. Tony and I transferred back to the big boat. Photography was easier and less bouncy there than in the small boat. Throughout the rest of the day, we passed through many more rapids that would have impressed us far more had it not been for Ashley Falls.[2] With the big one behind us, we seemed to become more seasoned river runners, and the scale of things diminished. I thought of this as we continued downstream through canyon walls that steadily grew higher and ran rapids that tossed and splashed and exhilarated us. When Tony turned to me and asked, "When do we come to Hell's Half Mile?" my sense of the scale of the

The *Brontosaurus* raft and crew running through Ashley Falls.

rapids took a turn in the opposite direction. If Ashley seemed big, what were the others like? On Les's scale, which rated rapids from one to eleven according to their fury, Ashley was a mere six. Ahead were many with ratings far higher than that: Hell's Half Mile, an eleven; SOB—nine; the Big Drop—nine to eleven according to the water stage; Hance—eleven; Unkar—nine; and Lava Falls, an eleven-plus.[3] There were more than a hundred eights and nines, each involving new struggles and risks.

Toward late afternoon, we approached a number six rapid—Red Creek.[4] We could again hear the roar far up the canyon. Don, Doc, and Fred in the small boat had lagged behind us shortly after lunch, and we had not seen them all afternoon. We were growing concerned—with the exception of Les, who said, "Aw, don't worry, they'll catch up." But they should have caught up with us long before. With the roar of Red Creek Rapid ahead, we really began to worry.

"Let's pull up and wait," Bruce said. With Les's "Okay"—which sounded as if he, too, was becoming concerned, we stopped far above the rapid and strained to hear, if we could above the roar of the river, the small boat coming. Les hobbled up the bank to a high spot where he could look far upriver. No sooner had he gotten up there than the small boat appeared around the bend. It had not been far behind, but because of the twisting of the river through the canyon walls, we had never caught sight of it. Don pulled in beside us.

"Where were you?" Cid asked. "We had begun to worry."

"Hiked up a side stream—took lots of pictures," Don answered. Fred wore an expression of guilt. I was sure he didn't approve, either, of such long separations, if for no other reason than everyone's peace of mind.

"Well, let's look over ol' Red Creek," Don said, ignoring our concern. We got out to walk down and see what lay ahead. Don and Bruce got to the rapid long before the rest of us, for along the banks cacti grew and were in full bloom. The sight of them delayed us. They were delicate bursts of color, and they seemed an anachronism here in this turbulent world. These flowers seemed so fragile among the ripped and crushed rocks hurled about helter-skelter from a monstrous slide of long ago. I thought, as I cautiously touched one of the ephemeral blooms with my fingertips, *If these can survive the turmoil, perhaps we can too!*

We reached the rapid just as Don was starting back. "I'm going to take Les to the other side—we can't see enough below from here."

We watched from upstream as the two took off across the river in the small boat. I wondered whether the motors would be powerful enough to get them to the other side before they were carried into the rapid. As they crossed, Don kept the boat headed upstream. They made no progress in that direction. But they lost no distance in the opposite direction, either. The motors were strong enough to hold them against the swift current, and they made it to the right shore, landing almost directly opposite where they had started. All sense of scale is lost in these canyons, and so it was a shock to see how small they looked as they climbed the ledges on the opposite bank. We had to strain our eyes to see them, but we could see well enough to spot Les as he returned to the boat. He was taking movies as he walked along the ledge. Apparently he was so interested in what he saw in the camera finder that he failed to notice how close he was to the edge. Over he went into the river—camera and all.

"Les is in the river!" Bruce shouted with laughter. Up bobbed his cap with Les still under it, and we could see Don give him a hand and pull him into the boat.

"Won't have to wash my feet tonight," Les commented with a chuckle as they returned to our side of the river. "Think I've ruined the film, Charlie?" he asked, standing up in the boat, dripping wet, holding his movie camera above his head.

"Not if it's as watertight as you!" I laughed.

Don told us that Red Creek would be a nasty one to run. We'd have to snake it through, starting out on the far right until we passed the first big rocks. Then we'd have to pull hard to the left to avoid crashing into other rocks, and then hard right again—hard, hard right this time—to avoid a big gravel bar right in the middle of the rapid. If we didn't negotiate that second hard, hard right, the current might carry us to the left and into sharp rocks, which would surely rip us up, for the river was spread over a wide area and shallow.

"Where did you get that number six rating, Les?" Don asked.

"From you," Les answered.

"Better change that to an eight—in this water stage anyway," Don advised.

Les sat down in the big boat and made a notation on his map. Then he took up his oars. "Think you can make it, Bruce?" he asked.

"Let's go!" Bruce shouted back. With that Tony jumped into the boat with the towline, Don gave us a shove, and we were off ahead of Don, Fred, and Doc. We headed upstream as Don had done in crossing before.

"Row hard, Bruce—row hard—PULL," Les puffed. "We've got to make it over there before we hit!"

I could hear the boatmen's grunts as I watched us approach. We lost ground fast. I could feel the surge of the boat as their oars dug hard into the water, and I could sense my own muscles flex as I saw from the corner of my eye the oars bending as the men pulled. A strong wind, cold and harsh, began to blow upcanyon and helped us in our struggle to reach the other side before hitting the rapid.

"Here we go!" Bruce shouted.

"Let 'er go!" Les called back. They stopped rowing, and the boat gave a surge into the drop as though someone had cut a rope holding her back. Between the two rocks we plunged. The nose of the boat dug into the kick-up wave at the bottom of the first drop, and water splashed high in the air.

"Hard left—pull, Bruce, pull!" Ahead was a big boulder covered entirely by a great mound of water. I thought for sure we'd hit it and go tumbling into the hole behind. "Swing her—left oar, pull, Les!" The rock approached the boat with the speed of a thundering steam engine. I heard a loud crash in the boat. I looked around. Les was clamoring back into position; his oar had missed the water, and he had tumbled.

"Pull out your oar, Les!" Bruce cried in fear that the rock would hit the side. He didn't realize that Les's oar was already out of its mount. Les was fumbling to get it back in when the boat tipped to a forty-five-degree angle. We grazed the side of the boulder and plunged forward. As we passed the monstrous thing, I looked over the high side and could see the hole behind it. Had we gone over, we would have been swallowed up and buried under tons of water. It was a lucky near miss!

Now Les was shouting to Bruce, "Get your oar back; hard right—hard—HARD—swing her, Bruce, swing her!" They pulled with all their might—I was sure an oar would crack. But the waves were high, and as often as not, the oars missed the water when each and every hard dig into it counted. We all knew we'd never make that hard, hard right Don had warned us about. we were stuck with the next best choice now: avoid the left side of the gravel bar at all costs. There was no stopping to figure it out, to rechart the course. We were in it, and there was nothing we could do. The inextricable current was carrying us along. All at once there was a horrible grinding sound on the bottom of the boat, and we suddenly came to a dead stop. The river was rushing madly all around us. Waves hit against the broad side of the boat and splashed into it. We were dangerously grounded right in the center of the rapid! We had to get off the bottom quickly; water was pouring into the boat fast.

"You stay—and hang on!" I shouted tersely to Cid as we jumped overboard to shove us off. "Hang on to the safety lines on the side," I yelled to the others. We stood up to our knees in the full force of the rapid. Water rushed about our legs, and the choppy waves broke against them, soaking us to the waist. No one thought about how cold the water was. We pushed and tugged, stumbled and fell over the rocks on the bottom. The *Brontosaur* would not budge. The force of the current against her side held her solidly.

Just then Don and the others came bounding through. Don had to veer sharply to avoid hitting us. Seeing our plight, Don headed for shore on a small island below us. They landed, pulled their boat up on the bank, and began to wade into the river toward us. The going was rough, and I saw Doc slip and fall face first into the water. He recovered quickly and scrambled on. Fred was up to his waist in a deep spot and had all he could do to force his body against the current. He managed to grab our long floating towline and pull himself to our boat. They made it, and with the help of the three extra men, we were able to push the *Brontosaur* gradually back upstream and off the rocks. As she hit deep water, the current grabbed the upper end of the boat, and it swung quickly into the river.

"Jump—JUMP!" Don yelled. Les, Bruce, Tony, and I all madly scrambled for the rear end of the boat. It was hard enough to climb over the high sides in still water, let alone in this thrashing foam. Cid grabbed whom she could, when and where she could, and with all her strength helped us back into the boat. Bruce managed to get in first and helped Les up. Cid held onto the seat of my wet dungarees as I straddled the side with one leg in and one out of the boat. I grabbed Tony's wrist. By the time we were all in, the boat was bounding down the rapids. I looked back to where we had been and saw Fred, Don, and Doc standing in the middle of the river. They looked strangely out of place and marooned; hopelessly abandoned, yet comical.

As we sat around our campfire later, Don said, "I felt just like Donald Duck! You know—like in one of those cartoons when Donald runs off the edge of a cliff, and he's out there in midair, and he turns around and runs back to the cliff before he starts to fall. That's just how I felt when the *Bronto* took off and there wasn't anything near us anymore—except water."

*Ten*

# BROWN'S PARK AND THE GATES OF LODORE

The night turned out to be as tumultuous as the afternoon had been. The wind began to rage during our supper, and rain started to fall as we turned in. About four in the morning, it came down full force, and the wind howled through the scrub cedars around us. I thought of Cid's boudoir. Would it hold? I thought my own tent would take off at any moment. The sides flapped, and the center pole wobbled back and forth. Lightning flashes lit the insides, and the thunder shook the earth. I could hear the echo and reecho of it in the canyon upstream.

I was glad we were camped at the end of Red Canyon and not in it, and remembered back to Carter Creek and the roar my rifle had made. What must the million-times greater boom of thunder sound like there now? The wind, too, must be far worse there, for the canyons act as great troughs, carrying the warm air up to the cool air above. There is always a wind in the canyons; it always blows upstream, even on the quietest day. Now there must have been a veritable hurricane in there.

I thought of Tony. "I'll take my wilderness raw," he had said, spurning my invitation to come into my tent if a storm blew up, knowing he had no protection against it. The others had tarps or tents that they could curl up in, but Tony had only his sleeping bag, and it wasn't waterproof.

I thought of the boats. Were they securely tied to those driftwood logs? It didn't seem so now that I felt the strength of the wind. But Les was near, I knew.

I thought of the others, spread out as they were. Were they wondering and worrying too about the rest of us? Were they okay in this Walpurgis

The crew in Lodore Canyon on the Green River.

Night? I thought of getting up to check, but I realized how silly that would be. The others would probably think I was nuts! What could I do? Spread my wings so the chicks could take cover under them? Each to his own problems! "Requirement: ruggedness" I remembered from my ad in the *Saturday Review*. In the boats, we each had a responsibility to all. Our boats tied us together like an umbilical cord, but ashore we were individuals—at least so far as keeping dry or getting wet in a rainstorm was concerned. So I held down my own tent.

The morning came with bright sun as though nothing had happened. We all seemed to crawl out at once—except for Tony; he had been up for hours and had a fire going strong, the coffeepot boiling atop it.

"Had a hell of a time," he admitted. "I guess I slept on the side of a hill 'cause I rolled down into some cactus. I ended up in a gully, and the water came pouring down and right onto me. Got soaked—my sleeping bag's all wet."

*Well*, I thought, *at least it got him up for a change*. As I was thinking this, I heard a loud sizzle from the fire and turned to see the coffeepot with its precious contents tip over into it.

"Good night, Tony!" I said with irritation. "You ought to know by now that wood burns and you can't expect a coffeepot to sit on it forever.

Prop it up with rocks!" I glanced over at Don, who had an amused expression on his face as he ran to the rescue. He gave me a quick, cynical smile, hooked the coffeepot with a stick, and went down to the river to fill it with water again. Tony ran for wood to resuscitate the fire.

"Who put out the fire?" Bruce mumbled as he came up from the spot where his sleeping bag lay. He was rubbing the sand and sleep from his eyes. Just then Cid appeared. She loved her cup of coffee first thing in the morning, and she admitted that this was the one luxury she had missed so far.

"Do I smell the sweet odor of coffee?" she asked with delight. Doc broke out laughing.

The sun bathed us with its warmth just long enough for us to have breakfast. Then, as if it felt it had done its duty for the day, it retired behind a heavy overcast. Occasionally during the day, it peeked through a break in the swiftly moving clouds to see that Earth was revolving in its proper way beneath. The wind began to blow again. We made slow progress down the river; the banks hardly moved even though both motors were running at full speed. With the strong wind, whitecaps formed on the river and splashed the sides of the boats and us. We huddled in our ponchos and spoke hardly a word all day as we passed through the open country of Brown's Park.[1] Just moving your body raised goose pimples.

But nature, even in her crueler moments, makes recompense. The big clouds moving swiftly across the sky; the sun's rays occasionally striking the earth with long shafts of light; the occasional flash of lightning and the accompanying clap of thunder: these elements created the perfect setting for our approach to Lodore Canyon.[2] The Gates of Lodore were spotlighted by the shafts of sunlight. It was a beautiful sight, yet a feeling of foreboding came over me. Inside those gates was one of our deepest canyons with walls rising three Empire State Buildings high and higher, that "dreadful canyon of Lodore," as Powell had called it. Beyond were Disaster Falls and Triplet Falls and Hell's Half Mile.

Yes, at last we'd come to Hell's Half Mile. Tony would be there finally; if he had asked once during the past two days, he had asked twenty times when we'd be coming to it! *Beyond those gates*, I thought, *beyond those gates, Tony, roars Hell's Half Mile—one half mile of hell, Tony—a number eleven rapid, Tony—one of the worst on the whole river. Why not ask about Disaster Falls, Tony? Powell lost a boat there, and there's one piled up on*

Bruce Lium writing notes while in camp.

*the rocks now. Tomorrow—tomorrow we'll see Hell's Half Mile and hear the deafening roar!*

"We'll come to Hell's Half Mile tomorrow, Tony," I said out of the silence. He gave me a puzzled look, for this time he hadn't asked. My words rang back into my ears, and I felt as though I had announced that we were about to enter Valhalla. Indeed, it looked as though we were!

Lodore cabin is just inside the boundary of Dinosaur National Monument, and during the summer, a seasonal ranger occupies it. But now it was deserted, and with permission, we chose it for our camp on the night of June 14. The cabin is fully equipped for moderately comfortable, civilized living. In one room are bunks with springs and mattresses. In the other are a large picnic table, chairs, a big wood stove, a sink, dishes, pots and pans, and a good supply of food. Even though we had been in the wilderness for only four days, we had lived lives close to the elements. We were a bit awestruck by the sudden jolt back into the civilized world. A chair felt almost foreign; the outhouse, an object of quaint delight.

We tried the well, but the water looked dirty and tasted strange, so we turned to the river again for our supply. The outhouse smelled, and it seemed ridiculous to shut the door and hide in darkness. But the warmth of the stove felt good. Cid pulled the big old rocking chair up to it and rocked away in regal comfort. Les put on a pan of water to boil, and while the water was still steaming, he proceeded to soak his sore toe in it. Don and Bruce cooked meatballs and spaghetti, seasoning the pot fully with pinches of this and that from every small bottle on the shelves. Doc, Fred, and I spread our cameras on the big table to clean and repair the damage the silt and sand had done. The field glasses had accidentally fallen into the bottom of the boat the night before and were soaked through.

"Better not take them apart—you'll never get the prisms lined up again," Doc warned.

"Well, they're no good this way," I answered, and began to take out all the available screws. The glasses had been made in Japan, and I was thankful for Japanese simplicity. Everything fit back together perfectly, and the glasses were as good as new after I had cleaned the silty scum from the lenses and prisms.

I was amazed to discover how dirty the cameras had gotten! Up to now it had been impossible to do a thorough cleaning. But when I took them apart, I found sand and silt in all the gears I could reach, even inside the magazines that were scrupulously protected when loading film. They were light tight, so it was hard to believe that sand and silt could get into them! Even though the lenses were protected in front by the glass number eighty-three daylight-conversion filters, they were dirty.

What surprised me most was that the CC 10M gelatin filters that were placed behind the lenses—between them and the gates of the cameras—were also covered with silt! This meant cutting new gelatins to fit—a tedious and exacting job, for nothing must touch their surface. Cutting the 10M filter for the Cine Special was simple compared to cutting one for the 70-DL. I had merely to cut a strip of the proper length and width. But cutting the 70-DL filter was another matter. It had to be cut in the shape of a circle the size of a dime. I carried a dime in the camera case especially for this job, and Tony referred to it as "Eggert's mad money—so he can buy an ice cream cone along the way." I cut the filters with the very sharp scalpel we carried in the medical kit.

"Clean up your junk, Eggert. Chow's on!" Don quipped just as I got the last camera back together.

The hour I spent eating was the worst I've ever experienced. Perhaps it was the tension I had built up fidgeting with all those small screws. Perhaps it was my sudden realization of how hard the water and silt had been on the cameras; of what a job of photography lay ahead, and the thought of twenty thousand feet of color film possibly being ruined by a few grains of sand. Perhaps it was simply a letdown from the tension of starting the expedition. It might have been the four closed-in walls of the cabin crowding the eight of us in when we had gotten used to open spaces, or the heat from the stove: it was hot, and the room suddenly seemed so small. Perhaps it was Tony's voice, which seemed high-pitched and whiny. He talked incessantly, and I thought if he mentioned his girl once more or passed one more picture of her around, I would pounce on him. I had to get out of that room and get out fast. I jumped up and gave Don a nod to come with me. He followed.

"What's the matter?" he asked when we got to the riverbank.

"I had to get out before I exploded—let's get into the boat and go downstream a ways."

"Okay," Don answered without further question.

"Let's pull up here and go to that spot where we were in 1952," I said, pointing to a high ledge overlooking the entrance to Lodore. We tied the small boat up and climbed together. When we got to the ledge, we sat and watched the shadows climb the east wall of Lodore. Finally Don spoke.

"Remember—here's where we were back in '52."

"Yeah, and here we are on the river."

"Guess dreams do come true, Eggert."

There was a long silence between us, and we both sat there thinking back to when I had asked, "How would you like to go down it all the way?" I looked into Lodore Canyon and heard the echoes of rapids boiling up their white water again. I relaxed, and the tension of an hour ago went away. I could think more rationally. "How do you think we're making out, Don?" I asked.

"Doin' fine, Charlie. I'm proud of Les and Bruce. I've been watching that boy, Bruce. He's a fine boatman—the tops!"

"I think so—decisive, too, about a rapid. Ol' Les, he's still figuring how to run a rapid when he's in the middle of it."

"Yeah," Don answered. "He's a good man, though—knows a lot about the river. And he's been through Cataract and Grand—that counts for a lot. Wish he'd let Doc take a look at that toe. Now, there's a swell guy, that Doc. But you know who I think is going to pull out? Fred."

"Fred!" I said in utter surprise. "What makes you think that?"

"I don't know—there's something about him that makes me think that."

"Scared?"

"No—not scared—it's worry; he's worried. Unsure of himself, too, maybe—but mostly worried, and I know a worried man can't take this for long."

"Gosh, I didn't think that—unsure possibly. But I think he's enjoying the trip."

"I tell you he'll quit if he keeps worrying."

"Well," I said, "I hope he won't. We'll have to quit if he does. We haven't got enough men as it is."

"Yeah, I know what you mean."

There was another long pause as we mulled this possibility over in our minds. Then I asked, "What do you think about Mrs. Sumner?"

"Quite a person for an old lady. She'll stick it out as long as we let her."

"How long do you think that will be?" I asked.

"She'll have to walk around Hell's Half Mile, that's for sure. Then through Split Mountain, she's going to have to ride. If she can take that, we can take her through Desolation and Gray. Dad tells me they are like Split. Actually it's too early to tell; Lodore will be rough on her. I really don't know, Charlie. I do know this: I won't take her through Cataract—I'm scared for myself. That's our big one—it's a big enough risk without her. I'm worried about her going through Lodore right now."

"I'd hate to lose her, Don. I'm liking her more and more."

"Better to lose her at Jensen or Green River, Utah, than in Cataract. I like her too. Didn't like the idea at first—taking her. But she seems to know when to keep out of the way. Thought she'd get in my hair at first."

"You know who's getting in my hair, don't you? Tony," I said. "Maybe there's something wrong with me, but he annoys the hell out of me at times. I thought I'd bat him when he let the coffeepot dump over for the fourth time this morning. And I thought I'd go nuts with his jabbering back there. Who gives a damn about his love affair? Not us certainly."

"Well, I sure don't, but he's just a kid."

"A kid is right! Am I getting so old and crotchety, Don, that I can't take that small talk anymore? Doesn't it bother you?"

"When you're stuck with people like I am on the Dinosaur runs, you bump into all kinds. I guess you learn to ignore them. It doesn't bother me—I let it go in one ear and out the other. Half the time I don't even hear him."

"Well, if he dumps that coffeepot once more, I'm going to give him the boot!"

"We'll straighten him out, Charlie. Don't let it bother you. Wait till he sees Hell's Half Mile—he'll come to."

"It's going to scare the hell out of him," I said, and I chuckled when the thought suddenly struck me that it would probably scare the hell out of me too! In any case, I felt relieved that I had blown off steam to Don.

It was almost completely dark when we returned to the cabin. It took a long time to get back upstream against the swift current even though the boat was unloaded. Tony was on the bank to greet us.

"Where've you been?" he shouted.

"Went down to look over Hell's Half Mile," Don answered.

"Gosh, how was it?"

"Well," Don kept kidding, "it was a little tough to get to—we had to run Upper and Lower Disaster and Triplet Falls first. Wasn't so bad going down, but comin' back was a ripsnorter, huh, Charlie?"

"Everybody's outside, rolled up asleep. I've been in the cabin writing letters." Tony added, "Wish you'd taken me."

"You were too busy talking when we left," Don answered.

*Eleven*

# HELL'S HALF MILE

Civilization, even in its less-pretentious form—as in Lodore cabin—has its complications. Breaking camp was far more involved and time-consuming than any day before. The cabin had to be put in order, the counters cleaned, the ashes taken from the stove, the floors swept, and, obeying the law of the wilderness, a new supply of wood had to be cut to replenish what we had used.

At eight o'clock I tried to reach the monument headquarters with the FM walkie-talkie that had been left under the table in the cabin, just as Jess Lombard had promised. "Field set KB 7235 calling KOD 793—Field set KB 7235 calling KOD 793—this is Eggert calling Dinosaur headquarters—calling Dinosaur headquarters—over," I called into the small microphone. I waited. All I could hear in the headphones was static. I hiked to a hill beyond the cabin and tried again. The result was the same—nothing but static. It was a strange sound. It made me feel even more remote than I was.

Off to the southwest, across the mountains and desert 150 miles, someone was alert and listening for my call. We had agreed that I would start calling in on the fourteenth at 8:00 a.m., at 11:00 a.m., again at 4:30 p.m., and at 5:00 p.m. Had they heard my call, and were they trying to answer me? Were they calling back, "This is KOD 793—you're coming through fine, 7235." Was it that I could be heard but not hear them? I checked the controls, tried another setting, and called again. Nothing. *Well,* I thought, *if they heard me, they know we're okay.* I looked up at the steel relay tower. A strange object; it looked lonely and forlorn.

I wondered what Powell would have thought if he had seen it standing there eighty-six years ago.

On my way back to the cabin, I decided to try the call again. I began to worry that park headquarters might wonder why they hadn't heard from me. I worried that they might have a message for us. Worried! Why, I hadn't worried about the outside world for the past four days! I had almost forgotten such a place existed. When I first saw the FM set in the cabin, I felt relieved to have communication—a crutch to lean on during our run through the canyons. I felt happier for having it, but now I began to wonder! I hadn't worried up in Red Canyon Rapid when we were in that tight spot. Even if we had lost our boat, we'd have made it out somehow. On our own, without KOD 793 or any other magical number, we'd have gotten out. But here I was—with no crisis—and I was worried, worried over the simple fact that I couldn't reach anyone with this electronic gadget strapped over my shoulder! *These things make us have less guts*, I thought. I began to resent having to carry the heavy thing.

The boats were finally loaded, and we were on our way into the Canyon of Lodore. Entering the gates was an event to photograph, so Tony, Doc, and I went ahead to climb a ledge overlooking the entrance where we could get shots of the *Brontosaur* going through. While we waited for the big boat, thick, purple clouds hung above, dropping intermittent rain upon us. The light created the proper ominous effect. I could imagine deep, Bach-like chords on a mighty organ sounding in my ears as the *Brontosaur* came cautiously around the bend far below us. It passed through the steep red rock portals and entered Lodore Canyon.

We returned to the little boat, and Don took up the oars. One motor had been packed in the *Brontosaur* before we left the cabin. The other was on the small boat to be used for emergency only. Tony shoved us off. Don pulled hard on the left oar, and the boat spun around to face south into the canyon. Where we had landed, the banks of the river rose gradually in rock terraces to gentle hills beyond. We hadn't gone a quarter of a mile when the tamarisk and sandy banks abruptly stopped. Out of the earth rose somber, purple rock, and the river was held between sheer walls several stories high. We could no longer see the horizon or the mountains ahead. Wherever there was an irregularity in the rock wall, the water made a deep, sighing swoosh as the strong current formed whirlpools as it passed by. All over the surface of the river, great boils heaved up ominously, causing large water mounds. With the undercurrents rose large tree limbs and logs that had been carried to the depths below. The river seemed to be gathering all its strength for the obstacles ahead. We could feel its power as it pushed the rubber bottom of the boat upward in a boil or sucked it down as we passed over an eddy. In the distance, deep in the canyon, we could hear the echoes of thunder and the forbidding, faint roar of white water.

Beside the boat was the sound of Don's oars dipping in and out of the river. The closeness of the sound gave dimension to the whole tone picture. It was like the opening passages of a great symphony, perhaps Richard Strauss's *Also Sprach Zarathustra.* The sighs the river made, the distant rumble of thunder and rapids: these were the deep sustaining chords of the basses of the orchestra we heard as we approached closer and closer. Suddenly ahead—like a mighty crescendo of the full orchestra—the Gates of Lodore soared up from the river. Beyond was the great canyon, a dramatic crevasse in the mountains split asunder by the Indian god, Ta-vwoats, to make a path to the forbidden land of paradise. And deep between the giant walls, at the bottom, ran the raging river the god had sent through the gorge. I recalled Cid's words: "[a] great monstrous marvelous joke the gods of the Indians left as a warning to the rest of humankind."

This was no canyon to travel alone, and so the *Brontosaur* waited below the gates for us to catch up. When we pulled up beside it, Doc went back to the big boat. I asked Fred to join Don and me in the small boat, changing places with Tony. Tony looked puzzled, but Don knew the reason for the move. I felt that perhaps with me, Fred might gain some of the confidence I thought he needed. Fred had said to me long ago, back in the East when he had discussed joining us, that the main thing he was worried about on the trip was whether there would be a shoulder—a sympathetic shoulder—where he might lean in the tight spots. I thought that perhaps now Fred found himself in that tight spot—what with Disaster Falls and Hell's Half Mile ahead. I would offer him my shoulder.

I watched him through the first few riffles. He held on tightly. As we approached a rapid, I said, "Remember, Don, this is the one we nearly tipped over in coming back upstream in that narrow metal boat we used in 1952?"[1]

"Yeah." Don laughed. "I thought I was going to get you wet then!" Just then we hit. The waves were higher than that earlier time. A wave crashed over the front of the boat, spraying us thoroughly. "Whoopie!" Don yelled. Then came another big one, and I heard a resounding crack. An oar had broken! Before either Don or I could remember where it was, Fred grabbed the spare oar and had it by the oar mount, waiting for Don to remove the stub of the broken one. He had moved as quickly as a dart!

"Good ol' Fred saved the day for us!" Don shouted enthusiastically to the others as he jumped ashore above Disaster Falls. "We broke an oar up there, and he grabbed the spare quicker than lightning." He turned to Fred. "Thanks," he said, "we'd have had it if you hadn't grabbed that oar." Fred gave him an embarrassed smile, but I knew that inside he was proud. We were all proud of him! I thought to myself, *This will help*.

Now for Disaster Falls.[2] After we tied the boats, we rested before walking down to look over the falls. Tony suggested we get out Powell's journal and read about his disaster before we set off. We all sat around him as he read:

> During the afternoon [of June 9, 1869] we come to a place where it is necessary to make a portage. The little boat is landed, and the others are signaled to come up.
>
> When these rapids or broken falls occur usually the channel is suddenly narrowed by rocks which have been tumbled from the cliffs or have been washed in by lateral streams. Immediately above the narrow, rocky channel, on one or both sides, there is often a bay of quiet water, in which a landing can be made with ease. Sometimes the water descends with a smooth, unruffled surface from the broad, quiet spread above into the narrow, angry channel below by a semicircular sag.[3] Great care must be taken not to pass over the brink into this deceptive pit, but above it we can row with safety. I walk along the bank to examine the ground, leaving one of my men with a flag to guide the other boats to the landing place. I soon see one of the boats make shore all right, and feel no more concern; but a minute after, I hear a shout, and looking around, see one of the boats shooting down the center of the sag. It is the "No Name," with Captain Howland, his brother, and Goodman. I feel that its going over is inevitable,

> and run to save the third boat. A minute more, and she turns the point and heads for the shore. Then I turn downstream again and scramble along to look for the boat that has gone over. The first fall is not great, only 10 or 12 feet, and we often run such; but below, the river tumbles down again for 40 or 50 feet, in a channel filled with dangerous rocks that break the waves into whirlpools and beat them into foam. I pass around a great crag just in time to see the boat strike a rock and, rebounding from the shock, careen and fill its open compartment with water. Two of the men lose their oars; she swings around and is carried down at a rapid rate, broadside on, for a few yards, when, striking amidships on another rock with great force, she is broken quite in two and the men are thrown into the river. But the larger part of the boat floats buoyantly, and they soon seize it, and down the river they drift, past the rocks for a few hundred yards, to a second rapid filled with huge boulders, where the boat strikes again and is dashed to pieces, and the men and fragments are soon carried beyond my sight. Running along, I turn a bend and see a man's head above the water, washed about in a whirlpool below a great rock.
>
> It is Frank Goodman, clinging to the rock with a grip upon which life depends. Coming opposite, I see Howland trying to go to his aid from an island on which he has been washed. Soon he comes near enough to reach Frank with a pole, which he extends toward him. The latter lets go the rock, grasps the pole, and is pulled ashore. Seneca Howland is washed farther down the island and is caught by some rocks, and, though somewhat bruised, manages to get ashore in safety. This seems a long time as I tell it, but it is quickly done.

Tony stopped reading and carefully closed the book. We sat listening to the roar of white water. I thought of the wooden boat wedged between the rocks on the other side of the falls. The name of the place still had meaning!

We all clambered over the rocks—perhaps some of us in Powell's footsteps—to look at Disaster. It was as though we had parked our car alongside the highway and were rushing to the scene of a big accident ahead. There she was—a roaring, boiling foam! Above the first falls, the river was wide, just as Powell had described, and there was the quiet pool. Then the river narrowed and, in a great semicircle, came the drop. Hundreds of tons of water leaped suddenly forward over and between huge boulders. Below this came the second drop. Water kicked high, splashing and bounding forward, leaving great sprays behind that the wind picked up and carried to shore to wet our faces. Below that were another falls and more spray and foam.

"Can't walk around this one, Charlie," Don told me. "All the current pushes to the other side. Too hard to land below—unless you want to walk a good ways down."

"Thanks, I prefer to ride anyway. Can we send the *Brontosaur* through first so I can get pictures?"

"Sure," Don answered. He turned to Bruce and Les to give them instructions: "Take her between those two big rocks, then straight ahead—go with the river; don't fight it. You'll hit a big hole down there, so keep her nose straight. The falls are easy in this stage—high water covers most of the rocks."

Tony and I set up the cameras on a vantage point overlooking the falls. Don with his Rollei and Fred with his 8mm movie camera positioned themselves so they weren't blocking us. I made a final check on my exposure and the spring wind of the cameras. They would have to be wound up tightly to get the whole sequence. "Start the camera running just before they hit the first falls," I instructed Tony, "and be sure to keep the boat in the center of the finder if you can." I leaned over my tripod, and with my finger on the trigger, I aimed the camera upstream to the place where the *Brontosaur* would appear. Soon she came; I spotted Bruce's white cowboy hat first. *It was a good marker*, I thought, though I wished he'd take it off ashore; his face was always in shadow.

Again, as in Ashley, the big boat seemed to hesitate before going over the drop, as though it were sniffing the edge like a dog to find out if it was safe to make the leap. Then it went! Between two big rocks, it plunged, gaining speed. I had a hard time keeping it in the finder. On through the tumult, the big hulk rode, plowing through the waves. Then it suddenly disappeared! With the camera still going, I lifted my eye from the finder to see what had happened. It had dropped down in that big hole. Now the boat was in sight again, climbing up the other side. The boatmen had held her straight; they had made it! I didn't realize until I saw the developed film that Cid was sitting up in the middle, waving away, enjoying every splash that hit her.

Now it was our turn in the small boat. We put the cameras in their cases and the cases in the big waterproof rubber bags. These we tied down securely with nylon cord. Then we checked the duffle to see that it was tied solidly. Over it all we put a rubber tarp. I took the front seat and discovered I could partly cover myself with the tarp. Don sat in the center to row. Tony and Fred held down the back. We headed into the falls back end first, and when we hit the bottom, a big wave back-splashed into the boat and soaked Tony and Fred. On through we bounced and tossed. Sometimes we were up in the air atop a wave; sometimes we were down in a trough, surrounded by waves ten feet high!

"Watch it!" Don yelled as he gave a hard pull, sending the boat swiftly around to face the other way. "We're going down in the hole!" I held tightly with one hand and checked the straps of my life preserver with the other. Ahead the river dropped from view for several feet, and beyond rose a huge wave caused by the rebound of water out of the hole. Down we went! I thought we were heading straight for the bottom of the river. But then up we climbed, over the big wave like a roller coaster. I felt it in the pit of my stomach. Then down again into choppy water, and it was all over. I didn't realize how wet I was until we landed.

"Where is Lower Disaster?" I asked as we pulled in beside the *Brontosaur.*

"We ran it," Don answered. "It's all one now with this high water."

"I've been cheated! I've been cheated!" Cid exclaimed. "I expected two of them. Let's go back and do it again!"

"There's plenty more ahead, Cid," Don said.

Tony went back to the big boat, and Fred, Don, and I went ahead to run Triplet Falls. "Keep to the left and watch out for the overhanging cliff on the right" were Don's instructions to the *Brontosaur.*

"You know this canyon well, don't you, Don?" Fred asked.

"Been through it hundreds of times, I guess. I know the rapids by heart. Dad taught me how to row a boat in this canyon." He added, "I've never been through in such high water, though—it's really kicking up. We won't have anything worse than these according to Dad—except in Cataract. Wish I knew that one as well as this. Practically nobody knows it."

Triplet Falls looked big as we approached.[4] From far upriver, we could see the waves tossing. "Won't have to stop for this one—looks big, but there aren't any rocks. All we have to watch out for is that overhang on the right. Hang on, Fred, and get ready to duck," Don said.

The waves were big—bigger than any we had seen before. Up and down we went, heading for the cliff. Don pulled hard on his right oar to get away. All of a sudden, an oar slipped out of its mount. Don had all he could do to hold the end of the oar. He pulled with all his might with the other to avoid the cliff. Fred jumped quickly, grabbed the oar, and slipped it back in the mount. We ducked as we passed the edge of the cliff. Fred again had saved the day! Because of his quick action, Don was able to pull just in time, and we were saved from being washed under the cliff and overturned by the big backwash there. I was amazed at Fred's quick thinking. He knew what to do and did it—without hesitation, as though it was instinct. We could use a man like that all the way, and I hoped in my heart he wouldn't leave us.

"Tony's going to see Hell's Half Mile at last!" Don shouted. "It's just around the bend." Suddenly, he began to row for shore as hard as he could. "Wonder whether Les knows!" he said in alarm. We hit the bank, and Don jumped out. "Hold 'er, Fred," he said, throwing him the line. He ran up the bank to a point where he could see upriver. With his hat he flagged the *Brontosaur* to land. Standing on the bank with Fred, I could hear echoing from the canyon walls the sound of Hell's Half Mile.[5] There was a boom to it that I hadn't heard from any of the rapids so far. I looked over at Fred. He was listening too. "Sounds big, doesn't it?" I said.

"Wow!" Fred answered. "I can't wait to see it."

The *Brontosaur* pulled in beside us. "How'd you like those waves, Les?" Don shouted.

"In Triplet? Must have been fifteen feet high!" he answered.

"Looked like more than twenty to me—they were wonderful!" Cid said.

"Well, let's look over the big one," Don said. We tied the boats and went downstream to our first number eleven rapids, Hell's Half Mile. The roar grew louder as we approached. When we got beside it, the sound shook our very insides. All Tony could say was "Gee!"

The river was a foaming, churning, boiling mass from one side to the other as far as we could see. *How are we going to make it through here?* I thought.

Charles Eggert (with camera) photographing at Hell's Half Mile Rapid, while other crew members check out the rapid.

Don, Les, and Bruce climbed out on some big boulders that stuck out into the rapid. I watched Don point out the hazards—a big drop here, a hole there, a hidden rock, rocks sticking up, a large dead tree caught out in the middle that seemed to complicate matters even more. I tried to figure out the route the boatmen would decide to run, if they decided to run it at all. Maybe we'd have to line or portage. Powell and his men had done that here; it had taken them four days to get around!

Don came bounding across the boulders to me. "Can't run it with that little boat—we'll have to line—partway anyway. I'll bring her down to here, where we'll unload." He pointed to a spot just above the first falls.

"We'd better get the cameras, Tony," I said. Together we hiked back to where the boats were tied. Tony was still repeating "gee." Cid was sitting in the big boat when we returned.

"Better go down and see the excitement, Cid," Tony said.

"I'm sitting right here! If I land, you may make me walk around."

"This one would wash you overboard for sure," Don told her. Disappointed, Cid climbed slowly out of the boat. I could see she wanted to ride the big rapid.

We got our cameras and started back with Cid. Don took off in the small boat, hugging the shore cautiously as he went. While I set up the cameras, the others began to unload and portage the gear to a point about a third of the way down the rapid. "Why just to there?" I asked Don.

"Saves work—we'll ride it the rest of the way. It's just this first part we can't make."

I could see that; the drop was steeper than the little boat was long, and the waves looked like giants beside her. There were also inescapable boulders that would tip her over. The rapid was easy on us in one way: the hardest part was at the beginning. We could run the rest of it. No doubt we'd be running into the opposite situation, with the hardest part at the end of the rapid. Then we'd have to portage all the way around.

When I saw that they were starting to line the little boat, I handed Tony the camera. "Catch what you can—I'll help them out," I said.

Lining a boat down the side of a rapid can be tricky business. I recalled Powell's near disaster at this very spot: "we are letting down the last boat," he had written in his journal on June 16, "and as she is set free a wave turns her broadside down the stream, with the stem, to which the line is attached, from shore and a little up. They haul on the line to bring the boat in, but the power of the current, striking obliquely against her, shoots her out into the middle of the river. The men have their hands burned with the friction of the passing line; the boat breaks away and speeds with great velocity down the stream." Luckily, Powell's boat, *Maid of the Canyon*, stayed upright and drifted into an eddy below the rapid where they recovered her.

We let our small boat down inch by inch with Don riding inside her, guiding her around the boulders close to shore. We were confronted with a hazard: we had to pass the boat between two huge boulders. A large driftwood log lay across the top of them. Don instructed me to get on the near boulder and lift the log to let the rope pass under as they lined the boat down. I climbed up and could see below—between those two great rocks. There was a sharp drop-off of six or seven feet where the water poured in with terrific force. I thought to myself, *When that boat drops, she's really going to go.* I warned Don. "We'll hold her," he shouted. He sent Les below with a towline attached to the back of the boat to hold her in case she got away from the men above. Don tied the line to the back of the boat and handed it up to me. I passed it under the log and handed it to Les. As I did, I suddenly realized I was in an impossible situation. The front line would be taut; I couldn't pass it casually under the log as the boat dropped down. I'd be holding up the heavy log with both hands so the front line could pass under it. But how was the line going to get past me? I would have to do a hop, skip, and jump to avoid its tripping me. The log was heavy enough just to hold, let alone dance around with! What to do? I was just about to yell to Don that this wasn't going to work when I heard Bruce shout, "There goes Les!"

I looked around to see Les riding down Hell's Half Mile freestyle—that is, without benefit of boat or oars! Les had slipped off a rock and was in the boiling foam! There was no helping him at that moment. I was on the rock; the others were holding the boat for dear life and didn't dare let it go. Tony was the only one who was free to move quickly, and he did. He dropped the camera, found a rope, and ran toward Les, who, by now, had gone more than twenty-five feet downstream. Down the rapids, Les bounded. He tried to grab onto rocks, but the current was too strong and the rocks too slippery. His head bobbed up here, then there. By this time Bruce had gotten the towline snubbed around a big rock, and he could hold it alone. The others ran down the bank after Les, stumbling over the rocks as they went. It seemed to take forever for Tony to get to a point where he could throw the rope to Les. Tony leapt over a few more rocks. He finally reached a good spot and threw the rope. Les caught it. Meanwhile, the others had gotten there—Fred, Doc, and Don—and together they pulled Les in to shore.

Les didn't seem a bit shaken up by his violent ride. "Next time I'll remember to take a boat along." He laughed as he stood on the bank dripping wet.

Now it was my turn to do tricks. How was I going to pass that taut towline under my feet and hold up the log at the same time? The others returned to their places. Bruce, still chuckling over Les's remark, yelled to him, "If you can make it through, Les, Charlie can!" *Well,* I thought, *at least I have the possibility of landing in the boat when the rope trips me—along with the log!*

"Here she goes!" Don shouted. I poised myself for the inevitable. Things went so fast that I didn't know what happened. I must have managed to jump the rope as it passed under me, for I wasn't tripped. Or did I jump at all? I only knew that the log was jerked abruptly from my hands and landed beyond the nose of the small boat. Had the rope snagged it? (Seeing the movie later, I discovered that when the boat had dropped over the falls, the nose had raised up and caught the log, taking it along.) Les, meanwhile—from a safer rock—pulled the back line in, and the boat landed safely. We carried her ashore, dumped the water out, and reloaded the gear.

"What happened to the rope?" I finally asked.

"We had to let the boat go—couldn't hold her back," Bruce explained.

It was the *Brontosaur*'s turn to run now. Don was concerned about how the big boat would ride through, loaded so heavily. For a while there was talk of portaging some of her gear around, but we were already tired. "This will be the big test," Don said to me. Then he turned to Les and Bruce. "Straight down the center—ride it out nose first," he told them.

Don, Cid, Fred, Doc, Tony, and I stood on the bank awaiting the big show. Cid remarked that we looked as if we were standing on a curb waiting for a parade to come along. Presently we could see Bruce's white hat appear above the first drop. The big boat slowly approached the falls. Again she seemed to pause and sniff the edge before going over. Then she came violently through! The *Brontosaur* poured over the falls in a great heap and dug her nose into the white water as she hit the bottom. The boat and the two boatmen were momentarily completely submerged in foam. Through one big wave after another, the boat plunged, under one wave, over another. Then she settled herself and rode through the rest, plowing a wide furrow down the river as far as we could see. "They made it! They made it!" we all shouted. We stood cheering long after the big boat had disappeared around the bend.

We clambered aboard the small boat to ride out the rest of Hell's Half Mile ourselves; we were anxious to hear the boatmen's tale of the *Bronto*'s run.

"We've still got quite a run ourselves," Don reminded us as he took his position at the oars. He then made a few changes in seating arrangements. He told Fred and Doc to sit at the back with Tony between. Cid was put atop the duffle in the middle. I was to sit on the floor in the nose to hold the front end down. Don warned me, "You're going to get wet. All of you got your life jackets on tight? Here we go—shove her off, Charlie."

I gave us a shove, jumped in quickly, and we were off. A wave hit us at once, and I got soaked. *Well, I won't have to look forward to that!* I thought

Don Hatch with his ten-man raft, the *No Name*, on the shore of the Green River at Hell's Half Mile Rapid.

as I felt the water in the bottom of the boat reach the only place on me that was still dry. As we bounded through, I could hear Cid's shouts of laughter. She was enjoying it more than anyone I had ever seen on the river. *Young in spirit, that old gal*, I thought. And Fred, he had a big smile on his face—an expression broken occasionally by the sudden shock of a wave splashing over him.

We were through Hell's Half Mile all too soon, and after we climbed ashore dripping wet, we looked back at the rapid. Funny thing about these rapids: for the most part, you're scared to death as you approach. You don't have time to think as you go through, but when it is all over, you look back and wish you could do it all over again.

"Well, Tony, that was Hell's Half Mile," I said.

"Gosh," he replied, "it was wonderful."

*Twelve*

# RIPPLING BROOK

On the right side of the river a mile below Hell's Half Mile, there is a small, clear stream. Major Powell saw it on June 16, 1869, and described the place in his diary:

> Just before us, the canyon divides, a little stream coming down on the right, and another on the left, and we can look away up either of these canyons, through an ascending vista, to cliffs and crags and towers, a mile back, and two thousand feet overhead. To the right a dozen gleaming cascades are seen. Pines and firs stand on the rocks, and aspens overhang the brooks. The rocks below are red and brown, set in deep shadows, but above, they are buff and vermillion, and stand in the sunshine. The light above, made more brilliant by the bright-tinted rocks, and the shadows below more gloomy by the somber hues of the brown walls, increase the apparent depths of the canyons, and it seems a long way up to the world of sunshine and open sky, and a long way down to the bottom of the canyon glooms. We sit on some overhanging rocks, and enjoy the scene for some time, listening to the music of falling waters away up in the canyon. We name this Rippling Brook.

On June 15, one day earlier but eighty-six years later, we made our camp here. I have quoted this bit of Powell's diary only to point out that if he saw the place now, he would write the same description. It is exactly the same. There are no billboards advertising he-man cigarettes, no fishing shanties or fancy motels. There are no telephone poles or power lines to mar the open sky above Rippling Brook. The wind sings the same muffled song Powell heard through the trees, and the music of cascading water still sounds magically. The rapids through which he and his men struggled day after day resound their forbidding voices from the canyon walls. The great pine forests of Michigan, which even I remember, have disappeared into split-level ranch houses crowding in the humanity of suburbia. Up the California coast, a mountain has been made into a thruway over streets that were once hills. Celilo Falls has seen the last of centuries of Indian fishermen, and the sun has made its final rainbow in the mist of falling water. But in this pine-filled grove, Rippling Brook still flows, and its pools and cascades are lined with moss and columbine. Here our children's children can come—to see and listen and experience—just as Powell did. Rippling Brook is in a national monument, part of our National Park System, and protected from selfish interests that would turn its pounding water into power, its trees into board feet of lumber, and its grass and flowers into forage.

We sat long around our campfire that night looking up at the slit of night-blue sky. The stars seemed so close in the crisp, clear air that I felt if I reached out, I might touch one. Rippling Brook was a welcome solitude from the turmoil of the day on the river. When I crawled into my sleeping bag and let my muscles relax, I realized how tired I was. Every muscle ached from the work of getting through the rapids. With that feeling, however, came a sense of accomplishment. Pitting my strength against the forces of nature gave me a sense of victory I had never felt before. Somehow I felt that Major Powell and his crew were close by us that night.

*Thirteen*

# ECHO PARK AND HARPER'S CORNER

It was only six miles from Rippling Brook to the junction of the Yampa River and Echo Park in the heart of Dinosaur National Monument.[1] At this place, the canyon walls open out, cottonwood trees line the riverbank, and in the open fields, a local rancher grows bright green alfalfa. We arrived there before lunch on June 16, having come 160 miles from our starting point. This to me was familiar country. I had camped here in the spring of 1952 and again in 1953. The river was high, and it swelled to even greater volume because of the Yampa River, whose silt content was much greater than the Green's. For a mile and a half, the waters of the two rivers ran side by side, the siltier water of the Yampa flowing on the left and the lighter-colored Green River water on the right, even though they now shared a single channel. Not until they rounded the prow of Steamboat Rock did they intermix to become a single river.

The side of that great rock peninsula called Steamboat Rock rose boldly and majestically out of the river across from our campsite. I could never understand why someone had named it Steamboat Rock. It only remotely resembles a ship. Powell named it Echo Rock, for every sound across the river resounds clearly from its flat, nine-hundred-foot-high Weber sandstone side. We, of course, tested the echo out first thing and, satisfied that nature was functioning properly, went about our business of setting up camp.

While the others were doing this, I took off with the FM radio to make another attempt at getting a message through to Monument headquarters to let them know we were here so a ranger might bring the Jeep.

Echo Park and Steamboat Rock located in Dinosaur National Monument at the confluence of the Yampa and Green Rivers.

I had no luck in the open field just beyond the camp, so I decided to hike across Rial Chew's alfalfa field, climb up the talus slope against the cliffs, and make another attempt.[2] Also I thought that being in the sight line of the relay tower on Harper's Corner might help me make better contact. I was apprehensive as I trod across the alfalfa field with the heavy radio on my back; this was a good place for rattlesnakes.

I was glad to reach the far end of the field, out of the thick growth and into open ground, where I might spot one more easily. Reaching the talus slope, I climbed to a point high above Echo Park and there had an uninterrupted view of Echo Rock. What a magnificent sight! The great river flowed gently around its base. To the west, Harper's Corner loomed and reigned twenty-five hundred feet above it all.[3] From here I could see into three canyons: Lodore, where we had been; Yampa, the source of the silty Yampa River, where I had already been twice; and Whirlpool Canyon, where we would eventually voyage. I couldn't help but sit for a while to ponder this wonder of the earth before I attempted to call on the radio.

"Field Set KB 7235 calling KOD 793—calling KOD 793—over." I sat and listened. For a moment, there was just the same static, but then I thought I heard a voice! Yes, it was a voice, a voice from the outside world! I heard it say, "This is KOD 793 . . . [more static] . . . you receiving—over."

"This is KB 7235—I can hear you, I can hear you!" I yelled triumphantly. "We're at Echo Park—we—are—at—Echo—Park," I repeated slowly and distinctly. "Can you hear—can you hear?—Over."

"Yeah, Charlie, we can hear you okay" came a voice so loud that it blasted my ear. *Must have been a sunspot to cause that reception*, I thought as I grabbed the volume knob to turn it down. "Your Jeep is on the way down. Cliff is driving your Jeep down now—should be there soon—over."

"Fine," I called back. "No news here—we're okay—over."

"Okay," the voice at the other end said. "We're working on . . ." and then the voice faded away, and static took over.

"I didn't get that—I didn't hear you," I called. But no more followed, and I finally gave up. *Fixing what?* I wondered.

We were having lunch when Cliff arrived. He was like so many other Park Service personnel I've met: friendly right off, amiable, dedicated to his work, and unfailingly enthusiastic about the wilderness country. These men have the joys and inspiration of being alone with the big trees, the deep canyons, and the majestic mountains. On the other hand, they must contend with swarms of vacation visitors who come to see the scenic "freaks" and often find nothing more; who look on the park ranger as a policeman who prevents them from carving their names on the trees and enjoying the good luck they'd get from throwing a penny into Morning Glory Pool. What patience and devotion the ranger displays when he tries to help tourists find just a glimmer of the deeper, spiritual values—when all they want to know is the source of the steam piped in for Old Faithful!

We told Cliff about our adventures in the canyons. He was full of admiration. "Why don't you come the rest of the way through Dinosaur with us? There's still Whirlpool to go through, and Split Mountain Canyon," I suggested.

"I wish I could—haven't been on the river yet—but the men in the truck working on the Mantle Ranch Road are going to pick me up later."

I realized that he had a lot of work to do to get the area in shape for the oncoming summer visitors so I urged no further. *Why hadn't I arranged with the superintendent to bring the driver of my Jeep back to headquarters via our boats?* I asked myself. It would have been a pleasure

Fred Wood, above Yampa Canyon in 1955, looking at the incredible view.

to have Cliff with us. *Twenty-twenty hindsight vision*, I thought. We all have that!

If we wanted to drive to Harper's Corner and be back before dark, we'd have to get going, so as soon as lunch was over, Cid, Fred, Tony, Doc, and I took off in the Jeep for the high country. Cid was never particularly keen on making side trips. "I see more than enough from the boat," she always said. But this time I insisted that she come along; the ride through and up the side canyons to the high plateau would be an experience in itself. The view from Harper's, overlooking three canyons, was not to be missed! Seeing the canyon country from above gave you a sense of perspective, of the vastness and depth of them that you could never appreciate from the bottom.

When we left Echo Park, it was very warm, but it was near freezing when we arrived at Harper's Corner, twenty-five hundred feet above our campsite. The wind blew sharply, and in the two hours it had taken to drive there, the sky had filled with clouds and was now heavily overcast. None of us had jackets, so Cid decided to stay in the car where it was warm while the rest of us hiked the half mile to the tip of Harper's. When we had almost arrived, we came upon a large sign across the trail that warned us not to go beyond that point. "Dangerous," it read in part. Here the trail made a sharp descent, and the world around us seemed to drop away into nothingness. Fred and Tony gave me an apprehensive look. "It's okay," I said. "They probably haven't got the trail cleared yet. I've been here several times—I'm sure it's fine," I said confidently.

After we had walked a few more yards, the trees thinned out, and finally there was just one that miraculously grew out of the solid rock that formed the tip of Harper's Corner. Now the sides of the world literally did drop away. On three sides, there was a precipitous drop to the canyons below. I was aware of Fred's and Doc's dislike of heights; we had had that discussion before. I didn't like high places either. I could never trust myself; I always felt compelled to jump.

"Come, we'll make it to the tree anyway," I urged. The wind was strong. It blew so hard I thought it might blow us off into space. But we held on and made it to the tree. There we sat huddled together. The tree offered little protection from the sharp wind. It, too, from the looks of its scraggly shape, was having a hard time surviving in this cruel, beautiful place.

With the heavy overcast, this was no time to photograph. I had seen the place in better light—better, that is, for Kodachrome film. I had never felt its beauty more profoundly than now, though. Harper's Corner, covered with thick gray clouds, with the wind screaming around the jagged rocks and in the gnarled tree, had never seemed so cruel or dangerous as now. Yet that danger and cruelty only intensified the beauty of the place. Perhaps it was the challenge of that which made me see the beauty more clearly.

Far to the west, the sun shone brilliantly on the snow-capped mountains. There seemed some possibility of a break in the weather. I suggested we wait for a little while in hopes that the clouds would blow over so I could take my pictures. The longer we waited, however, the worse it seemed to get, and in final desperation I said to Tony, "Well, let's go out to the tip and take pictures anyway." I took a deep breath. Even less than the other times I had walked those last few yards across the narrow knife edge to the tip of Harper's did I fancy going there now. The narrow stretch was no more than six feet wide—in one place, not more than three—and fifteen yards long. On either side, the drop was sheer. There was no room for error; one slip and that would be it for eternity. It was like the narrow granite wall around the observation walk atop the Empire State Building—except that there was no iron guardrail, the drop was twice as far, and the surface was a jumble of rocks, some of them loose. For nothing in the world would I have the courage to walk that flat granite wall on the Empire State, yet I had crossed this stretch twice before and was about to try it again. *Third time—three times, and you're out*, I thought grimly. Maybe I'd better forget it; I'd throw away the film on the cutting room floor anyway.

But there was something magical about that flat rock beyond the narrow stretch. For one thing, out there you could look straight down into Echo Park and Whirlpool Canyon. You couldn't do that by the tree. You were suspended out there—almost by a skyhook—and you were lord and master of all you surveyed. It was like standing on the prow of a ship with the entire ocean before and below you. For another thing, out there you were proud of yourself for having the guts to get there. Later, you could brag about it; that was nice too.

"Think you can make it?" I asked Tony. I took another deep breath and stood up. The wind hit my erect body. The wind! That would make it harder. Just so it blew steadily; we could compensate for that. A heavy sudden gust, maybe not. *Be prepared for it in any case*, I thought.

"Take it really slow, Tony, and follow every one of my footsteps across. Don't put your weight forward until you know the footing is safe." I started for the ledge. Then I remembered the worst part. I came close to Tony to make myself heard above the wind. "One other thing—and this is hard to explain—the perspective," I shouted into his ear over the howling wind. "The perspective is funny when you cross." How could I make him understand? "Tony," I shouted again, "look—the earth directly below you—where your feet are—will move in the right way when you move!" I motioned with my arms, moving them from in front to behind me to illustrate. "But the earth all around is going to look as though it is moving in the opposite direction!" I moved my arms forward from behind. "That's because the ground below doesn't move as fast as the trail does—the whole perspective is different—it's so far down!" I shouted. "It seems as complicated as Einstein's theory of relativity. That's what it is in a way. Objects at different distances move at different speeds depending on where you are. Here one plane moves backward, and the other forward," I went on. Tony smiled. *What a place to be trying to explain Einstein!* I thought. "Be prepared for it, Tony—it may make you dizzy."

It was an eerie feeling, this effect. I remembered well the first time I had crossed and experienced it. No one had warned me, and I had had to stop in the middle of the knife edge to get my bearings. For a moment, I thought I was walking backward.

Inch by inch, we made it out. I remembered suddenly that warning sign back on the path. Perhaps the winter frosts had loosened the underlying rocks. The whole thing might be ready to crumble. Maybe the Park Service had put the sign there for that reason! No, I reassured myself, it was to discourage the tourists; keep them off until a better trail was built for them to cross safely for a look, like that well-protected wooden walk out to Inspiration Point in Yellowstone. But even in my split second of terror over the possible frost damage, I was glad no such structure was here to spoil the delightful danger. What joy is there in walking up and down some wooden steps and across planks, coddled in the security of a high two-by-four fence? The scene is always more thrilling when you have to take your life in your hands to see it. Oh, the wooden walks are fine for the worriers, the older folks. It gives them a chance to see too. But there should always be a few places around to test the guts of those who are willing to take the challenge. "PROCEED AT YOUR OWN RISK," the sign ought to read, "DANGEROUS BUT PASSABLE."

I tested every rock with my feet to see whether it would hold. I pushed down on one, and it went tumbling down—down—down. I didn't hear it hit bottom. Even if there had been absolute quiet, I wouldn't have heard it. The bottom was too far below. I felt my heart pound as the rock fell away. I tried another rock. There wasn't much choice. One rock tipped unexpectedly as I stepped on it. *Remember that one on the way back*, I thought. "Watch that, Tony," I yelled out of the corner of my mouth. Then there was room to squeeze my foot between two big rocks. This felt secure, though I had to lean to keep my ankle from scraping the rock, and it was hard to keep my equilibrium with the heavy tripod and camera over my shoulder. Swallows dive-bombed us as we crossed, resenting our presence. They swooped past us from high above at incredible speed. Their wings cutting through the air sounded like jet planes.

I let out my breath when my foot reached the landing place at the far end. I wondered whether I'd been holding it all the while. I couldn't have been; it had taken too long to cross—longer than the other two times—and the distance seemed twice as far.

"Whew!" Tony exclaimed, "quite a bridge!"

"Only one bad thing about being safely out here, Tony—we've got to cross back again!"

"Should have brought parachutes; we'd get back to camp safer and quicker," Tony responded. Our camp was almost directly below us, or so it seemed from this great height.

I took my pictures, though I wondered why I was wasting the film. The light was too drab and flat to show the contours, the deep cuts of the canyons. The whole scene was two-dimensional; it was beautiful to me, but I wondered what Tony thought of it, never having seen it in sunlight and shadow.

Going back across the narrow stretch was harder. The wind was with us and blew us forward. We needed no push! The only nice thing about coming back was seeing terra firma come closer. I thought of Cid's words earlier, describing some loose rocks against the canyon wall. "The less firma, the more terra," she had said.

"You crazy guys!" Fred said when we got back to them. I thought I saw a look of envy on his face.

"You really ought to go out—after all, I was as scared as you are!"

When we arrived at camp, there was a large group around our boats. One of the Hatch River Expedition's scheduled trips had come down the Yampa and stopped to greet us. One of the boatmen was named Rasmussen. He was wearing swimming trunks, and I have never seen such a build on a man before. He was a solid mass of rippling muscles. I wondered whether he carried his barbells along in his boat. With Doc leaving us at Jensen, we'd be shorthanded, and I wished we could get this muscle man, Rasmussen, to join us. His passengers were from New York, members of the Appalachian Mountain Club. They had heard about our expedition, read about it in the *New Yorker* magazine. "I heard Lowell Thomas tell about it over the radio too," one of the women in the party said. "My, what a trip you're having!"

"You're making a pretty wonderful one yourself," I said.

"Yes, it is magnificent—but *you*, you're going through *all* those canyons! We have to stop at Island Park."

"That's too bad—you should go on through Split Mountain. There are some good rapids in there!"

"Oh, we had some terrific ones up there," she answered, pointing up Yampa Canyon. I looked over at Rasmussen. He gave me an understanding smile. "We started from Mantle's; the rapids were kid's stuff. You could ride them on an air mattress," he said.

It was getting toward suppertime, so I invited the river party to join us. Les already had a fire going. "No thanks," Rasmussen said. "This place is getting too crowded. We're making our camp downstream, on the other side."

I looked around and noticed several cars parked among the big cottonwoods. A family with several children was sitting at a table downstream eating, and dust rising from the road meant another car was coming in. Echo Park crowded! I could hardly believe it. Yet I remembered the controversy over the reclamation project. Dinosaur had received a lot of publicity since I spent days alone in this place in 1952. Hardly anyone came then; hardly anyone knew there were canyons here! Now the river men were camping elsewhere to find the solitude they sought on the river. The traditional river stop at Powell's campsite across from Echo Rock would soon be overrun with sightseers off the highway, coming in on the improved road. *They don't deserve the right!* I thought selfishly. Only those who had fought their way down the river deserved this island of solitude, this place of rest after the challenge of Lodore. Couldn't the Park Service restrict it for us and arrange for the others to have their picnics at the other end? Well, I consoled myself, everyone had the right to test the echo; the kids down below were, that was certain. Every few minutes a yell would come from below; then a few seconds later, the yell would repeat from the face of Echo Rock. "Testing, one-two-three-four," I said sarcastically to the others around our campfire. "The echo is working all right tonight!"

"We need more wood for the fire, Les," Don said. Les got up and hobbled over to some large cottonwoods. He picked up a dead limb from the ground, nearly twelve feet long and a good six or eight inches in diameter. He swung one end against the trunk of a tree. It gave a resounding crack that echoed several seconds later from across the river. When

Les had broken up the limb, he gathered up the pieces and carried them to the fire.

"Easier'n choppin'," he said with a grin as he stacked several pieces on the fire. The dry wood flared up, giving our campsite and the trees above a rosy glow. The light of the fire flickered mysteriously on the face of Echo Rock, way across the river.

"Shall I get out my cornet and play a tune?" Tony asked.

"Oh—it's so peaceful and quiet now that those kids have stopped yelling," I protested. "Why don't we just sit and listen to the murmur of the river?"

"Guess you're right," Tony agreed. Just then the blinding headlights of a car turned in and glared at us. It was as though we were suddenly spotlighted on a stage. The car drove almost into us. The motor stopped, and, with the lights still burning, a man got out and proceeded to put up a tent not thirty feet from us. When he got his tent up, he turned off his car lights. Then he lit a Coleman lantern, which he set on the next table. Its harsh, sizzling light overwhelmed the glow of our campfire in the trees and against the cliff. He sat down at the table beside the lantern and started to read a book.

We resented his presence. "Ought to know enough not to camp so close to others," Don said loudly enough for him to hear. That was true; there was a mile of riverbank, and there was plenty of space between campsites. There were many other groves of cottonwoods he could have picked. His presence threw a pall over our camp. I remembered the Rasmussen party downstream, and I began to feel that we, not our neighbor, were the intruders. Perhaps it was we who should have camped elsewhere. We were the ones out of place now; we were still back in 1869. This was 1955. The Coleman lantern was still sizzling as I fell asleep in my tent.

*Fourteen*

# PHOTOGRAPHING THE YAMPA RIVER AND JONES HOLE

June 17 was another day spent in the high country, on the plateau above Yampa Canyon. As I piled camera equipment into the back of the Jeep, I thought of Powell's photographer, E.O. Beaman.[1] What an easy job I had by comparison! To get views from above, he had had to scale the canyon walls, carrying cumbersome equipment: cameras three times the size of mine, wet plates of glass to register the photographic image, and a big tripod to hold the heavy camera. All in all, Beaman needed nearly a ton of equipment to take pictures during the voyage. Here I was with two cameras strung around my neck and another movie camera in a box half the size of Beaman's single camera, which also held four lenses, an exposure meter, several rolls of film, and all those gadgets the modern photographer thinks he needs but seldom uses. The whole shebang didn't weigh more than fifteen pounds! My pockets were stuffed with rolls of film, on which the emulsion had been coated weeks before in Rochester, New York. Beaman had to mix and apply his emulsion to pieces of glass on the spot. How did he manage to dry those wet plates in wind carrying almost as much sand as air? How did he have the energy in all this heat to climb two thousand—sometimes three thousand—feet to the rim of the canyon to expose his plates? In the desert heat, it was hard enough to carry the equipment a few hundred feet from the road to the rim of a canyon!

Fred and Cid remained behind in camp. They both wanted to catch up on their notes and their laundry. Bruce and Les stayed behind too, to repair boats and paint the platform and oars. Doc, Tony, Don, and I

Charles Eggert taking photographs at Mantle's Cave viewpoint on the Yampa River, June 17, 1955.

took to the high country. Tony rode in the front seat, and so it was his job to open the stretched-wire fence gates we had to pass through; to get where we were going, we had to cross two private ranches still maintained within the monument: Rial Chew's and Charlie Mantle's.[2]

The stretched-wire gate is an invention conjured up by the devil himself but a convenient one when the rancher doesn't want to go to the trouble of erecting a hinged gate. The wire gate is simply an extension of the fence itself, except that at one end, the three barbed wires are attached to a thin pole. This is held against the regular fence post by sticking the lower end into a wire loop near the bottom of the regular post and tying the upper end with a rope to the top. This arrangement is simple, for the rope needs only to be drawn tightly to keep the gate taut, but it becomes far more difficult when another wire loop replaces the rope at the top.

These gates are not by nature sloppy; at least they don't appear that way when they are up and stretched across the road. However, they do look that way when you see one open with the wire lying in a tangled heap on the ground. When they are stretched, they are as tight as the fence on either side. The problem comes when closing them. Seldom, if ever, have I closed one that seemed to have enough wire to get it close enough for the top loop to go over the small pole. Getting the small pole into the bottom hook is hard enough, but using your foot as well as both arms, you exert enough force to slip it in. At this point, after all, you have only one wire to stretch—the bottom one. To get the top in is another matter! Two wires need stretching, and the bottom one is working against you! To complicate matters even more, the main fence post is in your way so you can't pull the gate toward it with all your weight. A beginner usually pushes the small post instead. You have to use both arms to do this, and invariably one arm won't hold it there while you use the other to loop the wire over the top.

If you studied physics in high school, you may recall at this point that the lever is a handy gadget for moving the immovable. You then will wrap your arm around the big post and draw the little one to it. But normally someone who has spent fifteen minutes getting scratched while untangling the barbed wire that he casually tossed aside while opening the gate (a simple matter because a slight push usually creates enough slack to slip the top loop off) doesn't think of the lever, which is really the only sensible solution. Closing the gate is simple once you remember the lever. Unfortunately, many people like myself allow temper to take over rather than tap into past knowledge of the laws of physics, and it takes several encounters and losses of temper and many scratches before the value of the seemingly impractical knowledge gained in high school becomes apparent.

One way to learn the operation is to be told. The other, and the way I learned, is through firsthand experience. At least I was alone and thus saved from the embarrassment of making a fool of myself in front of others in my struggle. But there is a certain sardonic pleasure, once you have mastered the technique, in watching another struggle to learn. I was contemplating all this as Tony approached his first encounter with the adversary of the stretched-wire gate. At least he had one advantage over my first try: he didn't have to hold a horse by the reins at the same time. The three of us sat in the Jeep wishing and waiting for Tony to give us a good laugh. *Poor Tony,* I thought, *it's mean to let him make a momentary fool of himself.* But maybe this is part of the process of growing up. It's no big matter to make a fool of yourself in a small thing like opening a gate. It trains you to think things over carefully so that when bigger things come along, making a fool of yourself won't become a tragic matter. Besides, later on Tony would have the fun of feeling superior to someone else trying it. Don't we all laugh when a one-year-old's legs buckle as he or she attempts a first step?

Tony got the gate open all right. And he threw it back from the road with a gesture of bravado. We waved to him as he leaned nonchalantly against the main fence post waiting for us to pass through. When I stopped on the other side, we looked back to watch the struggle; there was bound to be one. Then I thought of Doc. Had he ever encountered these diabolic devices? Probably not in his world of hospitals and sterile, air-conditioned laboratories. In any case, if he knew how to close the gate, we'd save time, for Tony was as obstinate as the gate; if not, then the laugh would be twice as hearty and the joke only half on Tony.

Tony was untangling the barbed wire when Doc joined him. Doc helped pull some of the wire out of the sagebrush. The two aimed the end pole at the bottom loop, but it wouldn't fit. That was because they aimed the wrong end, for the wires were still twisted, and they had the gate upside down. Turning it over, they lined the wires up neatly in three rows. The post then fit easily into the bottom loop. Together they pushed the top. It was obvious that Doc had never tackled a fence gate! Tony let go to slip the loop over the top of the main post. With Tony's push gone, the gate didn't stretch. He jumped around to the other side.

"Watch this." I laughed. "Tony's going to end up on the wrong side of the gate!"

With Doc pushing with both arms and Tony pulling, they were able to draw the small post up to the main one; with his other arm, Tony slipped the loop over. Then he discovered he was on the wrong side of the gate. We all roared with laughter, including Tony, who now had the choice of climbing the fence and ripping his pants or opening the gate again. He chose to open the gate, being careful this time not to get it tangled.

Scratching his chin, Doc said, "There must be an easier way!" As Tony pushed, Doc wrapped his arm behind the main fence post and pulled up. It was easy. Doc had remembered the law of the lever. Tony was finally on our side of the gate, the loop was holding the three wires taut, and we drove on to the next gate.

"Guess I can manage this one," Tony joked as he jumped out to tackle the next stretched-wire gate.

We got back to camp very late. The others had already eaten. The book-reading neighbor had moved on. The other campers were gone too, and we had Echo Park all to ourselves. The only sounds other than our own camp noises and our laughter recounting the fight with the wire gate (and the echoing laughter from the cliff) were the soft murmurs of the Green as the water flowed past and the rustle of wind through the cottonwoods.

We retired late. Fred, Tony, and Bruce took a midnight swim. Cid recited lines from Shakespeare in the quiet:

> How sweet the moonlight sleeps upon this bank!
> Here will we sit and let the sounds of music
> Creep in our ears. Soft stillness and the night
> Become the touches of sweet harmony.[3]

Her mellow voice echoing back seemed as if it came from another world, like a voice from the sixteenth century coming from the stage of the Globe Theatre. Perhaps it was; who knew how time worked on this island of eternity?

A photograph of the entire 1955 crew on June 17, 1955. Shown left to right on the top row are Cid Sumner, Don Hatch, Les Jones, Fred Wood, and Bruce Lium. The bottom row includes (from left) Dr. Robert Parsons, Tony Tuttle, and Charles Eggert. Cid is holding the expedition flag, a camera lens with an arrow through it. Photograph courtesy of Robert Parsons Collection, J. Willard Marriott Library, University of Utah.

We slept late the following morning. This was a time for leisure after our struggles in the canyons. We, too, were vacationers in Dinosaur National Monument, and we had only a short run to our next camp, Jones Hole Creek, seven miles downriver. Don, Fred, and Doc went ahead, eager to fish for trout in the clear waters of Jones Creek. The rest of us took our time loading the big boat.

This was the first time the *Brontosaur* would ride in "planned solitude" on the river. We shoved off more than an hour after the others had left. Bruce and Les let the river carry us lazily around the prow of Steamboat Rock (we left the name Echo Rock behind with the echoes.) All of us lounged in the big boat watching the great cliff twist in the sky as we floated around its base. We looked up at Mitten Park fault, that mammoth synclinal fold in Earth's crust, and wondered at the great forces of pressure that had caused it. Our eyes followed it down to where it went under the river, and then, using the vertical slabs of strata on the other side, we followed the course of the fold back to the sky again, where it

A view of the Yampa River Canyon, approximately ten to fifteen miles above the Yampa's confluence with the Green River.

ended at Harper's Corner, twenty-five hundred feet above our heads. How small that rock bridge we had crossed looked now, yet just yesterday it had seemed miles across.

Soon the canyon walls closed in; we could feel them pressing in upon us even before we arrived at the head of Whirlpool Canyon.[4] Bruce and Les sat up and took the oars. The sound of splashing in the water seemed loud—an intrusion into the solitude around us. Very soon another sound took over, a sound that by now had become familiar: the rumble of distant rapids.

"Rapids—Ra-peeeds ahead!" Cid shouted.

We bounced through one, then another. We let the boat go as it would; it was too lazy a day to fight them. Their splash was refreshing in the heat. We wouldn't have minded getting dumped into one.

"Heads up for the next one," Les warned. "She's a churner. We'll have to pull hard across to make Jones Hole."

"It's gone," Bruce said.

"Gone? What do you mean, gone?" Les asked.

"When I went through earlier with Bus—he told me there used to be a tough one here, but high water took it out," Bruce explained.

I remembered that rapid from other trips through this canyon. We had had to enter from the left and go diagonally across the river to

Whirlpool Canyon on the Green River at the site of the proposed Echo Park Dam, 1955.

hit Jones Hole Creek campsite. If ever I had come close to tipping over, it was in those exceptionally high waves of Jones Creek Rapid. It was a toughie, even if you entered in the center. You couldn't enter on the right and make the landing: too many rocks. Even if you made the entrance correctly, you still had to ride the waves sideways, and they could flip your boat that way. On the ocean, crossing a wave diagonally is best, for there the wave motion moves across the water and carries you along. In a river rapid, it's different; it is the water that moves over the formed wave; the wave remains in place. The force of the moving water propels you up, over, and down, and the strength of that force is often enough to flip a boat, especially if it hits the wave broadside.

Bruce was right: the Jones Creek Rapid, rated a number three on the scale, was gone, and we so marked it on the map. It reminded us of those ever-altering changes on the river—and of the fact that our maps showed us only what had been. I recalled that huge fissure on the edge of Red Canyon and wondered if that slab had fallen by now.

When we arrived at Jones Hole Creek, we found Fred and Doc fishing along the bank of the Green.[5] "What are you doing there?" I yelled as our boat pulled up beside the small one tied to the bank. "I thought you'd be way up the creek."

"Don's up there," Fred said. "We didn't feel like going all the way up. The fishing is no good."

"No good!" I exclaimed. "Why this is one of the best trout streams in America!"

"It was," Fred explained, "but Don figures there's been a recent flash flood—it took out all the trout."

Late that afternoon Don returned to camp dejected. He hadn't caught any fish either. We were all disappointed.

We had a wonderful afternoon anyway. The clear water of the creek looked appealing, especially since our only baths had been in the silty river. After stating my intentions to Cid, I went beyond the creek, found a lovely, clear pool, and stripped. The sun was hot, but the water in the creek was almost freezing cold. I thrashed about with my hands and feet, deliberately attempting to get myself wet all over, but this was painfully slow. I finally gathered enough nerve and jumped in. The icy water took my breath away. Once I was used to it though, it was a soothing delight. I lathered myself completely with soap, and then, lying between two big rocks, I let the water pour over me to rinse myself off.

I used the last big bar of Ivory I had. The rest I had given to the others. They had lost their bars of nonfloating soap in the river. It hadn't occurred to me to bring floating soap; I had picked it out because it seemed like the biggest bar on the shelf at the time, but I realized what a convenience it was when Don's bar was the first to disappear in the silty water our first night out. He had yelled so loud when it went that I thought he had lost his Sierra Club drinking cup, a precious item, for besides holding water, hot chocolate, coffee, or grape juice, it also contained many memories.

As I held myself against the two big rocks to keep the swift water from carrying me downstream, its force beat against my neck and shoulders, cascading over my head and across my face. What a wonderful, wild feeling it was lying there with the velvety-smooth water pouring over me! I looked up at the narrow walls of the canyon Jones Creek had cut. They were bright salmon pink and climbed terrace upon terrace until stopped by the vivid blue sky. I felt like Adam: newly created.

Cid was reading when I returned to camp. The others were napping in the tall grass by the river under some big cottonwoods.

"Well, from the expression on your face, I can tell you enjoyed your bath!" she said, putting her book down. It was Wallace Stegner's *Beyond the Hundredth Meridian.*

"It was wonderful! You must try it—cold, though." I told her where I had been and how to find it.

"I most certainly will. My hair feels like hemp with all this silt in it." Her expression became much more serious as she looked down at the book she had been reading. "Charles," she said after a pause, "I've been reading Stegner—about Cataract Canyon. Do you think you will let me go through?"

I wasn't prepared for this. It hadn't occurred to me that Cid would want to know whether she could go beyond Jensen or not. We'd be there tomorrow; naturally she'd like to know soon. But Don and I had not discussed Cid since our talk at Lodore. We had been through a lot since then—Disaster, Triplet, Hell's Half Mile, and others that would have counted for more had it not been for those big ones—and Cid had been one of us, so much so that we hadn't given a thought to her being different from the rest of us. Cid had become one of the crew. The only thoughts I had had of anyone leaving were about Doc's departure at Jensen. I hated to see him go. I hadn't thought that Cid might leave us too. Though she couldn't line a boat the way Doc had done, she contributed something else to the expedition. It would be hard to pin down what that something was. Perhaps it was the bouquet of flowers she placed on the camp table every night. Perhaps it was her gentle voice that contrasted to the roar of rapids, her gaiety and femininity—even in her dungarees and shirt—in this chaotic world.

"You've had a pretty good taste of what's ahead," I said, feeling as if it was my job to plead for her to stay. "Would you go on if you could—if Don let you?" I asked, remembering that it was Don who had the final word.

"I certainly would!" she answered emphatically.

"Well, Cid, there's a lot of canyon ahead before we get to Cataract. Green River, Utah, would be the final place to decide about it."

"I'm in no hurry—it's just that I'd like to look forward to it."

"I'll have a talk with Don, Cid. Meanwhile we go through Split Mountain tomorrow, and it's a rough section."

"Fine!"

I looked at my watch; it was time to make my four o'clock test call on the FM radio. I called and got an immediate answer. The reception was very clear.

"We've been working on the transmitter—that's why you couldn't get us very well before," the chief ranger at Dinosaur headquarters said. Then he told me something that perked up the entire expedition. "Didn't you tell Jess you were looking for another man—a cook or something?" he asked.

"Yes, why?" I replied.

"There was a guy through here a couple of days ago—an Englishman. He wants to see the country. He read about your expedition in some magazine, and he stopped in to ask Jess when you were coming through. He wants to join you as a cook, I guess. Jess told him you were looking for one."

"That's right—when did Jess say we'd be through?"

"I think he told him on the nineteenth—that's right, isn't it?"

"Yes, we plan to get to Split Mountain Gorge around noon tomorrow."

"Well, the guy said he'd be in Vernal again on the nineteenth to be sure not to miss you. Jess said he was some kind of doctor." I looked over at Doc. Though we hadn't needed his services so far—except for Les, who rejected them—there was a lot of security in having a doctor along. That was another reason we hated to see him leave us. If this Englishman was a medical doctor, things were indeed looking up for the expedition!

"Hold him when he shows up—we're definitely interested," I said.

"How's fishing down there?" the chief ranger asked.

"Lousy—but the water's fine."

"Yeah—too bad about the flash flood there. Happened last week."

The others had gathered around for the radio call, and when it was completed, we all rejoiced over the possibility of another man to help us through the canyons ahead. Fred seemed particularly happy about it.

*Fifteen*

# WHIRLPOOL AND SPLIT MOUNTAIN CANYONS

"You know," I said to the others at breakfast the next morning, "we've never given a name to our little boat. I'm tired of referring to it as 'the small boat' in my notes. How about a name for her?"

"Well," Don suggested, "how about the *Plesiosaur?*"

"Good night! What's a plesiosaur?" asked Tony.

"A plesiosaur is—or, I mean, was—a seagoing dinosaur, sort of like the Loch Lomond sea serpent," Don answered.[1]

"That name is too hard to spell—it's a good one, though, matches the *Brontosaur.* But the Park Service already has a boat named that," I said.

"Powell had a boat called *The Maid of the Canyon,*" Cid suggested.[2]

"That's you," Fred answered.

"Well, why not name it after me?"

"Powell also had one called the *No Name*—our boat doesn't have a name, so why not call her that?" Tony suggested.

"Yeah, he lost it in Disaster Falls!" Don said.

We're past there now—no need to be superstitious—how about it?" I asked. "Tony's idea seems logical—the poor boat doesn't have a name."

"All in favor of christening her the *No Name* shout 'aye,'" Cid said.

"Aye!" we all shouted.

"Where's a bottle—Cid shall christen her!" Tony said.

"How about this?" Bruce asked, holding up a canteen.

We all marched down to the riverbank, and with the proper decorum due our staunch little craft made of rubber, Cid ceremoniously lifted the canteen over the prow of the boat. “I christen you the *No Name*,” she said solemnly, upending the canteen. Out poured purple juice.

“Ohmygosh!” Don yelled. “That’s my grape juice!” The christening turned out to be more of a ceremony than we had planned. All it lacked was the bubbles! Never was the christening of a boat surrounded by more laughter. It was impossible to turn serious until we entered Split Mountain Canyon, where we started to face big rapids again; Moonshine Draw would be another five, SOB a nine, and Schoolboy (named that because it looked tough but wasn’t) a number seven.[3] There were many others, all rough.

“What do you mean here, Les?” Don asked, looking up from his map. “You have a ‘plus two’ marked after the three.”

“I figure it’s worse in high water,” Les answered.

“They’re all worse in high water in this canyon,” Don replied.

Through the rolling hills and flats of Island Park, the river meanders for seven miles, seemingly undecided about which way to go after coming out of Whirlpool Canyon. It is as though the river determined to rest a while from its labors of cutting that great gash. As you approach Split Mountain Canyon, the mountain walls close in, the cliffs rise suddenly on either side, and you can feel the current beneath you gather force in preparation for the work ahead. Almost before you know it, you are drawn into the canyon, and before you’ve traveled a fast half mile, you are faced with the booming roar of Moonshine Draw rapids. The river makes a quick, sharp jog, and the full force of the current piles into the left cliff. Many a boat has been tumbled by the back-curling waves that pound upstream in defiance of the onrushing water.

“Hard to the right!” Les shouted to Bruce. They pulled with all their might to avoid crashing into those big waves. The boatmen knew they were there, and we entered the rapid from the far right. We were prepared. But even so, the force of the river carried us toward the cliff as though a powerful magnet were drawing us. The *Brontosaur* plunged through the waves, and the cliff passed close by. I hadn’t realized how fast we were going until I had such a close point of reference. We barely made it. So close we came that one of the big waves clipped the back end of the boat, hitting so hard that I thought it would spin us completely around. It shook us from stem to stern. The boatmen, yelling instructions to each other, had all they could do to keep the boat straight. We ended up below on the far left side of the river. It was amazing! We had approached that rapid on the far right, almost along the shore, but in spite of the hard pulling, here we were in just a few short seconds on the far left. What tremendous force and power were in that river!

What would have happened to us if we had not been prepared? I thought of others who had entered Split Mountain Canyon unaware of the peril ahead. This was no canyon for the novice to run. And I remembered back to that Sunday when I had stood on the banks of the river below Split Mountain Gorge watching for floating duffle and bodies of men who had been unlucky in the rapids of the canyon. It had been Moonshine that had gotten them, and from this point on, they had held on to the sides of their overturned boat, clinging desperately as they rode out SOB and Schoolboy and the rest. Out of control, they had somehow hung on, and they were picked up: gashed, cut, bleeding, and half drowned at the end of the canyon. In spite of that, they had been lucky![4]

In our struggle, we had momentarily forgotten about Don, Fred, and Doc. They were behind us above Moonshine. We looked back to watch them come through. They didn't appear; there was no sign of the *No Name.* Surely they hadn't stopped above the rapid. Where were they? We became alarmed.

"Better pull out to the center of the river, Bruce," Les said with concern. By this time, we were well below the rapids, and as the roar of them died away, we could hear shouts of "yooo hooo."

"There they are!" Cid cried. "There they are ahead!" Don had used the motor through Moonshine, and with the extra speed and power, he had managed to stay far right and passed us someplace in the rapid. The waves were so high that they slipped by us without being seen. It seemed incredible that they were ahead of us; we had gone through so fast!

SOB was next, and it lived up to its name. To make it worse, a high wind kicked up, making the boats tough to manage, especially the *Brontosaur* with its broad sides. SOB is especially difficult because the river makes an S-turn, and all of it is churning, angry, white water. No boat as heavily loaded as our *Brontosaur* had ever attempted to run it.

"There's only one way," Don shouted from the *No Name* as we approached. "Enter far, far left and try to stay there. Then as you go over, try to make it to the right bank—start pulling for it as you enter. You won't make it, but try; try like hell!" Don seldom swore; perhaps the name of the rapid demanded it. "We'll go ahead and wait below," he yelled as he sped up his motor. The boat crossed our bow to hug the left bank of the river. Just as he came upon the rapid, Don cut the motor and jumped for the oars. We lost sight of them as they went over the drop.

"Swing her around, Bruce," Les ordered. "We'll take her in backward." We made the approach as Don had instructed. Then I heard Les yell, "Heck, no, Bruce, swing her around the other way—quick!" Bruce gave a hard backward push on his right oar and a strong pull on his left. Les did the opposite.

"Other way!" Les shouted. "Other way!"

"Make up your mind, dammit!" Bruce yelled back. We went down diagonally with a plunge that I felt in the pit of my stomach. Since we were nearly broadside, we hit a wave hard. It splashed almost completely over the boat.

"Head for the right bank!" someone yelled. The men pulled hard on their right oars. We were in the middle of the river, halfway through the rapid. The right bank was flying past us. The current swung us around. We were facing downstream. I could see ahead a great pile of giant waves where the river made its final turn to the right.

"Keep her straight, Les!" Bruce shouted. The right bank disappeared behind us, but the swing of the boat had brought us close to its shore. Don had said we wouldn't make it, but I could see why he wanted the men to try hard for it. The big boat was now in the right position for the next turn.

"Left oar, hard, Bruce," Les yelled. I thought, *If Les pulls any harder on that oar he'll crack it for sure.* The current again forced us to the center of the river in spite of the efforts to keep the boat against the right bank. The left bank loomed straight ahead; we'd crash for sure against the cliffs!

"Swing her right!" Les cried. Around the boat went in the center of the river. The waves splashed over us as she hit them broadside. The maneuver left us a boat's length away from the left bank.

"Let her go—we've got her made now!" Les yelled triumphantly. We were still making good speed when Tony threw the towline ashore to Don. He had to run down the beach with it before he could pull us to a stop.

"How's that for a ride?" he asked Cid.

"It was wonderful—wonderful!"

For the next four miles, there were only three small rapids, and so we were able to sit back and enjoy the canyon scenery. It was amazing how different each of the four canyons in Dinosaur National Monument was. Lodore was majestic, purple, forbidding, and at times gloomy, with great ledges, one upon another, where tall Douglas firs grew. Yampa was a cheerful yellow and brown, gaily twisting and winding, with great overhanging cliffs where the rock was stained with long streamers of black from water dripping above. Whirlpool was dark, ominous, a great V cut through the mountains. Split Mountain Canyon was a combination of them all: a riot of color with razor-sharp flying buttresses and rock pinnacles high above. Fir trees lined the rim, appearing like a great army of men looking down as we passed by. The wind was still blowing, and all of a sudden a heavy cloud passed over the rim without warning and soaked us with rain. It blew over as quickly as it had come, but the color it left on the wet rocks made the momentary discomfort worthwhile. We had begun to peel off our ponchos when Don called to us from the *No Name*, "Better leave them on—Schoolboy's ahead." We listened; sure enough, we could hear the sound of white water. Schoolboy was just around the bend.

"It's a killer!" Don yelled with glee. "Whoopie!" he shouted as he stood up in the boat to see ahead. We all jumped up to look. We could see water splashing twenty feet in the air. The river dropped out of sight. The roar grew louder. "Sit down back there; you're rocking the boat!" Don yelled back at us. He waved his arm above his head, pretending to throw a lariat rope at us. Obviously, from his gay mood, Schoolboy had more fun in it than fear.

"Let's take it for all it's worth!" Bruce yelled to Les over the roar. "Hang on, everybody!" And so we did! Down went the nose of the boat. For a moment, Frog was completely submerged. Up she climbed over the first big wave, then down again! The *Brontosaur* spread the waves as her heavy nose hit, cascading water to either side. The wind picked up the splash and threw it back at us. We yelled, partly from the shock of cold water, partly out of exuberance. We knew now what that big boat could take, and we had confidence. Up and down the waves the old *Bronto* went like a caterpillar. Then she settled snugly into quiet water. That was it. And that would be it for the 138 miles to the next big rapid. We would not hear white water again until then.

Near the spot where the river exits from the canyon at Split Mountain Gorge is a huge cave. It cannot be seen from across the river at the campsite because of a hill, topped by jumbled rocks, that hides its entrance. As a matter of fact, if you stood on the right bank, you would never detect its presence at all. It is so well camouflaged that even Powell, with his keen eyes always alert to every feature of the canyons, missed seeing it though it lies only a few hundred yards from the riverbank. I had been told about it by a park ranger, who divulged its presence as though it were a secret palace of the gods. We would otherwise have missed it too. We yelled and motioned to Don and the others to stop, but they went on, misunderstanding that we were going to make a rest stop.

Bruce and Les decided to remain in the shade of a big cottonwood tree. There was no doubt that they were tired after the hard pull through the rapids, so I didn't urge them to join Cid, Tony, and me. Before setting off, we changed from our sneakers to high boots. We would be hiking through sagebrush and rocky talus, where rattlesnakes might lurk. As far as I was concerned, the rattlesnake was our greatest enemy, perhaps because I am more afraid of snakes than of rapids, especially rattlesnakes. The journals of river men are full of stories of encountering them, and although there is no record of any river traveler being bitten, the possibility is always there. A bite could be very serious business in these isolated places where immediate help is unavailable. We carried antivenin but certainly not enough to take a patient through several days without more extensive medical care. The two kits of serum we did carry were of dubious value anyway because we had no refrigeration to protect their potency. The best protection was caution: a wary eye and high boots.

"Lot of nonsense," Don had said when I had told him to get a suction kit to carry with him at all times. "And more nonsense to spend all that money on serum."

"Nonsense until you get bitten," I retorted.

The three of us set off in the direction of the cave. After a few yards of hiking, we were surprised to find we had come ashore on an island in the river and had to cross a broad, but seemingly shallow, stream. The water could not have been a creek coming into the river, for there were no side canyons. The walls of the big canyon rose sheerly all about us.

"No need to get your fine boots wet right off," I said to Cid. "Hop aboard." I leaned over to give her a piggyback ride across.

"Why, Charles, I'm too heavy." She laughed.

"No, you're not—come now—get on!" She hesitated for a moment, and I thought she must be thinking of the decorum. But we were in the wilderness, not on the main street in Duxbury, so we could all be kids together. So she climbed aboard my back, and we set off into the stream. I had expected the bottom to be sandy. It wasn't; it was full of rocks—big ones, some of them—so I slipped and faltered.

"We're going to fall in!" Cid yelled.

"And we'll both get soused—together we stand, together we fall!" At that moment, I dropped into a deep spot up to my thighs. I raised Cid's feet up to keep them dry.

She let out a shout. "Never mind the boots—it's the other end! I'm sitting in the water!"

"Hold on—we'll make it!" I exclaimed, feeling with my foot for shallower water. A few more stumbles, and we were across.

"Thank you, Sir Walter, for the ride," Cid said, curtsying to me.

"You're quite welcome, Your Majesty," I replied with a low bow and a sweep of my arm.

When we climbed the talus and arrived at the mouth of the cave, I was awestruck by its size.[5] The entrance was a mammoth arch with a span of nearly a hundred yards. At the center, it must have been three stories high. Above the entrance rose an overhanging cliff, smoothly concave, of unbelievable proportions. Near its top were jagged scars left by huge slabs of rock that had fallen in front of the entrance to hide it from view on the river. The whole place lay in the shadow of this great overhang, and the only light that entered was reflected from the outside, which gave a rosy tint to the Weber sandstone. Long, fat streamers of black stain streaked the surface of the rock where water had left its mineral dyes as it dripped from the cliff above, clinging to the undercut surface until it evaporated or no longer could withstand the pull of gravity.

The floor of the cave was deeply covered by the finest sand, powderlike in texture from thousands of years of continual grinding by the wind. The sandy floor extended back into the cave as far as we could see until the reflected light stopped, leaving the back in mysterious darkness. Inside, the place was cool and dank. It smelled of age. In the center was a high mound topped with rocks. I wondered whether it might have been used as a sacrificial altar by the prehistoric Indians who had made their home here centuries ago, hidden from enemies who had driven them into the security of the canyon country. Buried in the deep sand must be a treasure of Indian artifacts—pottery, utensils, clothing, perhaps—for very little exploration had occurred here since the Indians had left centuries ago.

I decided to do a little surface digging with my hands; I was sure the Park Service wouldn't mind as long as I didn't carry anything off; if I made an important discovery, I would bring it to headquarters for protection. As I plunged my hand into the soft sand, my mind was far, far off, dreaming of hundreds of years ago. Suddenly, there was a thundering roar, and the whole cave seemed to shake. My heart leapt into my mouth. I jumped up and ran wildly for the exit. We all seemed to take off in opposite directions at the same time. I could imagine myself being buried alive under hundreds of tons of rock from the falling ceiling. *Our presence has disturbed the delicate balance, and our voices have vibrated away the loose rock,* I thought! As I ran, I glanced back. Behind me a dust cloud was rising.

"It's an avalanche in the back," I yelled. "Run! Run!" Just then I saw five or six huge animals coming straight at me. I couldn't make out what they were in my confusion and haste. Bears? Cougars? Cougars! *Good God,* I thought, *an avalanche and wild mountain lions on top of it. Where will I run; where shall I go!* "Look out!" I cried. Then the animals saw me and bounded around the other side of the hill. All at once I realized what they were and discovered the source of the sound. Five huge sheep went thundering past—the biggest I have ever seen—and the pounding of their hooves on the sand had caused the thunderous sound. Tony and Cid saw them at the same time. But the question remained—were they running from something else or because we had frightened them? As they bounded out of the cave, the sound went with them. There was dead silence again, except for the pounding of my heart in my ears. I had had the wits frightened out of me!

"I thought the end was upon us," Cid said breathlessly. Tony stood high on a rock, his eyes as big as saucers. How he had climbed the sheer side, he didn't know.

We had been too frightened to laugh over the incident. Of all things, sheep! Those gentle, docile animals scaring us half to death! But the very surroundings—so mysterious, so ancient, so awesome—had contributed in no small measure to our fright. Probably the sheep were wild ones that had wandered down here from the grazing country up in the mountains years ago. They obviously hadn't been shorn for a good many years, if at all, and this made them look as large as bears. I'd never seen such big ones.

The dust raised from the frantic rush of animals and humans for the nearest exit made it impossible to go back in the cave again. Nor did any of us want to. There was something eerie about the place, sheep or no sheep. The great overhang, the long span of the entrance, the depth of the cave, all that rock above our heads—a whole mountain of it—made it spooky: too spooky, too unreal, too big for human beings.

"Let's get back to the boat," I suggested. No one needed urging. Cid wouldn't trust my carrying her back over the stream. "We're all too shaky for that," she explained. When we got back, we found Bruce and Les fast asleep under the tree. It seemed cruel to disturb their peace.

"Rise and shine," I whispered softly. Bruce opened one eye and smiled.

We had only a half mile on the river to the Split Mountain Gorge campsite, where we would complete the first quarter of our voyage. We had divided the trip into quarters, not according to length but by civilization points. To get to the other side of the river in the swift current and such a short distance was a pulling job for Bruce and Les.

"Pull into the back eddy around the cliff on the right," Les ordered. This was the same back eddy that Cid and I had studied ten days before. As we swiftly rounded the cliff, we saw a gang of people on shore waving and cheering our arrival. A Sierra Club river trip through Dinosaur was to start the next day, and a number of people were here to greet our arrival. Word of it had gotten around through my radio call from Jones Creek. We felt very important as we approached, our expedition flag flying beside Les in the front of the boat. Tony blew a few notes on his cornet—I believe they were from "Old Man River." We hit the back eddy and felt very slick and accomplished for making it across the river directly to our mark. But the eddy was bigger and stronger than we

Charles Eggert after getting soaked by the river. Note Cid sitting on the boat under a sun shade behind him. Photograph courtesy of Frederick Hoffman Wood Collection, Special Collections, J. Willard Marriott Library, University of Utah.

had anticipated. It caught us and whirled us around and around. Back upstream we went.

"Pull, Bruce!" Les shouted—but not loudly enough for those on shore to hear. The men pulled—and pulled! Still we stayed in the great whirlpool. We were carried back toward the bank where Don was waiting to catch the line, then upstream again, and back down. Every time we came close, the people on shore shouted a rousing cheer of welcome. Then we were carried upstream again. We simply couldn't get out, no matter how hard the boatmen pulled. What a sight we must have made!

"Get out of there, you bungling idiots!" Don jibed from shore. Fred and Doc stood there watching and laughing. The others began to laugh too. We looked as if we'd never handled a boat before.

"Stop fighting it," Don yelled. "Let her go way up—then pull out." Bruce and Les dropped their oars and sat back. The boat made another trip upstream. "Now pull!" Don shouted. Out of the eddy we popped into the main current. But now we were out too far.

"Pull in, Bruce, pull hard!" Les ordered. Don ran downstream to catch our towline. Tony threw it. We were still out too far; it missed Don.

"Jump, Tony," Bruce shouted as he ran forward to the nose of the boat and jumped in, grabbing the rope as he went over. He sank up to his chest. So did Tony. But the two, holding the towline, stopped the boat and pulled us back upstream to the place where we were supposed to land. It was too shallow to bring the nose of the boat completely to shore; she was too heavily loaded. Unceremoniously, we climbed into the water and waded ashore, where we received a gala welcome.

"We'd have been here a day sooner," said Les, "but another eddy caught us up in Lodore. I'm hungry—let's eat!"

*Sixteen*

# VERNAL INTERLUDE

The crowd that had come to greet our arrival at Split Mountain George gathered around the picnic table to hear about our experiences. We relished our role of adventurers. I was amused by how much we exaggerated! There was no need to; the truth was fabulous enough. But hearing our own descriptions of how high the canyon walls rose, how violently the waves tossed our boats, how gallantly we negotiated the fierce rapids, I thought of the written accounts of other travelers in the wilderness and questioned their veracity. Had things really been as bad as they had made them out to be? Well, perhaps they had been; perhaps the authors hadn't exaggerated at all.

Perhaps we, now, weren't exaggerating either. It only seemed that way—possibly because the experiences were so fantastic that the account of them sounded like a departure from the truth: utter fiction. Who was qualified to judge their credibility? Even we who had traveled through those canyons weren't. We had been in a dream, detached from our world and traveling in another. Now that our feet were planted back in a familiar place, we couldn't believe what we had done and seen.

The first 209 miles now seemed easy, and in retrospect there had been more fun than fury to it. Yet the separate experiences that made up the total didn't sound so easy when we heard ourselves tell about them. And it was the highlights you related—the things that made you sound gallant and daring. You left out the hours of lolling on the boat watching the rims of the canyons pass across the sky. You left out the eagle you saw gliding above in its private world of air. Nor did you tell about the family

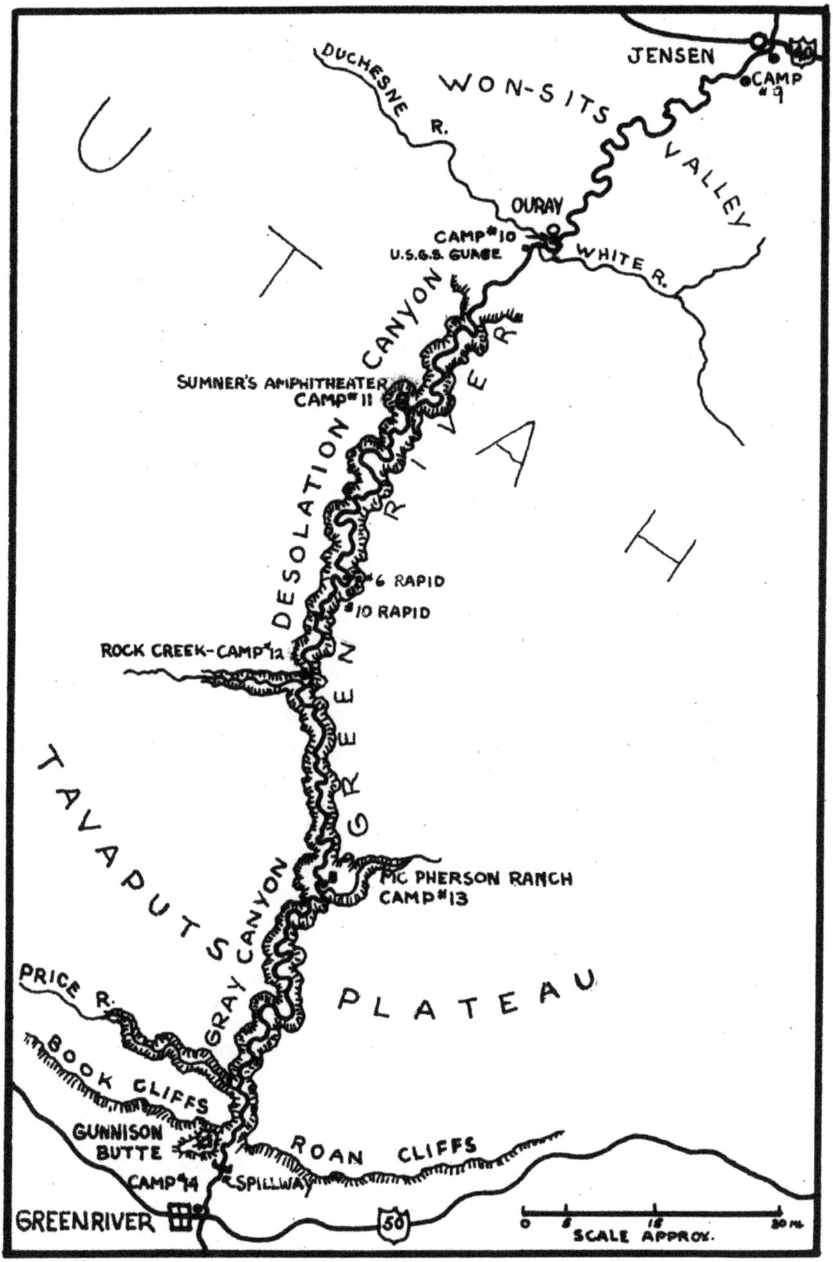


The second detailed map made by Charles Eggert to record their river trip. This one runs from Jensen to Green River, Utah, and includes the trip's camps and notable features.

of deer that bounded up the ledges of the canyon wall, startled by your sudden presence. You didn't mention the sense of peace you felt around you at first either. All of these things weren't exciting to talk about. Not yet anyway; not until after you got all the physical heroics out of your system. Turmoil and danger were the things that needed telling first, the stuff that wanted to be heard first. The rest would come later—in a book maybe. The aesthetic joys were, in the end, the important things—but only in retrospect, after the journey was all over, to be described in places where there weren't eagles soaring or deer leaping from cranny to cranny; where peace was a sought-after quality, not a part of the surroundings.

It had been easy—up to now anyway. There were no broken bones, no wrecked boats, only a few scars from bangs on rocks, a few blistered hands from tugging on ropes. That was all. It seemed easy—now that we had made it. But it hadn't been easy up there in Hell's Half Mile or at Ashley Falls. No, it hadn't been easy until it was over. Then it seemed simple, and to tell about it sounded exaggerated, even if you really told the truth.

After lunch a car took us to the dinosaur quarry to see the fossil diggings.[1] We were a motley-looking bunch—torn shirts, ripped dungarees, hunting knives and tin cups hanging from our belts. It wasn't hard to recognize us as the gang who were running the river all the way. Cid was the center of attention. There was nothing unusual about us men; any man with a certain amount of guts and no common sense might try such a thing, but a sixty-four-year-old woman—that was something else again! Too, she was much more incongruous looking in her outfit: dungarees, white shirt with one shoulder almost completely torn away, a cap, and draped over it, that indispensable nylon veil, no longer white but silty brown.

None of us cared how we looked; it was too hot for propriety. And we were away from the river, from the cool water that we could douse over us for relief. We found some comfort in pouring water from our canteens over our heads, much to the surprise of several well-dressed tourists. They were a bit amazed by our utter disregard for getting our clothing wet.

After our tour of the quarry, we went back to the parking lot, where I recognized the battered bus that had hauled our supplies to Green River. Rasmussen was at the wheel. Rasmussen! Almost anything seemed credible! Or was it that nothing was incredible anymore? Now here was

Rasmussen, the muscular giant, with the steering wheel of a battered bus instead of solid, heavy oars in his hands, waiting to drive us to Vernal. His presence was a bit of a shock. This was a different world from the one we had known him in. It seemed as though he must have been catapulted from a distant planet to this spot, just as we seemed to have been.

Rasmussen handled the bus as though it had just come from a factory, newly built. He was not in the least concerned that at any moment a wheel might go flying off into the ditch, or that its body might bounce from the frame into the highway. It certainly felt as though it might! As cars whizzed past, I felt that Hell's Half Mile was a far safer place. The bus ride was a frenetic change from the slow pace of the past nine days on the river.

Vernal, twenty-five miles inland from the river, was even hotter than the quarry, but the green grass and cool shade on the lawn at the Hatch house gave us some respite. Our arrival was a gala affair. Assembled for the Sierra Club river trip through the canyons of Dinosaur National Monument were friends from all over the States, many of whom I knew only through correspondence.[2] Charlotte Mauk was there from Berkeley, California; Fred Packard and his wife from Washington, DC; and Joe Penfold from Denver. There were also people from Buffalo, Seattle, Chicago, and St. Louis. And we had just come from the bowels of the earth. It was incredible that we should all meet at this hour in this spot in such a vast world—but, as before, incredibility was accepted without so much as a grain of salt!

Someone had a fine bottle of bourbon, so an impromptu cocktail party began. It was the beginning of further celebration. We were sitting in a big circle on the lawn swapping stories when Bus Hatch tapped me on the shoulder to tell me that the fellow from England who wanted to join our expedition had arrived. Dr. Leslie Emsden was on Bus Hatch's front porch waiting to talk with me.[3]

"The superintendent of the monument told me you were looking for a cook," Dr. Emsden said after our introduction. "I've come to America, and I want to get a very good look at it, so I hired myself out to drive a new truck across the country and deliver it to Salt Lake City. Your country is certainly big!"

"Yes, it certainly is, and the best way to find that out is to drive across it," I answered.

"I'm finding that out!" he exclaimed. "Why," he continued, "on the way out, after four days of driving, I expected to see the Pacific Ocean over the next rise, whereupon I came to a sign that told me I was only at the geographic center of the country. I almost gave up."

"Oh, you came on Route 36, right?"

"That's correct."

"It's about the dullest route but the straightest across."

"I know," Dr. Emsden answered, "but I was told to come that way—besides, I wanted to get here by the quickest route, for I had read about your expedition in the *New Yorker* and hoped by chance I might join it. I'm a doctor by profession, not a cook, I should warn you, but I've done considerable roughing it, so I can throw a pot of stew together. I assume your food is all tinned.

"That's right—we haven't refrigeration, of course." I was considering this man not as a cook but rather as another able crew member to help us through the worst part of the trip, which still lay ahead. I was also attracted by the fact that he was a doctor. As for his build, he looked sturdy enough; obviously he was no weakling. As far as his ability as a doctor went, I managed to get our present doc aside and asked him to check Emsden's qualifications. Doc found out where he had studied medicine, where he had interned, and other pertinent facts to make certain that this man, in fact, was a doctor.

Don interviewed him, too, and approved. "Well," I finally said to Doc Emsden, "come join us. This will be an unusual way to see America, but you'll certainly see a part of it very few others experience!" I took him around to meet our merry group and, after introducing him, poured him a drink.

"Just a short one, please," Doc Emsden said. "I must go into town for some boots and tennis shoes."

"Join us at dinner then—at the Vernal Hotel about seven."

I was still watching our new expedition member walk away when Fred came out of the house looking very dejected. In my excitement over seeing so many friends and meeting Doc Emsden, I had completely forgotten that we might also lose Fred. The elation I felt over the new doctor was negated by Fred's appearance. To lose Fred would be a very hard blow.

"I just talked with Esther," he said. "Things don't sound too good at home."

"Someone sick?" I asked.

"No—they're okay, but Esther sounds as if she has her hands full with the shop. I feel I ought to be back there helping her."

"Fred, we'd hate to lose you—I'm sure everything will be all right. I hope you'll not decide to leave. We need a good man like you, you know."

"Thanks, Chuck," he answered. "Let me think about it for a while. I'm not sure just what to do."

"Charlie," Charlotte Mauk interrupted, "I'm going to take your mermaid, Mrs. Sumner, with me to the hotel so she can use my shower."

Cid looked like a new woman when next we saw her in the dining room of the Vernal Hotel. Her shirt was mended, and her silver-gray hair again had a bright sheen that set off her suntanned complexion. Cid was a picture of health; we all were after those days of sun, water, and clean air! We looked as though we had lived on a steady diet of high-powered vitamins. But we ate as though we had just come from a concentration camp! One shrimp cocktail wasn't enough; we had to have two. Fresh meat we craved the most, so all of us ordered the largest steaks in the kitchen. Blueberry pie topped with two scoops of ice cream completed a meal we felt we well deserved.

Our meal was made even happier by Fred's appearance just before dinner arrived. He had disappeared just before we sat down and was gone a long time. Presently he came into the dining room with a grin from ear to ear. "Well, Eggert," he announced, "you're stuck with Wood for another 821 miles! I just talked with Esther again—and with the kids—and they said they'd never forgive me if I didn't go on. My worries are over!" And Fred looked it. There was no longer that expression that I had often mistaken for fear on his face.

We had a carefree time at dinner, unburdened of the worry of being shorthanded. Furthermore, we had another doctor to reinforce our sense of security, which would have otherwise been supported only by our abilities as river runners. Our first nine days had taught us to be cautious. We had become able; we had learned the hazards, and we were prepared to keep out of trouble, to hang on, to step cautiously. But always there lurked the possibility of sickness or an unexpected emergency when it would be necessary to have a good doctor immediately at hand.

Time went quickly, and there was not a moment to lose to get our original Doc to his plane. There was little time to regret his going, though all of us wished he had the time to continue. With his departure went something more than just a man. Doc, with his background where order and efficiency played such a large role, was in a sense the real leader of the expedition, and neither Don nor I could replace his qualities of leadership. I hadn't realized how much Doc had held us together, especially in camp; the single unit we had been on the river seemed to disintegrate as I stood there, feeling very much alone and responsible, after his plane had disappeared into the vast sky. "Well," I said weakly, "I guess we'd better get back to the boats."

It was pitch black with only the stars to guide the way when we reached the river at Jensen. Les and Bruce had taken the boats downstream from Split Mountain Gorge to Jensen, a distance of eighteen river miles (about five miles as the crow flies), while we were in town. They were to find a camp spot and set up—exactly where, we didn't know, but somewhere near the highway bridge. It would be easier and quicker to bring in our fresh supplies at Jensen rather than Split Mountain Gorge.

We had a hard time finding their camp in the dark. We drove some distance upriver from the bridge, along the right bank, but there was no sign of them. Finally, we stopped the car and yelled. In the distance downstream, we heard their answering call. In the quiet of the night, their voices seemed to come from the faraway buttes in the desert beyond. Finally, after several spot checks along the way, we found the camp on the left bank of the river below the bridge. It was conveniently located for supplies but otherwise was an ugly campsite. The noise of cars and trucks whizzing across the bridge on US 40 would keep us awake. The moment we got out of Don's car, the mosquitoes began attacking and fed upon us all night. They completely ignored the insect repellant. On the contrary, the repellant seemed to attract them!

The moment the sun rose over the hills, it blazed down on us with hot fury. There wasn't a cloud in the sky to give us a moment of respite from its burning rays. Tony volunteered to stay in camp to guard our equipment. Now that we were in civilization, we had to worry about things like that. I hated to leave him there in the broiling sun. There wasn't a tree to give shade, only a few scrubby tamarisk bushes lining the bank of the river. I was actually worried that he might perish. There was water in Jensen across the bridge; also a small store where he could buy cold drinks and ice cream. The shade of the porch at the post office offered some escape, and Tony told us he could spend the day there. From the porch, he could look across the river to our camp.

In Vernal we were less comfortable even than Tony. Not only was it just as hot, but we were confronted with people, and people meant dealing, making choices, and making decisions. There was dealing with telephone operators and busy long-distance circuits, and I sweated out an hour waiting for a call to New York. Along with the choices and decisions were all kinds of complications. Time crawled at a snail's pace. Doc Emsden had discovered he was allergic to his sleeping bag and had to exchange it for another. He had spent an uncomfortable night, he told me, and he looked drawn and tired. Cid, too, looked worn out and wan by midafternoon. The twinkle was gone from her eyes, and she seemed listless.

"Did you take your salt pills this morning?" I asked while we were having an ice cream sundae at the drugstore.

"Yes, I took my quota of two."

"Don't you feel well?"

"This heat," she answered, "perhaps it's that. I'll be all right. This air-conditioned drugstore is a help. Do you think we'll ever get back to the river?"

Finally, at four-thirty, we all packed into Don's car—seven of us in a coupe. We were stuffed in like sardines! The cans of gasoline for the motors were in the trunk, and the fumes added to our discomfort. By some miracle, we survived the ride to Jensen without someone passing out, and we were grateful to climb out into open space. Cid went immediately to the river and sat on the side of the boat with her feet in the water. Doc Emsden still looked terribly dragged out, so I told him to forget about his duties as cook for the evening. He joined Cid in the boat while Bruce dealt with the problems of cooking supper.

None of us ate much; we were too hot. Tony, whom I had expected to suffer more than we did, was the freshest among us. He had sat all day on the porch of the post office eating ice cream and writing letters to his girl. Cars and trucks continued to roar over the bridge, and the mosquitoes began their attack again. At seven o'clock, I made up my mind that we had had enough of Vernal and Jensen, and in spite of the late hour, I gave the order to break camp and set off on the river. We would travel on until dark and make camp at a more comfortable place.

This was probably the most popular decision I made on the whole journey. Everyone seemed to come to life. Camp was broken up rapidly, and we floated downstream, happy to get into the wilderness again. We felt like ourselves again and began to laugh and joke. A cool breeze came up, and we ran on until dark, when we found a suitable campsite. Don, Bruce, and Tony took to the hills and made their camp high above the river. There was a tamarisk thicket along the bank, but behind it was a flat area where the rest of us set up our camps. Les chose the *Brontosaur*. We were still annoyed by mosquitoes, which were even more voracious than the ones at Jensen. I put on my Levi jacket to protect myself while I put up my tent, but they bit right through the thick denim. The desert ground was so hard and dry that I could hardly pound my steel stakes into it. We had bug bombs with us, and I sprayed the inside of the tent well. I was grateful to have the tent for protection.

We had just gotten settled when I heard a great splash. My first thought was that Les had fallen into the river. Fred and I both jumped out of our tents to see. When we got to the boat, Les was lying comfortably inside. "It's just a darned beaver," he explained. "He resents my presence. Guess we parked over his house." The beaver continued to make loud splashes all night long. The flap of his tail on the water made a resounding smack, so Les got little sleep.

We awoke the next morning and sensed immediately that another hot day was ahead. This was no surprise. None of us were looking forward to the eighty-five miles of desert country and slow river between Split Mountain Gorge and Desolation Canyon. We knew the going would be slow, that it would be hot now that we had left the mountains behind, and that the sun would beat down on us unmercifully as we passed through the Uinta Valley.

One of the first things Les did when we got on the river was erect a tent over the platform on the *Brontosaur*. Two spare oars held up the front of the tent. It made a refuge for Cid. She sat in it most of the day, and with her nylon veil wrapped around her, she looked like a captured Egyptian princess being carried down the Nile by Nubian slaves. She dipped the veil into the water every so often and wrapped it around her head again. The evaporation of the water gave her a handy air-conditioning system. But toward noon, it got so hot that she came out of the tent and asked Bruce to douse her completely with a bucket of water. Bruce looked at her incredulously. "Go ahead, Bruce," Cid said. "Pour it all over me—it will really cool me off; otherwise my blood will boil and explode my veins!"

Cid leaned over the side of the boat, and Bruce reluctantly proceeded to pour a pail of water over her head, shoulders, and back. "It's the treatment, boys!" she shouted with glee. "Come and get it! It's so refreshing. Who's next?" Bruce was convinced, and he lay on his stomach while Cid poured a bucket of water over him. Don was attracted by the shouts and laughter in the *Brontosaur*. He turned the controls in the *No Name* over to Fred and climbed aboard the *Brontosaur*. Cid doused him. Then it was my turn, and then Tony's and Doc's. Doc seemed to be affected most by the heat. Cid earlier had given him a towel that he had soaked and wrapped around his head. He looked like a very-much-out-of-place Arab, very pale. He was also having a hard time breathing. It was an asthma attack, he explained, that came from an allergy to his other sleeping bag. He assured me it would soon disappear. But as the day went on, he grew worse. I became alarmed, broke out the medical kit, and gave him some pills for asthma.

The motor on the *No Name* droned on and on and on as it pulled the big boat. The heat and the sound of the motor seemed to hypnotize us, and we sat in silence most of the day, gritting our teeth to get through it and welcome the evening, when it would cool off again. Bruce and Les were the only ones who didn't seem to mind the heat. At first Les just sat, expending as little energy as possible. Finally, out of boredom or what I do not know, he took up the oars and began to row like fury. Perhaps he was eager to help the motor along and get us back into the canyons and fast water again. "Les! You'll kill yourself!" Cid protested, but he seemed not to hear and kept right on rowing. After about a half hour of this, he put down the oars, got out his Book of Mormon, and read to himself the rest of the day. We wished he'd read aloud, but he was in such deep concentration, completely oblivious to anything around, that none of us wished to disturb him by suggesting it.

Bruce busied himself with one thing or another all day. He couldn't remain still. He got out a long, thick board, a saw, and a large knife and made a new oar to replace the one we had broken in Lodore Canyon. Then he got out paint and touched up the designs on the *Brontosaur* again.

In spite of the heat and slow water, which made it seem as if we were dragging along, we made forty-nine miles and arrived in Ouray, Utah, in the early evening. Ouray, a very small settlement on the banks of the river, is the headquarters for the Ute Indian Reservation.[4] We found a comfortable campsite in a cool grove of cottonwoods close to the settlement. At the post office, I found several letters awaiting me—among them was one from my photo lab in New York, giving me a report on how I was doing with my footage. Several film clips were enclosed, and everyone gathered around to see the first bits of my film, *A Canyon Voyage*. The report warned that I should watch out for dirt in the gates of my camera. As if I needed the warning!

The postman, Mr. Wilson, one of the five white inhabitants of Ouray, came down to look over our boats. He struck me as a very lonely man who was hungry to talk to someone, so I invited him to have supper with us. He was delighted with the invitation.

After we ate, I decided it was time to have everyone become familiar with the medical kit. There hadn't been too much curiosity about it, but what with Doc Emsden feeling badly, and the heat of the day that had affected us all in one way or another, and the fact that we were going now into unfamiliar country, I thought it was time we knew what was in the kit. Up until now, a certain amount of security had come from knowing the country—at least Don, Les, and Bruce knew it—but from now on, all would be unfamiliar, and we had been told that the river through Desolation Canyon was very much like Split Mountain. That meant some rough rapids and the possibility of accident. We expected, too, that it would take from ten to fifteen days to get to our next civilization point: Green River, Utah.

I got the heavy kit off the boat. It was a large toolbox packed tightly with medical and surgical supplies. I took each item from the kit and explained what instructions I had gotten from my doctor on how to use it. Doc sat beside me and corroborated the information, which made me pleased to have remembered everything correctly. In the kit, on top of everything, was a card file that cross-indexed everything according to the diseases or disasters that each article matched. The first card read, "ADRENALIN—for injection. For severe shock, EXCEPT IN HEAD INJURY. Use only if caffeine and Coramine don't work, EXCEPT use this for SEVEREST heat prostration. This is a heart stimulant. Dosage: not more than one AMPULE." I got out the adrenalin and showed it to the group.

The next card read, "ALLERGY—see Chlor-Trimeton, Calagesic ointment, Neo-Cortef." Then there was "AMPHOJEL—for ulcer or upset stomach"; then "ANODYNE—for toothache. Fill cavity, mix anodyne powder with anodyne liquid to form a thick paste. Dry cavity with cotton and apply the paste," the card read.

"Wish I'd known about that sooner," Cid said with a sigh.

"Why? Did you have a toothache?" I asked.

"I had two horrible days with one. I had the tooth pulled in Vernal," she said.

"In Vernal!" I exclaimed. "When?"

"While you were all busy buying supplies and things. Maybe that was why I was a little pale in the afternoon.

"Are you all right—is it still bleeding?" I asked with concern.

"No—it's fine. I hated to leave part of me in Vernal, though."

"Well—of all things!" I exclaimed. "Why didn't you tell me?"

"I didn't want to. I thought you might leave me behind."

We all laughed. Leave? We had completely forgotten about deciding whether Cid should leave us in Vernal! The thought hadn't crossed my mind again since the discussion at Jones Creek. Cid was a definite part of us; she was no longer just a woman, aged sixty-four, accompanying us. She was not an extra on trial; she was one of the group.

"I knew there was something we were supposed to talk about!" Don said. "Too late now—you're stuck with us!" he added.

It was a few minutes before the shock of Cid's encounter with a dentist in Vernal left me. Had it been me, I am sure I would have announced bravely that I was about to have a tooth pulled. Then I would undoubtedly have bragged about how stoic I had been the rest of the trip! In disgust over my probable behavior in such a situation, I turned back to the card file. "ANESTHESIA" was the next card. The notation under it read: "See Xylocaine ointment—local, surface anesthesia. See PAIN." I turned to the card marked "PAIN" (to satisfy my own curiosity now, as well as for the others). It read, "See Codeine, morphine, APC, aspirin, Xylocaine ointment, paregoric." We were sure fixed for pain!

"If I'd known you had all that hop-up stuff, I'd have doped myself all day today," Don joked.

The next card was labeled "ANTIVENIN" and read, "Snakebite serum (Nearctic Crotalidae) for poisonous snakebites. See directions in box. THERE ARE TWO KITS OF THIS." This item seemed to deserve special attention because we were in the desert and about to enter the plateau canyons, and it wouldn't be too long before we'd be in diamond-back rattler country, among a species perhaps even more dangerous than the smaller, prairie rattler. Rattlesnakes, next to rapids, were our most serious concern. I thought we had all better know about snakebites and their treatment. I opened one of the kits and read the directions, taking out each item—the liquid, the powder, and the syringe—to illustrate exactly how to use them. Before I had half finished, I saw Cid slip away and retire to her tent.

When I had finished the directions, the conversation continued with snake stories around the campfire in spite of the late hour. We never got to "CODEINE," "CONSTIPATION," "INFECTIONS," "PENICILLIN," or "ZINC OXIDE." Our diseases and remedies literally went from *A* to *Z*, and without a doubt, we were the most elaborately outfitted expedition, so far as medicines were concerned, that had ever traveled on a river! *All very well*, I thought (in spite of the ribbing Don gave me about forgetting an X-ray machine). But as I laid my head on my inflated rubber pillow, I thought, *Who'll use that sharp scalpel and those sutures in case of a ruptured appendix? Doc Emsden?* I was happy that mine was out!

*Seventeen*

# UINTA BASIN

It was June 22, and ahead of us were Desolation and Gray Canyons and 128 miles to the next human beings. We thought of that as we bid our new friend William Wilson, the Ouray postman, goodbye. I shall always be grateful to Mr. Wilson for a letter he wrote to my wife after seeing us off. There is something special about receiving news from a stranger, a scent of truth and detached observation. If we were having trouble, I could have covered it up with nice things in my letters and telephone conversations with Betty. Mr. Wilson's letter gave her an objective report of our lives on the river.

He wrote,

> Dear Mrs. Eggert,
>
> Many thanks for sending me the card with the names of those who are with the River Expedition.
>
> They arrived here at Ouray evening of June 21, all in fine shape and in happy jovial mood. Was very pleased to meet them. When I got out of the post office, went down to the river to pay them a visit by invitation from your husband. Got there just in time for supper, and was it a feed.
>
> Then this morning, June 22, after the mail had left, went down to bid them luck on their way. They left fine after a night's rest.
>
> Bye now—As ever,<br>P.M. William W. Wilson<br>Ouray, Utah

P.S. Mrs. Sumner is having the time of her life, and enjoying the trip fine, is very well and happy.

Seeing them almost made me wish I was going along with them.

—W.W.W.

We did leave "fine" after a good night's rest. There was no report of nightmares over snakes following our long discussion, although I am sure we all took extra precautions as we made our morning trip into the bushes after breakfast. The day was again a hot one, but a fresh breeze kicked up from the river, air undoubtedly funneling out of the canyon ahead.

A short distance from the settlement we came upon a US Geological Survey (USGS) gauging station on the right bank of the river. It was nothing more than a cylindrical, galvanized tin structure on the riverbank. With its peaked top, it looked like a miniature farm silo—or one of those Commodity Credit storage bins I've seen so often in the West, only smaller in diameter. Up one side was the gauge, a strip of wood with numbers painted on it to measure the cubic feet per seconds of water in the river. The river level was up to the 9,500-foot mark, which we considered quite good, although we had expected it to be higher. By the middle of June, the volume of runoff from the snows in the watersheds should have been at full peak. Except for the rise we had experienced in Lodore Canyon, the volume of the river seemed to remain steady. The gauge went as high as 15,740 cubic feet per second. That apparently was the maximum height the USGS ever expected the river to rise at this place, but 9,500 was far down from that! That level was fine, from the reports we had, to travel through Desolation and Gray and even the next two canyons, Labyrinth and Stillwater. But we thought of Cataract Canyon. That was a long way off, and the water volume could change greatly by then.

Though we were momentarily satisfied with water conditions, we were puzzled about the future. The whole situation looked too "average." Was the river on its way up, or on the way down? There had been a lot of snow during the early spring—enough to make up for the lack of it during the winter, or almost so. And the warm weather had not come as quickly as usual, which would have made the runoff sudden and turbulent. Could it be that because of the gradual spring warm-up, the river would remain at a good level for a long time instead of having the usual short crest?

"I hope this thing either stays this way or goes up slowly," Don remarked as he turned back to the boat. "Otherwise we're in for trouble farther down."

"What do you mean, Don?" Cid asked.

"Well, we'd better not get the full crest of the runoff in Cataract. If that happens, we may as well get to work on our last wills and testaments, and if it drops from now on, we better take a bulldozer along to clear out the rocks to make a channel through there. Of course, there's the big Colorado coming in yet—she'll probably be at crest, or a bit below it from the runoff in the Rockies. But the Green better be on its way up if we're going to float through Grand Canyon. If it isn't, save your hiking boots for the occasion." His smile didn't quite hide the grim meaning behind his jokes.

Fred, Cid, Tony, and Doc Emsden weren't as concerned about the situation as were our boatmen, who understood the river. They wondered what had happened to the spring runoff. Had it come and gone? Was this it, or was it about to happen? Don looked forward eagerly to the Duchesne River, just below the gauging station. Perhaps its volume would tell us something; perhaps it was flowing at full crest. We stopped at the mouth of the Duchesne, one of the few tributaries of the Green, and found, to our shock, that it was nearly dry! The White River, another major tributary a mile below on the left, was our next hope.[1] It was nearly dry, too.

"We must have had it—what there was of it," Don said, referring to the spring runoff.[2] "It doesn't look so good for the lower canyons." I recalled his words at the head of Lodore, long before. "The river would never be right.... If you started up here in high water, by the time you got to Grand Canyon, the river would be too low," he had said then.

"Well," I said reassuringly, "there's still the big Colorado."

"Yeah—I'll be looking around the bend for it. She'd better be big!" Don answered. "I think I'll make nightly markings from now on to see what's happening."

"How?" someone asked.

"Put a twig at the water's edge," he explained. "We can see if she rises or falls during the night. It was easy to tell up in the other canyons. I know those. But I don't know where the river is supposed to be down here!"

The wind blew harder as the day went on, and though it was a physical relief to have the cool air, we made slow progress. Bruce and Les helped by taking up the oars and rowing even though the *No Name* was pulling us with the motor. The wind blew so strongly that we had to take the tent down. Tony suggested that we use it as a sail, but no one was clever enough to figure out how we were supposed to tack into the wind.

For a while we amused ourselves watching the wild ducks and geese, or an occasional beaver, on the river, just as we had done the day before. But soon the buttes and mesas closed in on us, and ahead loomed the great, gaping entrance to Desolation Canyon. As we approached closer and closer, our wildlife sightings became fewer and fewer, and when we entered the massive portals, they were gone altogether. There was a strange feeling about Desolation that hit us as soon as we got into the canyon. It was as though a heavy pall had fallen over the river. There were no signs of life except for the sparse vegetation. The ducks and geese and beavers were gone, nor was there an occasional deer's head popping up suddenly from the tamarisk to look at us with astonishment. Even the canyon walls seemed colorless, and everything was monochrome—even the sky, which became overcast with a thin veil of clouds.

The canyon seemed like a mammoth vaulted chamber of stone from the sixteenth century. Tony must have had this impression too, for he got out his horn and blew Gregorian chant-like passages that echoed forlornly from the cliffs as he played. Often the echoes blended with his playing, creating weird harmonies and dissonances. Otherwise we passed silently down the river. Even the motor seemed to be hushed as it smoothly droned on. Perhaps we were just no longer hearing it, for by now our ears had become so tuned to the frequency of its sound that we were oblivious to it. The canyon walls rose in huge terraces, each one set back from the previous one. Sometimes the walls were close to the river, proceeding upward from the talus along the edge. Sometimes they rose sheerly from the river or were set back far from shore. Heavy stone buttresses soared over the river in places, and occasionally, where the wind and water had eroded deeply, a hole or window was cut clean through the perpendicular walls.

In spite of the wind slowing down our progress, we were grateful for it. I felt that if it had not been blowing, this place would be a complete vacuum, where we could not breathe. With its bleak walls and sparse vegetation, Powell had done well to name it the Canyon of Desolation.[3]

Toward evening we came to a great curve in the river. The canyon wall on the outside of the curve was laid back in tremendous tiers, like a mammoth coliseum with imaginary rows upon rows of seats. Powell had named the place Sumner's Amphitheater after one of his men, Jack Sumner.[4] We landed on the opposite bank of the river, and as we prepared the camp, we felt like tiny actors playing before unseen giants. The wind died down during the evening, and with it went the only feeling of life in Desolation. I think we all had a compulsion to escape, but especially Tony. Looking up at the wall behind us (and knowing from the map that it was very narrow because the river ran directly behind as it completed the almost-circular curve), Tony announced that he wanted to climb to the ridge and look over at the river on the other side. Perhaps it was this urge to escape—escape to anyplace, but especially to get above, out of the oppression of the canyon, to get high up into open space—that made Tony insist that he could make it.

"It's harder than you think," I said, realizing that the narrow setbacks were higher than they looked and knowing, too, that Tony was far from an expert climber. "You can't make it, and I don't want you to try," I added.

"I tell you, I can make it up to the top," Tony insisted. He was determined he was going to climb. Don and I looked at each other. We both knew that it was dangerous. The situation was a tense one. Someone had to give way, apparently me. Perhaps a compromise would work.

"I'll tell you what, Tony," I said with forced enthusiasm, "try it to the third ledge—there by the big fallen slabs. I'll bet you'll find that's as far as you can go." Tony seemed satisfied, and off he went. Thick greasewood bushes surrounded our campsite, so it was a long time before we could see Tony again. Judging from the length of the time it took him to reach the talus slope, I realized that the canyon wall was farther away than I had judged, and so the ledges would be even higher and harder to climb. The immense scale of things had fooled me too.

Tony was easy to spot, for he had put on his red sweater when the air grew cool after the sun went behind the canyon wall. Had it not been for the sweater, he would have been completely lost to us in the maelstrom of jumbled rocks. We watched him climb agilely up the first obstacle. Then, with a little more difficulty, he made it to the second ledge. From where we were, we could see fairly easily the trail he had to take to reach the objective I had set for him. The ledge he was now on slanted and, at its high end, offered access to the ledge above it. The small red dot of Tony's sweater was moving slower now. I grabbed the field glasses to get a closer look. I could see that the route to the next ledge was fairly easy. I turned the glasses on Tony. He was being very careful, marking every footing, just as he had learned to do up on Harper's Corner. Then I looked up at the ledge above him, where I had told him to stop. I studied the fallen slabs carefully and saw that it would be difficult for even an experienced climber to scale them to reach the ledge above.

He was high now, far above us, and approaching the big slabs of rocks that precariously balanced on the ledge. I wondered whether Tony would heed my words, or whether he'd attempt to prove to us that he could make it to the top, which was still far above him. I am sure everyone else was wondering too, for silence fell on the camp as we watched him. I sensed that Tony felt he had to prove something to us, perform a brave act (if you can consider it brave rather than foolhardy; the two are closely allied) so he would shine in our eyes the way our boatmen did. There wasn't much bravado in being an assistant—carrying a camera around, packing and unpacking, handing me unexposed in place of exposed film, or building a fire. What's more, Tony had bungled a number of duties (especially supervising the coffeepot, which he still hadn't figured out how to set up so it didn't fall into the fire). After being this long on a voyage surrounded by heroic tales and in this canyon of Desolation, it seemed to all of us, not just to Tony, that some extra effort was required to prove there was such a thing as life, that we all existed and were useful for something. I felt Tony had chosen this moment to prove himself to us, to become brave and competent in our eyes. It was a mighty careless way to do it—risk his neck in this way—but in moments of stress, who knows what people choose to do?

Tony looked up at the great slabs of rock. They were twice his height. He put a hand up and grabbed one side. He tried several footholds. He looked above him again. Then he walked to the edge and looked down.

"Do you think he'll try?" Cid asked anxiously.

"I don't know," I answered. Then we heard a shout and saw Tony wave to us. We waved back to him and cheered as though we felt he had accomplished what he had set out to do. He started back down.

"Gee!" he remarked when he got back to camp. "You were right—I couldn't have made it higher. It's a lot harder than it looks from here—and bigger!"

"You were wonderful!" Cid said. To myself I thanked her for saying that. It was what Tony needed.

*Eighteen*

# DESOLATION CANYON

I slept fitfully, for Tony had pitched my tent on a slope, and my feet were higher than my head. My tent was made so that I could not turn around and sleep in the other direction. Because it was pitched among the thick greasewood—a scrubby, cedarlike bush—it would have been too much trouble to take it down and find a better spot. I had seldom asked Tony to "slave it" for me by pitching my tent, but I had gotten so far behind on my notes that I needed the extra time to bring them up-to-date. The more I rolled and tossed, the more annoyed I got with him as the night went on. *By now*, I thought, *he ought to have enough sense to lay a camp spot out on flat ground!* Funny how little annoyances can assume such huge proportions in the night.

In spite of the restlessness, I arose fresh. We were all up early and finished with breakfast before the sunshine hit the bottom of the canyon. We took particular care to lash the baggage tightly into the boat. There would be rapids today, and I think it was the prospect of white water again that spurred us to fast action.

For that short while during breakfast and breaking camp, we were not so depressed by our desolate surroundings. But as soon as we were on the river, rounding the lazy curve at the bottom of Sumner's Amphitheater and looking up at the barren cliffs, we felt again as though the eight of us were the only living things on the face of the Earth. Or were we on Earth at all? This place seemed no part of it. Desolation Canyon was a dismal abyss, the very end of all things. We had reached the limit of barren bleakness here, and as the boat carried us to the other side of the knife-edged precipice Tony had tried to climb the night before, I felt we were traveling on the River Styx. This canyon seemed to be that eternal place between Earth and the hereafter. Here time didn't tick away; we wouldn't hear a sound or feel anything; we would travel as lost souls—on and on—until the Day of Judgment, when the gates would open, and we'd be on our way again.

Perhaps this was the canyon of endurance, put here by the Indian god Ta-vwoats to test the psychological strength of the chief, Nu'-ma, to find if he was worthy of seeing heaven. Each canyon was a test of one kind or another. This one tested loneliness; it was a place so empty of all things that you could look straight into your soul, see the good and evil, and judge for yourself in the barrenness whether you were worthy of traveling nearer to the place you sought. And this place, along the wilderness river trail, was the right one to find that out. The upper canyons, above the Uinta Valley, were sort of pre-entrance exams: tests with enough bite to them—of danger, of endurance, of strength—to let you discover your capabilities. It was easy to call it quits after being tumbled out of the boiling waters of Split Mountain. From there on, it was not so easy to stop—and save face; from there on, you had to continue until you encountered defeat or success.

Surely the tests had begun. We had undergone the test of physical endurance as we passed through the hellish heat of the valley. This had been a test of our hides. Now, in Desolation, we were being tested on our insides, where our souls were hidden. Here we were not asking anything of each other but of ourselves.

I looked over at Doc Emsden. He was still suffering with his asthma and lay quite still in the boat, the towel wrapped around his head. Perhaps he should have had the pre-entrance exams. Jumping into the harder things might be too much for him. He had made an effort as our cook, but his struggle was almost painful to see. Bruce took over most of his duties, though Doc protested.

The river twisted and turned as it made its lonely way through the canyon. It was interesting to watch the marine compass that we now relied upon. It was easy to become lost here. You could mistake one bend for another on the map and run without warning into rapids, some of them nearly a mile long, with ratings of seven, eight, or nine. Don checked off each curve on the map as we went around. There were new vistas almost every moment, and each drifted out of sight before we could take a good look. Because we could not set our sights on one scene for long, we seemed to move quickly through the canyon.

Past Gold Hole we went, and Stampede Flat. The compass needle pointed north, and ahead was a large window in a narrow wall where the blue sky showed through. The needle pointed west, and ahead were three gaping side canyons, one of them called Rock House. It was well named, for it looked like a great city of apartment houses, all empty and deserted, half crumbled by eons of time. Then the river flowed south. Strange we should feel we were back on course again. How could we get off it? For a moment, we thought we were lost, for it was hard to judge the end of one curve and the beginning of another. It all looked simple on the map, but it was not that way on the river with the scale magnified 163,360 times! Small side canyons on the river appeared as big ones on the map.

"We better know where we are pretty quickly—there's a rapid around here someplace!" Don said anxiously. I checked the contours and the compass against the map the best I could. There were four side canyons on the left. We must be at mile point 313. I hoped so, and I was probably right, for soon the compass needle swung to the west.

"It's around the next bend!" I shouted to Don.

"Better land down there!" Don yelled back to Les and Bruce, and soon we pulled into shore to look over our eighty-eighth rapid. After checking it out, Don reported, "She's okay—fast water, so hang on! Life preservers everyone!"

In we plunged, and the surge of the big boat and the splashing waves gave new life to us all. It was Doc Emsden's first rapid, and it seemed to perk him up. We ran three more rapids in quick succession without inspection, except that Don stood up in the *No Name* to check them as we approached. In our depressed state, a little recklessness seemed in order. But as we approached the fourth one, Don yelled, "Land! Land!" and he pulled the towline free from the small boat and headed sharply to the left bank. Les and Bruce scrambled quickly for the oars. We knew it would be rough going because the roar filled the canyon. We all ran down the beach to take a look. Sure enough, this rapid would be tough, for several rocks as big as the *Brontosaur* lay midstream. Because they were staggered, it would be difficult to run.[1]

"Hang on hard, Doc," Bruce said as he climbed back into the big boat. "If we hit one of those rocks, you're liable to get bounced out. Maybe we better all have our feet ready to shove if we come too close."

Into the tongue of the rapid, we went with great speed, faster than we had experienced before. The boat didn't seem to make that hesitation we had felt in the big rapids upriver. We crashed and bounced through one wave after another. "Let 'er go with the current!" Bruce yelled to Les. We barely missed one big rock, then another. The boat bounced off the side of a big rock beneath the foaming river, and there were several others that we could feel scraping the rubber bottom as we went over them. I held my breath as the sound traveled the length of the boat. *The river*, I thought, *could be higher to ease our minds*. "Get ready to push!" Bruce yelled sharply. I quickly put down my camera, for I had been photographing the run. When I looked up, a massive wall of stone was passing close to my right shoulder. We had narrowly missed brushing against the cliff.

Then we were through the rapid, and the boat settled down in the quiet water below. The *Brontosaur* seemed to open out and relax, as though she had sat down and spread out her skirt after finishing a fast square dance.

"I hope there are more of those!" Cid said.

"Plenty more, Cid," Les answered. "This is only the beginning. The place is full of them. Say," he continued, "what time is it anyway? I'm hungry." Les was always hungry, but it really was time to stop and eat.

After lunch I suggested that Cid and Doc ride with Don in the *No Name* for a change. Cid enjoyed the small boat, but she seldom had a chance to ride in it. I wanted Don to know the way she was on the river better. I also wanted Don to observe Doc. I was worried about him. Besides, I had seen little of Fred; he rode with Don in the *No Name* nearly all the time now that I had abandoned it as a photographic vantage point. The *Brontosaur* was more stable, with less twisting and rolling.

No sooner had we gotten back on the river than a quick gust of wind lifted my cap and blew it into the water. "Stop the boat!" everyone seemed to yell to Don at the same time. He looked back in surprise. He must have thought someone had fallen overboard. Don cut the motor quickly while Bruce grabbed the oars and turned the *Brontosaur* broadside in the river. The current brought my cap to me. I felt foolish as I held it up to show Don what had caused all the excitement. He gave me a sarcastic smile. I felt more foolish a few minutes later when the wind grabbed my map,

The Eggert-Hatch Expedition stops for lunch in the shade of cottonwood trees.

with my ever-sharp pencil attached, and sent it into the river. We stopped again and waited for it to float to me. I grabbed it just in time, for in the silt-laden water, things floated only a short time before sinking to the bottom.

A gentle breeze continued to blow all afternoon, accompanied by occasional gusts that kept causing havoc. Don had brought along a very pretty pink-checked shirt that cheered the otherwise gloomy surroundings, and I thought he had picked an opportune time to wear it. During the afternoon, he stripped to the waist. In the middle of a small rapid, the wind picked the shirt up from the deck and dropped it into the river. Cid tried to grab it, but it got away and sank.

For a while things seemed settled, especially the wind, and we traveled a good distance without mishap. But suddenly and unexpectedly as we rounded a bend, a quick gust blew up, and I saw a white object fly past me. It was a sheet of Les's map set. The next thing I saw was Tony jumping headfirst into the river. I was stunned! Fred, hearing the big splash, looked around in utter surprise too. "Man overboard—man overboard," he shouted.

"Stop the motor—man in the river!" Bruce yelled to Don. He pulled the towline free and cut his motor. Tony was far behind now, retrieving Les's map. Bruce grabbed a line and threw it to him, and when Tony had hold of it, pulled him back to the boat. He looked like a well-soaked beaver as he came aboard. I was further shocked by the fact that he had jumped in with hat, dark glasses, wristwatch, hunting knife, and, worst of all, with his boots on.

I was enraged! "What the hell made you do that?!" I barked at him.

"Gosh, I don't know," he stammered. "Les lost some maps at Echo Park, and I thought . . ."

"You didn't think at all," I snapped, "or you wouldn't have jumped in. Didn't you notice how we picked up the other stuff a while ago? Did you know how deep it was?" I reminded him of Bruce's experience earlier in the day. Bruce had decided to go for a swim in the quiet water as the boats were traveling along, just as we had done during the heat in the Uinta Valley. Cautiously Bruce had measured the depth of the water with an oar. But between the time he measured and replaced the oar in the mount, the river became shallower, and when he jumped in, he hit the bottom hard. He bit his tongue severely and wrenched his neck. Bruce was lucky he didn't break it. In the light of this experience, Tony's act of recklessness seemed even worse.

"Guess it was kind of foolish," Tony said contritely.

"It sure was," Don piped in as he drew the *No Name* alongside the *Brontosaur.* "If you do anything like that again, I'll send you out one of these side canyons. You can kill yourself on your own then if you want to."

Tony remained quiet the rest of the day. I felt a little sorry that Don and I had jumped on him so hard. But this river was no place to act with abandon or lack of forethought. What if the river had been shallow? He might not have had the little luck Bruce had had. What if a big rapid had been directly ahead? We might not have had the time to stop for a rescue, for the current travels fast, and we had gone a half mile before we were able to get Tony back into the boat. Les's map was hardly worth risking a life for; we had other copies. I found it hard to forgive him. Yet who knows what someone will do on impulse? Perhaps, in the end, Tony had done us all a favor, for he made us even more aware of the dangerous possibilities that lie in wait for careless choices on this river.

We arrived at Rock Creek early in the afternoon.[2] It was, next to Carter Creek, our most attractive campsite so far. A grove of big cottonwoods grew by the mouth of the creek, and we made camp among them on the grass above the sandy shore. The mouth of the creek was full of smoothly rounded boulders over which the clear, cold water of the creek splashed. The sun shone brightly on the cliff opposite the camp, across the river. Up the side canyon cut by Rock Creek, we could see the high country, lined with pointed pines, and beyond, a blue mountain, topped with snow. I had an urge to climb and see the land above, but the thought of fresh trout for supper was more appealing.

Don and Les had already gone across the creek to a large field to hunt for grasshoppers. When Fred and I crossed the creek with our fishing tackle to join them, we were greeted by a strange sight. Don and Les were bending over with clubs in their hands, beating the ground. "What in the world are you two doing?" Fred asked.

"Pounding the earth to find out if there are any hollow spots! What do you think we're doing?" Don banged the ground with his club. "Got him!" he shouted. He leaned over and picked up a grasshopper.

"Isn't there an easier way?"

"Easiest way we've found. We tried every other method; we couldn't grab 'em with our hands; they were too quick for our caps, so now we're clubbin' 'em to death," Les explained.

"Grab a club if you want any fish!" Don laughed.

Fred and I got small tree branches and found them very effective. We must have been a strange sight there in the wild banging away at the ground. I was reminded of a scene from my childhood on the shore of Lake Erie, where we had a summer cottage. I hadn't thought of it in many years. The woman who lived in the only house near us—a quarter of a mile away—came rushing to my mother very early one morning, exclaiming in fright that a man was on the beach below her place, stabbing a long knife in the sand. He must be a murderer, the woman said, looking for a dead body! Mother grabbed the field glasses and the double-barreled shotgun at the same time and stood by the window watching as I clung to her skirts. Presently she saw the man get down on his knees and start digging in the sand. (I believe mother cocked the gun at that point.) Then he dragged a large burlap sack out of the hole. As mother pointed the gun, we saw the man open the sack, take out a whiskey bottle, and help himself to a drink. It was obvious now that this man was a bootlegger—for it was in the 1920s during Prohibition—and apparently the booze had been brought across the lake from Canada by boat earlier and buried there during a dark night. Now, nearly thirty years later in another wilderness, almost the same scene was taking place; the motive was different, but the actions were similar. I laughed out loud from the recollection. Fred looked up at me. I had to tell him the story that had surfaced in my memory.

I captured ten grasshoppers, Fred about the same, and off we went to the creek. Fred kept saying over and over, "Oh, just let me catch one trout—just one nice trout!" Soon we reached two productive-looking holes close together. Fred took one, I the other.

"Well, here's to Lady Luck," I said, spitting on the baited grasshopper—as I had seen my father do. That was sure to bring success! I had no more than gotten my line in the water when I heard Fred yell, "I got him! I got him!" I turned around to see Fred holding up a fourteen-inch trout. He looked exceedingly pleased.

"Well, you got your . . ." I was about to say "wish," but I didn't get it out; I had a strong strike and pulled my first fish, nearly as big as Fred's, out of the creek.

We figured we had frightened any others in those two holes, so we moved upcreek to the next ones. I heard Fred yell and knew he had caught another. So had I. Up the stream we worked, and I was surprised there were any trout biting in the holes we fished. Don, who was far above us, surely had dropped his hook in them too. I had six good-sized trout when I came to the most perfect-looking hole yet. It was very deep, and the water was blue-green in its innermost depths. Along one side was a big overhanging rock, and though I couldn't see, I knew a big fish must be lurking under it. On either side of the rock were small willows, and I knew that they would surely snag my hook. I was great for doing that, and I had already lost two hooks that way. This was my last one and my next-to-last grasshopper. Yet I had to stand behind the rock and drop my line over it into the creek if I didn't want to scare the big one lying in wait below—where I was sure he was. Carefully I lowered the line beyond my sight.

When I thought I had it down deep enough, I stood quietly waiting. Nothing happened. Slowly I began pulling the line up, being careful not to disturb the water too much. It had come only a short way when I felt a pull. *Damn it! Snagged my line*, I thought. But I quickly discovered otherwise, for no sooner had I felt the pull when my line suddenly ran out. The line gave a quick lurch, then rapidly crossed to the other side of the hole. I knew that I had a big trout with plenty of fight. *Oh, if only I can keep him on the hook!* I thought. Never had I felt such weight on the line. I let more line out and quickly made my way down to the bank of the creek. I could never pull him up over the rock. I lowered my pole close to the water, for I had no net. Then I saw his speckled body flash in the crystal-clear water. He was a big one, all right. He gave a pull, and I let out more line. Then I slowly drew it in.

The big fish flashed across the pool again, and my line swished sharply as it cut across the water's surface. Can't let him get under that rock now; he'll tangle the line for sure. In desperation I jerked the line. It was either he or I now. In I pulled, keeping the tip of the pole close to the water. He flashed before me again and broke the surface. *Oh no, you don't—you're not going to shake that hook!* I thought. I gave a hard pull, and he was still fighting as I landed him. Then the hook broke loose from his mouth. He fought furiously in the sand. I tried to grab him. My heart leapt when I saw how big and beautiful he was! And I felt his enormous strength in my hands as I tried to grab his slippery body. Three times I had hold of him, but each time he slipped out of my grip. Funny how a trout will fight its way back to water. It never flips or flops inland but always toward the water. Does the fish see it? Or is it instinct? Every flip brought him closer to his freedom.

I was on my hands and knees now, wrestling with him. At last I had a good hold, for by now he was covered with sand. Quickly, before he could get loose again, I hit his head on a rock and knocked him out.

We had had a fair fight. Yet I was sorry I had caught him; he was so beautiful. But the sporting instinct—or is the ancient urge to hunt and fish for food still carried in our blood?—made me continue the fight and win it.

Fred heard the struggle and shouts below from another spot where he was fishing. He came up to see what the trouble was. Standing on the opposite bank, he asked, "What was the fracas all about? Fall in?"

"This," I said, proudly holding up the trout, which I had just washed clean. His pink, yellow, and brown body glistened in the sun. He must have been a good nineteen inches long.

"Oh, my gosh! Oh, my gosh! What a beauty!" Fred exclaimed over and over.

"How's your luck? I asked.

"Five so far."

"This makes seven—I'm going to quit."

"I'll fish a bit upstream," Fred said, "and then I'll be back in a while."

I made my way downstream feeling very pleased with my catch. Never had I had such luck. Of course, in this vast wilderness the trout more than likely weren't wise to hooks and lines. Fishing required no artistry here. I had caught far more than I had expected—due not so much to my skill as a fisherman, but rather to the fishes' naivete about man and his traps.

I had one grasshopper left. *Why not just drag him along in the creek as you go?* I thought. I had let it down only a few feet in fast water, no longer serious about catching anything, when I got a strike. I said to myself, "Oh, no, not another one!" But I had another one, and I set off for camp with my catch strung on a willow branch.

What a fish fry we had that night! Fred came back with six. Perhaps he didn't believe in spitting on the bait, so it served him right! There was something strange about superstitions; sometimes they worked. Don came in with ten, and that made twenty-four trout in all: several rainbows, the rest browns or native cutthroats. I felt we were a gluttonous bunch, but we ate them all, and could have eaten more. The tang of the cedar and cottonwood we used for the fire gave them a taste of ambrosia fit for the gods! We ate by the light of our campfire, and in the last of the twilight, the new moon appeared in the western sky behind us, up the side canyon of Rock Creek.

*Nineteen*

# McPHERSON RANCH

Because we had made pigs of ourselves on trout the night before, I was sure we'd want a light breakfast. But not at all! Bruce had to make a second batch of his special pancakes—recipe: Bisquick (a couple of cups), powdered milk (a couple of shakes from the box if you had time and were in the mood), and river water well mixed with silt (enough to make the batter quite runny). Only Les did not appear for breakfast. As a matter of fact, he didn't show up at all. He stayed in the *Brontosaur.* I thought he was probably having one of his religious fast days. He seemed to have them every once in a while. But even then he had never before missed a drink of milk or hot cocoa in the morning. "Is he sick?" I asked Bruce.

"No—I guess not," Bruce answered vaguely.

Nor was Les on hand to load the boats. He remained quietly in the big boat, speaking to no one. I gave him a cursory look, but he seemed quite sullen. I thought it was better to leave him to himself; he'd come out of it. Had Don bawled him out for something I didn't know about? Perhaps, for Don had done that once before, and the result had been very much the same.

There was a big rapid immediately below Rock Creek. Don had looked it over while Bruce was frying his pancakes. As we shoved off, I noticed that Doc, who was feeling worse than ever, had no life preserver. He had left his in the *No Name* the day before. With a quick toss, Don threw it back to the big boat. The wind caught it, and away it went into the river. A life preserver was too important to lose, so Bruce jumped in after it. He got the preserver, but he lost his hat. There wasn't enough time to get both because the *Brontosaur* was heading into the rapid. I thought to myself, *This is going to be another day like yesterday!*

We got off to a bad start all right. The *Brontosaur* hit the rapid broadside and shipped a lot of water. I crossed my fingers and hoped we wouldn't continue to have bad luck all day.

We planned only a short run to the next clear water, and perhaps more trout, at Florence Creek, fifteen miles below Rock Creek and twelve rapids away. Only one rapid seemed bad enough to merit special caution: at mile point 342, where the water, according to a notation on our map, piled into the right cliff. I decided that I would walk around and photograph the boats going through. It was at this rapid that Powell and his boat, the *Emma Dean*, were upset due to lost oars.[1] The boat floundered and hit the rapid broadside. We were not the only ones to have troubles!

Our boats made it through the rapid in fine shape, although the big boat came within a hair's breadth of the cliff. Doc was kneeling in the front, ready to shove if necessary. They went through swiftly, and I had a hard time keeping them in the center of my camera viewfinder.

Don picked me up below in the *No Name*, and on we went; the *Brontosaur* was far ahead. We were alone, Don and I, so I had a chance to talk about Doc. "I'm really worried about him," I said. "He's a sick man."

"I know it. I hope he'll make it to Green River. We'll have to let him off there," Don answered.

"Gosh! I sure do hope he holds up! He doesn't ever get any better; matter of fact, he's far worse than he was at Ouray, where he assured me his asthma attack would be over in a day. Poor guy, he tries to pull his own weight too."

"Yeah, I know. Too bad—bet he'd be lots of fun if he felt better."

"I'm sure of it. He and Cid get along well together." Then I asked, "Did you bawl out Les for something?"

"No, why?" There was a suspicious tone in his voice.

"What's going on with him—one of his moody spells, do you think?" I asked.

"Maybe it's his toe. It hasn't gotten any better, I guess."

"I guess not—he limps as badly as he did at the start. We'd better get him to a clinic in Green River."

"I doubt if we can—he won't even let Doc Emsden look at it."

"It must be pretty horrible then. I can't get anything but an 'Oh, it'll be okay if I keep soaking it.' Well, Don, I won't let him go on until he has it tended to. We can't get through Cataract with him in that shape."

"Think we can get through without him?" Don asked.

"We'll have to—or get another boatman. That toe is going to get worse and worse if he doesn't take care of it, and you know that after Green River, there's nothing—no place to get a doctor until we end the trip."

"Les has been through Cataract, Charlie, and that would be a big help, you know."

"What help would a sick man be, Don? He'd be just another hazard."

"I doubt that we could get another boatman to replace him. Dad's got them all working on the Dinosaur trips."

"Well, start thinking about a solution. We're going to have to do something. We'll lose Doc Emsden too, at Green River—remember that. We're in pretty bad shape," I added after a long silence, during which I knew he was thinking that too. *I might as well say it out loud*, I thought. I suddenly felt depressed.

"We'll make out, Charlie. Les can still row, even with his bad leg," Don said. By this time, we had caught up with the *Brontosaur*. The others had waited on the bank above a big rapid. Don got out to look it over, so our conversation ended. I wasn't satisfied with Don's attitude. We'd have to hash it out later. I changed back to the big boat while Fred took my place in the *No Name*.

"Aren't you going to ride this one out in the big boat, Fred? You might get sopped in there!" I jibed.

"What! Ride the rapid in that big tub? Not me!"

"Well, don't get dumped—there's enough to worry about around here already!"

"Bet you get swamped before we do!" Fred said.

"Wanna bet? How much?" Les called to him. It was the first time I had heard him speak all day, and I was suddenly surprised to find Les in the boat. I had taken it for granted that he would be down looking over the rapid with Don and Bruce. This was odd, for surely he wasn't sick. I had seen him rowing like fury just a while ago.

"What are you doing here—no curiosity about what's ahead?"

"Oh, I thought I'd sit this one out, Charlie," he answered. I let it go at that.

We bounced through the big rapid and the next, and in our enthusiasm, we overshot our projected camp spot. Florence Creek appeared on the left, just ahead, with a big rapid immediately below it. We had planned to camp well above the creek.

"Pull in—pull into shore!" Don shouted. We hit the left bank, where there was hardly enough room to stand. The rock wall was directly beside us.

"We've got to go upstream for a suitable camp," Don announced. "It's the only place to camp—the cliff continues on like this below." We got back into the boats after studying the map. "Everybody row," Don ordered as he started the motor. Les and Bruce picked up the oars in the *Brontosaur*. Tony and I helped them pull. Fred towed us with the full power of the motor, and Don was at the oars in the *No Name*. Even with all that power, we made practically no progress against the current. Don decided that maybe the other side would be better, so we started straight across the river, hoping that the current there would be weaker. We found it just as strong. We were getting nowhere, simply holding our own against the river.

"Guess we'd better get out and push," Bruce suggested. Don kept the motor going while the rest of us, except Les and Cid, got out in waist-deep water and heaved. It was hard pushing, but we gained ground. We were almost directly across from the campsite Don had planned when we ran aground on a rocky shoal. Just as we did, we heard a big explosion in the bottom of the *Brontosaur*. Cid nearly jumped into the river. At first I thought it might be one of our insect bombs, but Bruce chuckled, "There goes Les's bug juice!" Sure enough, that must be it. Les kept his special brew of fruit juices in a gallon glass jug.

"Yeah, guess it was my juice," Les said. "It must have gotten too hot and blown up—it happens sometimes."

"Too hot, my eye!" I said. "We hit a rock, and that jug was on the bottom. Now we've got broken glass, and we'd better get it out in a hurry. Really, Les! You and your health and strength!" (Les thought this special concoction of juices—orange, lemon, papaya, apricot, and various others, including prune—did very special things for him, physically and mentally.)

"We can make it to the other side now," Don yelled. "Hop aboard." We crossed the river diagonally and landed on a wide, sandy beach strewn with driftwood. The wind blew up the fine sand, which blasted us. At first I thought it hardly worth the effort to land there.

Tony and Bruce got the lunch box out, and Cid volunteered to get lunch while we stripped down the *Brontosaur* so we could clear the bottom of broken glass. Everything had to come out of the boat. It was hard work to get the knots in the nylon straps loose and untie them. They had become almost welded together by the pulling and twisting action of the boat.

Doc Emsden was in the worst shape yet. As soon as he got off the boat, he sat on a driftwood log, struggling to breathe. His chest rose in great heaves. The cold water had done him in. He shouldn't have jumped in to help push. He should have let Les do that. I looked around and saw Les sitting on the side of the boat, one knee in his hand. The others were working with all their might to unload the boat before the glass cut into the sides. This was too much! It was all right for Les to be moody, but it was time he snapped out of it and went to work.

"Just what is the matter with you, Les? Why in the devil aren't you working too?" I demanded angrily.

"Well, Charlie, he said meekly, "as a matter of fact, I cracked my leg."

"You *WHAT?*"

"I cracked my leg."

"You mean you broke it?"

"Well, I don't know if it's broken or just cracked.

"When did you do it? Where?"

"Last night at Rock Creek."

"How?"

"I don't know. . . ."

"What do you mean you don't know? Surely you know how you did it!"

"I don't know—guess it just happened. I guess I may have put too much pressure on it shoving the boat around for the night."

"Well, for God's sake, let's get a splint on it right away!" I turned around to find the medical kit.

"He won't let us," Bruce broke into the conversation.

"You knew about this?" I asked.

"Yeah, Charlie—I wanted to splint it last night, but he wouldn't let me."

"It will be all right," Les interrupted.

"All *right?*" I exclaimed.

"I'll just sit here—I can row," he answered.

"For the next seven hundred miles?!" I asked incredulously. Then I turned to Don. "Why didn't someone tell me about this?"

"We didn't want to tell you—you've got enough to worry about," Don tried to explain. I knew he meant Doc Emsden. I was about to say that Doc could splint it—then I remembered that he had all he could do to breathe. I grabbed the medical kit and quickly opened it. "Do you want some of this Chlor-Trimeton, Doc? Would it help?" I asked.

"I may take some. I've run out of my capsules. But I'll be all right in a bit. Don't worry about me. I guess I shouldn't have gotten so wet. Tell Les to remain still; I'll take a look at his leg as soon as I catch my breath."

"I'm okay," Les called.

I thought to myself, *I've got to sit down.* I went up to Cid and sat beside her as she was opening a can of something. I had written her before the trip began that we could use her as ballast, psychological support, when the going got tough. She had written back that she had spent a good deal of her life being oil on troubled waters. Now in my moment of despair, I needed the kind of comfort only she among us could give. Like a child hiding under its mother's apron for protection, I sat beside her to receive the solace of her presence. "Les broke his leg," I said wearily.

"Yes, I know. Tony told me a few moments ago," she said quietly. "We'll get him to a hospital for an X-ray in Green River. Perhaps he just twisted it badly. An old break can hurt when you do that to it."

"I'm sorry I got so mad at him for not working," I confessed.

"He understands, I'm sure," she said.

We took everything out of the boat and helped Les to a log, where he sat while we hauled the *Brontosaur* on shore and turned her on her side to empty the water from the bottom. Then we carefully cleaned out all the broken glass. Luckily none had cut into the rubber, and there were no apparent leaks.

"Let's put her together later. I'm going fishing!" Don said.

"Hold on—I'll join you," I called. "Bring the camera, Tony. Let's get some pictures."

When we climbed up over the riverbank, we realized how far the valley opened out. We were still deep within canyon walls, but their lofty heights were spread nearly two miles apart. The wide valley contained gently rolling hills, and to the southeast, a high red butte rose like the massive ruin of a burned-out castle. We hiked a mile before we reached Florence Creek, which wound behind the hills. The creek was a disappointment, though. It was a small stream and choked with tumbleweeds. The only trout that we caught was too small, and we threw it back. We soon gave up and started back to camp, taking a shortcut over a hill spotted with sagebrush. It looked like a good place for rattlesnakes. "We better watch out through this," I said. "It looks snaky."

"Why, there's a snake now," Tony said nonchalantly, pointing to a wriggling object not five feet in front of us. I recognized it as a rattler immediately. So did Don. It was about three feet long and was well camouflaged by the brownish soil. A mad dash for rocks followed the shout, "Rattler!" We annihilated it with fury. When it was certainly dead, we bent over it, and with a stick, I pried open its mouth to see the fangs. Then I thought of the camera! What a perfect situation to get an exciting snake sequence! We had spotted it in time and could have had it under full control. We could have made it coil and strike. Don could have hammed it up a bit. I cursed myself for my twenty-twenty hindsight vision! The next snake might come under less-lucky circumstances for photographs. Furthermore, I was under control. Had I come upon a rattler under more surprising conditions, I might have run halfway across the country! I am more than willing to give any snake plenty of room, even a harmless garter snake. I'm scared to death of the darned things.

We had bashed the rattler so badly with rocks that it was hardly recognizable as a snake; it was certainly not a fit trophy to bring back to camp, and in the onslaught, the rocks had knocked off the rattles, and they got lost.

When we got back to camp, Bruce was full of excitement too. He and Fred had made an excursion to a deserted ranch near our camp.[2] We ought to see the place, he said. After supper Fred took Cid and me to it. Near the ranch we came upon a spring flowing from a cliff. It was almost hidden by a heavy cover of watercress. I have never seen such healthy watercress! The base of the plants was a good inch around, and the ground was literally covered with it. We ate several fresh sprigs before setting off through a deserted apple orchard to the ranch. Young apples were on the trees.

Beyond the orchard were several buildings, and to reach them, we had to cross a fence. The gate was there, but it was easier to step across the fallen, rusted barbed wire. The gate no longer worked. The first building we came to was a blacksmith's shop. The forge was there; harnesses and strips of leather hung from the rafters. Tools were all in place, ready to use. Everything had a thick layer of dust, and when I tugged on a strip of leather, it fell apart in my hand, rotten with age.

"Whoever it was left in a hurry. Didn't even bother to take anything," Fred exclaimed.

"Wonder why they left—Indian raid maybe?" I conjectured.

The next building we looked into was a small one-room cottage, heaped inside with rags. We poked among them, and Cid discovered a little girl's faded dress. It had been a gay print with puffed sleeves and ruffles around the edges. Then Cid found a small teddy bear and a doll with both arms missing. Scant bits of hair still clung to its china head, and its eyes still opened and closed. I felt suddenly sad and thought of my own children. Were they safe and sound now? What tragedy had befallen this child, this little girl, whose toys and pretty dress had been abandoned here? Surely, if they had planned to leave, they would not have left these things behind.

Then we saw what might have provided the answer. The main house stood solidly with all the rooms and walls and a chimney, but the roof was gone. The floors had caved in; the rain had rotted the beams. The walls were made of big stone blocks.

"The house burned. That's why they left—yet that wouldn't have hurried them away so fast," I said. "I wonder who they were?"

"He was a Scot—I know that," Cid remarked. She pointed out the peculiar way the surface of each block of stone had been chipped. Each one had been struck hundreds of times with a sharp object. Cid explained that this was to keep the stone from weathering. "It is exactly like the walls of Ardross Castle. Whoever built this house must have come from the north of Scotland," she said. "The family must have lived here around 1910 from the style of that little dress."[3]

Behind the house was the corral. Fred and I started for it. Cid was still examining the walls of the house, lingering there as though she had come upon something familiar in this strange world we were in. "Come along, Sherlock," Fred called to her.

One side of the corral was a natural rock ledge, and the other three sides were fenced with large poles, all in such good condition it could still have been used. The gate into the corral moved freely, in perfect balance, and it had that familiar squeak of wood rubbing against wood as we opened it. Along one side of the corral was another outbuilding—a hen house, we discovered when we entered. One huge log, more than two feet in diameter, had been split in half, and gouged out of it at equal distances were hollows, roosts where the hens had once sat hatching their eggs.

As we made our way back to camp, we stopped by the house again for another look. I noticed how, with such exacting care, each block had been precisely cut to fit the next. The cracks were hardly discernible. "This place was built with loving care," I said. "Only a disaster would take a man away from here."

"Gives you a queer feeling, doesn't it?" Fred asked.

"This is a lonely place," Cid answered quietly.

I couldn't get to sleep in spite of the fact that the night was cool and comfortable and the sand beneath me, soft. Cid's words, "This is a lonely place," kept ringing in my ears. I could hear them as plainly as if she were beside me repeating them over and over: "This is a lonely place . . . this is a lonely place . . . this is a lonely place." I got up and walked to the edge of the river. Even it, as the undercurrents rose and made soft swishes on the surface, seemed to moan in loneliness. The lapping of the water on the bank sounded like laughter, the mocking laughter of the Indian god Ta-vwoats. The canyon walls stood silent and awesome around me, holding me in. The more I looked at them, the closer to me they seemed to come. I could make out giant figures with folded arms and brooding faces in the rocks, and frolicking among them was a little girl in a pretty print dress with puffed sleeves.

I had a compulsion to go back to the ranch and pick up the teddy bear and the doll with no arms. It wasn't right for them to be abandoned. They seemed to cry out for the hand of a child to lead them out of this dismal place, where the pendulum of the timeless clock swung back and forth in silence.

A vision of my boys came to me. I could see them, hand in hand, walking through the meadow, lush with tall green grass, across from our house. They were smiling and gay, and little Seb was dragging a wooly teddy bear. I was homesick. I thought hard about them, hoping that the thoughts would soar over the canyon walls and across the great space that separated us. I told them I was all right. I tried to concentrate to get some vibration, some message, from them that they were well, that there were no broken bones, or cuts, or fevers. Three and nine were such perilous ages!

But these thoughts would never do! I had to pull myself together quickly lest I work myself into a real psychological stew! I went back to my tent and got my flashlight and maps. Walking down the beach to a place where my light wouldn't disturb anyone, I studied the maps. The below Florence Creek was rated a number six—pretty bad maybe; and the one two miles below it, a seven, with a notation: "Rocks!!! One entrance only."[4] Farther down was another, thirteen miles away. It was rated a number eight, and beside it in big print, the map said, "HAVE TO RUN—have to take a certain amount of heavy water." Then there was Coal Creek, and next, Poverty Canyon and Rattlesnake Creek—big rapids below each one! Well, it was better to get my mind on the dangers. These things meant daring and challenge. Better to dwell on these things than the thoughts of loneliness. Those thoughts were harder to combat. As I slipped back to my tent, I wondered if anyone had seen me wandering about this way—especially Les, bedded down in the *Brontosaur*.

*Twenty*

# GRAY CANYON AND GREEN RIVER, UTAH

I had not taken my cameras along on our visit to McPherson Ranch (we found the name on our map). It had been too late in the evening to get good pictures. I thought I would go back in the morning, but when the time came, I decided not to delay because of Les and Doc. The sooner we could get to Green River, the better. Besides, I didn't want to look on that deserted, lonely place again.

Many months later, while visiting Cid in Duxbury, I heard that she had found out more about the McPherson Ranch. In his account of his river run in 1911, Ellsworth Kolb had mentioned stopping off there and finding a Mr. McPherson, the owner, and two cowboys at work in the blacksmith shop. McPherson owned a large herd of thoroughbred cattle, and the men had just driven them down from the mountains to winter in the canyon valley. The house had burned down a short time before Kolb's visit, and the McPherson family had moved to Green River, Utah. Cid read the account aloud to me.

We ran Coal Creek Rapid; we had to run it, just as the map had noted, and we took plenty of heavy water. And we ran Poverty Creek Rapid and Rattlesnake in Gray Canyon—Gray Canyon now, for the wide valley of McPherson Ranch was the separation point between Desolation and Gray, though it all seemed like the same canyon to me.[1] There wasn't the marked difference the upper canyons had had. Below Coal Creek, the river jutted suddenly southwest, and after a mile, ran south again.

As we rounded this last bend, ahead of us, seeming to rise from the river, was the great tower of Gunnison Butte.[2] It marked the end of

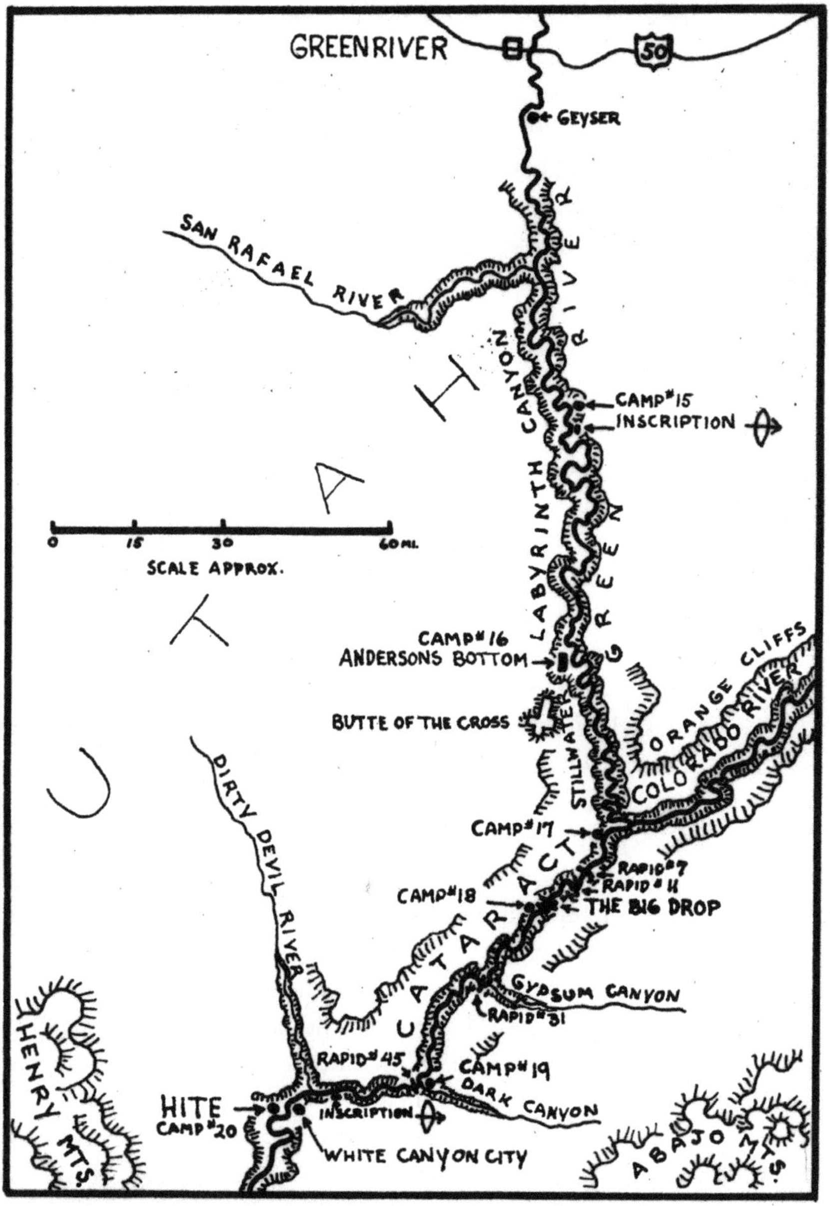


The third hand-drawn map made by Charles Eggert of the river trip, from the town of Green River, past the confluence with the Colorado River, and to the location of Hite, Utah.

the canyon and stood up like the Tower of Babel. As we came out of the canyon, we saw that it stood alone on the vast desert, which ran east and west for several hundred miles. Several miles separated the butte from the escarpment of the Book Cliffs, which were the end of the great risen plateau through which the Green River had cut Desolation and Gray Canyons. The butte was like some Romanesque cathedral and surrounding it, tier upon tier, were small chapels formed by talus and great stone buttresses. It was one of the most imposing sights along the river, and it remained long in view as the river twisted and turned, seemingly lost in the flats of the desert.

Very soon we saw signs of civilization. A road ran parallel to the river on the left, and we saw a shiny car pass by. It was a strange sight! Then a motorcycle roared past, leaving a long trail of dust behind. "There goes Les," Don yelled. We all roared. I think it was the first time we had joked since we had entered the portals of Desolation. Our laughter sounded good. We were relieved to get out of that chasm of barrenness. It had truly been a test of endurance.

Suddenly, we were aware that the current beneath us had stopped, and we were in dead water. "The spillway must be around here someplace," Don yelled over the roar of the engine.

"Good night, let's not go over it without looking," I yelled back. Don pulled us in to the left bank, and we all walked down to see. The river level had dropped, obviously, for the banks were soggy, and we had to step lively to keep from sinking in. Don had been keeping track of the water level, and up to now it had seemed neither to rise or fall but was holding its own. This encouraged us. Perhaps the men at the spillway had opened the gates recently; that would have caused the sudden drop.

Presently we came to a huge waterwheel nearly fifty feet in diameter. It was the largest in the world, we were told later. The wheel scooped up water in buckets attached to it. The buckets emptied into a trough, where the water was carried to the fields above the level of the river. The wheel was a clever contraption and reminded me of models of perpetual-motion machines I had seen on exhibit at the Chicago World's Fair.

Beyond the waterwheel, the spillway, or dam—to be exact—spread across the entire width of the river.[3] Here was the only man-made obstacle on the entire wilderness river trail of Major Powell from Green River, Wyoming, to the Virgin River and the Grand Wash Cliffs, where Lake

Mead now covers the channel the Colorado once cut through Iceberg and Boulder Canyons.

For the first time in many days, I remembered the other man-made obstacles scheduled to come in the future—Marble Gorge Dam, Glen, the one in Cataract called Dark Canyon Reservoir, Rattlesnake, where we had just passed, Desolation Dam above it, and Red Canyon and Flaming Gorge Dams—places where billions of tons of concrete would one day be poured, filling the canyon from wall to wall, flooding out all we had seen.[4] All these projects—and more—would be built if the reclamationists had their way. Reclamationists! Reclaiming what? Millions of acre-feet of water held back to feed a few thousand water-starved acres of land, where crops already producing a surplus could be raised! We felt we were enjoying the better kind of reclamation: refreshment of the soul. Ta-vwoats perhaps had the wiser plan. His canyon fed the spirit. There were the stony fields of New Hampshire, and the worn-out farms of New York, and the swamps of Louisiana. Why not reclaim them for hungry stomachs? Far cheaper too. These canyons were places to satisfy the hunger of the soul, to provide the intangible things humanity needs and seeks so desperately.

The spillway was approximately twenty-five-feet high, and it looked dangerous to go over it. Water flowed smoothly over the top and down the side. At the bottom was a big wave curling backward and beyond, many choppy waves.

I decided to take the risk of making movies from the *No Name* so I could get *Brontosaur* slithering down the spillway. Everything was carefully tied down, and the film box was rechecked to make sure it was fastened securely in case the boat flipped over. That would happen easily if the *Brontosaur* went down the drop sideways. I tied the cameras with nylon cord and fastened one end to the side of the boat. If we tipped over in the *No Name*, which was even more likely, we wouldn't lose them. If they did get dunked, we were about to come to Green River, and they could be cleaned, or even replaced, by sending to Salt Lake City for new ones. A shot of the *Brontosaur* coming down the 130-degree drop would be worth the risk—providing we in the *No Name* were still right side up to take pictures!

Don, Tony, and I started out first so we would be below. The *Brontosaur* was to follow close behind. As we approached the spillway, we saw seven or eight people standing along the bank, waiting to see us go over.

They waved and cheered. When we got to the edge, the drop seemed steeper than it had looked from shore. "Hold on—here we go!" Don shouted. Down the fall we slid. We crashed against the big wave at the bottom, and the spray covered us. Then we splashed through the next wave. When we got to the smaller riffles, I grabbed the camera from under the rubber tarp and aimed it at the *Brontosaur.* She was just approaching the drop. Down the spillway she poured, nose first, almost too politely. The fast water below the spillway carried us too far away to get good shots, but I was not unhappy; the *Brontosaur* had made it look too graceful! Her easy ride seemed like nothing at all. I was disappointed in the old girl. I had hoped she'd put on a good show, give us a big splash and a roll and a bounce at the bottom. Perhaps the old boat was getting too nonchalant about things now that she had run Disaster Falls, Hell's Half Mile, SOB, Rattlesnake, and the other 110 rapids. Well, there was Cataract ahead—the Big Drop, a number ten. Perhaps she'd show off then. (Little did I realize just how dramatic a performance lay ahead!)

It was twilight when the Green River bridge appeared, where US 50 crosses the river. Our maps were vague about exactly where the city was, but on the left bank, we could see the roof of a building above the thick growth of tamarisk. We pulled into the bank, and Tony and Don fought their way through the brush to find out where we were. It was nearly a half hour before they returned. Their shirts were ripped and their arms all scratched.

"Where have you been—in a fight?" Fred asked.

"These darned bushes—they're so thick we could hardly get through them," Tony answered.

"That's a roadside bar up there," Don reported. "The town is on the other side, down the road about a mile and a half. Guess we'd better cross the river and make camp over there."[5]

We crossed and stopped almost beneath the bridge. There was a flat place on the north side, and because we were so close to the road, we chose this as a convenient camp spot. Other people had certainly been here before us, and Tony remarked, "Our first sign of civilization—a garbage dump!" It was a filthy place, but I took no notice of it at the time. There were too many other problems that needed straightening out immediately. Don, Bruce, and I didn't stop to eat; we headed directly down the road toward town and the nearest telephone. It was dark now and very hot. The first gas station was closed, but another farther on was open, and we asked there about the town.

"Where is the hospital?" I asked the attendant.

He laughed. "Bub, the nearest hospital is at Grand Junction."

"How far is that?"

"About 110 miles."

"Is there a clinic in town—or a doctor we can get right away?"

"Nope, nothing like that here."

"Not even a doctor?" I asked in amazement.

"Nope—why? Someone hurt—had an accident?"

"We're on our way down the river, and we've got a man with a broken leg."

"Gosh!" he said, warming up a bit at last. Perhaps he had thought we were bums. We certainly looked it. "There's nothing in this town but a couple of bars and a post office," he continued. "And the train—you could get him out on the late train maybe. Too late for the bus."

"Do you have a phone?" Don asked.

"We'll call on my credit card," I explained quickly.

"Yep—right over there—help yourself."

"Better call Les's home—get his mother down here quickly," I told Don.

"Don't think he'd better go on, eh?"

"Of course not! Then call your dad for a replacement boatman."

Don called his dad in Vernal first. "Dad," I heard him shout into the phone, "Les broke his leg—we need another man." I could hardly hear the conversation over the racket that the gas station's air-compressor motor was making. It was in the same room with the phone. There was a long session of "uh-huhs" and "oh-is-that-so's," and then I heard him say, "Oh? Galloway? He'll be okay. How soon can he get here?" I held my breath. "Day after tomorrow? No sooner? Yeah, I get it—okay. Oh, we've done fine; nothing too bad yet—everyone is in good shape." *He has forgotten about Doc Emsden,* I said to myself. Don hung up.

"Well, what?" I asked.

"Al Galloway will come—he's on the river now.[6] He gets in late tomorrow. Dad thinks Al's wife can drive him and Les's mother down. Dad's going to call Al's wife now, and she'll call Mrs. Jones. I'm to call back tomorrow in case things don't work out."

So! Things would have to stand in suspended animation for two days! Nothing to do but sit it out. Well, I consoled myself, it could be worse. We might not have gotten a boatman at all—not that we couldn't do the rowing ourselves. But we needed that extra man—and another, if possible. Perhaps we could find a good man in Green River to join us.

I called home and found that everyone was well. I didn't mention our difficulties, and I was glad that the Ouray postman wasn't around to write a letter now! We each bought an ice cream cone and some cold soda to take back to the others. On the way back to the boats, I noticed a nice motel, and, remembering our terrible campsite, I told Cid and Fred about it when we got back. "It looks dark there now, but in the morning you could get rooms and ride out the duration," I suggested.

"We're okay," Fred said appreciatively. I felt he sympathized with me over the tough situation. Ever since discovering Les's broken leg, I had been worried that he and Cid might quit. The odds seemed so much against us. It would be a good time for them both to pull out. As paying passengers on the voyage, they certainly were under no obligation to stick with us.

I went to bed exceedingly comforted by the thought that Fred and Cid were willing to suffer the difficulties along with us. I planned in my mind the way the future would go. We'd get up early and do all the food buying to resupply ourselves. Bruce and I needed haircuts badly, and this was particularly noticeable with our crew cuts. Tony needed a haircut too, but it was hard to visualize him going to the barber. He should have gone to one even before we had started on the river! We'd fool around town a bit—perhaps have a cold, cold beer (that sounded so good!), and then it would be time to call Don's father again, and he'd tell us that Alden Galloway and Les's mother were on their way. They'd probably arrive late, but no matter; we'd be off day after tomorrow sometime, and that was the important thing. Doc could go back to Salt Lake City with Al's wife, too, and that would be that.

I was in for disappointment on every point! We had kept track of what date it was, but it had never occurred to us—nor did it seem necessary to know—what day it was. I discovered the day when I turned on the Zenith battery radio, which we hadn't played since Lodore Cabin. When I tuned in hoping to hear the news, the only loud station I could get came from Salt Lake City. The Mormon Tabernacle Choir was singing.

I recognized them immediately, for it is the one program I listen to faithfully. Not only are the choir and the organ beautiful to hear, but the provocative short talks that Richard Evans makes have always been a source of inspiration for me. This half hour of radio has been for many years my Sunday devotional; I find it far more inspiring than listening to some diehard fundamentalist preacher raving from the pulpit, bawling me out and assuming that I and everyone else in the congregation have done nothing all week except cavort with the devil!

"Is this Sunday?" I asked in complete horror.

"I don't know," Tony looked surprised.

"Let's see . . . what day was it when we left Jensen?" I asked. Taking that as a point of departure, we worked out a rough calendar and discovered that it was indeed Sunday—Sunday, June 26. There would be no grocery stores or barbershops open; we could do nothing but sit out the day!

US 50 was a roaring mass of traffic directly above our heads—mostly trucks, huge trucks from the uranium industry carrying supplies and equipment to and from the heart of uranium country around us. URANIUM ORE, DYNAMITE, or EXPLOSIVES said the signs printed in big letters on their sides.[7] The worst-looking of all were long thin big-wheeled tank trucks marked ACID. The very word is ominous enough, but to see it in big letters on these long black tanks whipping across the bridge at sixty miles an hour gave me a frightened feeling.

Since we were camped by the bridge, all the passersby saw us, and many people stopped to visit. Where had we come from? Where were we going? What was the idea? They all wanted to know. Some looked upon us with envy, others as though we were out of our minds. A reporter and photographer from the newly founded *Green River Journal* came down to interview us. We were told we'd be in the very first edition of the paper. The photographer lined us up on the *Brontosaur* around Les and took our picture.

Three men came and seemed more curious than the others. They hung around camp looking everything over with interest. I was suspicious of them at first, but they seemed genuinely interested in us. Uranium prospectors, they were, they said—they had claims all over southeastern Utah. It became obvious that they, like the Ouray postman, were looking for nothing more than the company of new people, and what better day than Sunday to pass the time this way. We got friendly enough to tell them about our troubles.

"You need a car," said the driver of the Mercury that had brought the three men down to our camp. Pointing to the car, he continued, "I won't be needing this one, so how about taking it while you're here? You'll need it to pick up supplies and get around."

"Oh, we can't do that," I said.

"Sure you can. Come along and drive us back to town. I have a Jeep I'll be using during the week. You can take this car to use as long as you need it. We call her the Uranium Cadillac." The two other men laughed with him. I was flabbergasted by such generosity and trust. What more convenient thing could we have than a car? It was a long, hot hike into town, and I had had visions of the hard work of hauling supplies and going back and forth for odds and ends. This was the West—and people were used to helping each other. Everyone out here needed help badly at one time or another, and they knew and appreciated what it meant, perhaps more than in any other part of the country.

I didn't even know the man's name, the owner of the Uranium Cadillac. It had slipped past me if we had ever even been introduced, so now I asked him, and I shall remember it the rest of my life. "Jim Nixon," he answered. I still carry his card in my wallet in hopes that someday I'll find some way to repay him for the help he gave us. I don't think I'll ever find anything to equal it.

Jim Nixon drove back into town with me, and I saw the place for the first time. There wasn't much to see! There were a bank and a post office on one corner and a row of stores running down a side street. That was about all. *A town on the skids*, I thought.

"We're going to build a whole new town across the bridge soon," Jim said. He must have recognized my disappointment about the place. "There's talk of building a uranium power plant and plans for a big refractor over there. The place will be jumping soon!" As he got out of the car, he said, "Say, since you-all are going down into that country, why don't you stop by here tonight? We'll show you 35mm color slides of it. We've taken a lot—from the ground and from planes."

This sounded like a wonderful idea, a fine way to spend an evening. In turn I invited them to have supper with us. They accepted gladly, and I seemed to see in their faces that same look of loneliness that had marked the face of our friend, the Ouray postman. That expression, it seems to me, comes from being too long under the big sky in wide-open, empty places. "About seven," I told him.

"We'll be there in the Jeep," Jim said with a smile. I thought he was the most generous man I had ever met.

As I drove back to camp, I gave the Uranium Cadillac a pat on its dashboard. "You wonderful thing!" I said out loud. Then I thought of Doc Emsden and the prospect of having to tell him he'd have to be leaving with Les. That would be hard to do. And there was Cid Sumner! What about her? This was the last stopping place before Cataract Canyon. I was sure Don wouldn't let her go on with us.

Suddenly, I wished we had never come to Green River, Utah! If there had been no Green River—if it had been erased from the face of the earth sometime between Jensen and now—there would be no decision to make, no question about taking Cid on from here. Of course she would go on, and she'd fight through it along with the rest of us. The responsibility would be great, yes; it would be harder and slower too—but we'd cope with it. But here, because we had a choice, a decision had to be made, and that was far harder.

We had no problems, no conflicts on the river. Civilization brought out all the superficial weak spots, traits people were most likely to judge others by. The really admirable things about us—the courage, compassion, strength—inner and outer—if we had them—were covered up in civilization as if by a coating of heavy oil.

When I arrived back at camp, the first thing Don said was, "I just heard of a guy with a plane who might fly our supplies into Hite. If we could do that, it would save us a lot of weight through Cataract. We've got too much stuff as it is without another couple hundred pounds of food."

"Where is he?" I asked.

"He runs a drugstore in town—Jim Hurst is his name. Maybe we can find him now and talk about it."

"Okay, let's go," I said. I purposely didn't ask anyone else to ride with us; I wanted to talk with Don alone.

"What about Cid? Are we going to take her on from here?" I asked as soon as we got off the embankment and on the highway.

"I won't risk taking her through Cataract," Don answered with finality.

"But I'd love her to be with us through Glen Canyon."

"Yeah, too bad. You know, she's worked out fine up to now, but if we run into trouble, it would be too risky for her."

We met Jim Hurst at his drugstore in Green River.[8] Yes, he'd fly our supplies in. Of course there was a landing field in Hite; uranium planes flew there all the time—it was the only way to get around. When would we get there? It didn't matter if we hadn't any idea. He'd just leave the stuff to be picked up, whenever that would be. Then the idea occurred to me.

"Is there any place you can land along the river just ahead of Cataract?" I asked.

"Sure—there's Anderson Bottom between Labyrinth and Stillwater Canyons. We've got an airstrip right by the river." Jim got out a map and showed us where it was.

"Could you pick up one of our passengers, Mrs. Sumner, on the way to Hite and fly her and the food there?" I asked.

"Guess so—it depends on how much your supplies weigh," Jim answered.

"This is our solution!" I said to Don. It sounded good to him. I felt happier as we returned to camp, yet there was still the difficult chore of telling Doc Emsden he'd have to leave. When we returned, I thought it best to get the thing over with right away, so I went straight to Doc and told him. He understood, though he was convinced his asthma would be gone soon. But we couldn't risk that possibility, I told him. Perhaps that is why I had a solemn look as I walked over to Cid. She knew what was coming when I sat down beside her. Don stood behind her.

"All right, come straight out with it. I know you had to argue with Les about his not going on, and it's been hard telling Doc he can't go—but me, I don't need soft-soaping. Just come out with it," Cid joked.

Don put his hands on her shoulders. "You're too precious to risk," he said.

"Don't you sugarcoat me, young man," she said.

"But we've arranged everything—we're going to fly you around Cataract," Don announced.

"*Fly* me around?" Cid asked in amazement. "In what kind of plane?"

"A very good one—the kind the uranium prospectors use," I said. "We've found a fellow named Jim Hurst who's going to fly our supplies into Hite, and he tells us he can pick you up at Anderson Bottom."

"Anderson Bottom! Where is that? Sounds like the tail end of the earth to me," Cid exclaimed.

"Well, it's an airfield beside the river—between Labyrinth and Stillwater Canyons. This way you'll only miss Stillwater and Cataract, and you'll be with us through Glen. You must see that one. It's just below Hite."

"I don't like the idea," Cid said. "I can't let you go through Cataract alone. You'll get reckless."

"No, we won't!" Don answered. "We won't because we've got to get through to meet you in Hite."

"What if you don't make it?" There was real concern in her voice. "And there I'll be in Hite—waiting and waiting like Penelope."

"We'll make it all right—don't you worry about that."

I sensed that Cid didn't like the solution very much. I was worried about it too. What if we didn't make it to Hite? And even if we did, Cid would be there for many long days, waiting in a godforsaken place in the middle of nowhere. We'd heard there was some kind of rooming house where she might stay, but we weren't sure. Perhaps she'd have to pitch her tent under a cottonwood tree and wait all alone beside the river. By flying her to the unknown, we were actually demanding far more courage of her than by taking her through Cataract. She was at least familiar with those dangers.

Jim Nixon and his two friends arrived on the dot of seven. We made a special effort cooking because of our guests. Don fried chickens and browned the sweet potatoes on the griddle. Cid made a salad of canned fruit, and we had a special treat of ice cream for dessert; also fresh milk, the first we had had. This was a real delight. Up to now we had had—those of us who could stand it—powdered milk, and Cid had remarked that if she ever had another daughter, she'd name her Starlac. "It is a beautiful name, in spite of the taste!" she said.

While we sat around the campfire, I got out the Hasselblad camera and took pictures. Between the fourth and fifth exposure, something happened, and the camera jammed. It had been behaving oddly for several days. No matter what I tried to do, the knobs were solidly stuck. *Well,* I thought, *I'll fix it in the morning.*

Our guests brought us a case of cold beer, which added to the festivities, and we all went down to the *Brontosaur* to toast Les and his future-healed bones. We tried to persuade him to drink a beer just this once—"now that your bug juice is gone," Bruce chuckled—but he wouldn't. Instead, he asked for a quart of milk and drank it down without stopping. "I'll be fine here—you all go see the pictures. Bruce brought me plenty of food, and I'll fall asleep quickly with such a full stomach," Les said.

"Won't you take a codeine pill to relieve the pain, Les?" I pleaded, offering one to him for the fourth time.

"There's no pain, Charlie, not if I don't move my leg. I feel fine."

"Well, I'll leave the pills with you just in case." I knew he wouldn't take them.

The remaining part of our evening at Jim Nixon's office was a delightful, yet frightening, one because of the pictures we saw. He showed us more than a hundred slides of the southwest country. The land looked even more fantastic than any we had seen: full of buttes, mesas, high plateaus, gullies, canyons, and mountains. It also looked lonesome and cruel, and I was profoundly concerned that we were about to go into a far vaster wilderness than we had yet seen. From Green River on, there was nothing but rocky desert: no roads, no people, no trees—except in the high mountains—for hundreds of square miles. We would be the only human beings in this vast nothingness, and buried deeply in the ghastly breach that cut through it—the river canyon—with no escape. Yet that was the only way to live and travel through this country. Here, surely, the Indian rumors were true. Here were the places where men had reached the brink of the canyon and vainly endeavored to reach the water below, only to perish with thirst while the river roared its mockery into their dying ears. We, at least, would be on that river. It was the only link between where we were and where we hoped to get. It would be suicide to try to cross that country on foot.

We felt uncomfortable cooped up in the small, smoke-filled room. It had been a long time since we had been so confined. I noticed Cid begin to nod after the first few sets of slides, and at one point, when Jim turned on the lights to find another box of pictures, Bruce gave a quick start and blinked his eyes as if he was wondering where he was. We were glad to get out into the open again, and even though the trucks marked EXPLOSIVES, GASOLINE, DYNAMITE, and ACID roared past, we all quickly fell asleep in spite of how miserable our campsite was.

The next morning, while Don and the others shopped, I remained in camp to fix the jammed camera. Nothing I did helped. I could not get the gears to mesh no matter what I did. The more I worked on it, the worse it got. I was distraught! I couldn't go on without this still camera. In desperation I decided I would make a quick trip to Salt Lake City to see if it could be repaired. This was a hard announcement to make, for it meant another day's delay. I began to think we'd never leave Green River!

When Don came back for lunch, I announced my decision. I knew he would be annoyed, and he was. This made me feel worse than ever. But this was a photographic expedition, after all, and there was no sense in making it without this important camera. "You'll just have to stick it out, that's all," I said in desperation. "I'll take the car and find out when the next train leaves."

"Wait, I'll come with you and get a haircut," Bruce shouted.

I discovered that I was too late for a train—it went in the early morning—but I could get a bus at seven o'clock that evening. So Bruce and I had plenty of time to get our haircuts.

I was amused by how fastidious Bruce was, how he wanted his crew cut just so. He continued to instruct the barber all the while he was cutting. This little streak of vanity surprised me. I didn't think he had it in him. It was surprising how little we really knew each other in spite of our close association on the river. I felt I ought to know Bruce better. The first impression I had had of him in Vernal had certainly changed! He had been overweight then, but now, with all the hard work, his six feet, two inches was a mass of muscle. He was a big fellow with exceedingly broad shoulders. By now he had acquired a golden tan, and his hair was light blond, bleached by the sun.

Bruce was as stalwart in character as he was physically handsome. He could be trusted; we could depend upon him in any situation. He was quick and seemed to have things figured out before they happened. Moreover, he didn't seem—and I was sure he wasn't—burdened by the problems of unrest and insecurity so many young people of his generation have. Perhaps I discovered in Bruce a truth: that it wasn't a complex background of big cities, of exposure to life in its many forms and diversities, that made a person mature, understanding, compassionate, and stable, but rather a simple life, directness, the absence of perplexing choices, and a strong moral background. Bruce always knew where he was going—on the river and, I am sure, through life. Looking over at him in the barber chair, I thought, *What a husband he's going to make for some lucky girl!*

Les's mother and his bride-to-be arrived while Bruce and I were still in town. They found us to say goodbye and good luck. Doc had finally won out and gotten a cast on Les's leg; Les was unable to make it up the bank from the boat and needed the cast to climb it.

I was sad to see Les go; his heart had been so set on this trip all the way down the river. He, like Don and I, had dreamed of making this journey one day. I felt cruel not to let him come, especially when he felt so sure he could make it. And as for Doc, I was sorry to see him go, too. Doc felt he had let us down, and he insisted that his asthma attack was about over. But it was impossible to take the risk. There would be risk enough with all of us healthy! I was disappointed, too, that our Englishman would not see the remaining canyons. But he had seen quite a lot, and certainly he had had an experience few Englishmen ever had in our country! "Besides," Cid said later, "he met Les, and I am sure there is no one like him in the entire United Kingdom."

We learned from Mrs. Jones that Alden Galloway was being driven down by his wife, Virginia, and would arrive in the evening. *Well,* I thought, *that point is settled too; our new boatman would be here waiting, and we could get off as soon as I returned from Salt Lake City.*

When we returned to camp, I asked Fred and Cid if they would like to come with me to Salt Lake City. Cid decided she would stick it out in camp, but I persuaded Fred to join me. He and I drove into town and ate at the café at the bus station to make sure we wouldn't miss the bus. It came on time, and we found ourselves headed for the big city. It struck me how strangely parallel our expedition was becoming to Powell's. He, too, had had to go out to Salt Lake for repairs—on his barometers.

It hadn't occurred to me how we were dressed until we got on the bus. What a sight we were to be going anyplace but on the river! Fred was a bit more respectable looking than I, for he had on street shoes and a clean pair of pants. I had just my moccasins, dungarees, and denim shirt, all ingrained with silt. *Well, so what?* I thought. There was nothing I could do about it; these were the only clothes I had. I was aware I'd have a hard time getting checks accepted in Salt Lake City. Perhaps my face was honest enough to carry me through. I hoped so! Aside from my telephone credit card and a couple of twenty-dollar traveler's checks, that was all I had to rely upon.

John Alden "Al" Galloway worked for Hatch for a few years running rivers and joined the Eggert-Hatch Expedition at Green River, Utah, to serve as a replacement boatman when Les Jones was forced to leave due to an injury.

We arrived in the big city after midnight and luckily found a room at the Little America Hotel in the middle of town. I was skeptical that they would let us into this place, one of the finest in the city, once they saw how we looked, so when I walked to the reception desk, I quickly explained that we were traveling down the river and had had an emergency. I needn't have said anything; it didn't matter. The advertising phrase some hotels and motels use, "Come as you are!" certainly applied here.

I took a long shower, the first in seventeen days. It was a physical delight! I looked forward to the foam-rubber mattress, but of all things, I had a hard time sleeping. Perhaps I had gotten used to what some wilderness enthusiasts claim is the world's best orthopedic mattress—the ground. (I never quite agreed!) And much to my chagrin, I woke at five o'clock. I was furious at myself. I was in the lap of luxury, where I could sleep late. Never had I appreciated comfort so much. Yet here I was, all twinkle eyed at that ungodly hour! I rolled over and tried to go back to sleep, but I couldn't.

Fred, much to my annoyance, had no such trouble. He was snoring away comfortably, and I had to shake him hard to awaken him for breakfast at seven. *Better able to adapt himself than I*, I thought.

I was glad my brains were ticking properly so early in the morning (for I don't usually work up to peak efficiency until around 10:30), and I felt smugly smart for going to Ecker's camera store immediately after I had left the Hasselblad with a camera-repair specialist.[9] I thought it highly unlikely the store would sell—or even have—one-third of a Hasselblad camera, the gearbox section, in case mine couldn't be fixed. I underestimated Ecker's! Not only did it carry these rather expensive cameras, but it also stocked single center sections. I gave the salesman the telephone number of my bank in the East and told him to call and verify my account in case I had to buy the new equipment.

Then I discovered that every noontime there is an organ recital at the Mormon Tabernacle. But I would have to hurry; the doors closed at 11:50, and it was now exactly 11:35! It seemed hopeless. Fred had said he was going to do some shopping while I was taking care of the camera. It seemed highly unlikely he'd be at the motel, but I grabbed a cab and told the driver to rush there. By happy coincidence, Fred was just coming out of the motel as we sped up to the curb. I yelled out of the window to him as we approached, "Fred! Hurry—jump in!" He looked at me bug-eyed.

"What's the matter—what's the matter now?" he asked excitedly as I pulled him in the door of the cab. He bounced into the seat as the cab took off with a fast U-turn.

"The Tabernacle organ—there's a recital at noon, and the doors close in just a couple of minutes!" I looked at my watch; it was 11:45! "We'll never make it!"

I had the money ready, with a generous tip for the fast service, and almost threw it at the cab driver as we jumped out and ran for the Tabernacle door, halfway across Temple Square. The doors were still open, and as we came to a quick stop and gathered our dignity, I noticed a sign which read, "Doors close at 12:10 sharp."

I was ashamed of my appearance in the Tabernacle, dressed as I was. Well, I consoled myself, the Mormon pioneers probably didn't have many hotsie-totsie clothes, either, and they came here. The ushers were very kind and seemed pleased that we had come, and only a few people gave us a disapproving look. *Tourists—easterners*, I thought.

I sat breathlessly awaiting the first notes from that great organ; I had waited a long time to hear a live performance. In the twenty minutes we sat in silence, I thought of the courageous Mormon pioneers on their hard, oft times tragic, and heroic migration across the Great Plains to this place. Even as they built their meager cabins to afford them a minimum shelter, they began erecting their Temple and Tabernacle. They were patient, inspired, and resourceful. The great blocks of granite they used for construction were cracked from the canyon walls by drilling holes and pouring water into them. When left overnight, the water froze and cracked the rock. There was neither dynamite nor pneumatic drills; this was the only way they had to mine the rock. The beams of the building we were in had been assembled with wooden pegs; there were no nails or bolts.

The organ was one of the first things they thought of. The great thirty-two-foot pipes weren't ordered and shipped out by freight. They were lovingly hand hewn from great trees brought down from high in the mountains. It was these pipes we heard first as they sounded the opening measures of Bach's great *Passacaglia* and Fugue in C Minor. With all these thoughts in mind, it was difficult to hold back the tears as Dr. Frank Asper began to play. It would be hard not to be moved by hearing that organ, hard not to visualize the pain and suffering and final reward of those valiant pioneers searching for the freedom to worship as they pleased.

I remembered one of the most moving experiences of my life, one that had occurred a few years earlier. We were making a trek down the valley of the Sweetwater River in Wyoming. We were nearing Devil's Gate when we came unexpectedly upon a small, tombstone-shaped monument sticking up from the sagebrush near the river. It had been put there in memory of a band of early Mormon pioneers, who, pushing handcarts all the way from the Missouri, had become trapped here and starved or froze to death in the bitter cold of a sudden blizzard.[10] Tears had come to my eyes then, too, as I stood there on a warmer day.

Now I thought of those men and women and children with their carts at that lonely spot by the Sweetwater as Dr. Asper played a concert version of the traditional Mormon hymn, "Come, Come, Ye Saints." As the sound of the organ soared in the vast space of the Tabernacle, I could almost hear those pioneers singing,

> No toil nor labor fear;
> But with joy wend your way.

Though hard to you this journey may appear,
Grace shall be as your day . . .
We'll find the place which God for us prepared,
Far away in the West,
Where none shall come to hurt or make afraid . . .
And should we die before our journey's through,
Happy day! All is well! . . .
But if our lives are spared again
To see the Saints their rest obtain,
O how we'll make this chorus swell—
All is well—all is well![11]

I wondered if they sang it then, as they lay huddled in the blowing snow, dying?

For our return to Green River, we found that the train was more convenient than the bus. The train departed at 5:30 and would get us to Green River near midnight. I was supposed to check back at the repair shop around four, so Fred and I had time to make a guided tour of Temple Square and do some souvenir shopping after the recital.

At four I returned to the repair shop and verified what I had surmised: the gearbox couldn't be fixed. "Someone tampered with it before I got it," the repair man said accusingly.

"Of course—I did!" I answered, explaining that under the circumstances, naturally I would try to fix it before running halfway across Utah to have it looked at! I put it back into a box, mailed it home, and bought a new section at Ecker's. The store had cleared my credit by phone; I wrote out my check and breathed a sigh. It could have turned out far more difficult.

I shall always remember our train back! It was the most beautiful one I've ever been on. It was a local, so I expected to find the same kind of equipment I have to endure on my trips to New York City from my house: old, dirty cars; no diner; uncomfortable seats; and the air-conditioning usually out of order. Not at all! This Denver and Rio Grande Western local had everything—including a vistadome car. Fred and I sat entranced in it while we wound through the high passes of the Wasatch Mountains. It was an experience comparable only to the river journey and incomparably more comfortable! We had ordered our dinner before going to the vistadome car, and it was awaiting us, steaming hot under silver covers, on our return to the diner. What service and superb food! We felt we were in the lap of luxury, and we had a good laugh at ourselves because of the way we were dressed.

In the middle of the night, our train pulled to a quiet stop at the Green River station. We felt very strange and lonely, getting off out here in this godforsaken spot. While riding trains, I have often watched people get off at places like this. I always wondered who they were, why they were getting off, and where they were going. Now here we were in the same situation, and I am sure the people on the train, going from one big city to another, must have wondered, too, about us as they watched us walk from under the lone light on the station platform and disappear into the dark.

We picked up the Uranium Cadillac and drove off to camp. When we got there, we found our situation had changed considerably. There were several cars parked and tents pitched near our spot. We found Don sleeping at the center of our camp. This was unusual, for he always sacked out away from things. We tried to pass him quietly, but he awoke with a start and jumped up. We quickly announced ourselves as he was grabbing a piece of lead pipe. There were "bums" in the other camp, Don explained, and our men were sleeping close to things, worried we might get robbed.

"Did Alden Galloway arrive?" I whispered.

"Yes, he's here," Don answered. He also told us that Don Harris, another river man, had passed through Green River on his way to Moab to take a party to Lee's Ferry.[12] Don said he had also talked with the USGS man and that both he and Harris had told him that the Colorado River was dropping fast, so if we expected to make Grand Canyon at all, we better get going. On that sour note, we went to our sleeping bags.

*Twenty-One*

# LABYRINTH AND STILLWATER CANYONS—CID LEAVES THE EXPEDITION

On the morning we shoved off from Green River, Jim Nixon said, "Charlie, you'd be foolish not to take a Geiger counter through Cataract Canyon. That is one place there has been no prospecting. None of us know what's down there, and you may run into a very good find."

The idea of prospecting for uranium did not particularly appeal to me, yet Jim knew what he was talking about. Perhaps the investment in a Geiger counter would be worthwhile; at least there would be no harm in taking one. When I proposed the idea, everyone was excited about the prospect of becoming millionaires! At the same time, we could foresee the possibility of disagreements unless we made some definite arrangements about how the millions would be distributed when we found our strike.

"Let's form a uranium company in which we'll share," I suggested. We all agreed and drew up a hastily scribbled document that we signed:

> June 29, 1955
>
> We the undersigned hereby agree to form the Hit-or-Miss Uranium Company in which we further agree to share and share alike in any and all expenses and in any and all profits resulting from this Company formation.

Alden seemed to be the most excited by the prospect of prospecting, so we named him chief prospector. As for Alden, I liked him from the moment I met him at breakfast. He seemed to have a keen sense of humor and had a decided twinkle in his eyes. We could stand some levity! Oftentimes we were far too serious. Alden already had a good start on a heavy black beard, and when he smiled through it, his white teeth glistened. And Al took particular care as we loaded the boats to see that our expedition flags were erected properly and Frog was safely tied to the prow of the *Brontosaur*. Bruce and I, up to now, had seemed to be the only ones who appreciated these minor details. Yet to me these were the symbols—the only remaining, tangible ones—of the journey, and perhaps Al realized this.

The last delay was a trip into town to buy a Geiger counter, a rock ax, and some claim-marker signs—the tools of our company—that were put into Al's care. Jim Nixon and his two companions gave us last-minute advice on prospecting and staking claims. "Good luck—and may you all be rich by the time you reach Hite!" Jim shouted as we set off once again on the river. Several cars tooted their horns as they passed over the Green River bridge and us, under it on our way into the great beyond.

We looked back upon the bridge with mixed feelings, for it would be our last night of civilization for the next five hundred miles—Hite counting as nothing from what we had heard. Ahead were our longest run, our greatest isolation, and our most dangerous canyon: Cataract. Only Al joked; the rest of us were solemn and glum. Cid, I felt, was unhappy over the prospect of flying and missing Cataract. Don was uneasy and unhappy about the three-day delay in Green River. His mind was on the report of water conditions on the Colorado. But mostly our gloom was caused by the memory of a remark a mysterious visitor had made to us in Green River. He was an old man, and he appeared suddenly in camp out of nowhere, like Elijah. "Not going on, are you?" he asked. "Not going to try Cataract? It's called 'the Graveyard,' you know." Yes, we knew; we'd read Clyde Eddy's account of going through there and knew that he had written that out of the fifty who had tried Cataract before him, twenty-nine had drowned. "The odds are higher now," our Elijah said, turning away after a penetrating look at our two boats and us.

"Who was that?" Cid asked.

"I don't know—some crackpot trying to scare us out," Tony answered.

"Probably one of those guys who had to climb out. He's just jealous of us," Don added. Yet we thought about him—and of the pictures we had seen at Jim Nixon's, and our maps, and the fifty-four rapids in thirty-nine miles of Cataract. "This will be the worst," Don's father had said, and he knew. I felt our old Elijah knew too—knew a lot more than we did.

The wind was against us the rest of the day, as though the Indian gods were resisting our progress. It was the strongest we'd yet experienced, and it blew fine sand off the plateau above, sandblasting us and making photography almost impossible. The wind and our slow progress added to our tension, for we had to make Anderson Bottom the following night if we were to meet Jim Hurst's plane the next morning.

For the first time, we had trouble finding a suitable campsite, but finally we stopped beneath a great overhanging cliff thirty-four miles below Green River. I built a fireplace out of shaley rocks I found around the campsite, and I believe that for the first time, our coffeepot did not dump into the fire. We had canned beef stew and a delicious salad of lettuce, peppers, carrots, and cucumbers, which Al concocted from our fresh supply. It was the hit of the evening. Don, Al, and Bruce picked a high flat ledge to camp on. The rest of us chose the bottomlands near the campfire, not being ambitious enough to lug our gear that high. Yet we admired the "eagle" boys for their perches.

It had been a horrible day in spite of the fact that we were finally on our way again. If there was an amusing event to remember, it was our experience at lunch. We had been told to be sure to see the geyser we'd pass five miles below Green River. We recognized the spot from the mineral deposits on the rock by the river. Above, a five-inch pipe protruded from a small pool of water. I rushed up, set up the cameras at an advantageous spot, and gave instructions about where everyone should go when the geyser went off—which it was supposed to do about every hour. The ground around the geyser, except for the small pool surrounding the pipe, was dry—indicating that it hadn't just gone off. Following some argument over whether we should move the heavy lunch box near the geyser—which meant a hard haul up the bank—or take a chance and eat in the boat, we lugged the box up to make sure we'd be on hand when the geyser went off. We had been told we'd have some warning from the sound of escaping carbon-dioxide gas, which would be emitted before the water exploded and rose 150 feet in the air.

It was a good thing we moved the lunch up! I was preparing a peanut butter sandwich, Fred was about to take a bite out of his, Don was stabbing a knife into the pickled pig's feet jar, and Cid was sprawled on the rock ledge. Suddenly, without any warning whatsoever, the geyser shot off a column of sparkling water straight into the sky. The column feathered out with the wind. It was quite a sight! We all scattered to the four corners of the area and couldn't grab our cameras fast enough. I managed to reach the movie cameras in time to get a few inches of exposure. Don was in the wrong position to get any picture at all, and by the time he got the geyser in the finder of his Rolleichord and had it focused, the performance was over. It stopped as quickly as it had begun! In the scuffle, Fred lost his sandwich, and Cid somehow ripped a huge hole in the seat of her trousers—how, we never found out. On our map the geyser had no name. Don gave it one: "F/4, 250th-of-a-second Geyser." "That's what it would take to photograph it!" he explained.[1]

We awoke the next morning with the thought of having to make fifty miles to Anderson Bottom. We had never attempted to travel so far on the river in one day! Jim Hurst had said he would check the river as he flew down to see where we were. If we were delayed, he would return and land the following morning instead. It was imperative, because of the canyon updrafts, for him to land and take off early in the morning—especially with the weight he would be carrying. We hoped to time it just right. We wanted to waste no time now that we knew the Colorado River was dropping. We had no extra time.

But soon after we left our campsite, we rounded a great bend in the river and before us, on the left canyon wall where there was a huge flat area, were carvings of the names and insignias of previous river parties.[2] The USGS survey party of 1915 had carved their names there; the Clyde Eddy party of 1927 was noted too, and the army engineers had put a huge replica of their castle-like insignia in the rock. Near it was carved a large and atrocious-looking angel, representing what or whom we didn't know. We decided we, too, must put a record of our passing. I do not approve of people carving names or defacing scenery (recall Mrs. Tietjen's name at Split Mountain Gorge), but in this case, the place was a traditional one—others had made it that—and traditionally, people have a compulsion to leave their mark on the landscape.

We spent nearly an hour with our rock ax, carving the lens and arrow of our expedition insignia into the sandstone, much to the annoyance of Don, who thought it was a foolish waste of time because we were of no

The crew carved the expedition's insignia in Labyrinth Canyon below the San Rafael River. Both Charles Eggert (left) and Don Hatch are shown standing in front of the carving.

particular historical significance. We were being presumptuous, he said. Nevertheless, Bruce and Al went to work with the ax after I first made an outline with a hard stone. It was hard work carving into the sandstone, but after it was done, we left the spot feeling that we had joined with other adventurous parties of the past, leaving our mark for adventurous parties of the future to see, though someday it would disappear, as Ashley's had, from rain and wind erosion, or else it might be buried beneath the surface of a reservoir.

The walls of Labyrinth Canyon grew higher and higher as we traveled on.[3] By afternoon they reached a thousand feet. Carved by nature from the canyon wall were many caves, amphitheaters, alcoves, and side canyons. But the space between the walls was wide, and we had a feeling of openness. The river was quiet and the current hardly noticeable. The riverbanks were lined with tamarisk and occasional cottonwood groves.

We were in butte country, and around and about us rose these tremendous rock monuments. As the sun went down, it threw red light upon them and made them even more dramatic. The land was like a

Labyrinth Canyon holds many prehistoric sites, including this remnant structure Tony Tuttle is checking out at Fort Bottom.

Buttes are common on this section of the Green River through Labyrinth Canyon.

scene from *Gotterdammerung*. The canyon walls reflected the pink sky of sunset, and, in turn, the river reflected the canyon and the buttes. It was one of the most beautiful times on the river.

The river in Labyrinth never ran a straight course, and rounding one of the bends, we suddenly noticed a man and woman with two small children standing on a ledge above the river. We were shocked to see people! It must be Anderson Bottom, we thought, though that place was supposed to be on the right side of the river. These people were on the left bank.

"Anderson Bottom? Is there a landing field here?" Don shouted to them. They stood gaping down upon us and did not answer. Perhaps they were as shocked to see us as we were at the sight of them. "Is there a landing field here?" Don shouted again, cupping his hands around his mouth.

"Yes—landing field back there," the woman yelled back, pointing behind her. From her accent, we gathered they must be Indians.

"Anderson Bottom?" Don asked.

"Down—down," the woman shouted, shaking her head as she pointed downstream.

"How far?" Don again yelled. "How many miles?" He received no answer, and we were by now well below them. We had lost our location on the river because of so many twists and turns, even though we had desperately tried to keep track of where we were. Our only landmark would be the Butte of the Cross.[4] When we could see it from the river, we would be near Anderson Bottom, Jim Hurst had said. I noticed also, from the geologic map we had bought in Green River, Utah, that we would be nearing the spot when the river began cutting into Navajo sandstone. Had we missed either sign?

As we were rounding another bend, worried that we might have overshot our destination, suddenly, like a great monster, the Navajo sandstone rose up from the river and before us, like a flaming cross rising above the purple horizon, stood the Butte of the Cross. A short distance below us, the right canyon wall receded, and we knew this must be the place. When we landed, Don jumped ashore and made his way through the thicket of tamarisk. When he returned, he said, "This must be it!"

"Could there be any question?" Cid turned to me and asked. "Surely you can't mistake a landing field!" I began to wonder, too, and went to look for myself. Getting through the tamarisk thicket was like fighting your way through thick mangroves. Scratched and bruised, I came to a clearing about half a mile wide and a mile long, covered sparsely with dried grass. Surrounding the area were low tan cliffs. Walking out into the flat field, I could just make out tracks on the ground that must come from airplane tires. *Yes*, I thought, *this must be Anderson Bottom.*[5]

A view from Gren River of Buttes of the Cross in Labyrinth.

"You'd think there would be a windsock or something," Tony said.

"Obviously there's not much choice in taking off or landing—so I suppose they don't bother," I observed.

We decided to camp beside the landing strip, and so it was necessary to hack a trail through the thicket to bring in our supplies. It was a hard job clearing the way. The brush and fallen limbs from the cottonwoods left hardly any room to swing an ax. It was pitch dark before we got our supper of spaghetti and meatballs on the fire. As we sat around the dying embers of the fire, we all were aware of something peculiar. "What makes it so eerie around here?" Cid asked.

"Aw, it's just you—thinking of that flight to Hite," Don chided.

"No—no, it isn't that. You just be quiet and listen," Cid said. We were still. "That's it!" Cid spoke again. "It's the quiet! Have you ever heard it so still?" We listened again. She was right; there wasn't a single sound to stir the air. "Why is it so quiet, I wonder?" Cid asked.

We thought for a moment, listening before we understood. There was no sound, no murmur from the river. Never before had we been so far away from it in our journey, or from other sounds—the babbling of the creeks, the roar of trucks at Jensen and Green River. The thicket of tamarisk insulated us from the sound of water. Here at Anderson Bottom, we all heard real silence for maybe the first time in our lives. There had been other quiet times on this journey, and in other places I had been, but always there was some sound, ever so slight, to give dimension to space. *Here there was nothing, and it was a weird feeling*, I thought as I strained my ears for some sound that I had gone deaf. "Well, let's sing or something," Tony suggested nervously. The absolute silence seemed unbearable.

Long into the night there was someone stirring in camp, and I realized that I was not the only one having trouble trying to get to sleep. But sleep finally took over, for the next thing I knew I awoke with a start at the sound of a roaring motor. It was a plane landing. I jumped out of my tent and saw a plane taxiing toward our camp. Don, Bruce, and Al broke out of their sleeping bags at the same time, and Fred popped his head out of his tent. We all expected this must be Jim Hurst to pick up Cid, though we hardly thought he'd arrive quite so early. The sky was just lighting up from the sun, which had not yet risen above the horizon. When the plane stopped in front of us, a man equipped with a backpack, a pick, and a canteen slung over his shoulder jumped out. As he did, the plane turned around and took off. The stranger gave the pilot a casual wave and turned toward us.

"What are you doing here?" he asked.

"We're on our way down the river. What are you doing here?"

"I'm on my way to do some prospecting," he answered as he turned away to head for the hills.

"Wait—wouldn't you like some coffee? It'll be ready in a minute."

"No thanks—I already had some. Good luck on the river," he said.

"Good luck to you," we answered emphatically. We were amazed and somewhat disillusioned by seeing this man. We thought we were the adventurers! We watched our sudden visitor become a tiny speck, then finally disappear into the hills. It was hard to believe that the whole incident had happened!

As soon as we started the breakfast fire, we heard another plane. It banked around the field and then came in determinedly, landed, and taxied up to us. Jim Hurst jumped out quickly, shouting, "Where's the lady? We've got to get going!"

"What's the rush?—Have some coffee," I said.

"Can't," Jim answered. "I've got to get this heavy load off the ground before it's too late. The sun will be hitting here in a minute, and the wind will start kicking up. If we're going, we've got to get up now."

We rushed Cid to the plane, and someone handed her a can with half an apricot left from supper in answer to her plea of wanting something in her stomach before flying off. She picked it out of the can with her fingers and stuffed it into her mouth as Jim boosted her into the plane seat. The door was slammed, and Jim revved the motor and taxied to the north end of the field. There he stopped and tested the motor. As he gunned the motor, dust blew up behind him in a cloud. Then the plane began to move, slowly at first, but faster and faster as it came down the field. It headed straight for a high cliff at the end of the field. *He'd better get off quickly if he's going to make it over the top*, I thought. I held my breath as the plane came closer and closer to the end of the field. Its tail was off the ground now, but the front wheels weren't. I heard Jim gun the motor harder in a last effort to make it off the ground. It roared, and I felt the vibration in the pit of my stomach. How different it was now from all the silence of an hour ago. Closer and closer to the cliff they came. *They'll never make it—why doesn't he cut the motor before it is too late?* I thought. But the wheels were finally off the ground, and in an instant Jim shot the plane nearly straight up, made a sharp bank at the same time, and barely missed the cliff. I let my breath out.

Then the plane went out of sight behind the tamarisk bushes and cottonwoods, and when Jim was safely above the canyon walls, he circled the field, dipped his wings, and set off to the south, and all was quiet again. We turned back to breakfast. Tony's meager fire had gone out, and so we had to start all over again. It was a lonesome breakfast without Cid, and we felt diminished without her. We were sorry we had sent her off. Yet under the conditions—the water dropping on the Colorado, the dangers and heavy risk of Cataract—the decision we had made seemed the right one.

About forty minutes later, just as we were about to break camp, we heard a plane. It was coming in for a landing, and as it taxied up to our campsite, we recognized Jim Hurst. "Just came back for that cup of coffee," he explained as he stepped from the plane. Jim said that the air was stable now, and without the heavy load, it was safe to land and take off. "Boy, we barely made it over that cliff!" he admitted. Then he told

Cid Ricketts was flown from Anderson Bottom to Hite, Utah, by pilot Jim Hurst to avoid taking her through the perils of Cataract Canyon. The plane is just taking off from Anderson Bottom in this photograph. Photograph courtesy of Hatch River Expedition Collection, Special Collections, J. Willard Marriott Library, University of Utah.

us he and Cid had had a fine time flying over Cataract. "I flew her low so she could see the rapids—some mighty big ones in there," he added. He went on to report that Cid had been deposited at the landing field and had gotten a ride into town in a truck. "She took the supplies with her. She'll make out okay—she's quite a woman!"

We made another pot of coffee, and when it was finished, Jim got up to go to his plane. "Well, anyone want to go back?—It'll be smoother than going on ahead," Jim said as he opened the door of the plane. We all laughed. His plane took off with far less effort than before; he was off the ground before he got halfway down the runway.

We broke camp and headed into Stillwater Canyon.[6] We had only thirty miles to go to the junction of the Colorado River, and anticipation mounted as we approached. The scenery became more dramatic, and the canyon walls rose to their greatest height, nearly twenty-four hundred feet above us. Finally, we rounded the last bend of Stillwater Canyon cautiously, our eyes and ears straining for the fearful sight and roaring sound of the mighty Colorado—the "world's most dangerous river."

We landed several hundred yards above the junction, wary of entering the big river without first looking it over. We had visions of being swept into a raging current that would carry us helplessly into Cataract Canyon, three miles below the junction. We jumped from the boats and ran across a mammoth sandbar to see the great river. Instead of the raging torrent we expected, we found a eunuch of a river! It was big, all right, but from shore it looked like a millpond. The mighty Colorado was insignificant compared to the Green: a lazy, placid stream. It seemed to us, from the geographical appearance, that it must be the Green that was the main stream. As a matter of fact, until the mapmakers changed it, the present Colorado from the junction upstream was called the Grand River. Only after the two rivers join does the mighty Colorado deserve that name.[7]

At 4:00 p.m., on July 1, we bade goodbye to the Green River. Cameras buzzed as the *Brontosaur* and the *No Name* rounded the bend and entered the mighty Colorado. The event marked the halfway point in our voyage. The boats looked small out in the middle of the river, buried deep between gaping canyon walls. Seeing them there, Tony and I got a better sense of scale and realized that this was indeed a big river! Below we could see the high walls of Cataract Canyon awaiting us.[8]

We sat for a while beside the boats after they landed to pick us up. Behind us were five hundred miles of canyon and some 126 major rapids. We had had 129 miles of quiet respite since the end of Gray Canyon: peaceful miles to prepare for what was ahead. Ahead? Another five hundred miles of canyons—Cataract, Glen, Marble, and Grand—and more rapids. In Cataract alone, there would be 54 of them and the biggest single drop in the whole river; in Grand, 365 rapids—one for every day of the year! We were by no means at the end of our experiences! Already we had come a long way and had lived, in those twenty days that were behind us, a life filled with adventure and beauty that very few ever get to experience. Yet there was more—much more—ahead of us.

"Let's go on to the first rapid," Don suggested. "I'm anxious to look a Cataract rapid over." So we went on for two and a half miles until we heard once more the roar of white water. In a way it sounded good; in another ominous, for it marked the beginning of the hardest single section of our journey, and the most dangerous. The roar came to our ears just as the rock strata changed from a golden hue to an ominous dark brown, and we knew this was the entrance to Cataract, a canyon that once entered would offer few exits—perhaps two in all its thirty-nine miles—and they were exits up to nowhere on the Great American Desert.

We pulled in to a sandbank and made our camp number seventeen. The rapid below was small compared to several others we had

Al Galloway holding a camera on a break from the river.

gone through in the upper canyons, but we decided not to risk going on. We had heard that often the canyon walls rose sheerly, and there might not be a campsite for miles. We would play it safe and stay here.

When we came ashore, we noticed beautiful and ephemeral lily-like flowers growing in the sand. They were the first flowers we had seen since the blooming cacti in the Uinta Valley. Such gentle flowers to be blossoming in this turbulent place! Fred got out his natural history guide and found that they were sacred datura, or jimsonweed.[9] After reading a description of them, we changed our minds about their gentleness. "All the parts of the plant are poisonous to cattle, sheep, horses, and human beings," it read. "Plant is sometimes grown as an ornamental, but it is dangerous." Singularly significant for it to be growing here, we thought, and it was a strange coincidence that we should see it for the first time as we entered Cataract Canyon! With sacred datura growing all around us, we had no choice but to make our beds in the midst of them and settle down for the night.

*Twenty-Two*

# CATARACT CANYON

As we left our campsite, the soaring walls of Cataract Canyon buried us deep in the earth. We ran the first rapid below our camp, and very soon we heard a roar that told us we were approaching a much bigger one. We landed on the right bank to inspect it. Above the rapid was a huge, quiet pool that encompassed the whole river. An almost straight line of boulders crossed the river, and the water plunged violently over them. Close to the left bank was an opening between two jagged rocks, where the water poured in a smooth, swift trough. The opening was just wide enough for the *Brontosaur* to fit through. Here Don chose to run.

"We'd better run the *Bronto* first," he said as he turned to the boats. "Then she'll be below to pick up in the *No Name* in case . . ."

Bruce and Al took their positions at the oars of the *Brontosaur*. Taking a deep breath, Bruce exclaimed in a determined tone," Well, here we go!" As we headed toward the rapid, Bruce ordered Al to help swing the *Brontosaur* around so that they faced the rapid as we entered. Because the river was quiet above the drop, it was easy to maneuver the big boat into position. Slowly we approached the tongue of the rapid. The men dipped their oars lightly into the water. As the nose of the boat went over the drop, the current grabbed its massive bulk. Into the foaming turmoil, we plunged full speed. There were immense kick-up waves at the bottom of the drop. Bruce and Al fought hard to avoid hitting them head on. Their oars dug in hard now. "Hard left, Al . . . pull! Pull!" Bruce shouted directions. We pitched at a sharp angle over the side of the first wave.

The expedition starts through the rapids of Cataract Canyon.

I was photographing the run, and luckily Tony grabbed me, or I would have been tossed off the platform on the boat.

The splashing wave caught the back of the *Brontosaur* and shoved her around. We were heading straight into the next mountain of water! We couldn't avoid it. The boatmen had all they could do, pulling with all their might, to keep the boat from veering broadside. Up and over the top of the big wave we went. As we came down the other side, I felt the drop in the pit of my stomach. "Keep her straight—keep her straight!" Bruce shouted almost hysterically. We were in the maelstrom of soaring waves now, and there was no escape. The only thing the men could do was keep the boat from turning broadside. Up and over we went, the big rubber boat undulating like a fast-moving caterpillar. Bruce and Al managed to keep the boat nosed into the waves even though many of their oar strokes missed the water because of the heaving of the craft as it was tossed about.

Don and Fred managed to escape the big waves completely in the *No Name.* As soon as they passed the rocks at the start of the run, Don gunned the motor and turned the boat sharply to the right to avoid them. He could do that with his small craft. They rode through with hardly a splash and missed all the fun. We got sopped!

I was watching the little boat follow when I heard Bruce shout suddenly, "Hey! There's another one! Watch out!" Just ahead we saw the river disappear, and beyond that, water was splashing high into the air. "We're too late—we've got to run her—hang on!" Bruce shouted excitedly.

The strong current carried us forward. There was nothing we could do but go with it. To attempt making it to shore now would make us hit the next rapid broadside. There wasn't time! Because we had missed the back eddy below the first rapid, there was no stopping now. With my cap, I waved a frantic warning to Don. He stood up in his boat to get a look at what was ahead. The last I saw of him, he had cut the motor and was grabbing the oars. We were in the rapid. Luckily it was mild with no jagged rocks sticking out of the water. But because we went through nearly sideways, we got another sopping. We headed for the bank as quickly as we could. Don and Fred followed closely behind, bouncing and splashing as they came.

"Let's not try *that* again!" Don said as he stepped from the boat with his maps in his hand. The three boatmen got together in a huddle to study what lay ahead. "No rating on the next one—we'd better walk down and take a look," Don said. The boatmen started to walk downstream.

"Mind if I go with them?" Tony asked me.

"Go ahead—see if we can walk around it. If so, I'll photograph from shore," I answered. I turned to Fred. "Well, here we are!" I said.

"Yep! Here we are," he answered. "Quite a canyon," he added as he strained his neck to look straight above him to the rim. The massive rocks looked frightening. Never had we been in a canyon where they were so disorganized. The other canyons had had a certain stability and order about them, but here the rocks were jagged, ripped, and torn. They seemed to hang in a delicate balance, waiting for the slightest jar to send them crashing into the river. "Hope that stuff stays up there until we get away from here," Fred commented.

"Scared?" I asked.

"No." He laughed. "But I'm prepared to be."

"Me too. Even Don is apprehensive about this canyon. We better not pull anymore stunts like that last one."

"No, you better not," Fred agreed. "Don wondered why you didn't land."

"I don't think we could have—the current carried us straight into it. Good thing it wasn't a bad one."

"Yep, good thing," Fred answered.

A view of the Colorado from the riverbank in Cataract Canyon. The *Brontosaurus* raft is running through one of the rapids.

The boatmen returned, and when they reached us, Don said, "The next one's nothing, but there's a ripsnorter coming up." He got into the *No Name* and started the motor, keeping it in neutral while Fred shoved off. Then Don headed the little boat upriver to await our start. "Don't forget to land below it," he shouted as we swung the boat around and headed downstream.

"Don't worry," Al yelled back. "Your ol' dad'll be headin' for terra firma in a hurry!"

The boatmen headed for the left bank before we were halfway through the rapid. They were taking no chances this time. Don followed closely behind. With the motor going full speed, he caught up and passed us in the rapid. He and Fred bounced over the waves and were splashed from every direction. Fred had a grin from ear to ear as he bailed the water from the boat.

Don landed the *No Name* and was stepping from the boat as we hit shore. After grabbing our towline and handing it to Tony when he got ashore, Don unstrapped his life preserver and threw it into the boat, glad to unburden himself of its bulky weight. He then picked up the plastic map case, and we gathered around to study and see what was ahead. Our fourth rapid was rated a number five, and from the contour lines on the map, we figured there would be a fifteen-foot drop in the rapid's quarter-mile length. Immediately beyond this rapid were two more, the first one of apparently no account, but the second again rated a number five. "May as well look over all three," Don suggested.

Tony and Fred stayed behind to hold the boats while the rest of us went down to inspect the rapids. When we reached a high place where we could look over all three, we were relieved to find that there were no protruding rocks or big holes.

When we got back to the boats, Don took another look at the map. "Land on the left side below the third one, you guys. There are two number sevens coming up below them. And don't miscount the rapids!"

With the thought of the two big ones below, we ran the three rapids as though they were riffles. "Sounds like we're about to come to a real rapeed!" Bruce shouted with enthusiasm as we landed again. The roar that came from downstream resounded from the canyon walls. There was a deafening boom to it that we hadn't heard before. The sound vibrated deep in my chest, and the whole canyon seemed to shake. Now, I felt, we were really in the canyon I had read about, had imagined in my nightmares before we started our expedition—the big canyon, the canyon of no escape, and the rapids that had to be run. I looked around me. There was no escape! We had just passed walls that soared straight up from either side of the river. There could be no going back. I looked up. There was no possible way to climb out. I felt suddenly hemmed in and momentarily frightened. We were trapped! Never before in our 509 miles of travel had I felt this way. "Let's look her over!" Don called, interrupting my grim thoughts.

It was a big rapid all right! Down its center were mountains of waves, twelve to fifteen feet high. The river was a mass of violent, splashing, foaming, silty water. Along the left, gigantic jagged boulders blocked the path. The boats certainly couldn't maneuver through them. "Looks like we can run the small boat on the other side," Don said. He climbed higher up the talus slope to get a better view. "Can't run the *Bronto* over there, though. Bruce, you'll have to take her down the center."

"Think she'll take those big waves?" Bruce questioned.

"Sure," Don asserted. "This one's sort of like Hell's Half Mile. She's going to do some plowing into the waves. Just try to keep her straight. You'll make it okay."

When we got back to the boats, we carefully tied everything securely. I made a second check of the latches on the film box and the nylon straps that held it down. Al and Bruce spread a tarp over the gear and crisscrossed ropes over it. Don tied a tarp tightly over the front end of the *No Name* to keep the water from pouring in and protect the duffle we carried there. I decided to cross the river with Don, taking all the cameras with me. His route with the small boat seemed safer. “Bet you’ll get a performance out of the ol’ *Bronto* in this one!” Don exclaimed over the roar of the motor as we crossed the river.

As soon as I got into position on the right bank, Don and I waved a signal for the *Brontosaur* to come through. Bruce, Al, and Tony had pulled the big boat upstream along the bank to give themselves more distance for their approach. On our signal, they headed her into the river and the rapid. Over the drop, the boat poured her great hulk. The *Brontosaur* was traveling faster than I had ever seen her go before. Up the first big wave, she climbed. Her nose shot into the air. Then she fell into the water with a big splash. The next wave poured almost completely over the boat as she dug into the river. The boat went up the next wave, and down, and into the next one, her blunt nose splitting the wave asunder. Over the next one, and the next, twisting and turning, pushing and splashing the river aside on her way. In the trough of the waves, she bent into a U and then, as she climbed up and over, she seemed to stretch out, curving into the opposite shape. The men pulled desperately to keep her straight. Oars seemed to fly this way and that, one time digging too deeply into the water, and another, thrashing the air above it. It was a great run, and we cheered when the boat finally settled down gently as she rode out the final surges of the river. My camera springs ran down just as the boatmen pulled into a back eddy. That would be about thirty-eight feet of film, which would mean one minute and a few seconds, I calculated. I could hardly believe the run had been so quick.

I returned to the *No Name*. “Going my way, bub?” I asked. “How about a ride?” I pointed my thumb downriver.

“Hop aboard and hang on! Give her a shove, Fred!” Don said. The motor on the small boat was propped out of the water, and Don was at the oars. He approached the rapid stern first so he could see ahead. Rowing upstream, he could slow down the speed and have extra leverage against the current to veer around the big rocks in his path. Don kept the boat close to shore, away from the huge breakers midstream. Even so, this would be a tough run: trying to avoid the rocks and deep holes behind them.

Bruce Lium, Al Galloway, and Tony Tuttle take a break after running a rapid in Cataract Canyon.

We banged against several, and the bounce of the rubber sent us careening about. Halfway through, we banged against one and were thrown into the current. Before Don could recover, we dropped over a submerged rock into a deep hole. The *No Name* hit with a hard bounce. I went over the back of the seat and landed in a foot of water in the bottom of the boat! I managed to hold the camera in the air. When he heard my yelp, Don reached around, grabbed the camera, and handed it to Fred. "Inflate your life preserver, Eggert, and you'll make it through!" Don shouted out of the corner of his mouth. We were bouncing and twisting so much that I couldn't recover my seat, so I rode the rest of the rapid in the bottom of the boat.

"Where's Charlie?" Bruce shouted as we approached the *Brontosaur.*

"Oh, he decided to swim through!" Don laughed as we pulled into shore.

I popped my head up from under the tarp. "Here I am—taking my bath," I said. Fred was already splitting his sides with laughter at my plight. He bent over, completely out of breath, tears streaming down his cheeks. Hearing Fred laugh was far funnier than my joke, and it was so contagious that we all began to roar—not at me but at Fred. There the six of us were, amid the most eerie and foreboding maelstrom of rocks and roaring rapids a person could imagine, all of us shaking with laughter! Humor was a relief, a solace, to our anxieties. Perhaps—perhaps the laughter wasn't so much from the silliness as from the letdown of tension over our first big trial in the rapids of Cataract Canyon.

Then came our next rapid, and our next, and still the next! Each one was bigger than the one before. The canyon walls reached awesome heights, and they came closer and closer together until they seemed almost to touch at the top. The roar of white water grew louder and louder as we progressed deeper and deeper into the canyon, as though a master hand were slowly turning up the volume. Fifty-four rapids in thirty-nine miles! These were the figures we remembered as we progressed on our way, almost yard by yard now instead of mile by mile.

Through another number seven, we went; then through the next, a number eight. Then a seven again, and another eight—with a notation on our map: "BIG!!" It was. They were all big, bigger than any before.

It was four o'clock when we came to mile point 13 in Cataract Canyon. The next drop was our fifteenth rapid and its rating, nine! We had already dropped 135 feet in those thirteen miles—a little more than ten feet per mile if you averaged it out. In the next half mile, we would drop twenty more feet. This was the biggest single drop on the entire river route from Green River, Wyoming, to Lake Mead.

We looked number fifteen over and decided that it could be run. We plotted our course through the inferno, put on our life jackets, and got into the boats. As at the earlier rapids, the river just above seemed to pause briefly to catch its breath before the plunge. Slowly we approached; then suddenly, the current grabbed us, and away we went, water splashing everywhere, the nose of the *Brontosaur* cutting first deeply into a twelve-foot wave, then rising high into the air, twisting and turning. Fear and elation at once gripped us. Down the center we went—Bruce shouting, "Hard left . . . pull hard . . . steady as she goes . . . watch that hole on the left . . . hard right, Al, pull, pull hard! . . . Oh, boy, we made it!" Then the frantic pull for shore as we rode out the tail waves.

Below rapid number fifteen, we stopped on the left bank to see what rapid number sixteen was like. This was the Big Drop—in fact as well as in name. Powell's account of it would rate it a number nine. Les Jones, who in August 1953 had gone through Cataract alone in a Penn Yan canoe had rated it a number nine. We rated it a number nine without qualification. Beside the rapid on our map was Les's notation: "The Big

Drop—worst in Cataract—shook my confidence." *If it shook Les's confidence, it must really be something!* I thought.

When we saw the rapid, we immediately discovered that it, plus the next one below, was all one big foaming maelstrom with a sharp drop right at the start that gave tremendous speed and force to the river. We could see that in higher water, the rapid we had just run would become part of it too, creating perhaps the biggest and longest rapid on the whole river. We were lucky there was a place to land between the two! At first look, we could tell that it would be impossible to run on the left. There were a number of deep drops behind the huge boulders submerged under the water. The holes were so big that the *Brontosaur* would be swamped, perhaps trapped, in them. And with the force of the current at the start, no maneuvering could avoid them. "We'll have to cross the river and try the other side. We sure can't run here!" Don exclaimed.

That was the first problem—to cross to the other side. The idea at first seemed fantastic. How could we do it with such a short distance between the two rapids and the current traveling so fast? "Batten down *everything!*" Don yelled over the roar in the canyon. We did, and while we worked, spray whipped up by the wind from the tossing waves soaked us. We dragged the boats upstream along the bank, stumbling, sliding, and falling over the wet boulders as we pulled. Slowly we pulled against the current until we reached rapid number fifteen. There we took turns resting and holding the boats against the choppy waves. "Well, let's go," Don ordered at last. We were ready to attempt it to the other side of the river, and God help us if we didn't make it before going over the brink of the Big Drop. The sun had already gone over the side of the canyon wall, and we were in shadow. Sopping wet, we were chilled to the marrow of our bones by the wind in the canyon twilight.

Don decided that we should try pulling the big boat with the *No Name*. The help of the motor seemed the only way the *Brontosaur* could possibly make it across. "I'll head my boat diagonally upstream into number fifteen while you fellows pull. Keep her nose upstream too; if you ever let her nose get caught in the current and she starts heading down, we're goners!" he shouted above the roar of the water. "And damned if I'm not going to cut you loose if you start going!" I had never heard Don so serious before—nor had I heard him swear. It made the situation seem even more crucial. He turned to me. "You better get your cameras and come with me. They will be safer here, and we don't want to lose them now!"

"That's okay with me," I answered.

"You'll have to row."

"That's okay too." I put the cameras in waterproof bags, tied them securely with nylon cord in the *No Name,* and sat down at the oars.

"Fred—you hold down the front end—we need weight there—and when we hit the other side, you get that rope snubbed around something as fast as you can," Don ordered.

"I'll be set," Fred answered.

"And be careful—don't slip, and don't jump too soon. Take your time—know where you're going before we hit. We'll probably hit hard and fast—and close to that drop. The important thing is to get your rope snubbed; the *Bronto* may start over the falls because we'll be so close." Then Don turned to Tony. "You stay in the *Brontosaur*—at the back end, there, with the line. As soon as the *Bronto* swings in, jump and hold her. You may have to jump into the water. Whatever you do, don't let go of that line—the water may be over your head. We'll try to make it so you can hit the shore, but that current is strong, and we can't putter around. Fred can't hold these two boats by himself."

"I'll jump right after Fred and hold too," I yelled.

"Okay, fine." Don turned to Al. "Is there another line we can throw from the front end?" Al found one, and it was tied on the ring beside the towline on the nose of the big boat. "You throw that one to Eggert as you come in," Don told Al.

"Okay, bub," Al answered. "Your ol' dad will be ready." By now Al was the only one with any sense of levity. He coiled the free end of the line and placed it on his seat.

Don started the motor. "Here we go! Don't let that towline snag in my prop!" he yelled to Tony. "Nose her out, Charlie—jump in, Fred!"

Fred jumped, I gave a hard pull on the right oar, back-watered with the left, and we headed upstream into the rapid we had run nearly an hour before. Don threw the motor into gear and opened the throttle. Tony gave a final shove to the *Brontosaur*, and we were off. I felt the big waves of the rapid bound against the nose of the little boat. Don let the towline out, and in a moment I felt the pull of the big boat behind. We'll never get her across in time, I thought.

I pulled with all my might. I could feel the muscles of my arms and back stretch and strain. I thought I would tear them from my bones. *Would I have the strength, the power, to help really?* I wondered. But the men in the big boat must have been pulling even harder, for I could feel the towline lag and tense, lag and tense, in rhythm with their rowing. Out of the corner of my eye, I could see rapid fifteen go farther and farther away from us. This must mean we were approaching the Big Drop. Would we make the other side in time? I glanced over my right shoulder. We were midway across. I looked around to the shore we were struggling to make. We were halfway. I pulled harder. We had to make it!

I gave Don a questioning look. He smiled broadly and made lunging motions with his shoulders, as though he were driving a horse into a gallop. He had one hand on the steering rod of the motor and the other on the emergency cord to cut the *Brontosaur* loose if necessary. Moments seemed like hours. Then I heard Don yell, "Fred! Get ready!" I could feel Fred get up from his huddled position in the front of the boat. I felt the boat lurch. Fred was jumping. Then we hit shore. Don cut the motor and jumped for my oars as I veered around to jump out. I leapt from the boat just as the *Brontosaur* began swinging around behind the *No Name.* Al dropped his oars, tossed the rope to me, and jumped into the river—grabbing the towline as he went. His weight nearly pulled me from the rocks into the river. Then there was a splash below. It was Tony. He was in the river up to his waist. He bounded to shore and pulled in the back end of the big boat. As the side of the *Brontosaur* hit the bank, Bruce jumped out and helped Tony hold. We had made it! And just in time. Directly below Tony was the Big Drop, waiting.

The sun's last rays were lighting the rim of the canyon when Don decided that we couldn't risk running the *Brontosaur* on the right side of the Big Drop either. It would be impossible to maneuver her into position for the falls so she would miss the main drop, which was almost as deep as the big boat was long. "We'll have to line her down," Don concluded. Line her down! How could we in this fast current! "It's the only chance we have," Don explained. "By holding her back, we may be able to scoot her alongside the hole before the current grabs her."

"Maybe we'd better camp here and do it in the morning," I suggested.

"No," Don answered. "I couldn't sleep with that problem staring at me all night. I'd rather do it now and get it over with."

"Whatever you want, Don," Bruce said, "only it's getting awfully late."

"Yeah, I know," Don considered. "No—let's get this one under our belts. We'll all rest better when it's behind us."

Tired as we were, Don, Al, Tony, and Fred grabbed the towlines and began letting the *Brontosaur* down the Big Drop. Bruce was in the big boat, guiding her around the rocks with an oar. I was ashore carrying the cameras around the rapid when it happened. Inch by inch, from rock to rock, the men were slowly lowering the boat over the falls when I heard a shout: "I can't hold her!" I looked up and saw Fred and Tony standing with a look of terror. Don was still running with the rope, but he could run no farther. There were rocks—big ones—and he could not leap across them. Al was in front of him, running, too, for he had the front line. The *Brontosaur*, with Bruce alone in her, was about to go over the drop. Al took a flying leap into the river. He grabbed the side of the boat and climbed in just as it went over. When the boat hit the bottom of the drop, I heard it crunch as it folded in the center. Bruce and Al, with his legs still half out of the boat, were holding on for dear life. Then the boat flattened out again as it poured down another fall and was lost in the waves that covered her completely. When next I saw the boat, Bruce and Al were still in her, scrambling for the oars. They fought desperately to recover themselves and the boat. Just in time they got her into an eddy at the end of the rapid and made it to shore.

Had it been a terrible error to attempt lining all that weight and holding the boat against the current? No one could answer. We had had no other choice but to try it that way. Lady Luck (or was it the favor of the Indian gods?) was with us. The *Brontosaur* made it, none of the gear was lost, and more important than anything else, both our boatmen were safe. We couldn't bring ourselves to think of what might have happened if Al had not made his heroic jump to the boat at that moment. There was no doubt that Bruce could not have recovered the *Brontosaur* alone. One man could not have stopped that boat from being dashed into the next—and probably the next—rapid. Luckily the *Brontosaur* had gone over nose first. Had she gone over sideways, she would have flipped for certain, and we would have lost everything. By lining we at least had prevented that.

Don was still white as a sheet as he brought the *No Name* through the rapid. This was a simpler matter; the small boat was able to squeeze between the boulders, close to shore, and avoid the big falls altogether. Even so, we held ropes attached to her—just in case.

We made camp just below the Big Drop among the huge boulders that lined the riverbank in a jumbled mass, rocks that had fallen from the canyon wall above us. The talus slope where we were forced to make camp (we had no other choice; this was where we had to stop—or run several more rapids in hopes of finding a better spot) slanted sharply up from the river to a height of a hundred feet. Above it rose the dark brown canyon wall. It went straight up three thousand feet! In the holocaust of jumbled rock, there was hardly room to lay out a sleeping bag. I managed to find a spot where I could squeeze my shape between two big rocks. Fred chose a spot below me with no more room than I had. Don and Bruce first intended to sleep on a narrow bank of sand no larger than their two sleeping bags. Then, on second thought, they decided that was no good. Suppose the river rose during the night?

The river rise during the night? That hadn't occurred to us until now! Then we remembered the night of horror that Clyde Eddy's party had at this very same spot on July 5, 1927. Our date was July 2, 1955. Eddy woke up to the sound of a thunderous rumble. The river was rising, and the violent force of the current was pushing the huge boulders under the water down the river. Though the stars were shining brightly where the men were, heavy rains had occurred far upstream, and the drainage of thousands of square miles was being narrowed and forced through Cataract. The river had no way to go but up. Eddy's feet were already in the river when he awoke because it happened so fast. The men moved their boats higher. Still the river rose and followed them up the talus slope, inch by inch, until they found themselves at the very top. They could go no farther. If the river had risen any higher, they would have had to take to their boats in the pitch-black night. "There was no rest for any of us until nearly morning, when, with our equipment hauled as high as we could get it, we stood in a group listening to the rush and sweep of the water which filled the canyon from wall to wall, a booming, roaring flood,"[1] Eddy wrote in his published account, *Down the World's Most Dangerous River*. The river had risen fifty feet before dawn came, and during the morning, it dropped back thirty feet. It was a flash flood of enormous proportions!

Bruce decided to sleep in the *Brontosaur* with Al. Don picked a spot just above the boats; he slept against a huge driftwood tree trunk that kept him from rolling down the slope. This was a safe place in case of an emergency. The boats were tied to the tree trunk.

I couldn't sleep that night. I rolled and tossed away the hours. First, I watched the shadow of the east canyon walls, which was cast by the full moon, recede down the west wall of the canyon. Then I watched the moon, which was so bright it helped keep me awake, rise and travel across the slit of sky above me. In its bluish light, the canyon looked four times higher. The walls seemed to lean in, and I remembered the rock slides we had seen along the way. Lying between the huge boulders made me feel even more insecure. To pass away the hours while the moon was over the canyon, I got out the binoculars and looked at it. I was amazed to discover how much detail I could see—craters, mountain ranges, the vast plateaus. When the moon went behind the canyon, I watched the shadow of the wall climb on the opposite side of the canyon. Then I saw dawn creep into the canyon. It was a beautiful sight, and I got up to get my camera and photograph it. Fred popped his head up. "What are you doing roaming around at this early hour, Eggert?" he whispered.

"Can't sleep—couldn't sleep all night!"

"I couldn't either. I'll make us some coffee." He crawled out of his sleeping bag. A "yoo-hoo" came from between the rocks below. It was Don.

"Doggone it, I couldn't sleep!" he complained.

"*You* couldn't?" Fred exclaimed.

"Nope—something about this place—it's real weird."

"I don't mind telling all of you," I admitted while we sat around the fire that Tony had built, "I was scared to death all night long."

"You needn't sound so exclusive," Al spoke up. "Your ol' dad was just as scared as you were. I'm still shaky, though ol' Sol is about to warm my achy bones."

"Were you scared, Fred?" I asked.

"You're darned right I was scared," he answered emphatically, "and I'll be mighty glad to get away from this place."

"Me too," Tony chimed in.

"I didn't feel very happy either," Bruce added with a frog in his throat, his eyes still puffy.

"Well," Don announced solemnly, "I was scared too. It's the first time I've ever felt that way in a canyon, and I've spent half my life in them.

It was those darned walls lit by that moon. I thought they were going to fall in on me any minute. It was doggone spooky."

"Well, I say, let's get the devil out of here—I'm anxious to find Mamma down in Hite!" Al said.

"Yeah! Let's get to Mamma—let's head for Cid!" Tony shouted.

"On to Cid Sumner and Hite!" Don announced, making a sweeping gesture with his arm toward the canyon below.

That was easier said than done; there were twenty-five more miles and thirty-seven more rapids in Cataract before then! We rode out ten rapids by the time we reached Gypsum Canyon Rapid.[2] There, a number seven with a ten-foot drop and fifteen-foot waves awaited us. We decided to have lunch above it. When we got the lunch box ashore, Bruce posed a question that took us aback. He asked, "I wonder whether those life jackets would really hold us up?"

"Well, old boy, it's about time we found out!" Al laughed.

"How about shooting this small rapid we just ran and find out?" Bruce suggested.

"I'll join you," Tony said. The three of them stripped bare—with the exception of Bruce, who still wore his red bandana around his head. They put on the life jackets and walked up the beach. They were a curious-looking sight dressed—or was it undressed—this way. Their mark of particular distinction (and a source of humor) was their bare white bottoms in contrast to the deep tans elsewhere. I was tempted to get a shot of them with the camera, but propriety got the better of me. How sorry I am that I didn't take that picture now! Perhaps it would not have been fitting subject matter for a film to be shown to the public, but what laughs we could have had privately!

But then—many things, many sights, many moments of high excitement and humor—had been and would continue to be missed by the camera. If there was one heartbreak from our canyon voyage, it was that: the things that the camera missed. One of these was Bruce, Tony, and Al prancing up the beach dressed only in life jackets.

I did get pictures of them floating through the small rapid. The jackets did indeed hold them up, and they bobbed through shouting and laughing merrily. They repeated the run several times before lunch.

At Gypsum Canyon, we had as incongruous a meal as anyone will ever have in the wilderness. "Let's break out that box of stuff Betty sent to us at Green River," I suggested. I opened it (for on the box, it read, "Open when you need something extra special—Your lovin' wife"). Inside, neatly packed in shredded paper were a jar of black caviar, a jar of pâté de foie gras, and a can of shrimp.

"Well! It's not quite Chambord's," I said to Fred, "but it's the closest thing to it here!" He greeted the remark with a roar of laughter. He inspired me to keep up the quipping. "Pâté de foie gras anyone?" I asked with an elegant air.

"What's that?" Al asked in disgust.

"Why, Alden, you uncouth man! If I have to be so common, it is goose livers, very fat goose, mind you, with truffles."

"And what exactly are truffles?"

"Don't you know what truffles are either? Truffles are a cross between wild mushrooms and wild potatoes. Pigs love them!"

"That's for me then. Idaho potatoes, did you say?" Al joked.

"Of course not! French potatoes. French mushrooms too. And now," I continued, "how about some fish eggs—I mean caviar? With a cracker, of course. James, James, where are the crackers?"

"Down in the bottom of the boat, sir, soggy with silt," Bruce chuckled.

"Rye crisp will do then—do we have any?"

"No," Don answered, "but we do have some nice, soggy graham crackers. Will they do? Or how about these cheezie crackers?"

"Say, how about that?" Al broke in. "How would that jar of cheese spread go with those fish eggs?"

"That plastic stuff?" Don asked. "Don't insult those baby fish that way!"

"Speaking of fish, will you have some crustaceans—in other words, shrimpses?" I asked.

"Oh—shrimp—I know what that is!" Don joked.

"Yeah." Al laughed, his white teeth shining behind his beard. "That's a cocktail—let's have some of that right now!" And so the banter continued.

So did the rapids that afternoon, and by evening we came to the one other big one that Don was worried about. Les had marked it a number eleven on our map. It was the only eleven in Ta-vwoats's forbidden passage until we hit Hance Rapid in Grand Canyon. There would be just one more—three in all—and that was Lava Falls, the last rapid on the river. There was just one thing worse than a number eleven rapid—a twelve, and a twelve rating meant something like Niagara Falls! What then would Dark Canyon Rapid, our first number eleven, be like? It was twilight—for twilight comes early in canyons thirty-five hundred feet deep—when we tied our boats to the driftwood on the left bank at the mouth of Dark Canyon Creek. Don couldn't wait to see it, and neither could the rest of us. Setting up camp could come later. We had to see what we were in for in the morning.

"This is the one I've been waiting for. Oh, boy!" Don exclaimed when we saw it.

At Dark Canyon, the mighty Colorado River and all its drainage from the western slope of the Rocky Mountains, and all the water that runs from the Upper Basin—from southern Wyoming and eastern Utah—drained by the Green River, flows around a sharp S curve where the river undercuts the canyon wall. Then it proceeds in a mass of foaming, crosscut waves around another big curve to the west. To make the situation worse, the stream that comes down the side canyon has carried enormous boulders into the main river.

When we looked at the havoc wrought by river and rock, we knew we would have a tough run. Furthermore, this rapid had to be run. Here was one of the few rapids on the entire trip that could not be walked around. On either side of the river, the canyon wall blocked passage at some point. It would be tricky, all right, but somehow it didn't seem as bad as the Big Drop. Les had noted on the map that there was a very bad drop at twelve thousand cubic feet per seconds of water. We had around sixteen thousand. Perhaps this accounted for the fact that Les's noted drop wasn't there. The water volume was great enough to smooth out the fall. Yet it was also great enough to make maneuvering the big boat around the S curve and then around the next curve without crashing into the sheer canyon walls very difficult. For with volume comes the momentum of a strong current.

Our boatmen stood for a long time studying the rapid. They threw several logs into the river to watch the natural course of the current as it caught them. "It's going to be a hard pull, Bruce," Don said. "Think you can make it?"

"That's for darned sure!" Bruce answered confidently. *Well, that's settled*, I thought, so I turned back to make camp.

We slept with the mighty roar of Dark Canyon Rapid vibrating the ground beneath us. But at this campsite, the side canyon gave us the

The crew at their Dark Canyon campsite eating breakfast.

feeling of space we had not had the night before, below the Big Drop. And we were on a sandy beach. All that helped, and it also helped to know that after this one, there were no more bad rapids in Cataract. We slept well.

"I didn't want to tell you last night," Al admitted at breakfast, "but I saw a hell of a big rattlesnake right up there in those rocks." He pointed to a spot not twenty feet away.

"Did you kill it?" I asked.

"Nope—that's the trouble. He sneaked between the rocks before I could grab his tail."

"Ohmygosh!" I exclaimed. "I'm glad you didn't tell me last night."

"Well, I figured you didn't want to know about it." Al laughed.

"Let's get out of here and run that rapid before that rattler gets hungry for some of your pancakes, Bruce," Don said.

I stayed behind to photograph the *Brontosaur*. We had landed well above the rapid, so the boatmen had plenty of room to get to the other side of the river to enter into it. The big boat went plunging and bounding through the big waves. They barely missed the cliff on the right. They were heading straight for it when they swung the boat around and passed a boat's length away from it. The men fought with all their might to stay on the right, fought against the current that was drawing them toward the

The two boats were tied up at the edge of the river while the crew carved the expedition's insignia at this location in Cataract Canyon.

sheer wall on the left where the river curved to the west. They managed to keep her in control, and we cheered them on as they bounced over the tail waves at the end of Dark Canyon Rapid.

Then Don, Fred, and I went through. We had an even easier time. With the power from the motor, we were able to take an opposite course and avoid the hazards the *Brontosaur* had had to face.

The rapid at Mille Crag Bend was our fifty-fourth and last in Cataract.[3] We gave a rousing cheer as we bounced merrily through. We took on extra—and unnecessary—splashes in celebration. We wanted to enjoy the thrill of white water to the fullest; there wouldn't be another rapid for 178 miles.

Below Mille Crag Bend, the canyon walls came so close together that I felt that I could just about touch either side with my fingertips. Powell named this section Narrow Canyon. Halfway through, on the left, we saw a large, flat area on the canyon wall where names were carved. We stopped to read them and found an almost complete record of the successful voyages through Cataract. Powell's name seemed to be the only one missing. This place had, through tradition, become the "official" registration place, so we again got out the rock ax and carved our insignia and the date—July 4, 1955.[4] It was the second time we had broken out a piece of our uranium company equipment; the first had been at the Dark Canyon campsite, where Al and Tony had done some minor—and unrewarding—searching with the Geiger counter. We had been too busy, too excited, too overwhelmed by Cataract. Until then, prospecting for uranium hadn't occurred to us.

Looking back at the insignia we had carved on the rock wall as we pulled out into the river, I felt we all had thankfulness to God in our hearts for having gotten through Cataract safely. We had had a far easier time than many whose names we saw carved on the canyon wall. We thought, too, of those others who had not gotten this far—to carve their names there!

*Twenty-Three*

# THE BIG DROPS, DARK CANYON RAPID, AND HITE

On our way down the river, we joked about putting signs in some of the more-desolate spots. We thought it would be mighty surprising for a future river expedition to come upon a sign along the riverbank reading SLOW DOWN—NAVAJO BLANKETS FOR SALE JUST AHEAD, or LAST GAS STATION FOR THE NEXT HUNDRED MILES, or CABLE CROSSING—DO NOT DRAG ANCHOR! About a mile above Hite, our proposed joke became even funnier. To our amazement, there on the bank was a big sign in red letters:

HITE, UTAH, AHEAD
CABLE CROSSING BELOW
ALL BOATS USE CAUTION!

We were coming into Hite, and the laugh was on us.[1] Our first thought—after stationing Fred as lookout for the cable crossing—was of Cid. Where would she be? How had she made out? Would she be there at all? We had estimated that it might take us ten days to get from Anderson Bottom through Cataract to Hite. We had made it in four. Perhaps Cid might have gone out, to a town somewhere, to wait out the time.

There was one way to find her if she was anywhere around—Tony's horn! He got it out, and as we floated down to the ferry, where the cable crossing was, he played "Dixie" as loud as he could. The sound filled the whole valley, which opened out from the river. But there was no sign of Cid—or of anyone else. Passing under the cable, we landed just below it on

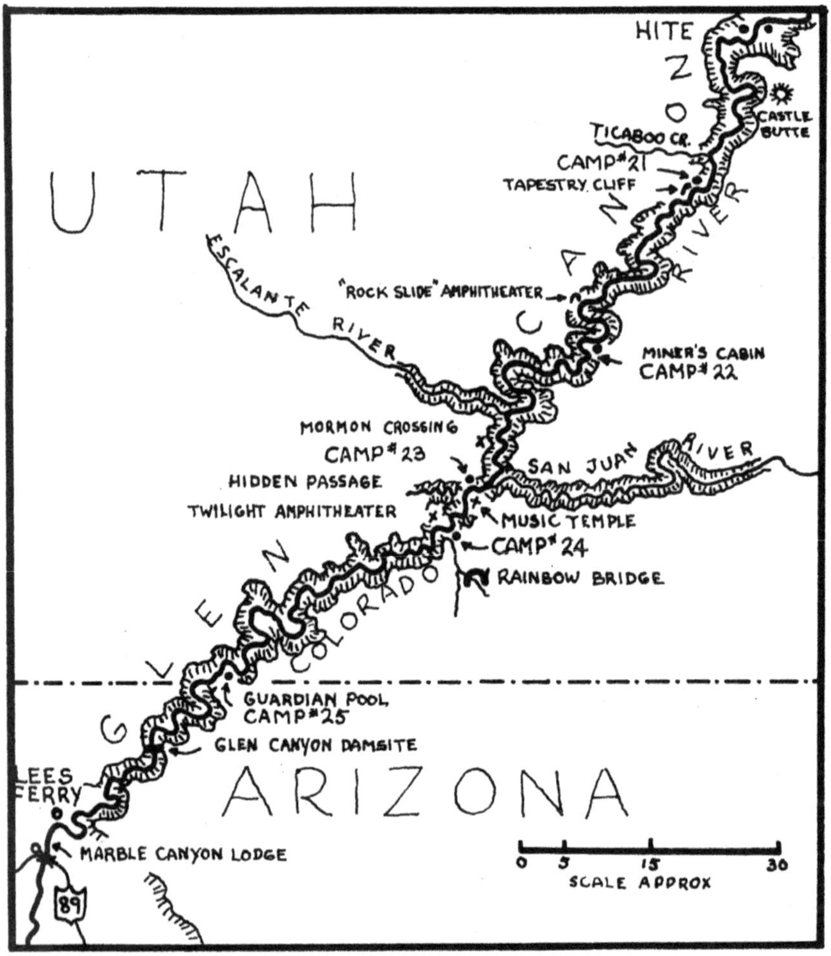


The last hand-drawn map made by Charles Eggert of the expedition's river trip between Hite and Lee's Ferry showing camps and important features.

the right side of the river. There was a house there, along with several small deserted cabins. Going to the house, we met Mr. Neilson, who operated the tumbledown ferry that took uranium trucks across the river. He had neither seen nor heard of a Mrs. Sumner, but he suggested that she might be across the river at a new settlement called White Canyon City. We had not heard of that place, and as we came down the river, we had missed seeing it because of a large island that separated it from us. White Canyon City was to the left of the island, a half mile or so upriver. Mr. Neilson offered to take us across the river on his ferry—at fifty cents apiece, which none of us had in cash anyway. We decided to go by boat, so we unloaded the *No Name* completely and took off. It would have been cheaper to take the ferry, what with all the gasoline we burned struggling to go upstream against the current. Tony blew "Dixie" on his horn all the way.

Soon we could make out a figure upstream in a white blouse waving frantically to us. We were no more than a few hundred yards away, but it took us nearly a half hour to reach her. In desperation Bruce, Al, and Tony jumped into the river and, up to their waists in water, pulled us to where Cid was. As we came ashore, she grabbed each one of us and gave us a big kiss and hug. "You made it! You made it!" she cried over and over. Then it occurred to her that we were all in the *No Name*. A look of horror came over her face. "The small boat! You lost the *Brontosaur* in Cataract!"

"Heavens, no!" Fred said. "It's at Hite."

"Hite? *This* is Hite!" Cid exclaimed.

"This is White Canyon." Fred laughed. "Hite is at the other end of the ferry."

"We came down the other side of the river, so we missed you," Tony said, "but we thought 'Dixie' would rouse you out of anywhere."

"I'd rattle my bones like castanets to that tune!" Cid answered. "Come, all of you—I know a place where I can treat you to a can of cold beer. I want to hear all about Cataract!"

"Leave it to Cid—she'll find a bar even out here in the desert!" Fred joked.

"Bet you've become the favorite barmaid in all of Utah by now," Don kidded her on our way to the "town," which we discovered was nothing more than a settlement of house trailers that itinerant uranium prospectors had brought in or rented. Cid had arranged to rent one and had lived in relative comfort during her stay. Comfort, that is, if you could ignore the heat and blowing sand. White Canyon City had just one thing to boast about: in the wooden building—the only permanent structure in this desolate, windblown spot—was the only bona fide bathroom within sixty miles.

"There's a restaurant here too," Cid said proudly, "and I want to throw a dinner party for all of you!" But after several very cold beers at the bar, Cid said with embarrassment that she'd have to withdraw her invitation: the dining room was closed. The cook, it seemed, had celebrated the Fourth of July a bit too vigorously and was in no condition to boil a pot of water, let alone cook a meal!

The Fourth of July! This called for further celebration. Half the town's population had gathered in the small bar and was overflowing into the grocery store area that adjoined it. Everyone had heard of us. We were the day's heroes, having made it through Cataract. We were congratulated by everyone.

I looked about me and was suddenly shocked to see Cid standing, laughing, and joking among the strangest assortment of men I have ever seen. Young men and old, they were—a motley, dungaree-clad bunch—and the contrast between her gentleness and their toughness made me ashamed that we had sent her off to live among this gang of barbarians. Only one or two had shaved within recent days. There were several with front teeth missing. Soap undoubtedly was the least sought-after item in the store. Their skins were tough as leather, weatherworn as the boots they wore, from the wind and baked by the hot sun under which they sought uranium and dreamed of becoming millionaires. Many had a strange, staring expression in their eyes, as though they had looked at infinity too long. The ones with happy looks were the drillers in their bowl-like, shockproof hats. They worked for someone else, drilling for the riches that probably weren't there. Little did they care; they got paid by the hour. Others were still searching in hopes of finding another Mi Vida, Charlie Steen's famous uranium mine. You could see it in their faces. Even when they peered down the hole in their beer cans, you could tell they were looking down an imaginary opening in the earth to a petrified river, a river of yellow-green uranium. They had looked so long for it that they could see nothing else.

I felt I had been transported back in time to the days of '49. This was nothing more than a mining camp, rough and tumble, temporary, full of adventurous, hopeful, disappointed men. The only thing missing were the tinkling piano and the buxom blonde singing risqué songs.

"What are you smiling at?" Cid asked.

"Oh, I just had a funny daydream of you among this gang. Why, you're the Mae West of White Canyon City! All you need is a bright red satin gown with long fringe!" I answered. "Weren't you frightened here?"

"Not at all! Why should I worry they'd harm me?" Cid answered. "After all, I think they admire all of us for what we are doing. We are just as adventurous as they are, risking just as much. The only difference is that we are seeking other kinds of riches."

Every so often a very loud explosion came from the direction of the river. It shook the building and rattled the bottles behind the bar. Cid explained that it was dynamite being detonated on the river. "They've been doing that for the past two days, celebrating the Fourth! They put a long fuse on a stick of dynamite and attach it to a board. Then they throw it into the river, and when it floats down, BOOM, off it goes! Oh, how I worried about that; I was sure the explosion would loosen the rocks in Cataract, and they'd come crashing down on you!"

There were still three cans of beer lined up in front of me when we decided we'd better get back to camp. We would cook our supper there. Even though Cid had all the supplies flown in by Jim Hurst with her, there were no pots or pans. As we left the building, I heard a young woman whom I had seen in the post office ask Cid, "Do you mean you are going off on that river with those wild men?"

"Yes, of course I am!" Cid replied.

"You are a brave woman, a very brave woman!" the other answered, shaking her head. Cid laughed.

We arrived at camp just as the sun went down. The seven of us in the small boat were packed in like sardines. I wondered why the navy had specified these as ten-man boats! The water came up to the top of the gunwales. It didn't occur to us that we might sink. If we had, it would have been the end of us all; we had nearly as much liquid inside us as the river did! Tony blew his horn all the way down while we shouted and sang to his tunes. Undoubtedly it was the gayest Fourth we had ever celebrated!

While we were eating, Bruce disappeared for a moment. He returned with a burlap sack in his hand. "Anyone want another beer?" he asked with a wink.

"Another beer!" Cid exclaimed. "I hope you didn't buy more after all that!"

"Course not," Bruce answered. "I collected all the extra cans we didn't drink at the bar."

"But they were open!" Cid exclaimed.

"I know—I plugged them up with—well, with toilet paper I had in my pocket," Bruce said shyly, with a blush on his face. Just then a tremendous boom came from the river close by. We nearly jumped out of our skins.

"Guess I'd better have one of those beers, Bruce," Al exclaimed. "My nerves need quieting."

The booming kept up all during supper. Then it stopped. We were in the peace and quiet we had come to know so well on the river. Gone were the sounds of rapids that had roared in our ears incessantly all through Cataract. And we knew we wouldn't hear that frightening sound again for the next 147 miles through Glen Canyon.

*Twenty-Four*

# HITE TO TICABOO CREEK

Ten miles below Hite, a butte rises from the river's edge like a great sentinel marking the entrance to Glen Canyon. Here, atop this massive rock pedestal, the mighty Indian god Ta-vwoats must have stood, arms outstretched, pointing the way to paradise, for if anywhere, that place was below—in Glen Canyon. We had heard that it was a land of enchantment, but little did we realize what exquisite and wondrous beauty was there until we saw it in the days that followed. If there is weeping to be done, cry over the destruction of this place! And destroyed it will be, for even as I write, blasts of dynamite are shaking its quiet solitude. Mighty earth movers are roaring over the desert above, and pneumatic drills are boring diversion tunnels in preparation for the Glen Canyon Dam.[1]

The reservoir will flood under hundreds of feet of water priceless gems of scenic wonder beyond comparison to anywhere else on the face of the earth. "The reservoir will make the beauty of Glen Canyon accessible to all," the propaganda tells us. We ask, "Is it not accessible now?" There is no canyon on the river more accessible than this one. What of the beauty will remain? It will all be at the bottom of a large lake! Everything will be flooded; there will be nothing to see except the desert country—the same kind of country you can see now from a car window on roads already built. I will wager that more lives will be lost in the construction of the dam than ever were lost on the river through here; already there have been four. If life and welfare—and beauty—be the concern, better that we should protect Glen Canyon, as we have protected other priceless scenic areas, as a national park: unimpaired, for the benefit and enjoyment of all the people. To these places, you and I—and our children's children—can come to look in wonder at our land, uncluttered by hot dog stands, road signs, and jive joints—or even the more handsome aspects of progress. Spread before us is the awesome wonder of natural things . . . the things God alone made.

Stand on the rim of the Canyon of the Yellowstone at dawn sometime and listen to the breeze singing in the pines around you. Smell their fragrance and the bright, crisp air, fresh from the Earth God created out of time and space. Feel on your face the spray sent up by the great Lower Falls. Look out across that chasm and up into the sky, still peppered with the brighter stars that outshine the dawn. Or some night lie at the mouth of a rock-carved amphitheater two or three times the size of anything you've ever been in. Look up the two-thousand-foot wall to the billion stars and listen to the murmuring of the river just beyond, still carving deeper the slot of canyon you're in. Think of nothing but what you see and feel and hear and smell. Something unexplainably wonderful will happen to you.

You won't find it in the stars, or in the sound of the wind or the river; nor is it hidden in a secret niche in an amphitheater. You can't say, "Well, here I am—what happens now?" You won't tingle all over or feel a chill go up your spine. Your hair won't suddenly stand on end. Very likely you won't be aware that something has happened to you right then—or within the next hour or next day, or perhaps for several years. But the farther away from the experience you get in time, the more aware you may become of the something that has happened to you . . . something you cannot buy or sell, share with another, learn from anyone, or read in a book. It just happens to you alone. The dictionary defines it as "serendipity"—finding something valuable that's not knowingly sought. Perhaps it is the discovery of intangibles we cannot describe.

You may find an immeasurable thrill in the sight and sound of the whirring generators at Hoover Dam (or at Glen Canyon Dam, when it is finished), or gasp at the unbelievable beauty of that sapphire gem in the desert called Lake Mead, and no doubt the supernatural and surrealistic reservoir that will be contained by the weirdly eroded hills and buttes of southern Utah and Glen Canyon Dam will stun your senses for a moment, but this is not serendipity. If the Glen Canyon reservoir ever fills and you go there to look, think a moment of those things beneath the surface of the water, the places of unmatched beauty—Music Temple, Twilight Amphitheater, Hidden Passage, Guardian Pool—where your chances of finding serendipity lie. The chances—those places to find it—are becoming fewer and fewer, and already the few remaining are becoming so crowded that it is even hard to see the scenery, let alone find nourishment for the soul. For all the acre-feet of water, for all the kilowatts of power, for all the crops to be grown, humanity can never be repaid for the loss of this priceless possession we will have destroyed beneath the surface of Glen Canyon reservoir.

There are a few years left to see these things on the bottom of Glen Canyon—for it takes a long time to build a dam. No longer can you boat through all of it, for the Bureau of Reclamation has forbidden passage beyond the dam site. Visit the places where you can still get by boat, and you may be blessed with serendipity.

It was two o'clock by the time we passed Castle Butte and stopped at Ticaboo Creek for lunch.[2] There was fresh water up the creek, our map informed us. There was a fresh-water well at Neilson's place in Hite, but he recommended not drinking from it. The river water, he said, was far more palatable—and, according to the Utah State Health Department, was pure. Neilson had sent a sample of river water to the department for analysis, and it had tested a minus-five bacteria count! This, I understand, is purer than New York City water! Nevertheless, the river water was heavily laden with silt, so Don decided he would hike up the creek and find the spring. He left as soon as he finished lunch. After nearly two hours had passed and Don still hadn't returned, we became concerned. It seemed unlikely he would be gone so long unless some disaster had occurred. Had a rattlesnake bitten him, and was he now lying and waiting for rescue? Or had a rock crashed down on him, knocking him out? Had he fallen and broken a leg? Could a cougar have attacked him? We knew they were around; we had seen their tracks.

All these things went through our minds as we waited for his return. Finally, we sent Bruce out to look for him. We waited. Bruce didn't return either. I got the revolver from the boat and strapped it around my waist. "Come on, Fred," I said. We left Tony and Al behind to guard Cid and the boats . . . against man, animal, reptile, and river.

There was enough sand in the creek bed to follow Bruce and Don's tracks for a long way. Eventually pebbles and rocks covered the ground,

Charles Eggert enjoying a happy moment on the river trip. Photograph courtesy of Sebastian Eggert.

Before Glen Canyon was dammed, the petroglyphs in Smith Fork Canyon were accessible from the river. Fred Wood is shown looking at the panel there.

and it was harder to trail them. We would lose the footprints, comb the area, then pick them up again in a patch of sand. Fred and I walked nearly two and a half miles—perhaps more, considering all the side trips and backtracking we did. We were in a narrow passage that the creek had cut when we heard, "Yoo-hoo—looking for someone?" It was Don, sitting on a rock above us. We were relieved to see him all in one piece.

"Are you all right?" I asked.

"Sure, why?" he answered.

"Where have you been so long?"

"Up farther—there's good water up there and a nice pool to cool you off."

"How far?"

"Oh, about a quarter of a mile. Bruce is up there now." I was too hot and too tired to admonish Don for being gone so long. Fred and I, both exhausted and wringing wet from perspiration, plodded up the creek bed. On and on we went. We would have turned back, but now we were in desperate need of a cool dip in that pool. Without it I was convinced I'd never make it back to the boats. After we had walked almost another mile, we met Bruce on his way back. "Good night! Where is that pool?" I asked.

"About a hundred yards more. It's not much, but it'll cool you off. There's a spring there too, with cold water." Bruce explained.

"Are you sure it isn't a mirage?" Fred asked.

"No—it's there." Bruce laughed.

Fred and I continued. Finally, we came to the pool. I was tempted to walk right into it, clothes and all, but I knew the shock of the cold water would probably fix me for good. First, we cooled our blood down by bathing our wrists and ankles. Then we stripped off our clothes and lay in the water. Nothing ever felt so good! We would have to satisfy our thirst here. In our anxiety, we had left camp without canteens—about as foolish a thing as anyone can do in desert county. Yet who thought we'd have to go so far?

The hike back to the boats seemed twice as far. The farther we went, the more I wondered why Don had come that distance for so little reason. Fresh water wasn't *that* important. The more I thought about it, the angrier I became. It wasn't like Don to delay us; he was the one who was always pressing us, wanting to get down the river because the water was dropping so fast. At Hite we had discovered that the river was lower than normal for this time of year. *Why should Don now take so much time just to get drinking water?* I wondered. He had never bothered to go so far for it at other times.

By the time we reached the boats, I was mad. I was convinced that Don had done an idiotic thing by delaying us for almost a half day. The fact that he had urged Fred and me on to that pool made me even angrier. The pool had refreshed us all right, but it was so much farther that we'd have been just as well off to return to the boats instead. Certainly we would have been no more exhausted; probably we'd have been less!

I greeted him with a frown and a complete lack of cordiality. As a matter of fact, I told him exactly how I felt about his running off. He resented my bawling him out, and we avoided speaking until we arrived at our campsite. Don was the first ashore, and I remarked sarcastically to him as he started up the bank that he'd better not disappear again. "We may just leave you behind this time," I added.

"If anyone is left behind, it'll be you!" he snarled back at me. I caught a glimpse of Cid looking at Fred with raised eyebrows.

Tension between us continued as we unloaded the boats. Everyone felt it. This wouldn't do; we couldn't go on this way. The situation would have to be ironed out, the air cleared, and good feelings restored. I knew that if they were not, the breach would grow wider. When all the duffle and camp supplies were ashore, I asked Don to join me alone in the boat. "Now," I said when we sat down, "this anger between us can't go on. Let's settle up right now. I got really mad at you for going off for so long. That was a very foolish thing to do."

"Well, I feel I have the liberty to do a little wandering on my own. That's my business," Don explained.

"Yes, but there are six other people to consider here. If you had planned to stay away so long, you should have told us. None of us is quite independent," I replied.

"I'll concede that," he said, "but I resent being jumped on or called an idiot!"

"I'm sorry for that, Don, but that was a hot hike you led us on. It was quite a jolt, too, to have you joke about it when we found you. We were damned worried about you. You'd be mad too," I answered.

"I didn't realize you'd be so worried about me."

"Of course we worried about you. After all, you never went off like that before. Can you imagine what went through our minds sitting there on the hot beach waiting and waiting for more than two hours?" I explained.

"I'm sorry."

"I'm sorry, too, that I got so mad."

"I don't blame you now that I look at it this way. Maybe we better make up."

"We *have* to make up, Don. Not only do I want to, but we are the leaders of this outfit, and above all, you and I have to get along. I'll grant you that we may get good and mad at each other at times. That's only normal—and it's okay—but if we're going to be successful, we have to swallow our pride and both be big enough to talk out our differences."

"Yeah, you're right. This expedition is bigger than both of us, Eggert."

"Now then, Hatch, let's get back to running this expedition. What's on the docket for tomorrow's run?" He and I turned to the maps and together we worked out our schedule. We returned to camp arm in arm. We arrived just in time for Bruce's call, "Supper's ready! Come and get it!"

Now that the tension had dissipated, I was able to notice the setting we were in. What a campsite we had picked! We were on a high place above the river, a rock-ledged terrace. The rock was a series of mammoth steps rising from the water. Each level was flat and large enough to accommodate all of us. We had made our campfire in one of the numerous potholes eroded in the rock. The one we picked made a perfect fireplace. The sky above was ablaze with sunset, which gave the canyon a rosy hue. Beyond us the river made a lazy curve to the left, and there the canyon wall rose straight up a thousand feet. For a mile and a half, the cliff followed the river before the wall fell back again. The face of the cliff was stained with long black streamers from water that cascaded over the rim in wet weather. It was an imposing sight: a gigantic backdrop—a hanging tapestry—behind us.

While we were having dessert, wildlife descended upon us. As I lifted my spoonful of canned pear to my mouth, I saw something move out of the corner of my eye—something very small. I took a better look. Lined up along a small ledge beside me was a group of field mice, looking down on our food. "Hey! Look, we've got visitors!" I exclaimed, not thinking what Cid's reaction might be. Just then from above, one of our empty tin cans came bouncing down the rock with two mice chasing it. Don threw his cap at them while I jumped up to scare the onlookers away.

Instead of pulling up the legs of her dungarees and running to the boats squealing—as I had expected her to do—Cid sat calmly laughing at the mice scurrying about. "Perhaps we better wash our dishes before we're overrun—if we aren't already!" she said. Hurrying about, we put away all the food and washed the dishes. This seemed to discourage the mice.

We were tired from the heat—and the afternoon hike up Ticaboo Creek. We laid out our sleeping bags on the ledges above the campfire. We each had a separate ledge. I was too tired to climb any farther up, so I laid my sleeping bag out near the fire. I was dozing off when I felt something scurry across my sleeping bag. A mouse! It occurred to me that one might—by mistake or choice—come into my bedding. Since I was inside and knew that getting out of a sleeping bag isn't a maneuver that can be done rapidly—at least not as quickly as this situation demanded—I decided I better get farther away from the place where the food had been. Small bits that had been spilled on the rock undoubtedly were what was attracting them again now that camp had quieted down.

I got up and carried my sleeping bag to a higher ledge, where I laid it out next to Don—for no other reason than that he happened to be there. I climbed back in and was just about to doze off when I heard Don's tin cup rattle. I opened my eyes, and in the light of the moon, I could see two mice having a merry time jumping in and out of the cup. They were licking out the last bits of flavor that remained. The last thing I remembered was that I must be sure to tell Don to wash out his cup before he ate breakfast.

*Twenty-Five*

# GLEN CANYON

Don's cup was heaped with canned Valencia orange slices, and he was raising his spoon for the first bite when I remembered the mice. "Stop!" I commanded. He froze.

"Whatza matter?" he asked almost in a whisper. His eyes were as big as saucers.

"Your cup—did you wash it out this morning?" I asked.

"No—why?"

"Mice were in it last night—lapping up what you left from supper."

"Oh, is *that* all! I thought you were going to tell me I was about to eat a scorpion." Don took his bite of oranges.

"Don!" I shouted. "Mice were running around in that cup. Spit it out!"

"Uh-uh, too good," he said with his mouth full. When he finished chewing, he swallowed and added, "Mice are clean little creatures."

"Well, I hope you noticed whether there was anything in there before you filled your cup!" I said.

"Nope—didn't notice there was anything there when I dipped it in the river before I brushed my teeth, either," he answered.

"I'm sure—" Cid laughed "—I'm sure the river did the trick, though it would have been more sanitary to boil the cup first."

"This cup has had just about everything in it, Cid, and I'm not dead yet," Don chuckled.

"Well, there's always a first time!" Tony said. Tapestry Cliff echoed to our laughter as we wiped the tears from our eyes.

Don Hatch, towing the *Brontosaur*, pilots the *No Name* in Glen Canyon on the Colorado River while another crew member looks at the stunning scenery.

Tony, Don, and I stayed behind when the *Brontosaur* set off on the morning run. Carrying the cameras and tripods, Tony and I climbed to the highest ledge—more than a hundred feet above the river—where I could get an uninterrupted view of its full sweep as it made its path through the red rock. Tapestry Cliff hung like a gigantic, supernatural curtain in the background. How amazingly ephemeral this solid mass of a million tons of sandstone looked!

The river below, almost the color of the surrounding rock, would have been lost in the scene if it had not been for the thin line of green tamarisk bushes lining its banks. In the boats we knew the river was a big stream, but high up where we stood, it was a thin, golden serpentine thread. The *Brontosaur* looked like a tiny dot. We could barely make her out as she traveled downstream. Seeing the boat there, and knowing how big she really was, gave us an idea of the scale of things. This country was big—big beyond imagination.

Bruce and Al were tired from rowing by the time we caught up with them in the *No Name.* They had rowed more than two miles. They got a fresh spurt of energy, however, when Don called, "We'll race you!" Four oars against one 7.5-horsepower Evinrude motor! The two boatmen pulled with all their might. For a while they were able to keep up with us, but in their excitement, they weren't watching where they were going

Tony Tuttle climbs a small side canyon in Glen Canyon in 1955.

and nearly rowed the *Brontosaur* up the riverbank. The *No Name* gained ground. (We could have overtaken them anytime if Don had opened the motor to full throttle—but then it wouldn't have been much of a race!) Al and Bruce finally gave up and begged a tow. This was an invitation for more fun. Don headed the *No Name* toward the *Brontosaur.* Just as Fred was about to throw the towline, Tony grabbed an oar, and with a well-aimed stroke, gave him a good soaking.

"Ah-ha, so you want a fight!" Al shouted. "Grab the oars, men! Water fight!" He pulled his oar from the mount. So did Bruce. Fred grabbed another oar, and Cid armed herself with a small paddle. They tried hard to splash back, but we were upwind, and their splashes blew right back at them. Tony, Don, and I were able to soak them thoroughly. In our shuffling from side to side in the *No Name*, the rubber gas line got cinched, and the motor conked out. Suddenly adrift, we found ourselves floating directly beside them, at their mercy and right in line of the full fire from three big oars and one small paddle. In my excitement, I somehow caught my oar in the current, which forced it under the boat. I couldn't pull it out, yet I refused to let go of it. Like a scene in a slow-motion movie, I was pulled overboard and into the river—hat, dark glasses, wristwatch, and all!

"Keep fighting, keep fighting!" I yelled. They did, and it was several minutes before I was picked up. In the meantime, Don had thrown me a life jacket. When I got back into the boat, the others, I found, were no less soaked than I was. What a water fight it had turned into! And how cool we felt as the water evaporated from our clothing in that hot, arid country.

It was late in the afternoon when we came upon a large overhang carved out of the canyon wall. We were continually testing echoes on our way down the river, and this formation produced a particularly startling one. I decided that we should stop and make a recording with the portable tape machine. The amphitheater was very much like a deep cave, yet it couldn't be called a cave because it didn't have that dug-out, enclosed shape associated with caves. Nor was it exactly an amphitheater, either, for people connect those with tiers of seats like the formation we had seen back at Sumner's Amphitheater. This place had a high-domed, half-rotunda shape. In the back, nearly a hundred feet from the river, was a spring surrounded by a thick growth of maidenhair fern. The river had built up a high bank of powdery sand across the entrance. The sandbank completely choked off the water coming from the spring, and so there was a clear, emerald pool, lined with cattails, at the rear.

The reverberation of our voices as we unloaded the sound equipment was eerie. Even when we spoke in a whisper, the sound was amplified many times, and if we shouted, the echo from the place reechoed from the canyon wall across the river. The voices we heard seemed not ours but those of great giants hidden within the walls of the canyon.

It is strange that you can't think of a thing to say when a recording is being made. We had to resort to reciting poetry. I recorded Cid quoting passages from "Lycidas." Tony spoke lines from a play he had performed at college just before coming on the voyage. Al read a paragraph from his current murder mystery. Don, in the meantime, had gotten out the canteens and was filling them at the spring in the back of the overhang. His voice coming from there was more phenomenal than ours out front, so I decided to go back with the recording equipment. Quicksand lined the pool, so it was tricky business to work our way back with the equipment we had to carry. We had to keep to a narrow edge of hard sand close to the wall, walking almost with our backs against it. Just before we got to the back, Tony lost his balance and stepped into the quicksand. His leg quickly sank into the muck, and he shouted "Help!" Bruce and Al grabbed him by the arms and dragged him back to firm ground. He was covered with dark muck up to his hips.

As I made a few tests on the recorder, I discovered the real pièce de résistance, soundwise, was the effect of voices from the sandbank, coming to us here at the back. "Why don't I go out and blow my horn!" Tony suggested. That was an excellent idea, so Tony, with Bruce as escort in case one or the other should slip into the quicksand again, went back to the boats. Tony got out his horn and began to blow it. Just as he did, there was a loud, ominous rumble above us. It sounded as though all the rocks were shifting and about to crash down upon us. Could it have been the blare of the horn that vibrated them loose? Certain sounds, I had heard, could shatter glass and cause avalanches. Perhaps Tony had blown the fatal note at just the right pitch to shake the precariously balanced rocks loose.

I gave Don a quick look. He was poised with his tin cup half-filled with spring water. His eyes were enormous. "Let's get the *H* out of here!" he whispered. We made a mad dash for the boats. We ignored the quicksand. How we made it out, I do not know, but apparently the sight of us flying out of there like a bunch of ballet dancers suddenly given a hotfoot was incredible—Al holding the microphone, me the recorder, Don with his tin cup high in the air, the long wire flying in every direction, and all of us tripping and skipping to avoid tumbling over it! The others, standing on the bank, were unaware of what we had heard and were amazed to see our quick exit. They couldn't imagine why we were running so fast.

"Take to the boats! Take to the boats!" someone shouted.

"What's the matter?" Cid shouted as we scrambled into the *Brontosaur* and the *No Name*.

"The place is about to crash down upon us!" Al yelled.

"Shove off—quickly!" I cried as Bruce fumbled around trying to get his oars in the oarlocks. He was sitting on the gunwale of the big boat. We hadn't given him time to get up.

We couldn't shove off—not until someone got out and pulled up the oars, which were still stuck in the sand holding the towlines. Al was about to jump out to get them when we heard the rumble again.

"Here come the rocks!" Don shouted.

"Is that what you heard?" Cid asked calmly.

"Yes—yes, that's it!" Tony's voice was high-pitched.

"Bruce," Cid said, "splash your legs against the side of the boat again." He did. The rumble reverberated from the overhang. "That's it—it's Bruce hitting his legs against the side of the boat," Cid explained.

"I was just washing the silt off my pants and shoes," Bruce explained, almost apologetically.

"We thought the world was coming down upon us!" I said.

"You should have seen yourselves running out of there." Fred laughed. "Oh, if only I had known how to run your cameras, Eggert! What a shot that would have made!"

"And you, Charles, with all that wire," Cid blurted out the words between bursts of laughter. "And the two of you leaping over it! I never knew all of you could be so graceful. Why, the three of you are budding Nijinskys."

"Look! Look at me!" Don held up his cup. "Not one drop spilled."

"Well, we had to step lightly! There was all that quicksand," Al remarked.

"Yeah—what about that? What happened to the quicksand?" Don added.

"You came out so fast," Bruce chuckled, "that you didn't give yourselves time to sink in!"

"I believe we could have run straight across the pool, we came out so fast," Don said.

It was twilight when we arrived at a good campsite. Nearby was an old deserted cabin, the home at one time of a gold prospector.[1] All along the way, there had been ruins of old mines where men had come and dug with hope. But their sights were aimed too short. The gold was here all right, but it wasn't the kind you can take to the assayer's office and get money for. If the miners left in poverty, it was because they were unable to see. The gold I speak of surrounded them wherever they chose to look.

The door of the cabin was ajar, and we entered. Inside everything was in order. The place looked as though its owner had simply gone away for the weekend—except that everything was covered with a heavy layer of sandy dust. Whoever it was had left this cabin long, long ago. It was built against a rock wall that formed one side of the cabin. The lovely texture of the rock gave the room a curious, but modern, look. *Our contemporary architects aren't so original after all*, I thought!

Outside, close by, we could distinctly see the outlines of what was once a vegetable garden, irrigated by the flow piped from a nearby spring. In the front yard grew several fig trees. They were loaded with ripe fruit, and Cid fell upon them with delight. "I haven't had ripe figs in thirty years!" she exclaimed, biting into one. "Try one, Charles," she added, turning to me.

"I don't like figs."

"But try one fresh from the tree," she said, biting into her second. "They're delicious!" She peeled back the skin of one, revealing the red fruit inside, and handed it to me. I bit into it. "Isn't it wonderful?" she asked.

"Well—" I answered, puckering my mouth. Cid picked another and bit into it. "Do you think you ought to eat so many?" I asked. "You better go easy."

Cid answered, "Listen, young man, I used to eat figs by the water bucketful before you were born!" I said no more. She gathered up all she could carry in her shirttails. "These will be wonderful with breakfast tomorrow morning," she commented.

"Perhaps by tomorrow morning you won't need them," I added.

Cid was the first one up the next morning. I found her leaning over a pot, stewing figs for breakfast. She continued to munch fresh ones throughout the day. Every time she took one, I gave her a look of disapproval. *Danger ahead,* I thought, but she just smiled and waved her hand, as if to shoo my look away.

We stopped at Navajo Creek, just above the Escalante River, for on our map was written, "Water falls—lovely pool." We hadn't had a freshwater bath in weeks. "Want to come along for a clean shower?" I asked Cid.

"No—I'll stay at the boat. You boys just go. I'll remain here to enjoy my figs in peace!" She laughed. The six of us hiked up the narrow canyon cut by the creek, and presently we came to an enchanting emerald pool, crystal clear, surrounded by mammoth boulders. At the far end of the pool, Navajo Creek cascaded in graceful leaps of sparkling white water. Around the pool, like a wreath of green, ferns grew. The place was so inviting that we could hardly get our clothes off fast enough. Clean, clear water! What a relief to get the silt washed off. I stood for a long while under the waterfall, letting the forceful spray pound down upon my head. Then for a while I lay on a large rock, sunbathing. The sun felt particularly soothing now that I was clean. We all sunbathed, and when I looked over at the others, I realized how tan we were. The color of our skin nearly matched the brown rocks we were lying on. We had used suntan lotion copiously the first week or two, and we were very careful not to get burned too quickly. But now we didn't have to worry any longer, except for the conspicuously white patch our shorts had left.

After a sunbath, we jumped into the water again, had a vigorous water fight which riled up the bottom of the emerald pool, and took another shower. Refreshed, we returned to the boats.

"Wouldn't you like to shower?" Fred asked Cid. "It's not far to the pool—hate to have you miss it."

Cid was sitting under the shade of a tamarisk bush, her wet nylon veil draped over her head. "No—there's been a nice breeze here in the shade. I'm too lazy to make the effort," she answered. There was no point urging. Cid seemed to prefer remaining by the boats when we went off. We hated to have her miss things, and sometimes we were a bit exasperated that she didn't explore more. Perhaps her age held her back; we always forgot to take that into account. Even we found ourselves exhausted just from the emotional impact of the scenery we were passing on the river. Perhaps that was enough for Cid.

We set off on the river again and made our next stop at the Escalante River to check the water volume.[2] There was no river there at all. The mouth was choked by a bank of silt, and cutting through it was a tiny stream of water, like the flow from a half-turned-on water faucet that ran into the Colorado. "Kind of dry in these parts," Don remarked cynically.

That afternoon we stopped, too, at Hole-in-the-Rock Creek, where the Mormons had come from across the slickrock desert to build a settlement in southern Utah. They had hardly begun to settle Salt Lake City after their heroic trek across the plains before the pioneers began spreading out to other parts of Utah. One brave party came suddenly one day in 1880 to this place on the Colorado River. Long and hard they searched for a passage down to the river from the plateau above, and, unable to find one, on January 26, they were forced to lower their twenty-six wagons and horses over the cliff to reach the river below. They had been two months on the way, and when they got here, the snow was falling, and few supplies were left. They carved steps in the rock wall, and 250 men, women, and children descended perilously to the river with a religious mission in their heads and a call to cross over and settle the San Juan desert beyond the canyon and the river.

We looked up at the place where the wagons, held by strained ropes and stretched muscles, were lowered down the twenty-five-degree descent. We could almost hear the frightened whinnying of the wild-eyed horses as they plunged down when the ropes broke. Nine were lost. We could almost hear, too, the screams of the women and children as they toiled and slipped down those steps in the blowing snow. Perhaps they, too, sang their hymn here—as they had when crossing the plains in other snows far north of this place.

*And how had they crossed the river*, I wondered, *to the other, less steep side where getting up would be easy?* We felt subdued as we left the spot. Our voyage down the canyon was small and easy by comparison. No one spoke as Don pulled the cord and started the motor to tow us away. Tony got out his horn and quietly played "Come, Come, Ye Saints." It didn't quite fit. The sound should have been coming from those hand-hewn pipes of the Tabernacle organ.

Then we passed the San Juan River.[3] The river was running full, its volume almost as great as the Colorado. The force of its current coming into the big river shoved us far over to the right bank as we passed. The sight cheered us up, yet the water level mark along the bank indicated that the river was dropping lower and lower. When we stopped for the night, Don told us we had traveled 643 miles and had just 76 to go to Lee's Ferry, Arizona. It was July 7. His remark sounded like a preliminary announcement that we would have to stop there. Already we were beginning to wonder whether there would be enough water to get us even *that* far. What if there wasn't? We might have to climb out—do a Hole-in-the-Rock in reverse. That was in all our minds, though we avoided discussing it. The river was below average in volume. It was too soon to have it drop so low. Unusual conditions, we thought. We hoped that something would happen to bring it back up.

Our camp, on the night of July 7, was again on a series of red rock ledges rising from the water's edge. Close by was the narrow slit of an entrance to a side canyon. After supper Fred and I hiked to explore it. To get to the mouth of the canyon, we had to climb high above the river along the top of a talus slope. Upon reaching the mouth, we came upon a scene of tremendous upheaval. A huge section of the canyon wall had fallen, and the surface of the big boulders that obliterated our path was so newly broken and cracked that they looked like freshly cut meat. The fall must have occurred within the past few days, for the leaves of the trees it had taken with it were still fresh, and sap was still running from the twisted, contorted, and broken branches. Tons upon tons of rock had come crashing down from high above, where a mammoth scar remained on the face of the canyon wall. Across the narrow canyon, the walls were gashed and scraped where rocks had bounded.

Fred and I were like ants crawling across the rockfall. When we came to the end of the debris, we found ourselves buried deep in a narrow passage into the rock beyond. The side canyon was no more than eight feet wide where we stood. It was nearly two thousand feet deep in the sandstone crust of the Earth! No sunlight had ever penetrated the depth of this place. Down the center of the canyon floor ran a trickle of a stream.

The hidden passage twisted and turned as we followed it through the rock, and presently we came to a sharp turn. Here the stream had cut diagonally through the rock. The sky was shut off from our view completely; only rock hung overhead. The canyon wall on the opposite side of the turn paralleled its companion wall upward, and the two sides were like giant pieces of a jigsaw puzzle jarred slightly apart. Fred and

I stood at the center of the turn, where we could look up and down the canyon as it wound its way through the rock. As we gazed up through the slit, the rock wall opposite seemed like the prow of a supernatural ship turned upside down. Behind us the stream had gouged out a deep cave, and a soft dune of powdery sand lay piled high in front of it. The air was dank and heavy with the green smell of fern.

On and on Fred and I wandered, quite unable to believe what we were seeing. In places the bottom of the canyon narrowed down, leaving only room enough for the stream to run between the walls. In other places, the stream had eroded deep potholes, where fingerling trout swam. We had to climb like flies along the slanting wall to get around these sections. At one place, there seemed to be a mild enough pitch to the wall to allow us to climb to a ledge above, but we could not. The rock was too slippery, for here small springs gushed from the wall. Wherever there was a seep in the canyon wall, ferns grew.

It was getting dark by the time we turned back; we had not yet come to the end of the narrow hidden passage, though we had walked a good two miles. We had been so entranced with the place that we had forgotten the time. Now we thought of that rockslide with the jagged-edged boulders we'd have to climb over to get back to camp. We hurried out as fast as we could. It was dark when we reached camp. The men were sitting around the campfire. Cid was sitting on her cot by the water's edge. We came upon her first. "You must see this place," Fred said. "No matter what, you must come with us tomorrow up that canyon!"

"We'll spend all day there exploring," I exclaimed. "It's incredible."

"Like the inside of a conch shell," Fred told her. His glasses reflected the deep blue light of the sky shining on the river, but I could see the excitement about the place in his eyes.

"You must see it," we urged.

"I'll go if it kills me!" Cid answered. "I can tell from your transfigured faces that it must be something! I've got to see anything that makes you two look like this!"

I could hardly sleep that night, thinking of this place we called Hidden Passage.[4] I couldn't believe that such a place of beauty existed and I had seen it.

*Twenty-Six*

# HIDDEN PASSAGE

I was brushing my teeth when Cid came to me the next morning. She was obviously very weak, and her face was pale. "Charles, I have had the most awful night. You were right—those figs! Do you have anything for it in the medical kit?"

"Yes—yes, of course," I answered, quickly putting my toothbrush aside. I stripped the waterproof covering from the medical kit and got out the card file to look up the appropriate medicine. Paregoric seemed like the right cure, so I opened the bottle and poured a teaspoonful and handed it to her.[1] "One every three hours. This should fix you up."

"What is it?" she asked.

"Paregoric."

"Paregoric! I haven't had that since I was a child."

"No? Nor fresh figs either! Here," I said, handing her the bottle, "take it. The two go together." As I closed the kit, I watched her walk to the table where Tony and Bruce were setting up for breakfast. I heard her tell Bruce that all she'd have for breakfast was a cup of hot coffee.

After breakfast I suggested that we run the boats down to the mouth of Hidden Passage. This would save us from having to climb over the debris of the rockslide. "Do you think you can make it up the canyon?" I asked Cid when we arrived.

"I said last night I'd go if it killed me, and from the expression you and Fred had on your faces, it is worth the risk. Of course I'll go! You set your own pace—I'll just follow along slowly."

A view of water, walls, and ferns in Hidden Passage, Glen Canyon, 1955.

Cid managed to keep up with Tony and me, for we stopped often to take pictures. She would either sit by while we photographed a scene, or walk ahead. Each time we finished shooting, we caught up with her and found her sitting with her notebook. "You know," she remarked, "this place is impossible to describe in words . . . prose anyway."

"Impossible to photograph too!" I answered. "It is too big even for the wide-angle lens. It is frustrating! How can such a place be portrayed?"

"Poetry, maybe. . . ." she said thoughtfully, returning her attention to her notebook. Tony and I left her sitting on the soft sandbank in front of the cave Fred and I had seen the night before. On up the canyon, farther than Fred and I had been the night before, we came to a deep pool, where the water filled the narrow bottom of the canyon from wall to wall. Here it would be necessary to wade—or possibly swim. Tony and I stripped down to our bathing trunks.

"I'll start and see how deep it is," Tony suggested.

"Good idea. If you can make it, then come back and pick up one of the cameras."

Tony started across the pool. In one spot it got so deep that Tony was up to his armpits in the water. Then it got shallow again, and he made

Charles Eggert wading through a pool in Hidden Passage with his cameras held safely above the water.

it to dry ground on the other side. As he returned, Cid caught up to us again. "Looks like the end of the road for you, Cid," I said.

"Why? I brought my bathing suit. I have it on under my dungarees." She took her white shirt and her dungarees off, and beneath them she had on a very pretty black silk bathing suit. I noticed that she had perked up surprisingly since breakfast, yet seeing her wearing a bathing suit, I wondered how she was managing. It seemed to me that she had put a great deal of reliance on that swig of paregoric.

"How do you feel?" I asked her.

"I feel fine now. You are a good doctor, even though you are a bit out of fashion prescribing *paregoric*."

"Not me—my doctor. Give him the credit—he outfitted the kit," I told her.

Tony and I waded up the stream with the cameras and tripods. Then we returned and took Cid's hands and helped her through. The bottom was rocky and slippery, so it was tricky going. Reaching dry ground again, we went on and on up the narrow slit through the rock. In places the stream spread out over the sand and rock; in others it cut a narrow passage—a miniature of the place we were in—through the rock creek bed. In some places, deep pools had been eroded, and in them young trout and polliwogs swam. Finally, almost three miles up, we reached a very deep pool with sheer walls on either side. At the head of it was a huge boulder that had fallen from above, blocking further passage for the camera equipment. There was no way to get it up without ropes, and we had failed to bring any. Bruce, Al, and Don climbed above the boulder by literally scaling the walls, which were so close together that, by pressing their hands and feet on opposite walls, the three men were able to make their way up. There was no immediate danger of falling, for if they did—as happened to Bruce—they merely fell into the deep pool below with a great splash.

Coming back down was easier; they simply worked their way down the big boulder as far as they could; then they dived into the pool. The three returned with eyes the size of platters. What they had seen beyond the place where we were forced to stop with the cameras was incredible, they said—deep, emerald pools, cascades, and a ribbon waterfall more than 120 feet high. Fred, Cid, and I thought we had seen more than we could believe already. It was hard to imagine there could be more. Yet there was, and we left Hidden Passage with the hope that one day—before it is all buried deep below the surface of Glen Canyon reservoir—we might return. I left with a feeling of frustration. I knew my pictures, or any words I could use, would be inadequate to describe this place.

Several months later I got a note from Cid. It contained the verses she had written as she sat in that narrow side canyon:

HIDDEN PASSAGE
To Hidden Passage come with reverence.
It is a holy place, this nautilus,
This mighty, spiral-chambered carven shell.
Step softly here where seldom man has trod—
So Adam walked in Eden's virgin dell
That lay still dewy from the hand of God.

All that's hidden leads us on and on—
The root and end of man are secret things,
But in this rocky heart of solitude,
The fearful deep primeval silence brings
A misty answer to our WHITHER, WHENCE,
A whisper that can almost tell us WHY.[2]

Cid was right—poetry described it best.

A short distance downstream from Hidden Passage, we came upon a huge alcove in the rock. If we searched the world high and wide and deep, we could find no grander temple. Here was a domed chamber in the yellow-brown sandstone, more than two hundred feet high, five hundred feet long, and at least two hundred feet wide. In the center was a high mound of rock and sand where a grove of box elders and cottonwood trees and ferns were growing. It was like a Japanese garden, and Fred remarked that it could not have been more perfect if it had been landscaped. He was right! At the far end of the vast chamber was a clear, still pool where, we were certain, a water sprite lived, for every few moments a tiny spout of water broke the surface, leaving behind a perfect ring that slowly enlarged and spread out until it reached the edge of the pool. The pool was deep—so deep we could not see the bottom, and around it, on the rock wall, grew a thick bank of maidenhair fern. Above the pool, through the ceiling and on up through the rock for a thousand feet, was a narrow, winding skylight that had been carved by a little stream that ran only when it rained. What a sight it must be to see it cascading in a two-hundred-foot free fall to the center of the pool below! And what a lovely sound it must make here, where the acoustics are perfect.

"We are pleased to find that this hollow in the rock is filled with sweet sounds," Major Powell wrote in his diary on August 1, 1869. "It was doubtless made for an academy of music by its storm-born architect; so we name it Music Temple."[3]

Here it was that Powell and his men camped and sang. And here it was, too, that Seneca and O. G. Howland and Bill Dunn, along with the others, carved their names on the rock wall, where they remain, almost as distinct as on the day they were made. Powell, on his second journey down the river in 1871, revisited Music Temple. Seeing the names of those three men from his first expedition, Powell thought this place would be a fitting memorial to Dunn and the Howland brothers, who had deserted him in the Grand Canyon. Thinking the party was doomed to disaster, they climbed out, only to be murdered by Indians when they reached the plateau above. As we stood looking at those names carved in the rock, we wondered what Powell would think if he knew that this place, too, would be destroyed by reservoir water and later by silt that would cover it forever from men's eyes. Powell was aware of the potential water resources of the Great American Desert, and he believed in utilizing nature in humanity's behalf. But he was also keenly aware of the resources that feed people's souls. This, too, was in humanity's behalf. How would he have felt about Glen Canyon reservoir? We thought we knew.

Five miles below Music Temple, we found hundreds of petroglyphs—ancient Indian drawings carved in the canyon wall.[4] This place was one of the hundreds in Glen Canyon where the prehistoric red men [*sic*] had left their marks in passing, like the GIs of a later day. "Kilroy was here," these told us in a different language.

"An almost universal human wish," Cid remarked, "to leave some sign that will last when we are gone; to hack away at the hard stone with the urgency of our mortality upon us."

Near the petroglyphs, another narrow side canyon cut its way back through the rock. We decided to explore it. Perhaps we'd find another Hidden Passage. Instead, we discovered an amphitheater of such astounding size that it left us speechless! We came upon it suddenly, unexpectedly. The narrow canyon took a sharp twist, and there it was—so big that Madison Square Garden could fit into it without having to squeeze. Again, as in Hidden Passage, where the creek curved in an almost complete circle, the rock was cut at a diagonal and had gouged deeply into the far side of the wall. The great domed roof above us must have been twenty stories high and a thousand feet across, and coming down the center of the chamber was a gigantic rock peninsula. Near its base in the dry creek bed was a flat area, large enough to hold a symphony orchestra and a full chorus. As we sat on the talus that rose high against the wall opposite, Tony and I speculated on what a glorious concert could be held here. "If Stokowski could only see this, I'll bet he would arrange it!" I said. "He has the imagination for such a thing—he's just the conductor to do it!"

"Yes, and we'd haul everyone down in boats. It would be the most magnificent concert ever given," Tony added enthusiastically. We sat back and pondered it. A fantastic idea? Perhaps, but a possible one. It would certainly be the music experience to end all music experiences, what with the anticipation the audience would feel just getting to the place. I closed my eyes and imagined the sound of a great orchestra here.

I sat with my eyes closed for a long time, unable to look, unable to fathom the fantastic bigness of the place. I opened them again when I heard Al yell for our attention. His voice seemed to come from everywhere—close to me, yet far, far away. "Where is he?" I asked.

"Over there—on the rock, climbing down. You can just make him out." Don pointed straight across the chamber to the rock peninsula. In the twilight of the place—for here, too, the sun had never entered—I spotted Al. He was nothing more than a small dot, no bigger than the period at the end of this sentence. And his small dot was in the same proportion to the landscape as that period to this page.

"Come across," Al shouted. "You can see the sky from here." We walked over and looked up to the crescent-shaped slit of blue winding around over us. Above the dome, where the chamber ended, a sheer wall of solid sandstone rose another thousand feet. Up there were tons upon millions of tons of rock, and we were in the very heart of it! All that weight above, the enormity of the place: it was too much for me—too superhuman, too vast. I felt reduced to nothing, a pygmy in a giant's world. I had to get out of the place, get back to where I was my right size again. I felt the way I had a few nights before, when I had lain on a rock ledge staring into the sky, where every star was brilliantly lit. The longer I looked up, the more three-dimensional the sky became, and I sensed the vast distances in it. Seeing the universe spread out above and around me that night made me feel as infinitesimally small as the sky was infinitely big. Now I found myself almost running to get out of this place called Twilight Amphitheater. I was glad to be in the open again, where I towered above something, even though it might be only the sagebrush.

"Gosh, what a place!" Tony said when he caught up with me. "It was like being in the belly of a whale!"

"It was more than that, Tony—more than that!" I replied.

While we were gone, a strong wind had come up. The wind kicked up high waves on the river, and we had a hard time fighting our way as

Five of the expedition members take a break in the quiet shade of Twilight Amphitheater in Glen Canyon.

we continued downstream. The waves tossed the *No Name* about, and the motor's propeller alternately dug into the water and whirled futilely in the air. In spite of the wind and the splash, the sun beat down upon us relentlessly. Don tried his best to steer us under the shadows of the overhanging cliffs along the river, but when we got into the shade, the splash was cold, and we shivered. Blowing sand from along the bank was carried by the wind and its blasting cut our faces. Cid tried to protect herself with her plaid umbrella, but the wind soon blew it inside out. Everything blew this way and that, and before Tony could tie them down, his dungarees, which he had momentarily laid on the platform, blew into the water and sank. After being in such sweetly quiet and peaceful places as Twilight Amphitheater, Hidden Passage, and Music Temple, I wondered whether the wrath of the gods was upon us for venturing there. It certainly seemed as though we were being punished for something, and that all hell had broken loose upon us. When we got to the point of being almost unable to endure it any longer, we saw Navajo Mountain hovering in the distance. We knew we were nearing the mouth of Aztec Creek, the entrance from the river to Rainbow Bridge.[5]

"Almost there!" Don shouted from the *No Name*. "Think you can stand it a little farther?"

"Yes, yes—go on, go on!" Cid shouted back to him from behind the piled-up duffle in the middle of the *Brontosaur*, where she was trying to shelter herself against the wind. Bruce was huddled as far down in the boat as he could get. He jumped up and grabbed his oars to help.

"Bruce! Bruce!" Cid shouted. "Put on a shirt or something—you'll be cut to pieces by the sand!"

"Haven't got one—it's wrapped up somewhere." He smiled. Cid scrambled around to find something loose to toss him, but everything was tied to something else.

Bruce rowed with all his might. His muscles glistened in the sun as the sweat poured off his skin. The blowing sand stuck to his flesh, and little rivulets formed where the sweat poured down through it. What stamina he had! The rest of us were exhausted from the physical effort of suffering the heat one moment and the cold the next. How long could a human body stand this kind of treatment?

It must have been another half hour before we pulled into a quiet bay that was sheltered momentarily from the wind by a sheer, high wall on the opposite side of the river. But as soon as we hit the beach, we were in the wind again. No one spoke as we unloaded the duffle. We couldn't speak; the sand was blowing too thickly. We dragged the food boxes across the flat, sandy beach to a wide, flat shelf of rock. Here we built the campfire in the shelter of a small crevasse and set the table up as the sun went behind the cliff on the other side of the river. "At least we'll be in the shade," Don remarked caustically.

"Yes, we'll at least be cool. Now if only the wind will die down as usual with the sun gone," Fred added. But the wind didn't die down as usual. We ate our canned chicken and sweet potatoes along with the swirling sand, and we had trouble keeping our dishes from blowing off the table.

On that hot night, we all huddled in our sleeping bags like pupae in cocoons. The blowing sand was more discomforting than the heat. How, I wondered, would I have the strength to hike the seven hot miles to Rainbow Bridge the next day? This day had been so full that I imagined I had had all I could take. Yet beyond us, hidden up the side canyon, was one of the wonders of the world—Rainbow Bridge; Nonnezoshie, the Indians called it, a rock arch like a rainbow in the sky, a place held sacred and secret by the ancient Indians. I dared not be so close and miss it. As I lay huddled in my sleeping bag thinking of that place, the wind suddenly stopped, and all was at once quiet, so quiet that I could again hear the murmur of the river. I popped my head out of my bag to listen to that soothing sound and breathe the clear air again.

When I looked up, I saw the stars. To the northeast was the Big Dipper that had followed us all those 650 river miles we had come. Only on one night had it deserted us—back in Cataract, where we had slept on the rocks below the Big Drop. It hadn't occurred to me until now that on every night except that one, I had looked up at that familiar constellation. Was that why I had been frightened then? Every night I had looked into the night sky and seen that one familiar thing in this unfamiliar world, and I had felt at peace, at home, in the universe—secure. This night, seeing the Big Dipper there, I felt my place again after the day of incredible events.

*Twenty-Seven*

# RAINBOW BRIDGE TO LEE'S FERRY

"I'll be all right, right here," Cid said. "It will be nice to be alone for a change."

"But it is only seven miles. We'd hate to have you miss Rainbow Bridge!" Don urged.

"And seven back? Too much—you'd have to carry me!"

"We sure could!" Bruce said.

"We may stay overnight. You better come along," Fred said.

"No—no, I'll just wait here, and you can tell me all about it when you return. There's nothing to bother me. It isn't nature—it's human beings you have to be afraid of, and I'm quite sure there'll be none of them here!" she said decisively.

"Well, okay," Don said, giving up, "but keep out of trouble!"

Cid gave him a hearty laugh. "You keep out of trouble. I know you boys—climbing around on narrow ledges. You just watch out for yourselves."

We gathered some oranges and a few cans of food—anything that would fit conveniently into our pockets—and were off. As we entered the mouth of Aztec Canyon, I looked back at our camp and saw Cid sitting alone on the rock ledge, watching us disappear. She gave us a final wave. How tiny she looked, so infinitesimal, a diaphanous white dot. Should I go back to her? *No, no—she would be safe*, I thought, *far safer than at Hite*. She was a woman with nerve, that gal. How fortunate we were to have her with us; how good was the turn of fate that had made her be here! She knew when to be independent—and when to be dependent;

when to talk and when to keep quiet. "Cramp our style," someone had worried at first. We all thought she might in the beginning, before we met her. What exactly did that phrase mean anyway? Prevent us from saying things we otherwise might say? Well, we never used those words anyway. "Dammit to hell" maybe, when one of us scraped some skin off a shin climbing about in the boat—but they were punctuation marks of speech, and Cid was no prude.

As far as "managing"—as they term it in polite society—taking care of those normal bodily functions in the morning and during the course of the day, we had no conflicts. If occasionally there seemed a time when wandering off might be misunderstood, someone simply warned the others by asking, "Does anyone know where the bathroom is?" We each had our own roll of toilet paper (on the advice of my doctor, who said it would be best in case of dysentery), and we simply disappeared someplace into the beyond. We had a small shovel with us, and that also helped to announce where we were going. We made enough stops during the day to take care of that other type of management. However, we all seemed to have little need in this hot, arid climate. We perspired profusely, and the problem of supplying our bodies with liquid was far greater than relieving them of it.

But more important than these insignificant things—which anyone can negotiate properly—was the rapport we established among ourselves. Cid, first of all, was a true adult—one of the few I have met. She had all those qualities—understanding, wisdom, tolerance, wit, and compassion—that are necessary to reach adulthood. Perhaps it takes age and a lot of living to acquire these things; I don't know. I do know that the few people I've met who have them never seem old. The old are those who are decrepit—mentally—in their outlook; those who have given up, who find no meaning in the future, who revert to second childhood, who fail to attain understanding and tolerance.

Cid needed no pampering; she never got in the way, never complained. If something didn't suit her, she adjusted herself or said so. Or, if in her wisdom, she realized that actually things suited none of us, she suggested something different—and she had a clever way of doing it to make it appear that her idea was what we had all had in mind in the first place. She was never domineering, nor was she rancorous. She took her place among us, shaped herself as a cog in the wheel of the expedition, exactly the same size and shape as the rest of us. Except for our complete misjudgment of both her and Cataract Canyon in not letting her go through with us, we never treated or looked upon this woman as someone who was being carried along . . . certainly not as a favor or for a price. She was a member of the crew just as much as the rest of us.

Cid was old enough, as she wrote, "not to be disturbed in the company of men." Also the men were not disturbed by her company. Not that Cid had no sex appeal—quite the contrary. Aside from the fact that our ages separated us from the whole idea of sex, there was enough spark to excite our libido and keep us men from becoming slovenly—in our appearance or our actions. Yet, on the other hand, and so important on an expedition where it was important that we act together, there was none of that manly sexual competition to cause us to be individual show-offs. There was no vying for attention, no "I can row harder than you can," nor "I'm braver than you are." There was no spreading of the neck and tail feathers like the male grouse in mating season. Vying for female admiration—competing among ourselves—could have become very uncomfortable, even disastrous, for our human relationships as well as the ultimate success of the voyage.

Even though Cid looked small and lost sitting on the rock ledge in the vastness of Glen Canyon, I knew she'd make out all right in our absence. Being alone would give her the opportunity to write up her notes, to contemplate if she wanted to, to reflect on the purposes for which she had joined us—whatever they were.

We headed into Aztec Canyon, and before we were a quarter of the way, I began to feel the heavy load of the camera I was carrying. The muscles in my shoulders and neck started aching. I looked back at Tony. He was carrying twice my load, plodding along without a complaint, without a grimace. Fred and Bruce were walking far ahead at an even, rhythmic pace. It was obvious they had both walked long distances before—Bruce on a ranch in his early youth, and Fred in the woods of Maine, where he had been brought up. They never slowed down, never sped up, never broke the long, even strides they took.

We followed the course of a shallow stream. It was so hot that the rocks burned through our boots, and when we could, we deliberately walked in the water to cool our feet. We plodded through thick sand that was worst of all—it was hot, heavy walking through it—and over cobblestones that twisted our ankles, and flat rocks; between boulders, and up and over them.

Rainbow Bridge was in a side canyon that ran off to the left of Aztec. We thought we had come to it and began making our way up a side canyon. We had gone almost a mile when the canyon narrowed and the incline became very steep. Soon the way was choked with a thick growth of greasewood bushes, and we knew this couldn't be the right canyon. We turned back.

We went another mile till we came to another, larger side canyon. By now it was noon. I wasn't hungry, but my mouth was as dry as cotton in spite of the many cups of water I had drunk from the little stream. We decided to rest a while. Holding out until the last minute, I finally took out an orange and peeled it. When I bit into it, I felt I had never tasted anything so good. The juice was a balm to my parched tongue and dry lips. I took small bites to make it last. When I had finished the first one, I was very tempted to take out the other orange I carried and eat it. *No—no, I must save it for the trip back*, I thought.

Bruce wandered around looking for some indication of our route to the bridge. Scribbled on the canyon wall, he found a small sign that read, "To the Bridge." We made our way into what we knew now for certain was Bridge Canyon. The mouth of the canyon was very narrow, and the canyon itself, deep. Bruce's massive figure was small as I watched him walk into it ahead of me. A stream rambled down this canyon too, and in places it had eroded large, deep potholes. We stopped, peeled off our clothes, and swam to cool ourselves from the heat.

When we got cooler, we dressed and walked on and on. The incline became steeper, the terrain rougher, and the walking harder. I thought we'd never come to the bridge, and I was beginning to wonder whether the trip was worth it. Tony and I fell far behind the others because we were carrying so much weight. We also often stopped to get shots of the towering surroundings we were in. When we caught up with the others, they were resting on a high ledge. We paused to catch our breath too. I sat for some time before I noticed; then I saw it! Far ahead up the canyon was Rainbow Bridge, spreading its great stone arch. "Hey!" I shouted in surprise. "There it is!"

"What—where?" the others asked, pretending to be excited. They had already seen it, but they acted as though they hadn't—just to see the surprised look on our faces.

"Gosh! What a sight!" Tony exclaimed almost reverently.

Strange one should walk so far and suffer so much to see a mass of stone arched across the sky. Perhaps this was why it was such a thrill. It was something you had to exert yourself to see. I wonder whether we aren't making a big mistake in making it so easy for people to see things. Nearly every week I receive press releases informing me that this road or that one in our national parks is being improved, widened, paved, made into a superhighway. It is getting so that you can see almost everything from a car window. People boast about how many parks they have covered during their vacation. Only recently I spoke to a couple who, in the course of their auto trip across the country, had seen Yosemite, Sequoia, Death Valley, the Grand Canyon, Bryce and Zion Canyons, the Tetons, and Yellowstone! Seen them! I thought. Felt them? Understood them? Never! Their pictures showed it. Almost everything had been taken from their car window or an overlook beside the road. They might just as well have stayed home and looked at pictures in a travel magazine. Their appreciation of what they had seen was in exact proportion to the time they had spent.

You have to get out of the car and walk—feel the ground under you, the earth around you, smell the air, hear the sounds. What is a waterfall without the spray in your face? What is a forest without the spongy feel of the thick layer of pine needles under your feet? What is a desert without the sand burning through the soles of your shoes or a cactus spine pricking your leg? All these are part of the whole, and more specifically, if there is effort involved, the appreciation is enhanced.

We continued to the bridge, stopping at every new vantage point just to sit and look. The closer we got, the more beautiful and graceful it appeared. There was a simple explanation of how the arch had been formed: a rock wall, a stream, the wind, softer rock eroding and cracking away; the stream finally making its way through, instead of around, the rock wall; more erosion—all that. But that mattered little; the arch was there, spread across the canyon, framing all of Navajo Mountain in its span, and its beauty superseded any geological explanation.

We spent a long while at the foot of the bridge, sitting there in awe of it, feeling its presence.[1] Then we climbed to one of the abutments, where the National Park Service had left a register log. We signed our names, drew a picture of our insignia beside them in the log, and read a few of the two-thousand-odd names of those who had seen it before us—most of whom had come by horseback down a fourteen-mile trail from the plateau above. In the column headed "Remarks," we read others' reactions. A number of people had composed poetry in praise of the bridge—most of it bad. The only comment several made was that it had been a hot, hard ride.

One person wrote, "Not worth it!" *Poor soul*, I thought. But then there are those people who have become so bogged down with the contrivances of civilization that they can no longer focus on the beauty of nature. I think often of the man who wrote that. Perhaps now that the blisters on his rear from the rubbing of the saddle leather have healed, he sits in his foam-rubber desk chair looking out his office window at the mass of humanity trying to fight their way across the street, bucking traffic, hating to have to rush back to their jobs. Could it be that now, trapped in the maze of his business world, he thinks back to Rainbow Bridge and wishes he could erase what he wrote there?

Near his remark, another, later visitor had quoted George Mallory:

> It is not the summit
> That matters, but the fight
> For the summit; not the
> Victory, but the gain itself.

It was too bad that this was written after the other man had come here. I'm sure the man who thought it was not worthwhile now sees the gain: peace of soul, a place he can turn his thoughts to, a quiet niche in his memory where he can reflect.

Bruce considered climbing the shallow-carved Moki Indian steps in the rock to the top of the bridge, but I had been advised we should not try it without proper climbing equipment. Near the top, the wall became very steep, and without ropes it was almost impossible to get up. I persuaded Bruce not to chance it, even though it would have been spectacular to get a picture of him on top of the 309-foot-high arch. With a man standing atop it, we could have had a real sense of the massiveness of the bridge, so huge that the dome of the capitol of the United States in Washington could fit beneath it.

Bruce and Fred started back to camp ahead of us, and when the rest of us got a half mile below the bridge, we discovered another ancient trail the Indians had carved into the steep canyon wall. Before the discovery of America by the white man, the ancient Indians had used these steps to climb high above and worship their sacred Nonnezoshie—Rainbow Bridge. Al suggested he climb up and see the view. Don said he would go too. The steps were on too sharp an angle against the steep canyon wall to climb with a camera in one hand, so Tony and I remained below to photograph them from the opposite side of the canyon. Al and Don made their way down to the creek bed below to cross to the other side of the canyon. The canyon was deep here, and we were a good hundred feet above its bottom. It took Al and Don some time before they reached the other side.

Al started gingerly up the steps, which were no more than shallow toeholds in the rock. Don followed. If ever there was a time when two men got off on the wrong foot, this was it! Al got halfway up when I heard him shout, "Hey, what's above me? I've run out of steps!" There was fear in his voice. Then I heard him yell to Don, "I can't get my leg back—come quickly and hold me!" Al was rimrocked! He had put his inner foot forward—and his weight—expecting to get a toehold in the next step, but the next step wasn't there. It had been eroded away. Al was too far out of balance to get his foot back to the step below. All he could do was press his weight against the canyon wall, hoping to hold himself there, digging his fingernails into the rock until Don could reach him and possibly help him back. Tony and I stood spellbound, watching, helpless to do anything.

"Hang on—hang on," Don shouted encouragement.

"I can't hang on—there's nothing to hang on to!" Al gave a nervous giggle. "Anyone got a skyhook?" he tried to joke. Gradually Don worked his way to Al. Then he found he, too, had his wrong foot forward.

"Wait a minute while I change feet," Don said.

"Good night! This is no time to trip the light fandango! Get your ol' dad down from here," Al said.

By juggling his toes—barely one toe alone would fit into the carved slots—Don finally got his feet changed around and pressed his own weight against Al. Al slowly and carefully got his suspended leg back to the step behind him. It was torture watching them move so slowly and knowing that at any moment, Al could plunge more than 150 feet to the rocks below.

Slowly they made their way backward to the flat ledge at the start of the steps. Al was still white, and sweat was pouring down his forehead when he got back to us. "What did you say those steps were called, Charlie?" he asked.

"Moki steps," I answered.[2]

"You know what *Moki* means in Navajo, don't you?" Al replied. "Moki means *dead*—and your ol' dad nearly had it! They were well named, I'm telling you!"

"Next time you'd better look before you step." Don laughed, patting him on the back.

"Son," Al answered, "there isn't going to be a next time. I'm keeping away from that Moki business."

The little stream and its deep pools were our lifeblood on our return to camp. We nearly died of the heat. We had avoided taking a thermometer with us; undoubtedly the psychological effect of knowing exactly what the temperature was would have killed us! Long ago the fever thermometer in the medical kit had exploded, and so had our marine compass in the relative coolness of the river. What must the temperature have been here in this closed-in canyon! It must have been at least 110 degrees, perhaps 120. We walked as much as we could in the water, and we peeled our clothes off and swam many times in the pools to refresh ourselves. We got back to camp at dusk. Since Fred and Bruce had left the bridge before us, they had arrived much earlier. Supper was on the fire, and Cid was cooking.

"You missed it all!" Tony said with excitement. "Al tried to kill himself on the Moki steps." So we told what had happened to the others.

"See—see! I told you to keep out of trouble. You better mind your mother from now on!" Cid exclaimed.

"And we're going to need a mother from now on too," Bruce spoke seriously. "Have you seen the boats?"

"No—what's the matter?" Don asked with alarm.

"They're high and dry on the beach—completely out of water," Bruce answered. All of us ran down to the river to see. Bruce was right! The boats were high and dry. When we had arrived at our camp, we had dragged only the nose of the *No Name* ashore. The river had dropped so quickly that the shoreline was some twenty feet beyond the *Brontosaur*!

"Boy! We're going to have some job dragging her back into the water tomorrow morning!" Don observed.

He was right; his remark was almost an understatement! We pulled, hauled, and tugged. We unloaded the boats to make them lighter. When we got them into the water, it wasn't deep enough to float them. We had to drag them into the deep channel, halfway across the river. We sank into the quicksand and muck to our knees as we pulled.

"We've only got sixty-nine more miles to go to Lee's Ferry, but I'll be darned if we'll make it if this keeps up!" Don growled.

"We've got to make it!" I said.

"Got to make it is right! Even if we have to drag the boats all the way, we've got to make it. We can't leave this river—not so long as there's enough water in it to drink!" Don answered.

Throughout the day, we found the sandbars to be larger and more numerous. We had had them before, and occasionally we had run aground. We had organized a guessing game with a reward for the one who could pick the side where the channel was, and we had joked about it. But there was no joking now! No matter which side we chose, we often had to drag the boats—especially the heavy *Brontosaur*—through the shallow water. Now we had a real crisis, and we were in a far more critical situation than any we had experienced before on the river, worse even than Cataract. Run out of river now? There was only one route through this desolate land—the river. What would we do if that route failed us? Would we have to leave our boats in the canyon with all our supplies and equipment and walk out? No—no, we didn't dare do that, not this far from any highway. It would be suicide to try to make it across the desert, up and down and around the hundreds of side canyons that cut into the barren, hot land. It was only sixty-odd miles to Lee's Ferry by river. How far would it be to get there on foot?

But as much as the water crisis, we thought of the canyons ahead—Marble Gorge and Grand Canyon. It hardly seemed now that there would be enough water in the river to get us through there—not with the *Brontosaur*. We needed a minimum of ten thousand cubic feet per seconds of water to get her through, we had been advised. With less than that, there would be too many rocks, and to get through with the big boat would be like trying to thread a hundred scattered needles. How much water did we have now? There was no way of telling exactly. The river was wide. Perhaps there was still enough water, and squeezed into the narrow gorges below, it would certainly be deeper. Then there was the

Little Colorado River coming in not far below. On the map it was a big river. The volume from it would help, we were sure. So before we allowed ourselves to think of abandoning hope of going on, we would wait until we saw the gauge at Lee's Ferry. Besides, for the first time since we had left the Uinta Mountains, we had clouds in the sky—heavy rain clouds, and at one point, rain fell. This gave us further hope that heavy rains in the vast area around us would bring the river up.

Yet when we pulled into our campsite at the mouth of a side canyon at mile point 685, where there was a wide sandbank, we all were resigned to the fact that we'd undoubtedly have to quit at Lee's Ferry. We began to think of civilization again—and our reentrance into it. We wondered what the impact would be like on us who had traveled in the wilderness for thirty days. Cid reorganized her gear—brought things she'd need—her crumpled suit, lipstick, nylon stockings, walking shoes—nearer the top, where they'd be accessible again. Al decided to shave off his heavy, black beard. "So I won't scare people," he exclaimed, "especially my wife!"

After supper I walked off by myself to explore the side canyon behind us. Going into it, I found myself in the narrowest canyon I'd visited on the whole journey. For long stretches, there was hardly room between the two walls to keep my shoulders from scraping the sides. It was a deep canyon and seemed even more so because of its narrowness. High, high above me was just a ribbon of purple sky. The stars shone though it wasn't yet night. I had to crane my neck to see them. As I looked, a heavy cloud passed over the canyon. I gave a quick glance at the narrow walls around me. This was a precarious place to be in if a flash flood came avalanching upon me! I turned and ran back.

As I came near the mouth of the canyon again, I noticed another small side canyon entering the one I was in. I looked above to a wider sky now that the canyon had opened up. It was clear, so I took a chance and started up it. The ground was wet—water seeping from somewhere—and tall grass grew all about. *Snakey place*, I thought, and so I watched my step. Several times a rustling in the grass startled me. Mice, perhaps, but yet? I was leery and almost turned back, thinking nothing was worth the risk of being frightened to death by a rattlesnake.

But I went on, almost as if drawn by a magnet, to where the walls narrowed down to a slit of a portal. I peered into the opening and entered, feeling as though I were an intruder in another's house. I came upon a place of such perfection that I exclaimed out loud, "Oh!" Before me was a vast chamber, almost perfectly round, with a domed roof of golden sandstone, and cut through it to the sky was a crescent-shaped slit in the rock. Edging one side was the blood-red light of the setting sun. The color seemed to melt into a thousand hues as it ran down to the floor of the chamber, where it was a soft yellow. In the center was a pool, a round emerald, surrounded by a band of golden sand. The water's surface was so still that it reflected a mirror image of what was above it. Low on the walls circling the pool grew lacy, maidenhair fern.

Nothing was stirring, not the slightest ripple on the water, not a leaf on the fern. Even the molecules of air seemed suspended in silence. The sound of my "oh" had no place here, and its echo bounded back and forth, back and forth, as though it were the first sound ever to enter this place. I thought it would never diminish, never escape. Yet it did finally cease, and I felt a heavy silence. I thought I had entered the very soul of the Earth. Was this the heaven the Indian god Ta-vwoats had showed the chief Nu'-ma? Yes, yes—this must be it! Could it be otherwise? No place could be more perfect in beauty than this.

I stood for a long while, hardly breathing, barely able to believe what I was seeing. Inside, my heart pounded, almost in fear. I felt hypnotized, in a trance. I made myself move across the sand. My footsteps made no sound on the hard-packed sand, nor left an imprint there. An eerie feeling came over me again as I stood at the opposite end. I felt no human had ever been in this place before. I felt I was looking into the dark secret of the world as I stared into the pool. There was no bottom; it just went deeper and deeper, the color on the sides changing from green around the edge, to blue, to purple, to violet, to blackness—beyond there I could not see. I became dizzy looking down into the depth. I thought I might be looking into my own soul!

I sat in silence for nearly an hour, entranced, and it was dark by the time I came back to camp. "Where have you been?" someone asked.

"I've just been to the secret soul of the Earth," I replied.

"Oh, come now, Eggert—you've been eating too much locoweed!" Fred laughed.

"No—no, you must go there tomorrow; after you see this place, there is nothing more to see. If any of you are seeking something from this voyage, you will find it there."

Fred Wood with his duffle bag in camp.

We camped on the long sandbank that ran from the mouth of the side canyon. Close to the wall of Glen Canyon, scrubby greasewood grew high on the talus slope. Their wood gave our fire a pleasant aroma. Cid put her cot up close to the boats, which were tied to rocks at the lower end of the sandbank. Tony chose a spot close to the canyon wall to sleep. He was nestled down in a depression in the sand. Bruce, Al, Don, and I chose to sleep by the mouth of the side canyon. There was a draft of air coming out of it that made it the coolest spot. Don looked up at the sky as he laid out his ground cloth. "If I feel one drop of rain—just one drop, I'm heading for the boats," he exclaimed. The sky was filled with dark ominous clouds, and in the distance we saw flashes of lightning. Thunder rumbled far off. The wind began to blow, and I felt uneasy. We were in a precarious place!

I had no more than fallen asleep when I was awakened by a violent wind and shouts from Cid. Sparks from our fire, which had been whipped into life again by the wind, were flying all around. Our dishes, pots, and pans banged and crashed as they were blown about. The rain began to fall. Don jumped up and ran toward the boats, dragging his sleeping bag and ground sheet behind him. "Mamma! Mamma!" he shouted. "I want my mamma!"

Bruce followed. "Head for the boats, men!" he yelled. Al and I followed quickly.

"We'd best sleep by the boats—just in case we hear a roar coming down that canyon!" Don shouted against the wind as the rest of us ran about gathering up the dishes. Then we all bedded down in a half circle around Cid. Wrapped in whatever protection we had against the wind and rain, we were all close together, side by side, closer than we had ever been during our voyage. As I lay there feeling everyone's presence, I thought of each one. To my right was Fred, always willing to pull more than his share, conscientious, always keeping a watchful eye on Cid for us, being more aware of her needs. How he had changed since we started out! Now he was full of the self-confidence I thought he lacked at the beginning. Now the West was more than just a hobby to him. It was a challenge, and he was able to stand up against it.

Bruce was at my left—Bruce, the youngest, perhaps the most admired, handsome, quiet, solid mentally and physically. I smiled to myself thinking back to my first impression of him: so fat, so young! I couldn't have been more wrong! Then there was Tony, four years Bruce's senior, yet younger seeming somehow. He was still searching his way, trying to find a path in life, impressionable. Often he seemed completely in a fog, as if the experience was too much for him. I regretted that I could do so little to help him find a way. But the experience wasn't physically too big for him. I remembered the way he had lugged so much heavy equipment to Rainbow Bridge. He would always have my admiration for that!

Next to Tony was Al: jovial, lighthearted, easygoing. It was so like Al to be reading paperback murder mysteries while we floated through the canyons. While running the rapids, he would lay the book down beside him, run the rapid, then pick it up again. Nothing bothered Al . . . except losing the last page of a mystery when the wind tore it from the book's binding. He never knew who the murderer was! Then came Don, my partner and coleader: cautious, sharp, quick to figure things out. With boats he had a talent beyond compare and an almost superhuman sense about the river. We had put our lives in his hands, and he was worthy of our trust on the river. Cid came next, completing the circle with her cot but more so with her gentleness, wisdom, understanding, and compassion. Cid was the keystone, the psychological ballast, that held us together.

I thought of the seven of us who had traveled so far together these thirty days, who had become such close companions. Beyond all the wonders, all the beauty, was the miracle of people—these seven people huddled together here in the wind and rain. Only Don had I known before the expedition began, and even then, I had known him only slightly when you came right down to it. We had had an enormous amount of luck on the river, perhaps more than anyone else who had traveled this far on it; but the greater luck was in getting together this diversified group of seven people who had come to know and love one another. We had gained much from this voyage: physically, mentally, and spiritually. But most of all, each of us had gained six true friends. This circle of seven people was bound by a common experience, an experience that would perhaps overshadow any we would ever have again. Unlike friends you acquire aboard ship crossing an ocean and lose as soon as you set foot ashore, these friends would last forever. Robert Louis Stevenson wrote, ". . . and the best that we find in our travels is an honest friend. He is a fortunate voyager who finds many." Certainly above all else, we were fortunate voyagers!

We began July 11 with our thirty-first batch of pancakes, made as usual by Bruce with his special recipe: Bisquick and river water. As the silt became thicker in the river, the pancakes got tougher. These were the toughest yet. "Bruce," Don remarked, "if we do go on through Grand, I'm going to have to sharpen my teeth!" Near the bottom of the food box, we found several cans of corned-beef hash, which we cooked along with our other breakfast regulars: eggs and canned bacon. It was a welcome addition!

The rest of the day was passed like the one before: fighting the low water, pushing and tugging, running the motor through deep water, dragging the boats through the shallows. To make matters worse, a strong wind blew against us and kicked waves up from the river, and sand, blowing over the canyon rim from the Painted Desert beyond, blasted and cut our faces and hands.

Near the end of Glen Canyon, the walls reached their maximum height, and rounding a big bend, we came upon some shanties and a ladder built up the side of the canyon wall to the top. This was the site of the Glen Canyon Dam. We passed it, trying not to notice; we didn't dare think of those millions of tons of concrete that will be poured here, blocking the river, backing up the water, creating the reservoir, flooding all that we had seen: Music Temple, Twilight Amphitheater, Hidden Passage, and the place where the Earth's soul was hidden, Guardian Pool.

At four o'clock, we came to one of the gauges of the USGS station at Lee's Ferry, Arizona.[3] The water was so low that we had to dig a trench to bring it to the gauge so we could read it. The water came to the fifteen mark. "Fifteen what?" we wondered. Fifteen thousand cubic feet per seconds of water? Hardly; there couldn't be that much. Fifteen feet deep? Not likely either!

Below the gauge, on the other side of the river a quarter of a mile downstream, was a house and several outbuildings and a boat dock. We pulled in just as a high-powered outboard motorboat came fighting upstream against the current. Landing beside us, a man got out and introduced himself as Dean Tidball of the USGS. "You must be the Eggert-Hatch expedition," he said. Yes, we were, we answered. "You're not going to try to go on are you?" he asked.

"We hope to," Don answered. "What are the water conditions?" We held our breath for the answer. I'm not sure what each of us wanted to hear. Certainly we wanted to complete our voyage, yet—yet we had seen a lot. With Guardian Pool crowning it all, we felt we had seen the ultimate. There we had seen the mythical heaven of the Indian gods, we were certain. No matter what was ahead, there could be nothing more rewarding than Glen Canyon.

"Terrible—worse this year than last," Tidball answered Don. "You've got sixty-eight hundred now, and it's dropping fast."

"Sixty-eight, did you say?" Don asked.

"That's all; I wouldn't advise Grand on that little," Dean Tidball answered. "And it has been dropping steadily for the past two weeks. No chance of a rise this time of year either."

"We had some rain last night," Tony exclaimed.

"Did you?" Tidball asked. "Well, it must have been local. You'll never get the kind of rain you need to bring this river up now."

"But what about the Little Colorado—there will be a lot of water coming in there, won't there?" Tony asked eagerly.

"The Little Colorado?" Tidball laughed. "That river dried up a month ago! It only runs three months out of the year."

"What did that gauge upstream read?" Don asked.

"That's surface level—it read about fourteen or fifteen feet, didn't it?" Tidball replied. "That's depth out in the center of the river.

"Well," Don said with resignation, "it looks like we've had it." He turned to Tidball and asked, "Is there a telephone around?"

"Not here—the nearest one is forty-one miles away at Jacob Lake; the other is at Cameron, seventy-one miles south."

We learned there was a bus to Flagstaff at four in the morning. It stopped at Marble Canyon Lodge, seven miles above us on U.S. 89, which ran across the plateau.

"Is there any way we can get up there?" Fred asked.

"I'm going up in a half hour to get the mail. Be glad to take you," Tidball answered. "Won't go up again for two more days."

Two more days or a half hour! It was Cid and Fred's chance to get out and call Vernal for transportation. Hectically they got their things together. Phone numbers and messages were quickly scribbled for Fred to pass on when he got to a phone. There wasn't time to say good-bye except for a quick handshake with Fred and a kiss from Cid, and they were gone. It was just as well, this fast good-bye. It was strange that they should go just as quickly as they had appeared. No time for sentimentalities. No rehashing of experiences. We would be together again. We could never say good-bye and really mean it.

After Dean Tidball's truck had pulled away, we floated the boats downstream to a spot where there were a couple of cottonwood trees. There we made camp, the five of us who were left, and there we remained for a day and two nights awaiting transportation out. When Dean Tidball returned from his trip to the top, he brought cans of cold beer and soft drinks that Fred had sent down to us. We drank a toast to Fred and Cid as we sat around our dwindling campfire, thinking of them up there with all the wide world spread out around them, waiting in the night for the bus. We would be spread out on the sandy bank of the river, surrounded still by canyon walls, listening to the soft murmur of the river, sleeping under only half of the stars.

*Twenty-Eight*

# *L'ENVOI*—GRAND CANYON

June 27, 1956: Fred and I stood at the Powell Memorial on the south rim of the Grand Canyon, looking down into that immense place.[1] "Can you believe we made it, that we were down there a couple of days ago?" he asked.

"No," I answered. "No, I can't." We sat down together, silently reflecting as the shadows changed the contours of the inverted mountains below.

Before we had left Lee's Ferry in July of 1955, we had stashed away our boats at the gauging station, and on June 11, 1956—a year to the day when we had left Green River, Wyoming—we again set off on the river. As I stood on the riverbank the night before we left on the last 312 miles of our voyage, I felt the earth beneath my feet tremble from the surging force of the river that had ten times the volume it had had when we had camped here the year before. My only solace was in knowing that the higher the water, the deeper the rocks would be covered. On the other hand, the greater the volume, the greater the force and turbulence—so I had no more feeling of confidence that we'd come out alive than anyone else who had dared challenge this river.

We went down those final 312 miles: through Marble Gorge and Grand Canyon; past mile point 760, where Bert Loper's wrecked boat remains above the high water mark as a memorial; past Stanton's Point and Peter Hansborough's grave by the seven-hundred-foot column; past mile point 782, where Boyd Moore had been drowned in May 1955. And we stopped and stood for a moment in silence at Separation Canyon,

Lava Falls, a major rapid on the Grand Canyon stretch of the Colorado River is shown. This was taken on the 1956 trip. Photograph courtesy of Frederick Hoffman Wood Collection, Special Collections, J. Willard Marriott Library, University of Utah.

where the two Howland brothers and Bill Dunn had abandoned the Powell Expedition.[2] We fought through more than 365 rapids—Unkar, Sockdolager, Hance, Horn Creek, Lava Falls. We saw sights of beauty and peacefulness—compared to the tumult of the canyon and the rapids: the vivid blue water of the Little Colorado River where it joined the silty-brown Colorado, a scene of such incredible color that we couldn't believe it even as we stood there looking at it; Deer Creek Falls, cascading more than a hundred feet over the canyon wall to the river below; Havasu Canyon, filled with sky blue water held in by walls whitewashed by nature; Elves Chasm, so magical we were convinced the wee folk did indeed inhabit it.

We broke oars in the wild water, and we nearly lost a boat in Hance Rapid. On the night of June 17, at ten minutes to twelve, we had to take to the high rocks when the river rose suddenly and washed the sandbar away from under us so quickly that we hardly had time to rescue our boats and grab the cameras and duffle.

Crew members of the 1956 trip with their boats in Marble Canyon on the Colorado River. Jack Brennan, of Harris-Brennan River Expeditions, joined them for the Grand Canyon in his outboard boat *JAX*. Photograph courtesy of Frederick Hoffman Wood Collection, Special Collections, J. Willard Marriott Library, University of Utah.

From the time we left Lee's Ferry until we came into Lake Mead, we fought the river, and it fought back. There was little time for the quiet, peaceful moments we had enjoyed in the other canyons. Almost all of it was like Cataract, except we were two thousand feet deeper in the earth, and the canyon around us was so immense that we lost all sense of scale.

We knew when we started that things wouldn't be the same; we could never recapture the experience we had had before. Don left us at Bright Angel Trail in Grand Canyon National Park early one morning to go to Pakistan on a special assignment to run the Indus River.[3] On the way up the trail to the north rim, he met Smuss Allan coming down en route to replace him as head boatman. Al was with us again, and Bruce, and ten new people. Cid might have come, but an operation at the last minute prevented her.

Though the same flags flew from the boats, and Frog was tied again to the nose of the *Brontosaur*, it wasn't the same expedition that had left Green River, Wyoming. There are those who will say that the

The Hatch's *Brontosaurus* raft being towed in the flat water of Lake Mead during the 1956 trip. Photograph courtesy of Hatch River Expedition Collection, Special Collections, J. Willard Marriott Library, University of Utah.

The crew of the 1956 expedition, top row from left to right: Philip Hyde, Doug Harvey, Fred Wood, Phil Sterns, Smuss Allen, Al Galloway, Bruce Lium, and Clark Lium. Second row, left to right: Charles Eggert, Nancy Gilmore, Mary Dorsey, Jack Brennan, Harvey (?), and Janet Hosse. Photograph courtesy of Sebastian Eggert.

The three members of the expedition that went on both trips in 1955 and 1956: Fred Wood (left), Charles Eggert (center), and Bruce Lium. Photograph copyright 1956 by Philip Leland Hyde, used with permission.

Eggert-Hatch River Expedition didn't make it all the way at all, that we were defeated by the river at Lee's Ferry, Arizona. In a way they are right; the river did defeat us, but not in the violent way it had so many others. Rather, it captured us in a spiritual way, and none of us will ever be the same again. We hadn't reached our goal in 1955, and I remember standing beside the riverbank feeling defeated in July of that year. Then I remembered the Mallory quote had I read at Rainbow Bridge: "It is not the summit that matters . . . not the Victory, but the gain." The gain? Serendipity.

We had more than enough excitement—physical excitement—on our voyage through Marble Gorge and Grand Canyon—the same kind of excitement we had had in Cataract. But there was little of the *other* kind of excitement—the serendipities—we had shared during those thirty-one days in 1955. And those are the excitements that count, that remain with you always: the ones you talk about and think about after the harum-scarum stuff has been told.

We had seen Ta-vwoats's forbidden passage through the Earth's crust that he split asunder. We can consider ourselves blessed to have made it safely all the way. And we accomplished what we set out to do—to make a motion picture record of those eighteen canyons that Major Powell first traveled through in 1869. Not one foot of film was lost, and so far as I know, ours is the only complete record of that entire route.

"Let's line up for a picture," someone suggested the morning after we docked at Temple Bar, Arizona, on Lake Mead. The fourteen of us stood before the camera.

Not thinking of how our original party had diminished, I suggested that all those who had started from Green River, Wyoming, get together for a picture. Bruce Lium, Fred Wood, and I stood before the camera. We three were the only ones left from the original party and the last to go all the way down Ta-vwoats's forbidden passage.

# NOTES

INTRODUCTION

1. Charles Eggert is D491, the four-year-old boy who was duped into surgery by his mother and aunt, in Helen Flanders Dunbar, *Emotions and Bodily Changes: A Survey of Literature on Psychosomatic Interrelationships, 1910–1953*, 4th edition (New York: Columbia University Press, 1954), 672–73.
2. Charles Eggert to author, April 29, 2000, email message. Later in that message Eggert elaborated on his evolving relationship with the dance: "It wasn't until Alvin Ailey and his troupe, Dance Theater of Harlem, came along that I saw in dance the real opportunity it offered in expressing masculinity. God-a-Mighty! I remember the first time I saw those dancers—up at the Saratoga Performing Arts Center. I damned near went ape-shit right there in my front-row-center seat. The comparisons began and grew, and today, ballet turns me off. I SHOULD qualify that: Classical Ballet turns me off."
3. Kenneth Grahame, *The Wind in the Willows* (London: Methuen, 1908; reprint Avon: The Bath Press, 1987), 10.
4. Stuart MacMackin, "Phidelah Rice School of the Spoken Word," *Dukes County Intelligencer* 23, no. 1 (August 1982): 18–30. Phidelah Rice operated a winter school, the Phidelah Rice School of Voice, in Cleveland, Ohio.
5. Eggert to author, January 12, 1999, email message. Tennyson first published "Crossing the Bar" in 1889 and requested that it be included as the last piece in any collections of his work posthumously published.
6. Eggert to author, February 26, 2000, email message.
7. Eggert to author, February 26, 2000, email message.
8. "First Lady In San Juan," *New York Times*, March 9, 1944, p. 19, col. 2.
9. Eggert to author, November 30, 1998, email message. Eleanor Roosevelt, "My Day," March 15, 1944. Courtesy of Christopher Alhambra, Eleanor Roosevelt Papers Project, The George Washington University, Washington, DC.
10. Eggert to author, February 25, 2001, email message.
11. Eggert to author, February 25, 2001; November 23, 1998, email messages.
12. Eggert to author, February 25, 2001, email message.
13. Eggert, "We Came to Shell, Wyoming, via Connecticut," typewritten manuscript signed, n.d., 3–5. Author's files, courtesy R. Sebastian Eggert.
14. Eggert to author, February 25, 2001, email message.
15. Freeman Tilden, *The National Parks: What They Mean to You and Me* (New York: Alfred A. Knopf, 1951).
16. Eggert to Ansel Adams, January 5, 1952, typewritten letter carbon copy, p. 2. All correspondence between Eggert and correspondents other than the author has come from the Charles Eggert Papers, ACCN 1659, Manuscript Division, J. Willard Marriott

Library, University of Utah, Salt Lake City. The Marriott Library extended the author generous access to Eggert's papers before they had been formally processed, consequently box and folder citations are not provided here.

17. Ansel Adams to Charles Eggert, n.d., typewritten signed letter.
18. US Department of the Interior, "The Colorado River: A Natural Menace Becomes a National Resource; A Comprehensive Departmental Report on the Development of the Water Resources of the Colorado River Basin for Review Prior to Submission to the Congress," March 1946, 116–17.
19. The name "Little Stinker" has passed from use, supplanted by "Winnie's Rock," probably because the boulder is lodged in the river at the mouth of the side canyon Powell named "Winnie's Grotto."
20. Charles D. Eggert, interviewed by Robert Sebastian Eggert, July 28, 1995, tape recording. Author's files, courtesy Charles Eggert.
21. Fred M. Packard, National Parks Association, Washington, DC, to Richard H. Pough, American Museum of Natural History, New York, New York, December 30, 1952.
22. The Dinosaur Cooperators included the Sierra Club, the Izaak Walton League, the Wilderness Society, the National Parks Association, the National Wildlife Federation, the Garden Club of America, the General Federation of Women's Clubs, the Wildlife Federation, and the CIO.

    Through the decades scholars have accorded *Wilderness River Trail* increasing credit. Owen Stratton and Phillip Sirotkin, *The Echo Park Controversy*, The Inter-University Case Program, (University: University of Alabama Press, 1959) mentioned it repeatedly but declined to interpret its importance or effect. Richard Edward Baird, "The Politics of Echo Park and Other Water Development Projects in the Upper Colorado River Basin, 1946–1956," Ph.D. dissertation, Political Science. (Urbana: University of Illinois, 1960) acknowledged the film's role but devoted more attention to shifts in voting patterns by members of Congress than to the realm of public opinion. Mark W. T. Harvey's *A Symbol of Wilderness: Echo Park and the American Conservation Movement* (Albuquerque: University of New Mexico Press, 1994) deftly blends political wrangling and the steering of popular sentiments. An administrative history of the North Cascades National Park singled it out for special mention: "The two most effective weapons in the Dinosaur campaign were the film, *Wilderness River Trail* and the book, *This is Dinosaur*, [edited] by Wallace Stegner; these were Brower's ideas." See David Louther, "Contested Terrain: The Establishment of North Cascades National Park," Chapter 1 in *Contested History: North Cascades National Park Service Complex, An Administrative History* (Seattle: National Park Service, 1998), note 59.
23. Eggert to Bus Hatch and Don Hatch, November 18, 1954, typescript letter carbon copy. Don Hatch to Charles Eggert, November 28, 1954, typescript letter signed.
24. Powell's trips have spawned an enormous list of writings. His own telling of the tale is readily accessible today in John Wesley Powell, *The Explorations of the Colorado River and Its Canyons* (New York: Dover, 1961). The Galloway trip of 1896–97 is documented in a series of letters back to his hometown newspaper the *Vernal Express* between June 30, and October 6, 1898. The Flavell voyage is documented in George F. Flavell, *The Log of the Panthon*, Neil B. Carmony and David E. Brown, eds., (Boulder: Pruett, 1987). Julius Stone's *Canyon Country: The Romance of a Drop of Water and a Grain of Sand* (New York: G. P. Putnam's Sons, 1932) chronicles this historic expedition in Stone's prose and hundreds of photographs by Raymond A. Coggswell. Vince

Welch, Cort Conley, and Brad Dimock's *The Doing of the Thing: The Brief, Brilliant, Whitewater Career of Buzz Holmstrom* (Flagstaff: Fretwater Press, 1998), one of the finest boatman biographies yet written, covers Holmstrom's glorious and enigmatic life exceptionally well. Roy Webb's *If We Had a Boat: Green River Explorers, Adventurers, and Runners* (Salt Lake City: University of Utah Press, 1986) briefly discusses the Nevills expedition of 1940. See also Nevills's journal from the 1940 trip, available in Roy Webb's edited collection, *High, Wide, and Handsome: The River Journals of Norman D. Nevills* (Logan: Utah State University Press, 2005), 61–94.

25. Don Hatch to Charles Eggert, 9 December [1954], autograph letter signed.
26. Eggert to Don Hatch, December 21, 1954, typescript letter carbon copy.
27. Eggert to Personals Department, *Saturday Review*, March 30, 1955, typescript letter carbon copy. The advertisement ran on April 16 and 30 on p. 57 and 36, respectively, and on May 7, 1955, p. 66.
28. Eggert to Patricia Fretwell, May 9, 1955, typescript letter carbon copy.
29. Eggert to author, January 1, 1999, email message.
30. [Richard Roevere], "Adventurama," in "The Talk of the Town" section, *The New Yorker* June 11, 1955, 24–26; Charles Eggert to author, July 21, 2001, email message.
31. Wallace Stegner, *Beyond the Hundredth Meridian: John Wesley Powell and the Second Opening of the West* (Boston: Houghton, Mifflin, 1954).
32. Eggert to author, February 13, 1998, email message.
33. Don Hatch, "Eggert-Hatch River Expedition—Green River, Wyo. to Lake Mead," autograph journal in daybook calendar photocopy. Author's files, courtesy of Don Hatch River Expeditions, Vernal, Utah.
34. Donald Worster, *A River Running West: The Life of John Wesley Powell* (New York: Oxford University Press, 2001), 437–39.
35. Adventurama Productions, "List of Engagements," 1955–1960, typescript photocopy. Author's files, courtesy Charles Eggert.
36. Historic American Building Survey, HABS NY,14-RHINB.v,2, Library of Congress, Washington, DC.
37. J. M. Thompson, *The Synoptic Gospels: Arranged in Parallel Columns* (Oxford: Clarendon Press, 1910; reprint, London and New York: Oxford University Press, 1969).
38. Eggert to author, February 17, 1998, email message.
39. Cid Ricketts Sumner, *Traveler in the Wilderness* (New York: Harper & Brothers, 1957; London: Macdonald, 1958).
40. Anthony Tuttle, *This Time in Twilight* (New York: New American Library, 1966). Anthony Tuttle, interviewed by author, October 16, 1999. Tape recorded telephone interview. Author's files.
41. Eggert, *The Sculptured Earth* (Red Hook: Charles Eggert Productions for the National Park Service, 1962).
42. Thomas G. Smith, "The Canyonlands National Park Controversy," *Utah Historical Quarterly* 59, no. 3 (Summer 1991): 216–242.
43. *A Canyon Voyage*, script by David Brower and Charles Eggert, cinematography by Charles Eggert, (Red Hook: Charles Eggert Productions for the Sierra Club, 1965); Charles Eggert to author, 1 October 1, 1997, email message.
44. Roy D. Webb, *Riverman: The Story of Bus Hatch* (Rock Springs: Labyrinth Publishing, 1989).
45. Eggert, "Forbidden Passage," *Sierra Club Bulletin* 43, no. 9 (November 1958): 44, 52.

CHAPTER ONE

1. This bill, passed by Congress and signed by President Eisenhower in 1954, called for a series of dams that would tame the Green and Colorado Rivers and many of their tributaries. Within the next two decades, two major dams—Flaming Gorge and Fontenelle—were built on the Green River, Glen Canyon dam was built on the Colorado, along with the Navajo Dam on the San Juan River, and no fewer than three dams were constructed on the Gunnison River in Colorado.
2. What began as a "hell on wheels" railroad town in 1868 had become, by 1955, the launching point for virtually every major expedition down the Green River. The reasons were simple: the upper end of the Colorado River is all but impassable due to rapids, and the town of Green River, Wyoming, is easily reached by train. John Wesley Powell started the trend in 1869 and came back for his 1871 expedition. Julius Stone (1909), the Kolb brothers (1911), and the USGS surveyors (1922) followed him. These and many other river runners are memorialized at Expedition Island, a national historic landmark within the city limits of Green River.
3. Eggert is counting river mileage downriver from Green River, Wyoming; thus, these locations are in the Grand Canyon, more than seven hundred miles downstream. All of these notations refer to Bert Loper, an early Colorado River boatman. Specifically, they refer to his 1949 Grand Canyon trip where he lost his life. The first notes that he capsized his boat, with Wayne Nichol as his passenger, in 24.5 Mile Rapid; the second describes the last time he was seen, floating into 25 Mile Rapid, and the last notes where his boat was found, fifteen miles downstream, just above Buck Farm Canyon. Loper was not seen alive again, but a hiker found his skeleton thirty miles farther downstream, near Cardenas Creek, in 1975.
4. Peter Hansborough, who drowned along with George Richards in 25 Mile Rapid in July 1889, was the only victim of three whose body was found. Franklin M. Brown, the leader of the expedition, had died just below Soap Creek Rapid a few days earlier. All were members of the Brown-Stanton expedition, which was seeking a route for a water-level railroad from Colorado to California. Robert Brewster Stanton, the engineer, abandoned the river after Hansborough and Richards died and climbed out of the Grand Canyon, only to return the next year and finish the trip; during this expedition, Hansborough's skeleton was found at the foot of President Harding Rapid. Hansborough's grave can still be visited today. The burial spot is shared by the grave of a Boy Scout who died in Glen Canyon in the 1950s, and whose body was found in the same eddy as Hansborough's.
5. This would be Skull Creek Rapid in Red Canyon on the upper Green River. Hook was a prospector who died trying to follow Powell in 1869.
6. Carlton Boyd Moore was a twenty-two-year-old student at Northern Arizona University. While on a trip with legendary Grand Canyon hiker Harvey Butchart, Moore tried to cross the river on an inflatable air mattress somewhere above the Little Colorado River. A poor swimmer, Moore was swept away and drowned. His body was never found.
7. Clyde Eddy, *Down the World's Most Dangerous River* (New York: Frederick A. Stokes Company, 1929).
8. Major John Wesley Powell (1834–1902) was a teacher, soldier, scholar, explorer, author, and founder of government bureaus. In the context of this book he is important

because of his pioneering voyages of exploration down the Green and Colorado Rivers in 1869 and again in 1871. His account of these journeys, *The Exploration of the Colorado River and Its Canyons,* was the first written description of the canyons of the Green and Colorado; it has gone through numerous editions and is still in print. No one connected with the Colorado River has been written about more than Powell, and his influence reaches to the present. Powell and his men named most of the canyons and many of the rapids and other features along the rivers that Eggert traversed in 1955 and 1956. It should be noted that while Powell's book is purported to be an account of the 1869 voyage, the narrative actually combines the two trips that he made, and many of the names he includes and the incidents he relates came from the 1871 expedition. No satisfactory explanation has ever been given for this.

9. John Colter, a famous mountain man, was a member of the Lewis and Clark expedition who went off on his own before the travelers returned home in 1806. He is generally considered to be the discoverer of what later became Yellowstone National Park.
10. George Leigh Mallory, who disappeared while trying to climb Mt. Everest in 1924.

CHAPTER TWO

1. Vernal was founded in 1878 by, among others, Jeremiah Hatch, grandfather of Bus Hatch. It is the county seat of Uintah County, Utah, and is the center for river running in Dinosaur National Monument.
2. Robert Rafael Hatch (1902–67) was known as Bus for most of his life. A carpenter and contractor by trade, Bus ran rivers first as a hobby and later as a business from his first trip in 1931 until shortly before his death in 1967. He was the father of four sons, two of whom, Don and Ted, were responsible for building Hatch River Expeditions into one of the best known, and at times the largest, river running company in the country.
3. The Hatch boatyard, at the corner of 200 North and 400 East streets in Vernal, is still a busy place during the river season and looks largely the way it did when Charles Eggert pulled up there in 1955. It occupies the location of the original settlement of Vernal, which was for a time known as Hatchtown
4. Another of Bus's sons, Frank, worked occasionally on the river but later became a CPA in Salt Lake City, Utah.
5. Bruce Lium, seventeen years old, was one of two brothers from Salt Lake City who worked for Hatch during the summers.
6. The *Brontosaur* was a twenty-seven-foot bridge pontoon, purchased as surplus from the US Army after World War II. The inflatable pontoons were designed to be hooked together side by side and a track laid over them, thus forming a temporary bridge. Hatch was one of the first to adapt these pontoons to river running by adding a wooden frame and two sets of oars and, later, an outboard motor. The basic design, albeit with many subsequent modifications, is still in use today. Although almost impossible to maneuver efficiently, it had several advantages over wooden boats: it was cheap, very sturdy, easily repaired, and could carry up to a dozen passengers. The other boat was a ten-man surplus military raft, about sixteen feet long and capable of carrying five people comfortably.
7. Cid Ricketts Sumner (1890–1970) was the only woman passenger on the trip. An author and traveler, she added an element of grace and humor to the journey and,

despite Eggert's initial doubts about her suitability for such an adventure, became much beloved by all of the crew. Her book, *Traveler in the Wilderness* (New York: Harper and Brothers, 1957), has, up to this point, been the only written account of the trip. For more on her life, see the section "After the River" at the end of this book.

8. The Echo Park Dam was one of the units of the Colorado River Storage Project. It called for a massive dam on the Green River, just downstream from its confluence with the Yampa River, and thus in the middle of Dinosaur National Monument. The proposed location of the dam set off a grassroots antidam firestorm that raged for several years and ultimately led to the decision not to build the dam at all. This defeat of the plans by the Bureau of Reclamation for a major dam is today considered the genesis of the modern American environmental movement. Eggert had been closely involved in the antidam efforts, and his films *This is Dinosaur* and *Wilderness River Trail* are considered by some historians to be among the major deciding factors that swung public opinion against the dam. Support for the dam, and disappointment when it was defeated, was still very strong in Vernal at the time when Eggert was writing, as his experiences at the state employment office demonstrated.

CHAPTER THREE

1. In June of 1955, the Green River near Jensen, Utah, was discharging almost ten thousand cubic feet per second, about ten times the amount that is now released from Flaming Gorge Dam.
2. Petroglyphs are the incised drawings left by Native Americans. Virtually all of those in Dinosaur National Monument—and they are extensive—were created by the Fremont culture, who inhabited the area around one thousand years ago. However, since these petroglyphs depict horses, which were unknown at that time, they must be much more recent, probably Ute.
3. Today this spot is the location of the Split Mountain boat ramp, where all river trips through Dinosaur National Monument leave the river.

CHAPTER FOUR

1. Leslie Jones, a distant cousin of the Hatch family, who had been working for Hatch for several summers by then. Jones later became a civil engineer and a noted river runner in his own right, famous for his solo trips in a modified canoe. He became well known in the river community for his scroll maps. More on Les Jones appears in the "After the River" section.
2. Frederick Hoffman Wood (1904–86), a Connecticut book dealer and the oldest man on the trip. More on him also appears in "After the River."

CHAPTER FIVE

1. US 191 and Utah 44.
2. The Red Canyon Overlook Visitor's Center is just off Utah 44, a few miles south of Manila, Utah. The view—and the gaping fissure that Eggert describes—is still there, but today paved trails lead to an overlook surrounded by guardrails, and the view looks down into a canyon partially filled by Flaming Gorge Reservoir.
3. Today Utah 44 bypasses the steep Sheep Creek Canyon road, but you can still travel the road through what has been designated as the Sheep Creek Canyon geological area.

4. Anthony Marchant Tuttle (1933–2001) was a student at Bard College in Rhinebeck, New York, when Eggert hired him to join the trip as a photographer's assistant. More about him appears in the "After the River" section.

CHAPTER SIX

1. Dr. Robert Jerome Parsons (1907–86). Dr. Parsons was Fred Wood's brother-in-law, and had an interesting and varied career. More about him appears in "After the River."
2. Frog survived the trip and is now part of the Charles Eggert collection in the Special Collections Department, Marriott Library, University of Utah.

CHAPTER SEVEN

1. For about seventy miles below Green River, Wyoming, the Green flowed through open country lined with cottonwood bottoms and dotted with ranches, houses, and ferries. The only relief in the landscape was provided by the Firehole Towers, a section marked by badland buttes, where Eggert's party camped their first night.

CHAPTER EIGHT

1. John Wesley Powell named Flaming Gorge in 1869 for the red color of the rocks. It was only about a mile long, but the swirling currents where the river entered the canyon gave rise to the legend of the deadly "Green River suck," dating from the mountain man days.
2. Powell also named this canyon in 1869. Another short canyon, it was cut through gray limestone and so called because it was just a big U-shaped curve.
3. Nielsen Flat was an open area on the left bank just below Horseshoe Canyon. There had once been a ranch there, but by the time the Eggert party passed through, it had long been abandoned. Access was by way of Sheep Creek Canyon.
4. In 1869 Powell noted so many of the eponymous birds that he named the canyon after them. Although not nearly as common, they can still be seen today in the river canyon below Flaming Gorge Dam.
5. Red Canyon cuts through the Uinta Mountains in a west-to-east direction and was named for the deep red color of the Uinta Mountain quartzite, a very hard Precambrian rock. It is the longest of the canyons of the upper Green River and was the first place where river travelers encountered significant rapids.
6. Carter Creek was but the first of many clear trout streams that entered Red Canyon; all of them were popular camping spots because of the clear water and abundance of fish. The Eggert party's bad luck was unusual; in 1922 Ralf Woolley noted that his party caught thirty-five trout in two hours in the same spot. Cid Sumner wrote of Carter Creek: "[H]ere at last I had arrived at perfection."

CHAPTER NINE

1. Ashley Falls was one of the biggest rapids on the Green. It was formed by huge boulders that had fallen from the canyon wall and got its name from the inscription—"Ashley 1825"—left by William Ashley, a fur trader and explorer. Powell saw the inscription in 1869 and gave the rapid its name. Over the years, many others added their names, so that by the time the Eggert party passed by, there was a "river register" at the site. Although it appeared dangerous, Ashley Falls was actually a comparatively easy run. It is now covered by Flaming Gorge Reservoir.

2. Just a few miles below Ashley Falls, near the mouth of Carter Creek, the party passed the site where construction for Flaming Gorge Dam started the next year. The dam was completed in 1963.
3. The Les Jones scale of one to eleven for difficulty of rapids is his own. Rapid ratings today are standardized on one of two scales: the international scale of one to six, where Ashley Falls was a three or a four at the most, and the Grand Canyon scale of one to ten.
4. Red Creek Rapid is formed by the outflow from Red Creek, which drains a large area of southwestern Wyoming and northeastern Utah. Boulders from the many floods have filled in the channel of the Green, creating what is still today a major—and, at times, even deadly—rapid. The stretch of Red Canyon below Flaming Gorge Dam is very popular today with recreational boaters and fly fishermen, and Red Creek Rapid is the main hazard remaining in the canyon. Ironically, many early boaters worried about running Ashley Falls, made it through that rapid, then went downstream in a more relaxed mode and wrecked their boats in Red Creek Rapid.

CHAPTER TEN

1. Brown's Park is a large open area below Red Canyon and above the Canyon of Lodore. It is about forty miles long and ten to twenty miles wide and is surrounded on all sides by mountains. A prime ranching area, it straddles three state boundaries—Utah, Wyoming, and Colorado—and was once the haunt of numerous outlaws, including the famous Wild Bunch. Today there are few ranches but a number of state and federal wildlife refuges.
2. The Canyon of Lodore is a seventeen-mile stretch of the Green River in western Colorado. Lodore was named by Andy Hall, one of John Wesley Powell's crewmen in 1869, who said it reminded him of a poem, "The Cataract of Lodore," written by Robert Southey, poet laureate of England, about 1820. After flowing to the east through Brown's Park, the Green River makes a turn to the south and cuts right across the axis of the Uinta Mountains, through the same deep red Precambrian rock that forms Red Canyon. The result is a deep, gloomy, atmospheric canyon where the sun only shines for a few hours each day and the rapids are, as in Red Canyon, frequent and difficult. The Gates of Lodore is the term used to describe the dramatic entrance to the canyon, which one of Powell's men described as "a mountain drinking a river."

CHAPTER ELEVEN

1. Eggert does not name the first rapid in Lodore, but the one he says almost capsized them is probably Winnie's Rapid. In 1871 John Steward, one of the crew members on the second Powell expedition, asked to have the charming grotto on the right side of the river named for his daughter, Winnie. The outwash from this steep side canyon created a rapid at its mouth. It consists of some large rocks in the middle of the river and, though seemingly easy to run, has been the scene of more than one accident.
2. Disaster Falls is the first major rapid in Lodore, and Eggert's extensive quote from Powell describes the 1869 incident that led to its name. It actually consists of two rapids, Upper Disaster and Lower Disaster. In the upper section, the river squeezes between two big boulders, and the constriction creates large waves and holes. Just downstream from it, the lower section used to be much more difficult to run in low

water and was often lined or portaged. The river washed up against an undercut cliff on the right side of the canyon, and it was difficult to keep boats out of danger. The floods of 1983 and 1984, however, changed the channel, and Lower Disaster Falls is now much easier to run.

3. Powell is describing what is today called the "tongue" of the rapid.
4. Another rapid named by Powell because it consists of three separate drops. There are a number of historic inscriptions on the cliffs on the left side of the river at Triplet Rapid.
5. Hell's Half Mile is the most difficult rapid in Lodore, if not on the entire Green River. The river drops over a boulder dam and then cascades over smaller rocks for a long distance downstream. Powell's crewman John Steward was again responsible for the name of this rapid. In 1871, after they had spent two arduous days portaging their supplies and lining their boats around the rapid, Powell asked his men what they thought the name should be. Some of them suggested Boulder Falls, but when Powell asked Steward, he replied, "Would Hell's Half Mile suit?"

CHAPTER THIRTEEN

1. The Yampa River is the last undammed major tributary of the Green. It rises in western Colorado, enters Dinosaur National Monument west of the town of Craig, Colorado, flows through a spectacular sandstone canyon, and ends in the middle of the monument. Because it is not dam controlled, the Yampa is still subject to annual spring floods and thus can only be run during a short window from about April through June. However, its wild nature also makes it very popular with river runners, and permits to run it are highly prized. Echo Park is the open area at the confluence of the Green and Yampa. Locally known as Pat's Hole after Pat Lynch, a hermit who lived there in the 1800s, Echo Park today has a car campground, ranger station, and water source for river runners and campers. It is one of the most beautiful places along the Green River, but it can be reached only by river or a long and sometimes treacherous dirt road from Dinosaur, Colorado.
2. At the time Eggert was there, the Chew family operated a ranch just up Pool Creek Canyon a few miles from Echo Park. The Chews had a hay field and occasionally ran stock in Echo Park. In the 1970s, the National Park Service bought the ranch, but the buildings are still maintained as a historic ranching exhibit. A later generation of the Chew family still operates a ranch on the east bank of the Green, just downstream from the Split Mountain boat ramp.
3. Harper's Corner is an overlook that juts out into the upper end of Whirlpool Canyon. It is reached by a thirty-five-mile paved road from Dinosaur National Monument headquarters and provides stunning views of the Yampa River canyon, Lodore, Whirlpool, Island Park, and the Uinta Mountains.

CHAPTER FOURTEEN

1. Elias Olcott Beaman was an experienced photographer from New York who was hired by John Wesley Powell to accompany his second expedition in 1871. Beaman took the first photographs of the Green and Colorado River canyons, but at Lee's Ferry, he and Powell had a disagreement, and he left the expedition, although he stayed in the West and took numerous other photographs. The process Beaman used,

to which Eggert is comparing his own relatively easy efforts, was a wet-plate one where the photographer needed glass plates, containers of various chemicals, and a portable darkroom just to take a picture.

2. The Mantle ranch is about ten miles up the Yampa River from Echo Park. First settled by Charlie Mantle in 1917, it is still owned by the Mantle family and operates as a working ranch and dude ranch. It can be reached only by river or a very difficult dirt road.
3. Shakespeare, *The Merchant of Venice*, act 5, scene 1, lines 54–57.
4. Whirlpool Canyon is another Powell name: June 21–23, 1869: "The Green is greatly increased by the Yampa, and we now have a much larger river. All this volume of water, confined, as it is, in a narrow channel and rushing with great velocity, is set eddying and spinning in whirlpools by projecting rocks and short curves, and the waters waltz their way through the canyon, making their own rippling, rushing, roaring music . . . [We] decide to call the canyon . . . Whirlpool Canyon."
5. All of the water in Jones Hole Creek comes out of the ground in a huge spring about four miles up the canyon. Today there is a Utah State Fish Hatchery at the springs, and it is a popular spot for river runners and fisherman. There are different versions of the origin of the name; one is that Powell named it after Stephen Vandeveer Jones, one of his crewmen in 1871; the other is that it was named for a local rancher, who hid out there after a domestic dispute. Using soap in the creek, as described by Eggert, is today strictly forbidden.

CHAPTER FIFTEEN

1. Don obviously means Loch Ness.
2. Powell's four boats on his 1869 expedition were the *Emma Dean*, the *Maid of the Canyon*, *Kitty Clyde's Sister*, and the *No Name*. It was the latter that was wrecked at Disaster Falls.
3. Powell named Split Mountain Canyon; after considering Craggy Canyon, he rejected that name in favor of one that described the geological setting. River runners such as Bus Hatch and Buzz Holmstrom named the rapids in Split Mountain; Moonshine because there was an illegal still nearby; SOB because there is no clean run through it; and Schoolboy because, although it looks difficult, it is so easy that a schoolboy could run it. The rapid Eggert does not mention is Inglesby, just above the end of the canyon, named for Dr. Arthur Inglesby in the 1930s.
4. This was a party in a single boat led by Roy DeSpain of Springville, Utah. DeSpain was a friend of Bus Hatch and an experienced boatman, but in the high water of June 1953, he went over a barely submerged rock at the lower end of Moonshine Draw and capsized. Today this is still called DeSpain Rock.
5. This cave, or more accurately overhang, is directly across from the Split Mountain boat ramp but is seldom visited anymore. The digging that Eggert describes is today strictly forbidden by the National Park Service.

CHAPTER SIXTEEN

1. It was at this site that Earl Douglass found the tailbones of a brontosaur in August 1909. Dinosaur National Monument was created in 1915, but it consisted only of the 80 acres surrounding the quarry. The monument was expanded to 236,000 acres in 1938 to protect the canyons of the Green and Yampa Rivers.

2. The Sierra Club had begun arranging river trips through Dinosaur with Hatch River Expeditions during the Echo Park Dam controversy. It was these trips that introduced people to the river canyons and helped to stop the dam from being built.
3. Dr. Leslie Emsden (1925–96). For more about him, see the "After the River" section.
4. As Eggert notes, Ouray is the headquarters for the Uintah and Ouray Indian Reservation, which stretches down the left, or east, bank of the Green almost all the way through Desolation and Gray Canyons. It was named for Ouray, a famous Ute chief.

CHAPTER SEVENTEEN

1. The White and the Duchesne Rivers are the last two major tributaries to enter the Green before it meets the Colorado some 250 miles downstream. Neither is very large, however. The White rises in western Colorado and flows west; the Duchesne on the south slope of the Uinta Mountains and makes its way east. Their mouths are within a few miles of each other on opposite sides of the Green. The area the party was now floating through had long been a favorite wintering ground of the Utes, and later the mountain men.
2. Don was right; the Green had reached its peak runoff that year in May at 9,115 cubic feet per second. By the time they reached Ouray, the river had dropped to 9,080 and was falling rapidly.
3. John Wesley Powell, July 8, 1869: "The walls are almost without vegetation; a few dwarf bushes are seen here and there clinging to the rocks, and cedars grow from the crevices—not like the cedars of a land refreshed with rains, great cones bedecked with spray, but ugly clumps, like war clubs beset with spines. We are minded to call this the Canyon of Desolation."
4. John Colton Sumner (1840–1907), one of Powell's crewmen on his 1869 expedition. Sumner rowed the *Emma Dean,* Powell's scout boat, and remained loyal throughout the expedition. He later turned against Powell, as did most of the crew from the 1869 trip, and ended his life embittered and destitute.

CHAPTER EIGHTEEN

1. Although Eggert does not name any of the rapids in the upper end of Desolation Canyon, from the description, it seems certain that this one is Steer Ridge, one of the first big rapids in Desolation Canyon. None of the rapids from the start of the canyon down to Steer Ridge are very significant, but Steer Ridge has caught unwary or inexperienced boatmen and caused a number of accidents.
2. Rock Creek is indeed one of the most pleasant spots in Desolation Canyon. A beautiful stream comes out of the Tavaputs Plateau to the west, and there has long been ranching at the site. Today camping is not allowed, but most river parties stop there to explore the old ranch buildings and enjoy the orchards.

CHAPTER NINETEEN

1. It's unclear why Eggert was so certain that this was the rapid where Powell's boat capsized on July 11, 1869, for later generations of scholars have been unable to pinpoint the exact location. From the description, this could be either Moonwater or Joe Hutch Canyon Rapid, also known as Cow Swim because later ranchers used to herd their cattle across the river here.

2. This is the McPherson Ranch, started by Jim McPherson around the turn of the twentieth century. The ranch lay near the Outlaw Trail, and McPherson, as was common with ranchers in such remote areas, often befriended outlaws such as Butch Cassidy and the Wild Bunch. The McPherson family owned the ranch until the 1940s, when the United States government bought it and added it to the Ute Indian Reservation.
3. Historians today agree that some of the rock work on the house that Cid Sumner admired was done by a Swiss-trained mason, Eugene Eyraud, known as Frenchie, but most of the construction and masonry were completed by Jim McPherson, whose father, incidentally, came from Scotland. There are similarities between the masonry at Rock Creek and Florence Creek, and apparently Frenchie also helped with that house, but again, according to family history from the Seamounts, who originally settled at Rock Creek, most of the work was done by the two brothers, Ed and Dan.
4. Three Fords Rapid.

CHAPTER TWENTY

1. John Wesley Powell, "July 13: This morning we have an exhilarating ride. The river is swift, and there are many smooth rapids. I stand on deck, keeping careful watch ahead, and we glide along, mile after mile, plying strokes, now on the right and then on the left, just sufficient to guide our boats past the rocks into smooth water. At noon we emerge from Gray Canyon, as we have named it, and camp for dinner under a cottonwood tree, standing on the left bank." Powell at one point thought about calling this stretch Coal Canyon because of the seams of coal in the canyon walls; then the name Lignite Canyon was considered, but the name was changed to Gray Canyon in 1872.
2. Named for "the lamented Gunnison," as Powell described him. Captain John Gunnison of the US Army's Corp of Topographical Engineers crossed here in 1853 while conducting one of the Pacific railroad surveys. He and most of his party were killed by Indians in central Utah not long after. Native Americans, Mexican traders using the Old Spanish Trail, mountain men, Mormons, and other travelers had long used the crossing at the foot of Gray Canyon. Frederick Dellenbaugh, who was a member of the 1871 expedition and later chronicled Powell's journeys in two books, said that it was originally called Cathedral Butte, but they later changed the name to Gunnison Butte.
3. The diversion dam was built in the early 1900s to channel water to the melon fields around Green River, Utah. The rapid below it is called Tusher Rapid. Running boats over the diversion dam is not recommended. The waterwheel that Eggert mentions can still be seen, although it is on private land and can be visited only with permission.
4. Of all the Bureau of Reclamation projects Eggert mentions, only Glen Canyon and Flaming Gorge Dams were ever built. Dark Canyon and Rattlesnake Dams in Gray Canyon never made it past the drawing boards, and the Marble Canyon Dam, planned for the Grand Canyon, set off an environmental controversy similar to the Echo Park Dam with the same results.
5. The town of Green River, Utah, where the Eggert party spent the next few days, was originally two towns: Blake on the west side of the river, and Elgin on the east. Both settlements were later combined to form the present town. Settlement began in the

1870s, but it was not until after the Denver and Rio Grande Railroad bridged the Green River in 1883 that the town began to grow. The first wagon bridge was built in 1910.

6. John Alden Galloway (1928–62) worked only a few summers for Hatch, but river running was in his blood: he was a great-nephew of the famous river runner Nathaniel Galloway. For more about him, see the "After the River" section.
7. By the time the Eggert party landed here, the uranium boom in southeastern Utah was in full swing, and there were around eight hundred active uranium mines in the region, along with mills, reduction centers, and other support facilities. Within a few years, however, the Atomic Energy Commission stopped buying uranium, and the boom went bust.
8. Hurst is a legend among canyon-country bush pilots. For a biography of him, see *Rim Flying Canyonlands with Jim Hurst* by Pearl Baker (A-to-Z Printing, 1973).
9. Ecker's Portraits and Photographic Equipment, 270 S. Main St., Salt Lake City.
10. Known as the Willie and Martin handcart companies, they were trapped by snow on the plains of Wyoming in the fall of 1856. More than two hundred people died in the two companies before the survivors were rescued by parties sent from Salt Lake City.
11. "Come, Come, Ye Saints" by William Clayton (1846); music by Jesse White (1844).
12. Laphene "Don" Harris (1911–2004), one of best known and loved of all the early Colorado River boatmen. He got his start with Norman Nevills in 1938 and went on to run the Green and Colorado and many of their tributaries, often in the company of Bert Loper. In the 1950s, he started his own company with his friend Jack Brennan, called Harris-Brennan River Expeditions, and conducted commercial trips until the 1970s.

CHAPTER TWENTY-ONE

1. Crystal Geyser, about five miles downriver from Green River, Utah. Powell noted mineral deposits when he passed there in 1869, but it was no longer flowing. In 1936 a company looking for oil drilled a hole about twenty-four-hundred feet deep but found nothing. They left the drill pipe there, however, and since then, the geyser has periodically erupted a stream of cold water to a height of about sixty feet.
2. This "river register" is just above Bowknot Bend and contains many names and inscriptions. Modern travelers are encouraged not to add to the register, however.
3. John Wesley Powell, July 15, 1869: "There is an exquisite charm in our ride today down this beautiful canyon. It gradually grows deeper with every mile of travel; the walls are symmetrically curved and grandly arched, of a beautiful color, and reflected in the quiet waters in many places so as almost to deceive the eye and suggest to the beholder the thought that he is looking into profound depths.... At night we camp on the south side of the great Bowknot, and as we eat supper, which is spread on the beach, we name this Labyrinth Canyon."
4. Actually two separate buttes. Named by Powell because from the river, at a certain angle, the two seem to form a fallen cross.
5. Anderson Bottom, about seventy miles below Green River, is still a favorite camping spot for river travelers, although the airstrip is no longer used. During the halcyon days of the Friendship Cruise, a powerboat race that went down the Green to its

confluence with the Colorado, and then back up that river to Moab, Utah, Anderson Bottom was a fuel stop and campsite where a huge party was held, with bonfires, bands, dancing, and a steak dinner.

6. The last of the canyons of the Green, Stillwater was named by Powell for the peaceful flow of the river. There are no rapids in its entire thirty-seven-mile length.
7. Before 1922, the Colorado River above the confluence with the Green was known as the Grand River since it rises in Grand Lake and flows past Grand Junction, Colorado. In that year, the Colorado legislature persuaded the Board on Geographic Names that the entire river, from its source to the sea, should be called the Colorado River.
8. Below the confluence of the two rivers, the geology changes from soft sandstones to hard limestones, and the character of the river changes as well. Powell wrote on July 23, 1869: "On starting, we come at once to difficult rapids and falls, that in many places are more abrupt than in any of the canyons through which we have passed, and we decide to name this Cataract Canyon." Smooth flows give way to tumultuous and even dangerous rapids. As noted by the stranger who came into their camp at Green River, Cataract was by this time known as "the Graveyard of the Colorado" because of the many men who had lost their lives in its rapids and falls. Since Eggert's time, Lake Powell has backed up into Cataract Canyon, drowning all but eleven miles of rapids—including such treacherous torrents as Dark Canyon Rapid, considered by some to be the worst in the entire canyon—but Eggert and his party had to face every one of those rapids. Compounding their concerns was the fact that not even Don Hatch, let alone any of the rest of them, had been through Cataract Canyon. The rapids of Cataract Canyon were rated by the 1921 USGS Survey, and those numbers are still in use today. Many of the rapids have since acquired names from more recent boatmen, such as Mile Long Rapid, the North Sea, the Big Drops, Satan's Gut, and Little Niagara, which give an idea of their size. During Eggert's time, these names were not in use, and thus it is hard to track the party's progress through the canyon.
9. *Datura wrightii* or sacred datura, a member of the nightshade family.

### CHAPTER TWENTY-TWO

1. Clyde Eddy, *Down the World's Most Dangerous River* (New York: Frederick A. Stokes Company, 1929).
2. Gypsum Canyon was also named by Powell because of the quantities of that mineral he found there. All of the rapids below the Big Drop are now covered by Lake Powell, including Gypsum and Dark Canyon.
3. John Wesley Powell, July 28, 1869: "At three o'clock we arrive at the foot of Cataract Canyon. Here a long canyon valley comes down from the east, and the river turns sharply to the west in a continuation of the line of the lateral valley. In the bend on the right vast numbers of crags and pinnacles and tower-shaped rocks are seen. We call it Mille Crag Bend."
4. This river register, which contained names dating back to the early 1900s, is now, alas, covered by Lake Powell, but it was extensively documented by the Glen Canyon salvage surveys in the late 1950s.

### CHAPTER TWENTY-THREE

1. Hite, Utah, was one of the few places where a road could reach the Colorado River all the way from Moab, Utah, to Lee's Ferry, some 180 miles downstream. It was

sometimes called Dandy Crossing because it was such a "dandy" place to cross the river, but it was later named for Cass Hite, a prospector who settled there in the 1880s. By the time the Eggert party passed, it had a ferry, a general store, a post office, and, just upriver at White Canyon, a uranium mill.

## CHAPTER TWENTY-FOUR

1. Construction on Glen Canyon Dam began in 1956 and was completed in 1963, but the reservoir—named Lake Powell—did not reach its maximum elevation until 1980. The flooding of Glen Canyon, coming so soon after the defeat of the Echo Park Dam, turned an environmental victory into a bitter defeat, one that is still hotly debated today.
2. After Hite became a town with a post office, Cass Hite felt it was too crowded and moved to a cabin on Ticaboo Creek, where he died in 1914.

## CHAPTER TWENTY-FIVE

1. Although it's not identified, this could have been the cabin of Bert Loper, who lived downriver from Cass Hite at Red Creek. Loper lived in this cabin for many years and had a small orchard. Glen Canyon was littered with cabins, placer workings, and other evidence of the mining activities that had gone on there since the 1890s.
2. The Escalante River was the last-discovered and last-named tributary of the Colorado and today is a popular destination for backpackers. It originates at the southern edge of the Aquarius Plateau and flows generally south until it meets the Colorado in Glen Canyon.
3. The San Juan is one of the major tributaries of the Colorado. It rises in the San Juan Mountains of southwestern Colorado and flows some four hundred miles through three states before it enters the Colorado in Glen Canyon. Today Lake Powell covers the scenic lower canyon of the San Juan, but the stretch between Bluff, Utah, and Clay Hills Crossing is still a popular river for rafters.
4. Like many place names in Glen Canyon, there is no documentation on who first used the name Hidden Passage, but a 1945 *Sierra Club Bulletin* article by Randall Henderson claims that it was Norman Nevills, pioneer river outfitter on the San Juan and through Glen Canyon, who originated the name.

## CHAPTER TWENTY-SIX

1. Paregoric was an opium-based treatment for diarrhea. Taken in liquid form, it was effective and once commonly available over the counter, but it is now restricted to prescription only.
2. Cid Ricketts Sumner, "Hidden Passage." Copyright 1957. Quoted by special permission of the author.
3. Music Temple was a popular stop for river runners in Glen Canyon for many years because of the wonderful acoustics. River parties left notebooks in a can in the sand, where many signed their names. These notebooks were later preserved and are now in the Special Collections Department, J. Willard Marriott Library, University of Utah. Unfortunately, the Eggert-Hatch party did not sign their names.
4. Probably the panels at Twilight Canyon. The petroglyphs here were produced by the Anasazi culture, Native Americans contemporary with the Fremont.
5. Named by later river runners for the small Anasazi ruins found at the mouth of the creek. Aztec Creek flowed through Forbidding Canyon, which hikers followed to

Bridge Creek, then up that to Rainbow Bridge. Most Glen Canyon river runners stopped for the hike to Rainbow Bridge, even though it was fourteen miles roundtrip.

CHAPTER TWENTY-SEVEN

1. Though long known to the Navajo, Rainbow Bridge was discovered in 1909 by a party led by Byron Cummings, a dean at the University of Utah, who was guided to the bridge by Nasja Begay. Many river parties who hiked to the bridge then climbed up a buttress and let themselves down with fixed ropes to the top of the bridge, but this has since been prohibited by the National Park Service at the request of the Navajo tribe. Today Lake Powell floods Aztec and Bridge Canyons and at high water reaches under the bridge itself. The registers that the Eggert party read through are now in the possession of the National Park Service at the Glen Canyon Recreation Area headquarters in Wahweap, Arizona.
2. *Moki steps* is the term applied to shallow footholds cut into the rock by the ancient Anasazi people. Before the adoption of the term *Anasazi,* which is Navajo for "ancient enemy," the prehistoric people were referred to as Moki.
3. Lee's Ferry was the next place downstream from Hite where a wagon could reach the river and had been a crossing point since John D. Lee had settled there after he was exiled because of his role in the Mountain Meadows Massacre in 1857. The first ferry service was an informal one, using one of John Wesley Powell's boats that he had left there in 1871, but by the turn of the century, the LDS Church had built a road to the spot and a ferry that was used to transport settlers and livestock over the river to the Mormon settlements on the Little Colorado River. A highway bridge replaced the ferry in 1927, and by the time the Eggert party reached there, the site was inhabited only by an engineer who monitored the water gauge for the USGS. In later years, however, Lee's Ferry became the launching point for Grand Canyon river trips, and now thousands of people pass through there each year.

CHAPTER TWENTY-EIGHT

1. The Powell Memorial is on the rim of the Grand Canyon, west of Grand Canyon Village. It was dedicated in 1918.
2. At the end of John Wesley Powell's 1869 expedition, tensions that had been growing for the entire trip split the group apart. Oramel and Seneca Howland and William Dunn left the river and climbed out to the north in an attempt to reach the Mormon settlements in southern Utah. They were never seen again. The canyon they climbed out of was later named Separation Canyon.
3. Don left the trip to help his father, Bus, who had been asked by Lowell Thomas to be the boatman for a trip on the Indus River in Pakistan. The crew that Thomas sent was making a Cinerama film called *The Search for Shang-ri-la,* and Bus and Don ran the boats for the camera crew.

# AFTERWORD

## After the River

*by Sarah McDaniel Holcombe*

As the sixth-century Greek philosopher Heraclitus observed, no man ever steps into the same river twice, for it is not the same river and he is not the same man. Seasoned river runners know that the river can change with the tumble of a rock or a hard rain. By the same token, a life can be forever altered on one river trip. Those daring rafters of the 1955 Eggert-Hatch River Expedition found their lives altered because of the friendships they made and the chances they took.

Although the members of the 1955 Eggert-Hatch Expedition were as diverse as a group could be with different ages, origins, and paths to follow, they are bound in history and river lore because of their unique journey to retrace John Wesley Powell's path before the floodwaters from Flaming Gorge and Glen Canyon Dams erased their tracks. Each person carried the river experience forward with them, forever changed by the things they saw, the trials that tested them, and the bonds they made, both with man and nature.

### Charlie Eggert

In 2005, when queried by his son Sebastian about how he spent the last fifty years of his life, eighty-seven-year-old Charles Donald Albert Eggert said in his typical humorous fashion, "I spent the last fifty years answering your questions." A more accurate truth might be that Charlie spent his life searching for answers to his *own* questions about the earth and about life. Insatiably curious about what was around the next bend, he spent his life in quest of the unknown, the unseen, and the unheard. Wherever he saw beauty, he strove to preserve it through motion pictures, photographs, and words.

The full-length Cinemascope film that was made during the first leg of the Eggert-Hatch Expedition in 1955 was called *A Canyon Voyage* and was shown for the first time at the Cosmos Club in Washington,

D.C. Although all the people featured in the film were invited, only Cid, Fred, and Tony were able to attend the premiere. In a letter written on November 26, 1955 to Don Hatch, bemoaning his absence, Charlie said, "It had them yelling in the aisles and applauding all the way through every time there was a particularly outstanding shot. You wouldn't have known us—as a matter of fact, we hardly recognized each other, we were all so dressed up! Cid had a long evening dress on and looked so lovely. Fred was all perked up, and I couldn't help but remember him in dungarees and a red bandana around his head. We all looked at each other and laughed—we were all so out of character!"

Charles toured the country showing the film and giving talks about the rafting trip, always with his faithful companion Frog, the trip mascot, by his side. He was the subject of several radio and print interviews. He and Cid Ricketts Sumner were interviewed together on the Mary Margaret McBride radio program.

After the completion of the second portion of the Eggert-Hatch Expedition in 1956, Eggert returned to the lecture circuit with his film called *Danger River*, the sequel to *A Canyon Voyage*. All told, he made four transcontinental lecture tours with his films, narrating them in person to enthusiastic crowds. Although these films were his best-known works, he also made at least sixteen other films including *Acadia*, a film about the Acadia National Park in Maine; an art film about the Lincoln Memorial in Washington, D.C.; and films featuring Yellowstone, Yosemite, and the Great Sand Dunes National Monument. The National Park Service hired Eggert in the spring of 1962 to make a film promoting creation of a new national park near Moab, Utah. Eggert spent forty-two days in the wilderness photographing country that few had ever seen. The result of that wilderness odyssey, *The Sculptured Earth*, premiered in Salt Lake City in October 1962, and the park, Canyonlands, was officially designated on September 12, 1964.

Ever the lover of beauty and preservation, in 1961 Eggert purchased Wyndclyffe (also known as Linden Hall), an abandoned estate on the Hudson River near Rhinecliff, New York. He restored the estate's 1852 carriage barn for use as a studio and later, after his divorce from his wife, Betty, it served as his residence. Wyndclyffe, it is said, gave rise to the expression, "keeping up with the Joneses." The house was originally built for Elizabeth Schermerhorn Jones, a relative by marriage to the wealthy Astor family, and aunt to writer Elizabeth Wharton.

In 1964 Eggert purchased and restored Maizefield, a Federal period brick home built in 1797 in Red Hook, New York. This home is listed on the National Register of Historic Places and remained in the family until 1986.

In 1965 the Bureau of Reclamation proposed the construction of two new dams on the Colorado River. Marble Canyon and Bridge Canyon dams would have flooded portions of Grand Canyon National Park. In an effort to heighten awareness and drum up support for halting the construction of these dams, the Sierra Club hired Eggert, a lifetime honorary member of the club, to work with David Brower to produce a film to oppose the project. Portions of Eggert's films *A Canyon Voyage* and *Danger River* were combined and a new narration by Brower was added to explain the need to preserve the canyons. Thanks to the repeated showing of the film on Capitol Hill, the proposal for the dams was defeated.

Without fear of solitude or the unknown, Eggert continually challenged himself. In 1969, he made a two-thousand-mile motorcycle trip from New York to Nova Scotia and back on his Moto Guzzi Interceptor.

Eggert tried his hand at many different jobs. For several years beginning in 1970, he worked with his dear friend David Brower at the Friends of the Earth office in New York City. He worked as a federal law enforcement officer at the Roosevelt-Vanderbilt National Historic Site in Dutchess County, New York, as well.

During a trip west in 1984 to show his film at the Canyonlands National Park anniversary, Eggert made a surprise visit to the Hatch River Expeditions headquarters in Vernal. Don Hatch turned the surprise around when he proposed a day trip through Split Mountain Gorge the next day. With Don Hatch at the oars and Charlie's sons Kip and Seb as passengers, Eggert and Hatch made their final run down the river together as a team.

Charlie was enjoying a quiet retirement in his studio with his faithful pets, Zacharias, a standard poodle, and Herman, a tuxedo cat, and concentrating mostly on his huge model railroad layout when he met Roy Webb, an archivist with the J. Willard Marriott Library at the University of Utah, who was writing a photo history book of river running on the

Green and Colorado rivers. Thus began a friendship that lasted until Charlie's death. Eggert agreed to donate his entire collection of photographs, film, writing, and correspondence regarding the Eggert-Hatch Expedition to the Marriott Library Department of Special Collections.

Eggert was asked to participate in a history trip in 1998 with Hatch River Expeditions on the Green River through Lodore, Whirlpool, and Split Mountain in Dinosaur National Park. Many members of Charlie's extended family were on the trip along with friends—Meg and Clark Hatch, Al Holland, and Roy Webb.

The Colorado Plateau River Guides invited Charlie in 2000 to lecture at their annual training seminar in Green River, Utah. He showed *A Canyon Voyage* to an enthusiastic audience of river guides at the John Wesley Powell Museum. The next day he showed the film again in Moab at a rally to support the decommissioning of the Glen Canyon Dam. Other presenters at the rally included fellow conservationists: David Brower, Katie Lee, Ellen Meloy, Ken Sleight, John Weisheit, Owen Lammers, Ann Zwinger, and Kent Frost.

In 2002, "River Rat" Charlie moved to Port Townsend, Washington, to be near his son, Seb. He died there on December 21, 2005, at age 87, still graced with his magnificent shock of silver hair and his unyielding, wry sense of humor. He requested that his ashes be divided and scattered in the two places he loved most: the Hudson Valley region in New York and the western desert he fought to protect. He is survived by his son, Robert Sebastian "Seb" Eggert; granddaughter, Katrina Blair; and great-grandson, Stone Stringham. His eldest son, Charles Christopher "Kip" Eggert, died in 2014.

Those interested in Charles Eggert, his work, and the ongoing efforts to restore his films can find more information at www.charleseggert.org.

### Leslie Emsden

In spite of the asthma that plagued Leslie Herbert Clare Emsden throughout his life, he logged many miles in travel and lived a challenging life, both personally and professionally. At the time of his association with the Eggert-Hatch party, he had already earned a master's degree in history in Oxford, England, and a medical degree from McGill University in Montreal, Canada. After being awarded a grant to work in Heidelberg,

Germany, he went there for a year, becoming one of the first civilians to spend time in East Germany after World War II.

In the years following his rafting trip, Emsden practiced medicine in Haiti and the Bahamas, always seeming to prefer situations that challenged him. He eventually worked at both Harlem Hospital and Castle Point Veterans Hospital in New York. After his marriage, he moved his family to Colorado in 1969 to take a position at the National Asthma Research Center in Denver, followed by a long period of time in practice at a state mental hospital there. Eventually, he found himself back on the East Coast in Syracuse, New York, at a public walk-in clinic in a low-income area, still seeking out the people who seemed to need his help the most. Shortly before his death, he was planning his retirement.

Good-humored, witty, and intellectual, Emsden made the most of his life and filled it with diversity, challenge, and service to his fellow man. Though he lived in many places, he never lost his clear British accent or his love for his boyhood home in Clare, Suffolk, England, as evidenced by the fact that all three of his children bear the middle name "Clare." A memorial stone for Emsden was placed in the parish cemetery there after his death in 1996 at age 71.

## Al Galloway

John Alden Galloway's too-short life was filled with service to his country, family, and community. As a high school student in Roosevelt, Utah, he excelled in athletics and was the state low hurdles champion. Though he spent only two summers as a boatman for the Hatches, river running was in his blood; his great-uncle, Nathaniel Galloway, was famous as a white water boatman on the Green and Colorado Rivers as early as the 1880s. Al had a variety of other jobs, such as well driller, railroad worker, and installation technician for Western Electric. His college education at the University of Utah was interrupted by a call from Uncle Sam. For two years he served in the US Army in the Korean Conflict, after which he resumed his engineering studies at Brigham Young University in Provo.

Galloway went to work for Thiokol and worked on the revolutionary Minuteman Intercontinental Ballistic Missile project that was contracted in 1958. His children have memories of their father driving them out to watch the testing of the missiles from the safety of their automobile.

Al was a loving husband and the devoted father of four small children at the time of his death on a cold December night in 1962, just seven years after the Eggert-Hatch Expedition. He was killed at age thirty-four on his way home from work when his car left an icy road and plunged down an embankment. Before the month was out, his widow, Virginia, would bear their fifth child.

His family remembers him as a man with a steadfast love for life and everything in it. The members of the Eggert-Hatch Expedition remembered him as a man who was quick to laugh, seeing humor in every possible situation.

### Don Hatch

Although Don Hatch is known well for his river expertise, it was only a small portion of who he was. Perhaps his profession as an elementary teacher helped to prepare him for herding groups of inexperienced people through dangerous rapids. He was dynamic and a man of action, preferring the living, breathing classroom to the positions as principal he was offered (and declined) over the years. Shortly after the death of his father, Bus Hatch, in 1967, Don left his teaching career to operate the family-owned Hatch River Expeditions.

When Don left the second leg of the Eggert-Hatch Expedition in 1956 before it was completed, he and his father ran the Indus River in Pakistan at the behest of Lowell Thomas for a film directed by Otto Lang. It was one of the earliest Cinerama films, called *Search for Paradise*, and was released in 1957. Bus and Don's filming trip on the Indus and Gilgit Rivers was one of the most difficult either had ever undertaken. While running one difficult stretch, the large camera boat capsized, losing the entire camera apparatus. One of the actors was lost, and his body was never found. Neither Bus nor Don ever felt the same about river running after that.

Don's devotion to conservation was a major driving force throughout his life, as he loved the outdoors and was committed to doing his part to protect it. His opposition to the Echo Park Dam, which threatened the beauty and navigability of the rivers he loved, sometimes made him unpopular in an area that, for the most part, welcomed the dam. But he was unmoved by the opinions of those who were shortsighted about preserving those things that are not manmade or replenishable. An avid snowmobiler, he volunteered for the US Forest Service in avalanche patrol. A beloved memory that Don would relive and retell throughout his life was the time he spotted a goshawk in the wild, a rare pleasure for just a few people because it is a bird whose habitat is increasingly threatened.

Don loved music, especially jazz, and played vibraphone and tenor sax, often playing in local bands. Before his death from cancer at age sixty-four, he told his family, "I've had a full life and I've done everything I ever wanted to do." At his funeral in Vernal, Utah, in 1994, hundreds of river runners, who wished to pay their respects, packed the church where the service was held.

**Les Jones**

It would appear that Leslie Allen William Jones was on to something when he drank his specially concocted "bug juice" for his health and strength during the Eggert-Hatch Expedition, because his injured leg healed up nicely and didn't slow him down for long. He went on to marry the young woman who came to rescue him that day in Green River, Utah, when he left the expedition early.

Jones worked as an engineer and made thousands of river maps for rafting enthusiasts. He is especially well-known for his scroll maps. In 1990, he began work as a surveyor, which he continued until his retirement. His commitment to conservation and respect for the rivers always remained strong. His friends affectionately call him "Buckethead Jones," so named because of the innovative helmet camera he sometimes wore to film his trips down the river.

In 1994, he was one of the legendary river runners honored with a two-week "Old Timers' Trip" down the Grand Canyon, along with some of his fellow river runners.

Kathryn, his beloved wife of sixty-one years, died in 2016, and is buried in Afton, Wyoming. Les, now ninety-six, lives in Afton near his niece, Jenny Hansen. Though he has lost his ability to see and walk, his mind is still sharp, and he still loves remembering his years on the river. A writer of prose and song, the epitaph on his and Kathryn's gravestone contains a piece Les wrote: "Ride the wilderness white waters in reverence before

God, with a prayer His strength will be in you." He also included such phrases on his hand-drawn maps.

Reflecting upon his years of devotion to the river and the hardships that sometimes go along with it—like rafting with a broken leg—Jones is practical. "Whatever you are, whatever you believe, you ought to be true to it."

**Bruce Lium**

Little did Bruce Lium know when he met Don Hatch in 1955 that this association would lead to a friendship of a lifetime, as well as an enduring love and respect for rivers that wound their way through his education and profession. Over a twelve-year period, he was a guide for the Hatch River Expeditions and the United States Geological Survey. He made many rafting trips with people from the United States, as well as some foreign countries, on the Green, Yampa, Colorado, Middle Fork of the Salmon, Main Salmon, and Snake rivers, logging around twenty thousand river miles. His graduate work at the University of Utah in environmental biology emphasized the study of rivers and streams, and his research was conducted all across the country, much of it used for his PhD dissertation.

In 1986 Lium established American Water Resources, a consulting firm in Hailey, Idaho. His company's work emphasizes riparian system restoration, along with fisheries habitat improvement, wetland enhancement, and water rights issues. Officially retired only recently, Lium still acts as a consultant from time to time, even though he has seen his eighty-first birthday. He and his wife, Kay, live in Challis, Idaho, in a cabin next to a healthy stream.

Lium says of the life that he has built, "Rivers have been my whole life since I was seventeen years old. I enjoyed working with them on a daily basis and rarely did I ever miss a day without being near these fascinating wonders of nature. They captured my heart completely and never do I want to be away from them for as long as I live."

**Bob Parsons**

Robert Jerome Parsons was head pathologist, director of laboratory training, and head of the intern program at Highland Hospital in Oakland,

California, until his retirement in 1975. Though he might have been more successful monetarily in a private practice, he was a public-minded individual who wanted to serve where he was needed most and the bulk of his practice as a pathologist was done for the Alameda County System. He also liked the challenge and diversity of the work in that setting. He worked on many interesting projects over his career, such as testing the Salk vaccine. During his service in the navy as a lieutenant commander during World War II, he did malaria research.

Born in 1907, Parsons had many varied interests and excelled in most. He loved gardening (particularly roses), he was a pianist, and he enjoyed dancing. He knitted, and his specialty was argyle socks. He was free to indulge his love of travel after his retirement, and over the years he saw places such as Africa, Alaska, Hawaii, and Japan, exploring his interest in birding on some of the trips.

The Parsons family had traveled together in the past to national parks on vacations, but "Doc Parsons" was so moved by his experiences on the Eggert-Hatch Expedition that he took his wife and children back to the Glen Canyon area that he had grown to love, so they could see the landscape before the dam was finished and the land flooded.

Parsons died of cancer in 1986.

**Cid Ricketts Sumner**

Bertha Louise Ricketts Sumner was affectionately called "Cid" after her birth in Brookhaven, Mississippi, because of her "placid" disposition. It was a characteristic for which she was known throughout her life. Already an established writer when she joined Eggert-Hatch, Sumner's book about her experiences, *A Traveler in the Wilderness*, was published in 1957. In her lifetime she wrote fourteen books.

Three of her novels were made into successful motion pictures. The much-loved Tammy Tyree character from *Tammy Out of Time* and *Tammy Tell Me True* had quite an impact on popular culture: In the 1960s, "Tammy" was the thirteenth most popular name for baby girls. *Tammy and the Bachelor* starring Debbie Reynolds and *Tammy Tell Me True* starring Sandra Dee were the most popular of the Tammy films. A television series called *Tammy* was made in 1965 based on the character and ran for twenty-six episodes on ABC. The last in this series of books, *Tammy in*

*Rome*, was published in 1970. Cid's book, *Quality* was one of the first of its kind to deal with issues of race and the film made from it was called *Pinky*. Somewhat controversial for the times in 1949 because it was the first film to portray an interracial romance, it received three Academy Award nominations.

Cid's intrepid spirit carried her through many adventures which included a donkey ride through the Cevennes, following Robert Louis Stevenson's route in *Travels with a Donkey*, which she detailed in her book, *Saddle Your Dreams* (1964). She also pony-trekked through Invernesshire, Scotland, and rode a horse for seven days over Hardangervidda, Northern Europe's highest mountain plateau. She spent a winter in the Hebrides; summered on a farm in Valdres in Central Norway; and was lashed to the mast of a ship during a wild storm when crossing from the Isle of Harris to the Isle of Berneray. She was a frequent visitor at Ardross Castle in the Scottish Highlands and a resident many times at the MacDowell Colony in Peterborough, New Hampshire. Cid lived and traveled until she died with her characteristic style and enthusiasm, leaving enamored people in her wake.

Despite the worry her family had for her rambling adventures all over the world, Cid's death came in 1970 in her own home in Duxbury, Massachusetts. She died at the hands of her sixteen-year-old grandson, who lived next door to her. Placid to the end, she didn't fight back, but held a pillow up to try to ward off his blows. Her dying words were, "Why are you doing this when I love you so much?" She was eighty years old.

### Tony Tuttle

After graduating from Bard College, Anthony Marchant Tuttle worked as an actor, a jazz musician, a limo driver, and as a maître d' in a successful Manhattan pub. The son of Day Tuttle, a well-known theatrical and radio producer and director, it was natural that Tony would be inclined toward the theater. However, the career that brought him the most fame and success was that of writer. His first book was a work of fiction, inspired by his experiences with the Eggert-Hatch Expedition, about a river rafting trip, *This Time in Twilight* (1966), which he worked on in Los Angeles while he was a fellow with the Huntington Foundation. Among his other published works were *Songs from the Night Before* (1972) and *The Drive for the Green* (1969). He edited *The Journal of Andrew Bihaly* (1973), the diary of a young Hungarian man who came to the United States after the horrors of World War II.

Anthony Tuttle died in New York City in 2001 at age sixty-eight.

**Fred Wood**

Born in 1904, Frederick Hoffman Wood was the oldest male member of the Eggert-Hatch Expedition. To a degree, this might explain his air of caution about an expedition of this magnitude. But at the same time, perhaps it is for this very same reason that he looked at the trip as the chance of a lifetime and a reason to step outside his life as a mild-mannered bookseller and into the dreams of the West that had always lived in his head.

The trip agreed with Wood. He came home not only with tanned skin and strong muscles, but also with a confidence and fullness of life that he had not before realized. Although he felt that he had met the challenge well, as it turned out, his greatest challenges still lay in the years ahead of him when he and his wife, Esther, struggled to survive the deaths of their two sons, Colby, at age twenty-two, and Paul at age thirty-three—hardships far greater than any river rafting expedition could ever demand of a person.

Around 1970, the Woods sold their bookstores, The Open Book, in Southport and Bridgeport, Connecticut. Though they were retired, they still led active lives by donating time to local causes. A particular charity that was dear to Fred's heart was the annual book sale at Pequot Library, which began in 1961 in Southport. That very first year the sale consisted of six thousand volumes and it took three weeks to sell everything. Fred Wood donated his time to sort and price donated books and library discards with assistance from a handful of volunteers.

Fred died in 1986.

*If my ship sails from sight, it doesn't mean my journey ends, it simply means*
*the river bends.*

—British statesman John Enoch Powell